Lecture Notes in Computer Science 2050

Edited by G. Goos, J. Hartmanis and J. van Leeuwen

T0210980

Springer
Berlin
Heidelberg
New York
Barcelona
Hong Kong
London
Milan
Paris
Singapore
Tokyo

Jean-Yves Le Boudec   Patrick Thiran

Network Calculus

A Theory of Deterministic Queuing Systems
for the Internet

Springer

Series Editors

Gerhard Goos, Karlsruhe University, Germany
Juris Hartmanis, Cornell University, NY, USA
Jan van Leeuwen, Utrecht University, The Netherlands

Authors

Jean-Yves Le Boudec
Patrick Thiran
EPFL
INN Ecublens
1015 Lausanne, Switzerland
E-mail:{jean-yves.leboudec/patrick.thiran}@epfl.ch

Cataloging-in-Publication Data applied for

Die Deutsche Bibliothek - CIP-Einheitsaufnahme

Le Boudec, Jean-Yves:
Network calculus : a theory of deterministic queuing systems for the
Internet / Jean-Yves Le Boudec ; Patrick Thiran. - Berlin ; Heidelberg ; New
York ; Barcelona ; Hong Kong ; London ; Milan ; Paris ; Singapore ; Tokyo :
Springer, 2001
  (Lecture notes in computer science ; Vol. 2050)
  ISBN 3-540-42184-X

CR Subject Classification (1998): C.2, D.4.4, D.4, E.4, H.3.5, H.4.3

ISSN 0302-9743
ISBN 3-540-42184-X Springer-Verlag Berlin Heidelberg New York

Springer-Verlag Berlin Heidelberg New York
a member of BertelsmannSpringer Science+Business Media GmbH

http://www.springer.de

© Springer-Verlag Berlin Heidelberg 2001
Printed in Germany

Typesetting: Camera-ready by author
Printed on acid-free paper   SPIN 10781496   06/3142   5 4 3 2 1 0

A Annelies
A Joana, Maëlle, Audraine et Elias
A ma mère
— JL

A mes parents
— PT

Pour éviter les grumeaux
Qui encombrent les réseaux
Il fallait, c'est compliqué,
Maîtriser les seaux percés

Branle-bas dans les campus
On pourra dorénavant
Calculer plus simplement
Grâce à l'algèbre Min-Plus

Foin des obscures astuces
Pour estimer les délais
Et la gigue des paquets
Place à "Network Calculus"

— JL

Contents

Introduction

What this Book is About

Network Calculus is a set of recent developments that provide deep insights into flow problems encountered in networking. The foundation of network calculus lies in the mathematical theory of dioids, and in particular, the Min-Plus dioid (also called Min-Plus algebra). With network calculus, we are able to understand some fundamental properties of integrated services networks, window flow control, scheduling and buffer or delay dimensioning.

This book is organized in three parts. Part I (Chapters 1 and 2) is a self contained, first course on network calculus. It can be used at the undergraduate level or as an entry course at the graduate level. The prerequisite is a first undergraduate course on linear algebra and one on calculus. Chapter 1 provides the main set of results for a first course: arrival curves, service curves and the powerful concatenation results are introduced, explained and illustrated. Practical definitions such as leaky bucket and generic cell rate algorithms are cast in their appropriate framework, and their fundamental properties are derived. The physical properties of shapers are derived. Chapter 2 shows how the fundamental results of Chapter 1 are applied to the Internet. We explain, for example, why the Internet integrated services internet can abstract any router by a rate-latency service curve. We also give a theoretical foundation to some bounds used for differentiated services.

Part II contains reference material that is used in various parts of the book. Chapter 3 contains all first level mathematical background. Concepts such as min-plus convolution and sub-additive closure are exposed in a simple way. Part I makes a number of references to Chapter 3, but is still self-contained. The role of Chapter 3 is to serve as a convenient reference for future use. Chapter 4 gives advanced min-plus algebraic results, which concern fixed point equations that are not used in Part I.

Part III contains advanced material; it is appropriate for a graduate course. Chapter 5 shows the application of network calculus to the determination of optimal playback delays in guaranteed service networks; it explains how fundamental bounds for multimedia streaming can be determined. Chapter 6 considers systems with aggregate scheduling. While the bulk of network calculus in this book applies to systems where schedulers are used to separate flows, there are still some interesting results that can be derived for such systems. Chapter 7 goes beyond the service curve definition of Chapter 1 and analyzes adaptive guarantees, as they are used by the Internet differentiated services. Chapter 8 analyzes time varying shapers; it is an extension of the fundamental results in Chapter 1 that considers the effect of changes in system parameters due to adaptive methods. An application is to renegotiable reserved services. Lastly, Chapter 9 tackles systems with losses. The fundamental result is a novel representation of losses in flow systems. This can be used to bound loss or congestion probabilities in complex systems.

Network calculus belongs to what is sometimes called "exotic algebras" or "topical algebras". This is a set of mathematical results, often with high description complexity, that give insights into man-made systems such as concurrent programs, digital circuits and, of course, communication networks. Petri nets fall into this family as well. For a general discussion of this promising area, see the overview paper [30] and the book [24].

We hope to convince many readers that there is a whole set of largely unexplored, fundamental relations that can be obtained with the methods used in this book. Results such as "shapers keep arrival constraints" or "pay bursts only once", derived in Chapter 1 have physical interpretations and are of practical importance to network engineers.

All results here are deterministic. Beyond this book, an advanced book on network calculus would explore the many relations between stochastic systems and the deterministic relations derived in this book. The interested reader will certainly enjoy the pioneering work in [24] and [10]. The appendix contains an index of the terms defined in this book.

Network Calculus, a System Theory for Computer Networks

In the rest of this introduction we highlight the analogy between network calculus and what is called "system theory". You may safely skip it if you are not familiar with system theory.

Network calculus is a theory of *deterministic queuing* systems found in computer networks. It can also be viewed as the *system theory* that applies to computer networks. The main difference with traditional system theory, as the one that was so successfully applied to design electronic circuits, is that here we consider another algebra, where the operations are changed as follows: addition becomes computation of the minimum, multiplication becomes addition.

Before entering the subject of the book itself, let us briefly illustrate some of the analogies and differences between min-plus system theory, as applied in this book to communication networks, and traditional system theory, applied to electronic circuits.

Let us begin with a very simple circuit, such as the RC cell represented in Figure 1. If the input signal is the voltage $x(t) \in \mathbb{R}$, then the output $y(t) \in \mathbb{R}$ of this simple circuit is the convolution of x by the impulse response of this circuit, which is here $h(t) = \exp(-t/RC)/RC$ for $t \geq 0$:

$$y(t) = (h \otimes x)(t) = \int_0^t h(t-s)x(s)ds.$$

Consider now a node of a communication network, which is idealized as a (greedy) shaper. A (greedy) shaper is a device that forces an input flow $x(t)$ to have an output $y(t)$ that conforms to a given set of rates according to a traffic envelope σ (the shaping curve), at the expense of possibly delaying bits in the buffer. Here the input and output 'signals' are cumulative flow, defined as the number of bits seen on the data flow in time interval $[0, t]$. These functions are non-decreasing with time t. Parameter t can be continuous or discrete. We will see in this book that x and y are linked by the relation

$$y(t) = (\sigma \otimes x)(t) = \inf_{s \in \mathbb{R} \text{ such that } 0 \leq s \leq t} \{\sigma(t-s) + x(s)\}.$$

This relation defines the min-plus convolution between σ and x.

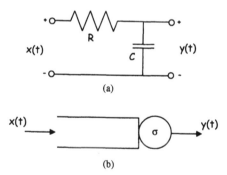

(a)

(b)

Figure 1: An RC circuit (a) and a greedy shaper (b), which are two elementary linear systems in their respective algebraic structures.

Convolution in traditional system theory is both commutative and associative, and this property allows to easily extend the analysis from small to large scale circuits. For example, the impulse response of the circuit of Figure 2(a) is the convolution of the impulse responses of each of the elementary cells:

$$h(t) = (h_1 \otimes h_2)(t) = \int_0^t h_1(t-s)h_2(s)ds.$$

The same property applies to greedy shapers, as we will see in Chapter 1. The output of the second shaper of Figure 2(b) is indeed equal to $y(t) = (\sigma \otimes x)(t)$, where

$$\sigma(t) = (\sigma_1 \otimes \sigma_2)(t) = \inf_{s \in \mathbb{R} \text{ such that } 0 \le s \le t} \{\sigma_1(t-s) + \sigma_2(s)\}.$$

This will lead us to understand the phenomenon known as "pay burst only once" already mentioned earlier in this introduction.

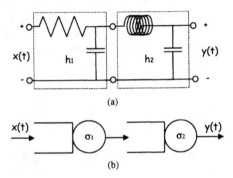

(a)

(b)

Figure 2: The impulse response of the concatenation of two linear circuit is the convolution of the individual impulse responses (a), the shaping curve of the concatenation of two shapers is the convolution of the individual shaping curves (b).

There are thus clear analogies between "conventional" circuit and system theory, and network calculus. There are however important differences too.

A first one is the response of a linear system to the sum of the inputs. This is a very common situation, in both electronic circuits (take the example of a linear low-pass filter used to clean a signal $x(t)$ from additive noise $n(t)$, as shown in Figure 3(a)), and in computer networks (take the example a link of a buffered node with output link capacity C, where one flow of interest $x(t)$ is multiplexed with other background traffic $n(t)$, as shown in Figure 3(b)).

Since the electronic circuit of Figure 3(a) is a linear system, the response to the sum of two inputs is the sum of the individual responses to each signal. Call $y(t)$ the response of the system to the pure signal $x(t)$, $y_n(t)$ the response to the noise $n(t)$, and $y_{tot}(t)$ the response to the input signal corrupted by noise $x(t) + n(t)$. Then $y_{tot}(t) = y(t) + y_n(t)$. This useful property is indeed exploited to design the optimal linear system that will filter out noise as much as possible.

If traffic is served on the outgoing link as soon as possible in the FIFO order, the node of Figure 3(b) is equivalent to a greedy shaper, with shaping curve $\sigma(t) = Ct$ for $t \ge 0$. It is therefore also a linear system, but this time in min-plus algebra. This means that the response to the minimum of two inputs is the minimum of the responses of the system to each input taken separately. However, this also mean that the response to the sum of two inputs is no longer the sum of the responses of

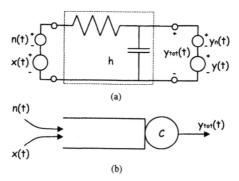

(a)

(b)

Figure 3: The response $y_{tot}(t)$ of a linear circuit to the sum of two inputs $x + n$ is the sum of the individual responses (a), but the response $y_{tot}(t)$ of a greedy shaper to the aggregate of two input flows $x + n$ is not the sum of the individual responses (b).

the system to each input taken separately, because now $x(t) + n(t)$ is a nonlinear operation between the two inputs $x(t)$ and $n(t)$: it plays the role of a multiplication in conventional system theory. Therefore the linearity property does unfortunately not apply to the aggregate $x(t) + n(t)$. As a result, little is known on the aggregate of multiplexed flows. Chapter 6 will learn us some new results and problems that appear simple but are still open today.

In both electronics and computer networks, nonlinear systems are also frequently encountered. They are however handled quite differently in circuit theory and in network calculus.

Consider an elementary nonlinear circuit, such as the BJT amplifier circuit with only one transistor, shown in Figure 4(a). Electronics engineers will analyze this nonlinear circuit by first computing a static operating point y^* for the circuit, when the input x^* is a fixed constant voltage (this is the DC analysis). Next they will linearize the nonlinear element (i.e the transistor) around the operating point, to obtain a so-called small signal model, which a linear model of impulse response $h(t)$ (this is the AC analysis). Now $x_{lin}(t) = x(t) - x^*$ is a time varying function of time within a small range around x^*, so that $y_{lin}(t) = y(t) - y^*$ is indeed approximately given by $y_{lin}(t) \approx (h \otimes x_{lin})(t)$. Such a model is shown on Figure 4(b). The difficulty of a thorough nonlinear analysis is thus bypassed by restricting the input signal in a small range around the operating point. This allows to use a linearized model whose accuracy is sufficient to evaluate performance measures of interest, such as the gain of the amplifier.

In network calculus, we do not decompose inputs in a small range time-varying part and another large constant part. We do however replace nonlinear elements by linear systems, but the latter ones are now a lower bound of the nonlinear system. We

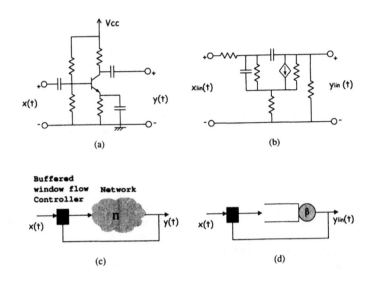

Figure 4: An elementary nonlinear circuit (a) replaced by a (simplified) linear model for small signals (b), and a nonlinear network with window flow control (c) replaced by a (worst-case) linear system (d).

will see such an example with the notion of service curve, in Chapter 1: a nonlinear system $y(t) = \Pi(x)(t)$ is replaced by a linear system $y_{lin}(t) = (\beta \otimes x)(t)$, where β denotes this service curve. This model is such that $y_{lin}(t) \le y(t)$ for all $t \ge 0$, and all possible inputs $x(t)$. This will also allow us to compute performance measures, such as delays and backlogs in nonlinear systems. An example is the window flow controller illustrated in Figure 4(c), which we will analyze in Chapter 4. A flow x is fed via a window flow controller in a network that realizes some mapping $y = \Pi(x)$. The window flow controller limits the amount of data admitted in the network in such a way that the total amount of data in transit in the network is always less than some positive number (the window size). We do not know the exact mapping Π, we assume that we know one service curve β for this flow, so that we can replace the nonlinear system of Figure 4(c) by the linear system of Figure 4(d), to obtain deterministic bounds on the end-to-end delay or the amount of data in transit.

The reader familiar with traditional circuit and system theory will discover many other analogies and differences between the two system theories, while reading this book. We should insist however that no prerequisite in system theory is needed to discover network calculus as it is exposed in this book.

Acknowledgement

We gratefully acknowledge the pioneering work of Cheng-Shang Chang and René Cruz; our discussions with them have influenced this text. We thank Anna Charny, Silvia Giordano, Olivier Verscheure, Frédéric Worm, Jon Bennett, Kent Benson, Vicente Cholvi, William Courtney, Juan Echaguë, Felix Farkas, Gérard Hébuterne and Milan Vojnović for the fruitful collaboration. The interaction with Rajeev Agrawal, François Baccelli, Guillaume Urvoy and Lothar Thiele is acknowledged with thanks. We are grateful to Holly Cogliati for helping with the preparation of the manuscript.

Part I

A First Course in Network Calculus

Chapter 1

Network Calculus

In this chapter we introduce the basic network calculus concepts of arrival, service curves and shapers. The application given in this chapter concerns primarily networks with reservation services such as ATM or the Internet integrated services ("Intserv"). Applications to other settings are given in the following chapters.

We begin the chapter by defining cumulative functions, which can handle both continuous and discrete time models. We show how their use can give a first insight into playout buffer issues, which will be revisited with more detail in Chapter 5. Then the concepts of Leaky Buckets and Generic Cell Rate algorithms are described in the appropriate framework, of arrival curves. We address in detail the most important arrival curves: piecewise linear functions and stair functions. Using the stair functions, we clarify the relation between spacing and arrival curve.

We introduce the concept of service curve as a common model for a variety of network nodes. We show that all schedulers generally proposed for ATM or the Internet integrated services can be modeled by a family of simple service curves called the rate-latency service curves. Then we discover physical properties of networks, such as "pay bursts only once" or "greedy shapers keep arrival constraints". We also discover that greedy shapers are min-plus, time invariant systems. Then we introduce the concept of maximum service curve, which can be used to account for constant delays or for maximum rates. We illustrate all along the chapter how the results can be used for practical buffer dimensioning. We give practical guidelines for handling fixed delays such as propagation delays. We also address the distortions due to variability in packet size.

1.1 Models for Data Flows

1.1.1 Cumulative Functions, Discrete Time versus Continuous Time Models

It is convenient to describe data flows by means of the cumulative function $R(t)$, defined as the number of bits seen on the flow in time interval $[0, t]$. By convention, we take $R(0) = 0$, unless otherwise specified. Function R is always wide-sense increasing, that is, it belongs to the space $\mathcal{F}$ defined in Section 3.1.3 on Page 128. We can use a discrete or continuous time model. In real systems, there is always a minimum granularity (bit, word, cell or packet), therefore discrete time with a finite set of values for $R(t)$ could always be assumed. However, it is often computationally simpler to consider continuous time, with a function R that may be continuous or not. If $R(t)$ is a continuous function, we say that we have a *fluid model*. Otherwise, we take the convention that the function is either right or left-continuous (this makes little difference in practice).[1] Figure 1.1.1 illustrates these definitions.

Convention: A flow is described by a wide-sense increasing function $R(t)$; unless otherwise specified, in this book, we consider the following types of models:

- discrete time: $t \in \mathbb{N} = \{0, 1, 2, 3, ...\}$

- fluid model: $t \in \mathbb{R}^+ = [0, +\infty)$ and R is a continuous function

- general, continuous time model: $t \in \mathbb{R}^+$ and R is a left- or right-continuous function

---

If we assume that $R(t)$ has a derivative $\frac{dR}{dt} = r(t)$ such that $R(t) = \int_0^t r(s)ds$ (thus we have a fluid model), then r is called the rate function. Here, however, we will see that it is much simpler to consider cumulative functions such as R rather than rate functions. Contrary to standard algebra, with min-plus algebra we do not need functions to have "nice" properties such as having a derivative.

It is always possible to map a continuous time model $R(t)$ to a discrete time model $S(n), n \in \mathbb{N}$ by choosing a time slot δ and sampling by

$$S(n) = R(n\delta) \tag{1.1}$$

In general, this results in a loss of information. For the reverse mapping, we use the following convention. A continuous time model can be derived from $S(n), n \in \mathbb{N}$ by letting[2]

$$R'(t) = S(\lceil \frac{t}{\delta} \rceil) \tag{1.2}$$

---

[1]It would be nice to stick to either left- or right-continuous functions. However, depending on the model, there is no best choice: see Section 1.2.1 and Section 1.7

[2]$\lceil x \rceil$ ("ceiling of x") is defined as the smallest integer $\geq x$; for example $\lceil 2.3 \rceil = 3$ and $\lceil 2 \rceil = 2$

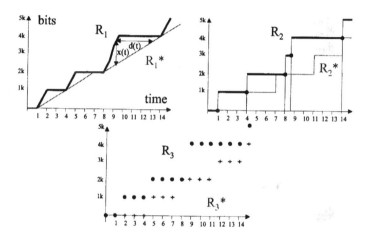

Figure 1.1: Examples of Input and Output functions, illustrating our terminology and convention. R_1 and R_1^* show a continuous function of continuous time (fluid model); we assume that packets arrive bit by bit, for a duration of one time unit per packet arrival. R_2 and R_2^* show continuous time with discontinuities at packet arrival times (times 1, 4, 8, 8.6 and 14); we assume here that packet arrivals are observed only when the packet has been fully received; the dots represent the value at the point of discontinuity; by convention, we assume that the function is left- or right-continuous. R_3 and R_3^* show a discrete time model; the system is observed only at times $0, 1, 2...$

The resulting function R' is always left-continuous, as we already required. Figure 1.1.1 illustrates this mapping with $\delta = 1$, $S = R_3$ and $R' = R_2$.

Thanks to the mapping in Equation (1.1), any result for a continuous time model also applies to discrete time. Unless otherwise stated, all results in this book apply to both continuous and discrete time. Discrete time models are generally used in the context of ATM; in contrast, handling variable size packets is usually done with a continuous time model (not necessarily fluid). Note that handling variable size packets requires some specific mechanisms, described in Section 1.7.

Consider now a system S, which we view as a blackbox; S receives input data, described by its cumulative function $R(t)$, and delivers the data after a variable delay. Call $R^*(t)$ the *output function*, namely, the cumulative function at the output of system S. System S might be, for example, a single buffer served at a constant rate, a complex communication node, or even a complete network. Figure 1.1.1 shows input and output functions for a single server queue, where every packet takes exactly 3 time units to be served. With output function R_1^* (fluid model) the assumption is that a packet can be served as soon as a first bit has arrived (cut-through assumption), and that a packet departure can be observed bit by bit, at a constant rate. For example, the first packet arrives between times 1 and 2, and leaves between times 1 and 4. With output function R_2^* the assumption is that a packet is served as soon as it has been fully received and is considered out of the system only when it is fully transmitted (store and forward assumption). Here, the first packet arrives immediately after time 1, and leaves immediately after time 4. With output function R_3^* (discrete time model), the first packet arrives at time 2 and leaves at time 5.

1.1.2   Backlog and Virtual Delay

From the input and output functions, we derive the two following quantities of interest.

Definition 1.1.1 (Backlog and Delay). *For a lossless system:*

- *The* backlog *at time t is* $R(t) - R^*(t)$.

- *The* virtual delay *at time t is*

$$d(t) = \inf \{\tau \geq 0 : R(t) \leq R^*(t + \tau)\}$$

The backlog is the amount of bits that are held inside the system; if the system is a single buffer, it is the queue length. In contrast, if the system is more complex, then the backlog is the number of bits "in transit", assuming that we can observe input and output simultaneously. The virtual delay at time t is the delay that would be experienced by a bit arriving at time t if all bits received before it are served before it. In Figure 1.1.1, the backlog, called $x(t)$, is shown as the vertical deviation between input and output functions. The virtual delay is the horizontal deviation. If the input and output function are continuous (fluid model), then it is easy to see that $R^* (t + d(t)) = R(t)$, and that $d(t)$ is the smallest value satisfying this equation.

In Figure 1.1.1, we see that the values of backlog and virtual delay slightly differ for the three models. Thus the delay experienced by the last bit of the first packet is $d(2) = 2$ time units for the first subfigure; in contrast, it is equal to $d(1) = 3$ time units on the second subfigure. This is of course in accordance with the different assumptions made for each of the models. Similarly, the delay for the fourth packet on subfigure 2 is $d(8.6) = 5.4$ time units, which corresponds to 2.4 units of waiting time and 3 units of service time. In contrast, on the third subfigure, it is equal to $d(9) = 6$ units; the difference is the loss of accuracy resulting from discretization.

1.1.3   Example: The Playout Buffer

Cumulative functions are a powerful tool for studying delays and buffers. In order to illustrate this, consider the simple playout buffer problem that we describe now. Consider a packet switched network that carries bits of information from a source with a constant bit rate r (Figure 1.2) as is the case for example, with circuit emulation. We take a fluid model, as illustrated in Figure 1.2. We have a first system S, the network, with input function $R(t) = rt$. The network imposes some variable delay, because of queuing points, therefore the output R^* does not have a constant rate r. What can be done to recreate a constant bit stream ? A standard mechanism

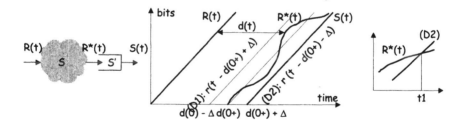

Figure 1.2: A Simple Playout Buffer Example

is to smooth the delay variation in a playout buffer. It operates as follows. When the first bit of data arrives, at time $d_r(0)$, where $d_r(0) = \lim_{t\to0,t>0} d(t)$ is the limit to the right of function d[3], it is stored in the buffer until a fixed time Δ has elapsed. Then the buffer is served at a constant rate r whenever it is not empty. This gives us a second system S', with input R^* and output S.

Let us assume that the network delay variation is bounded by Δ. This implies that for every time t, the virtual delay (which is the real delay in that case) satisfies

---

[3]It is the virtual delay for a hypothetical bit that would arrive just after time 0. Other authors often use the notation $d(0+)$

$$-\Delta \le d(t) - d_r(0) \le \Delta$$

Thus, since we have a fluid model, we have

$$r(t - d_r(0) - \Delta) \le R^*(t) \le r(t - d_r(0) + \Delta)$$

which is illustrated in the figure by the two lines (D1) and (D2) parallel to $R(t)$. The figure suggests that, for the playout buffer S' the input function R^* is always above the straight line (D2), which means that the playout buffer never underflows. This suggests in turn that the output function $S(t)$ is given by $S(t) = r(t - d_r(0) - \Delta)$.

Formally, the proof is as follows. We proceed by contradiction. Assume the buffer starves at some time, and let t_1 be the first time at which this happens. Clearly the playout buffer is empty at time t_1, thus $R^*(t_1) = S(t_1)$. There is a time interval $[t_1, t_1 + \epsilon]$ during which the number of bits arriving at the playout buffer is less than $r\epsilon$ (see Figure 1.2. Thus, $d(t_1 + \epsilon) > d_r(0) + \Delta$ which is not possible. Secondly, the backlog in the buffer at time t is equal to $R^*(t) - S(t)$, which is bounded by the vertical deviation between (D1) and (D2), namely, $2r\Delta$.

We have thus shown that the playout buffer is able to remove the delay variation imposed by the network. We summarize this as follows.

Proposition 1.1.1. *Consider a constant bit rate stream of rate r, modified by a network that imposes a variable delay variation and no loss. The resulting flow is put into a playout buffer, which operates by delaying the first bit of the flow by Δ, and reading the flow at rate r. Assume that the delay variation imposed by the network is bounded by Δ, then*

1. *the playout buffer never starves and produces a constant output at rate r;*

2. *a buffer size of $2\Delta r$ is sufficient to avoid overflow.*

We study playout buffers in more details in Chapter 5, using the network calculus concepts further introduced in this chapter.

1.2 Arrival Curves

1.2.1 Definition of an Arrival Curve

Assume that we want to provide guarantees to data flows. This requires some specific support in the network, as explained in Section 1.3; as a counterpart, we need to limit the traffic sent by sources. With integrated services networks (ATM or the integrated services internet), this is done by using the concept of arrival curve, defined below.

Definition 1.2.1 (Arrival Curve). *Given a wide-sense increasing function α defined for $t \ge 0$ (namely, $\alpha \in \mathcal{F}$), we say that a flow R is constrained by α if and only if for all $s \le t$:*

$$R(t) - R(s) \le \alpha(t - s)$$

We say that R has α as an arrival curve, or also that R is α-smooth.

Note that the condition is over a set of overlapping intervals, as Figure 1.3 illustrates.

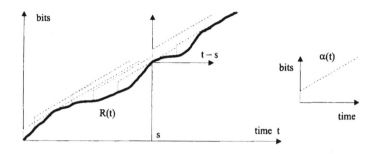

Figure 1.3: Example of Constraint by arrival curve, showing a cumulative function $R(t)$ constrained by the arrival curve $\alpha(t)$.

Affine Arrival Curves: For example, if $\alpha(t) = rt$, then the constraint means that, on any time window of width τ, the number of bits for the flow is limited by $r\tau$. We say in that case that the flow is peak rate limited. This occurs if we know that the flow is arriving on a link whose physical bit rate is limited by r b/s. A flow where the only constraint is a limit on the peak rate is often (improperly) called a "constant bit rate" (CBR) flow, or "deterministic bit rate" (DBR) flow.

Having $\alpha(t) = b$, with b a constant, as an arrival curve means that the maximum number of bits that may ever be sent on the flow is at most b.

More generally, because of their relationship with leaky buckets, we will often use *affine* arrival curves $\gamma_{r,b}$, defined by: $\gamma_{r,b}(t) = rt + b$ for $t > 0$ and 0 otherwise (see Section 3.1.3 for an illustration). Having $\gamma_{r,b}$ as an arrival curve allows a source to send b bits at once, but not more than r b/s over the long run. Parameters b and r are called the burst tolerance (in units of data) and the rate (in units of data per time unit). Figure 1.3 illustrates such a constraint.

Stair Functions as Arrival Curves: In the context of ATM, we also use arrival curves of the form $kv_{T,\tau}$, where $v_{T,\tau}$ is the stair functions defined by $v_{T,\tau}(t) = \left\lceil \frac{t+\tau}{T} \right\rceil$ for $t > 0$ and 0 otherwise (see Section 3.1.3 for an illustration). Note that $v_{T,\tau}(t) = v_{T,0}(t + \tau)$, thus $v_{T,\tau}$ results from $v_{T,0}$ by a time shift to the left. Parameter T (the "interval") and τ (the "tolerance") are expressed in time units. In order to understand the use of $v_{T,\tau}$, consider a flow that sends packets of a fixed size, equal to k unit of data (for example, an ATM flow). Assume that the packets are spaced by at least T time units. An example is a constant bit rate voice encoder, which generates packets periodically during talk spurts, and is silent otherwise. Such a flow has $kv_{T,0}$ as an arrival curve.

Assume now that the flow is multiplexed with some others. A simple way to think of this scenario is to assume that the packets are put into a queue, together with other flows. This is typically what occurs at a workstation, in the operating system or at the ATM adapter. The queue imposes a variable delay; assume it can be bounded by some value equal to τ time units. We will see in the rest of this chapter and in Chapter 2 how we can provide such bounds. Call $R(t)$ the input function for the flow at the multiplexer, and $R^*(t)$ the output function. We have $R^*(s) \leq R(s - \tau)$, from which we derive:

$$R^*(t) - R^*(s) \leq R(t) - R(s - \tau) \leq kv_{T,0}(t - s + \tau) = kv_{T,\tau}(t - s)$$

Thus R^* has $kv_{T,\tau}$ as an arrival curve. We have shown that *a periodic flow, with period T, and packets of constant size k, that suffers a variable delay $\leq \tau$, has $kv_{T,\tau}$ as an arrival curve.* The parameter τ is often called the "one-point cell delay variation", as it corresponds to a deviation from a periodic flow that can be observed at one point.

In general, function $v_{T,\tau}$ can be used to express *minimum spacing* between packets, as the following proposition shows.

Proposition 1.2.1 (Spacing as an arrival constraint). *Consider a flow, with cumulative function $R(t)$, that generates packets of constant size equal to k data units, with instantaneous packet arrivals. Assume time is discrete or time is continuous and R is left-continuous. Call t_n the arrival time for the nth packet. The following two properties are equivalent:*

1. for all m, n, $t_{m+n} - t_m \geq nT - \tau$

2. the flow has $kv_{T,\tau}$ as an arrival curve

The conditions on packet size and packet generation mean that $R(t)$ has the form nk, with $n \in \mathbb{N}$. The spacing condition implies that the time interval between two consecutive packets is $\geq T - \tau$, between a packet and the next but one is $\geq 2T - \tau$, etc.

Proof: Assume that property 1 holds. Consider an arbitrary interval $]s, t]$, and call n the number of packet arrivals in the interval. Say that these packets are numbered $m + 1, \ldots, m + n$, so that $s < t_{m+1} \leq \cdots \leq t_{m+n} \leq t$, from which we have

$$t - s > t_{m+n} - t_{m+1}$$

Combining with property 1, we get

$$t - s > (n - 1)T - \tau$$

From the definition of $v_{T,\tau}$ it follows that $v_{T,\tau}(t - s) \geq n$. Thus $R(t) - R(s) \leq kv_{T,\tau}(t - s)$, which shows the first part of the proof.

Conversely, assume now that property 2 holds. If time is discrete, we convert the model to continuous time using the mapping in Equation 1.2, thus we can consider that we are in the continuous time case. Consider some arbitrary integers m, n; for all $\epsilon > 0$, we have, under the assumption in the proposition:

$$R(t_{m+n} + \epsilon) - R(t_m) \geq (n+1)k$$

thus, from the definition of $v_{T,\tau}$,

$$t_{m+n} - t_m + \epsilon > nT - \tau$$

This is true for all $\epsilon > 0$, thus $t_{m+n} - t_m \geq nT - \tau$. □

In the rest of this section we clarify the relationship between arrival curve constraints defined by affine and by stair functions. First we need a technical lemma, which amounts to saying that we can always change an arrival curve to be left-continuous.

Lemma 1.2.1 (Reduction to left-continuous arrival curves). *Consider a flow $R(t)$ and a wide sense increasing function $\alpha(t)$, defined for $t \geq 0$. Assume that R is either left-continuous, or right-continuous. Denote with $\alpha_l(t)$ the limit to the left of α at t (this limit exists at every point because α is wide sense increasing); we have $\alpha_l(t) = \sup_{s<t} \alpha(s)$. If α is an arrival curve for R, then so is α_l.*

Proof: Assume first that R is left-continuous. For some $s < t$, let t_n be a sequence of increasing times converging towards t, with $s < t_n \leq t$. We have $R(t_n) - R(s) \leq \alpha(t_n - s) \leq \alpha_l(t - s)$. Now $\lim_{n\to+\infty} R(t_n) = R(t)$ since we assumed that R is left-continuous. Thus $R(t) - R(s) \leq \alpha_l(t - s)$.

If in contrast R is right-continuous, consider a sequence s_n converging towards s from above. We have similarly $R(t) - R(s_n) \leq \alpha(t - s_n) \leq \alpha_l(t - s)$ and $\lim_{n\to+\infty} R(s_n) = R(s)$, thus $R(t) - R(s) \leq \alpha_l(t - s)$ as well. □

Based on this lemma, we can always reduce an arrival curve to be left-continuous[4] Note that $\gamma_{r,b}$ and $v_{T,\tau}$ are left-continuous. Also remember that, in this book, we use the convention that cumulative functions such as $R(t)$ are left continuous; this is a pure convention, we might as well have chosen to consider only right-continuous cumulative functions. In contrast, an arrival curve can always be assumed to be left-continuous, but not right-continuous.

In some cases, there is equivalence between a constraint defined by $\gamma_{r,b}$ and $v_{T,\tau}$. For example, for an ATM flow (namely, a flow where every packet has a fixed size equal to one unit of data) a constraint $\gamma_{r,b}$ with $r = \frac{1}{T}$ and $b = 1$ is equivalent to sending one packet every T time units, thus is equivalent to a constraint by the arrival curve $v_{T,0}$. In general, we have the following result.

Proposition 1.2.2. *Consider either a left- or right- continuous flow $R(t), t \in \mathbb{R}^+$, or a discrete time flow $R(t), t \in \mathbb{N}$, that generates packets of constant size equal to k data units, with instantaneous packet arrivals. For some T and τ, let $r = \frac{k}{T}$ and $b = k(\frac{\tau}{T} + 1)$. It is equivalent to say that R is constrained by $\gamma_{r,b}$ or by $kv_{T,\tau}$.*

---

[4]If we consider $\alpha_r(t)$, the limit to the right of α at t, then $\alpha \leq \alpha_r$ thus α_r is always an arrival curve, however it is not better than α.

Proof: Since we can map any discrete time flow to a left-continuous, continuous time flow, it is sufficient to consider a left-continuous flow $R(t), t \in \mathbb{R}^+$. Also, by changing the unit of data to the size of one packet, we can assume without loss of generality that $k = 1$. Note first, that with the parameter mapping in the proposition, we have $v_{T,\tau} \leq \gamma_{r,b}$, which shows that if $v_{T,\tau}$ is an arrival curve for R, then so is $\gamma_{r,b}$.

Conversely, assume now that R has $\gamma_{r,b}$ as an arrival curve. Then for all $s \leq t$, we have $R(t) - R(s) \leq rt + b$, and since $R(t) - R(s) \in \mathbb{N}$, this implies $R(t) - R(s) \leq \lfloor rt + b \rfloor$, Call $\alpha(t)$ the right handside in the above equation and apply Lemma 1.2.1. We have $\alpha_l(t) = \lceil rt + b - 1 \rceil = v_{T,\tau}(t)$. $\qquad\qquad\square$

Note that the equivalence holds if we can assume that the packet size is constant and equal to the step size in the constraint $k v_{T,\tau}$. In general, the two families of arrival curve do not provide identical constraints. For example, consider an ATM flow, with packets of size 1 data unit, that is constrained by an arrival curve of the form $k v_{T,\tau}$, for some $k > 1$. This flow might result from the superposition of several ATM flows. You can convince yourself that this constraint cannot be mapped to a constraint of the form $\gamma_{r,b}$. We will come back to this example in Section 1.4.1.

1.2.2   Leaky Bucket and Generic Cell Rate Algorithm

Arrival curve constraints find their origins in the concept of leaky bucket and generic cell rate algorithms, which we describe now. We show that leaky buckets correspond to affine arrival curves $\gamma_{r,b}$, while the generic cell rate algorithm corresponds to stair functions $v_{T,\tau}$. For flows of fixed size packets, such as ATM cells, the two are thus equivalent.

Definition 1.2.2 (Leaky Bucket Controller). *A Leaky Bucket Controller is a device that analyzes the data on a flow $R(t)$ as follows. There is a pool (bucket) of fluid of size b. The bucket is initially empty. The bucket has a hole and leaks at a rate of r units of fluid per second when it is not empty.*

Data from the flow $R(t)$ has to pour into the bucket an amount of fluid equal to the amount of data. Data that would cause the bucket to overflow is declared non-conformant, otherwise the data is declared conformant.

Figure 1.2.2 illustrates the definition. Fluid in the leaky bucket does not represent data, however, it is counted in the same unit as data.

Data that is not able to pour fluid into the bucket is said to be "non-conformant" data. In ATM systems, non-conformant data is either discarded, tagged with a low priority for loss ("red" cells), or can be put in a buffer (buffered leaky bucket controller). With the Integrated Services Internet, non-conformant data is in principle not marked, but simply passed as best effort traffic (namely, normal IP traffic).

We want now to show that a leaky bucket controller enforces an arrival curve constraint equal to $\gamma_{r,b}$. We need the following lemma.

Lemma 1.2.2. *Consider a buffer served at a constant rate r. Assume that the buffer is empty at time 0. The input is described by the cumulative function $R(t)$. If there*

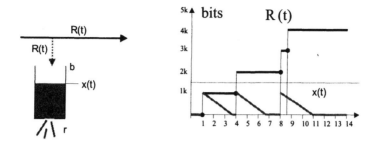

Figure 1.4: A Leaky Bucket Controller. The second part of the figure shows (in grey) the level of the bucket $x(t)$ for a sample input, with $r = 0.4$ kbits per time unit and $b = 1.5$ kbits. The packet arriving at time $t = 8.6$ is not conformant, and no fluid is added to the bucket. If b would be equal to 2 kbits, then all packets would be conformant.

is no overflow during $[0, t]$, the buffer content at time t is given by

$$x(t) = \sup_{s:s \leq t} \{R(t) - R(s) - r(t-s)\}$$

Proof: The lemma can be obtained as a special case of Corollary 1.5.2 on page 40, however we give here a direct proof. First note that for all s such that $s \leq t$, $(t-s)r$ is an upper bound on the number of bits output in $]s, t]$, therefore:

$$R(t) - R(s) - x(t) + x(s) \leq (t-s)r$$

Thus

$$x(t) \geq R(t) - R(s) + x(s) - (t-s)r \geq R(t) - R(s) - (t-s)r$$

which proves that $x(t) \geq \sup_{s:s \leq t}\{R(t) - R(s) - r(t-s)\}$.
Conversely, call t_0 the latest time at which the buffer was empty before time t:

$$t_0 = \sup\{s : s \leq t, x(s) = 0\}$$

(If $x(t) > 0$ then t_0 is the beginning of the busy period at time t). During $]t_0, t]$, the queue is never empty, therefore it outputs bit at rate r, and thus

$$x(t) = x(t_0) + R(t) - R(t_0) - (t - t_0)r \qquad (1.3)$$

We assume that R is left-continuous (otherwise the proof is a little more complex); thus $x(t_0) = 0$ and thus $x(t) \leq \sup_{s:s \leq t}\{R(t) - R(s) - r(t-s)\}$ □

Now the content of a leaky bucket behaves exactly like a buffer served at rate r, and with capacity b. Thus, a flow $R(t)$ is conformant if and only if the bucket content $x(t)$ never exceeds b. From Lemma 1.2.2, this means that

$$\sup_{s:s\leq t}\left\{R(t)-R(s)-r(t-s)\right\}\leq b$$

which is equivalent to

$$R(t)-R(s)\leq r(t-s)+b$$

for all $s \leq t$. We have thus shown the following.

Proposition 1.2.3. *A leaky bucket controller with leak rate r and bucket size b forces a flow to be constrained by the arrival curve $\gamma_{r,b}$, namely:*

1. *the flow of conformant data has $\gamma_{r,b}$ as an arrival curve;*

2. *if the input already has $\gamma_{r,b}$ as an arrival curve, then all data is conformant.*

We will see in Section 1.4.1 a simple interpretation of the leaky bucket parameters, namely: r is the minimum rate required to serve the flow, and b is the buffer required to serve the flow at a constant rate.

Parallel to the concept of leaky bucket is the Generic Cell Rate Algorithm (GCRA), used with ATM.

Definition 1.2.3 (GCRA (T, τ)). *The Generic Cell Rate Algorithm (GCRA) with parameters (T, τ) is used with fixed size packets, called cells, and defines conformant cells as follows. It takes as input a cell arrival time* t *and returns* result. *It has an internal (static) variable* tat *(theoretical arrival time).*

- *initially,* tat = 0

- *when a cell arrives at time* t, *then*

```
if (t < tat - tau)
    result = NON-CONFORMANT;
else {
      tat = max (t, tat) + T;
      result = CONFORMANT;
      }
```

Table 1.1 illustrate the definition of GCRA. It illustrates that $\frac{1}{T}$ is the long term rate that can be sustained by the flow (in cells per time unit); while τ is a tolerance that quantifies how early cells may arrive with respect to an ideal spacing of T between cells. We see on the first example that cells may be early by 2 time units (cells arriving at times 18 to 48), however this may not be cumultated, otherwise the rate of $\frac{1}{T}$ would be exceeded (cell arriving at time 57).

In general, we have the following result, which establishes the relationship between GCRA and the stair functions $v_{T,\tau}$.

Proposition 1.2.4. *Consider a flow, with cumulative function $R(t)$, that generates packets of constant size equal to k data units, with instantaneous packet arrivals. Assume time is discrete or time is continuous and R is left-continuous. The following two properties are equivalent:*

arrival time	0	10	18	28	38	48	57
tat before arrival	0	10	20	30	40	50	60
result	c	c	c	c	c	c	non-c

arrival time	0	10	15	25	35
tat before arrival	0	10	20	20	30
result	c	c	non-c	c	c

Table 1.1: Examples for GCRA(10,2). The table gives the cell arrival times, the value of the `tat` internal variable just before the cell arrival, and the result for the cell (c = conformant, non-c = non-conformant).

1. *the flow is conformant to GCRA(T, τ)*

2. *the flow has $(k\, v_{T,\tau})$ as an arrival curve*

Proof: The proof uses max-plus algebra. Assume that property 1 holds. Denote with θ_n the value of `tat` just after the arrival of the nth packet (or cell), and by convention $\theta_0 = 0$. Also call t_n the arrival time of the nth packet. From the definition of the GCRA we have $\theta_n = \max(t_n, \theta_{n-1}) + T$. We write this equation for all $m \leq n$, using the notation $\vee$ for max. The distributivity of addition with respect to $\vee$ gives:

$$\begin{cases} \theta_n = (\theta_{n-1} + T) \vee (t_n + T) \\ \theta_{n-1} + T = (\theta_{n-2} + 2T) \vee (t_{n-1} + 2T) \\ \dots \\ \theta_1 + (n-1)T = (\theta_0 + nT) \vee (t_1 + nT) \end{cases}$$

Note that $(\theta_0 + nT) \vee (t_1 + nT) = t_1 + nT$ because $\theta_0 = 0$ and $t_1 \geq 0$, thus the last equation can be simplified to $\theta_1 + (n-1)T = t_1 + nT$. Now the iterative substitution of one equation into the previous one, starting from the last one, gives

$$\theta_n = (t_n + T) \vee (t_{n-1} + 2T) \vee \dots \vee (t_1 + nT) \tag{1.4}$$

Now consider the $(m + n)$th arrival, for some $m, n \in \mathbb{N}$, with $m \geq 1$. By property 1, the packet is conformant, thus

$$t_{m+n} \geq \theta_{m+n-1} - \tau \tag{1.5}$$

Now from Equation (1.4), $\theta_{m+n-1} \geq t_j + (m+n-j)T$ for all $1 \leq j \leq m+n-1$. For $j = m$, we obtain $\theta_{m+n-1} \geq t_m + nT$. Combining this with Equation (1.5), we have $t_{m+n} \geq t_m + nT - \tau$. With proposition 1.2.1, this shows property 2.

Conversely, assume now that property 2 holds. We show by induction on n that the nth packet is conformant. This is always true for $n = 1$. Assume it is true for all $m \leq n$. Then, with the same reasoning as above, Equation (1.4) holds for n. We rewrite it as $\theta_n = \max_{1 \leq j \leq n} \{t_j + (n - j + 1)T\}$. Now from proposition 1.2.1,

$t_{n+1} \geq t_j + (n - j + 1)T - \tau$ for all $1 \leq j \leq n$, thus $t_{n+1} \geq \max_{1 \leq j \leq n}\{t_j + (n - j + 1)T\} - \tau$. Combining the two, we find that $t_{n+1} \geq \theta_n - \tau$, thus the $(n + 1)$th packet is conformant.   □

Note the analogy between Equation (1.4) and Lemma 1.2.2. Indeed, from proposition 1.2.2, for packets of constant size, there is equivalence between arrival constraints by affine functions $\gamma_{r,b}$ and by stair functions $v_{T,\tau}$. This shows the following result.

Corollary 1.2.1. *For a flow with packets of constant size, satisfying the GCRA(T, τ) is equivalent to satisfying a leaky bucket controller, with rate r and burst tolerance b given by:*

$$b = (\frac{\tau}{T} + 1)\delta$$

$$r = \frac{\delta}{T}$$

In the formulas, δ is the packet size in units of data.

The corollary can also be shown by a direct equivalence of the GCRA algorithm to a leaky bucket controller.

Take the ATM cell as unit of data. The results above show that for an ATM cell flow, being conformant to GCRA(T, τ) is equivalent to having $v_{T,\tau}$ as an arrival curve. It is also equivalent to having $\gamma_{r,b}$ as an arrival curve, with $r = \frac{1}{T}$ and $b = \frac{\tau}{T} + 1$.

Consider a family of I leaky bucket controllers (or GCRAs), with parameters r_i, b_i, for $1 \leq i \leq I$. If we apply all of them in parallel to the same flow, then the conformant data is data that is conformant for each of the controllers in isolation. The flow of conformant data has as an arrival curve

$$\alpha(t) = \min_{1 \leq i \leq I} (\gamma_{r_i, b_i}(t)) = \min_{1 \leq i \leq I} (r_i t + b_i)$$

It can easily be shown that the family of arrival curves that can be obtained in this way is the set of concave, piecewise linear functions, with a finite number of pieces. We will see in Section 1.5 some examples of functions that do not belong to this family.

Application to ATM and the Internet Leaky buckets and GCRA are used by standard bodies to define conformant flows in Integrated Services Networks. With ATM, a constant bit rate connection (CBR) is defined by one GCRA (or equivalently, one leaky bucket), with parameters (T, τ). T is called the ideal cell interval, and τ is called the Cell Delay Variation Tolerance (CDVT). Still with ATM, a variable bit rate (VBR) connection is defined as one connection with an arrival curve that corresponds to 2 leaky buckets or GCRA controllers. The Integrated services framework of the Internet (Intserv) uses the same family of arrival curves, such as

$$\alpha(t) = \min(M + pt, rt + b) \tag{1.6}$$

where M is interpreted as the maximum packet size, p as the peak rate, b as the burst tolearance, and r as the sustainable rate (Figure 1.5). In Intserv jargon, the 4-uple (p, M, r, b) is also called a T-SPEC (traffic specification).

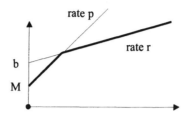

rate p

rate r

b

M

Figure 1.5: Arrival curve for ATM VBR and for Intserv flows

1.2.3 Sub-additivity and Arrival Curves

In this Section we discover the fundamental relationship between min-plus algebra and arrival curves. Let us start with a motivating example.

Consider a flow $R(t) \in \mathbb{N}$ with $t \in \mathbb{N}$; for example the flow is an ATM cell flow, counted in cells. Time is discrete to simplify the discussion. Assume that we know that the flow is constrained by the arrival curve $3v_{10,0}$; for example, the flow is the superposition of 3 CBR connections of peak rate 0.1 cell per time unit each. Assume in addition that we know that the flow arrives at the point of observation over a link with a physical characteristic of 1 cell per time unit. We can conclude that the flow is also constrained by the arrival curve $v_{1,0}$. Thus, obviously, it is constrained by $\alpha_1 = \min(3v_{10,0}, v_{1,0})$. Figure 1.6 shows the function α_1.

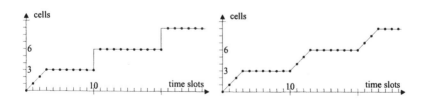

Figure 1.6: The arrival curve $\alpha_1 = \min(3v_{10,0}, v_{1,0})$ on the left, and its sub-additive closure ("good" function) $\bar{\alpha}_1$ on the right. Time is discrete, lines are put for ease of reading.

Now the arrival curve α_1 tells us that $R(10) \leq 3$ and $R(11) \leq 6$. However, since there can arrive at most 1 cell per time unit , we can also conclude that $R(11) \leq R(10) + [R(11) - R(10)] \leq \alpha_1(10) + \alpha_1(1) = 4$. In other words, the sheer knowledge that R is constrained by α_1 allows us to derive a better bound than α_1 itself. This is because α_1 is not a "good" function, in a sense that we define now.

Definition 1.2.4. *Consider a function α in cal$F$. We say that α is a "good" function if any one of the following equivalent properties is satisfied*

>   *1. α is sub-additive and $\alpha(0) = 0$*

>   *2. $\alpha = \alpha \otimes \alpha$*

>   *3. $\alpha \oslash \alpha = \alpha$*

>   *4. $\alpha = \bar{\alpha}$ (sub-additive closure of α).*

The definition uses the concepts of sub-additivity, min-plus convolution, min-plus deconvolution and sub-additive closure, which are defined in Chapter 3. The equivalence between the four items comes from Corollaries 3.1.1 on page 144 and 3.1.13 on page 151. Sub-additivity (item 1) means that $\alpha(s + t) \leq \alpha(s) + \alpha(t)$. If α is not sub-additive, then $\alpha(s) + \alpha(t)$ may be a better bound than $\alpha(s + t)$, as is the case with α_1 in the example above. Item 2, 3 and 4 use the concepts of min-plus convolution, min-plus deconvolution and sub-additive closure, defined in Chapter 3. We know in particular (Theorem 3.1.10) that the sub-additive closure of a function α is the largest "good" function $\bar{\alpha}$ such that $\bar{\alpha} \leq \alpha$. We also know that $\bar{\alpha} \in \mathcal{F}$ if $\alpha \in \mathcal{F}$.

The main result about arrival curves is that *any* arrival curve can be replaced by its sub-additive closure, which is a "good" arrival curve. Figure 1.6 shows $\bar{\alpha}_1$ for our example above.

Theorem 1.2.1 (Reduction of Arrival Curve to a Sub-Additive One). *Saying that a flow is constrained by a wide-sense increasing function α is equivalent to saying that it is constrained by the sub-additive closure $\bar{\alpha}$.*

The proof of the theorem leads us to the heart of the concept of arrival curve, namely, its correspondence with a fundamental, linear relationships in min-plus algebra, which we will now derive.

Lemma 1.2.3. *A flow R is constrained by arrival curve α if and only if $R \leq R \otimes \alpha$*

Proof: Remember that an equation such as $R \leq R \otimes \alpha$ means that for all times t, $R(t) \leq (R \otimes \alpha)(t)$. The min-plus convolution $R \otimes \alpha$ is defined in Chapter 3, page 134; since $R(s)$ and $\alpha(s)$ are defined only for $s \geq 0$, the definition of $R \otimes \alpha$ is: $(R \otimes \alpha)(t) = \inf_{0 \leq s \leq t}(R(s) + \alpha(t - s))$. Thus $R \leq R \otimes \alpha$ is equivalent to $R(t) \leq R(s) + \alpha(t - s)$ for all $0 \leq s \leq t$.   □

Lemma 1.2.4. *If α_1 and α_2 are arrival curves for a flow R, then so is $\alpha_1 \otimes \alpha_2$*

Proof: We know from Chapter 3 that $\alpha_1 \otimes \alpha_2$ is wide-sense increasing if α_1 and α_2 are. The rest of the proof follows immediately from Lemma 1.2.3 and the associativity of $\otimes$. □

Proof of Theorem Since α is an arrival curve, so is $\alpha \otimes \alpha$, and by iteration, so is $\alpha^{(n)}$ for all $n \geq 1$. By the definition of δ_0, it is also an arrival curve. Thus so is $\bar{\alpha} = \inf_{n \geq 0} \alpha^{(n)}$.

Conversely, $\alpha \leq \bar{\alpha}$; thus, if $\bar{\alpha}$ is an arrival curve, then so is α. □

Examples We should thus restrict our choice of arrival curves to sub-additive functions. As we can expect, the functions $\gamma_{r,b}$ and $v_{T,\tau}$ introduced in Section 1.2.1 are sub-additive and since their value is 0 for $t = 0$, they are "good" functions, as we now show. Indeed, we know from Chapter 1 that any concave function α such that $\alpha(0) = 0$ is sub-additive. This explains why the functions $\gamma_{r,b}$ are sub-additive.

Functions $v_{T,\tau}$ are not concave, but they still are sub-additive. This is because, from its very definition, the ceiling function is sub-additive, thus

$$v_{T,\tau}(s+t) = \lceil \frac{s+t+\tau}{T} \rceil \leq \lceil \frac{s+\tau}{T} \rceil + \lceil \frac{t}{T} \rceil \leq \lceil \frac{s+\tau}{T} \rceil + \lceil \frac{t+\tau}{T} \rceil = v_{T,\tau}(s) + v_{T,\tau}(t)$$

Let us return to our introductory example with $\alpha_1 = \min(3v_{10,0}, v_{1,0})$. As we discussed, α_1 is not sub-additive. From Theorem 1.2.1, we should thus replace α_1 by its sub-additive closure $\bar{\alpha}_1$, which can be computed by Equation (3.13). The computation is simplified by the following remark, which follows immediately from Theorem 3.1.11:

Lemma 1.2.5. *Let γ_1 and γ_2 be two "good" functions. The sub-additive closure of $\min(\gamma_1, \gamma_2)$ is $\gamma_1 \otimes \gamma_2$.*

We can apply the lemma to $\alpha_1 = 3v_{10,0} \wedge v_{1,0}$, since $v_{T,\tau}$ is a "good" function. Thus $\bar{\alpha}_1 = 3v_{10,0} \otimes v_{1,0}$, which the alert reader will enjoy computing. The result is plotted in Figure 1.6.

Finally, let us mention the following equivalence, the proof of which is easy and left to the reader.

Proposition 1.2.5. *For a given wide-sense increasing function α, with $\alpha(0) = 0$, consider a source defined by $R(t) = \alpha(t)$ (greedy source). The source has α as an arrival curve if and only if α is a "good" function.*

VBR arrival curve Now let us examine the family of arrival curves obtained by combinations of leaky buckets or GCRAs (concave piecewise linear functions). We know from Chapter 3 that if γ_1 and γ_2 are concave, with $\gamma_1(0) = \gamma_2(0) = 0$, then $\gamma_1 \otimes \gamma_2 = \gamma_1 \wedge \gamma_2$. Thus any concave piecewise linear function α such that $\alpha(0) = 0$ is a "good" function. In particular, if we define the arrival curve for VBR connections or Intserv flows by

$$\begin{cases} \alpha(t) = \min(pt + M, rt + b) & \text{if } t > 0 \\ \alpha(0) = 0 \end{cases}$$

(see Figure 1.5) then α is a "good" function.

We have seen in Lemma 1.2.1 that an arrival curve α can always be replaced by its limit to the left α_l. We might wonder how this combines with the sub-additive closure, and in particular, whether these two operations commute (in other words, do we have $(\bar{\alpha})_l = \overline{\alpha_l}$?). In general, if α is left-continuous, then we cannot guarantee that $\bar{\alpha}$ is also left-continuous, thus we cannot guarantee that the operations commute. However, it can be shown that $(\bar{\alpha})_l$ is always a "good" function, thus $\overline{(\bar{\alpha})_l} = (\bar{\alpha})_l$. Starting from an arrival curve α we can therefore improve by taking the sub-additive closure first, then the limit to the left. The resulting arrival curve $(\bar{\alpha})_l$ is a "good" function that is also left-continuous (a "very good" function), and the constraint by α is equivalent to the constraint by $(\bar{\alpha})_l$

Lastly, let us mention that it can easily be shown, using an argument of uniform continuity, that if α takes only a finite set of values over any bounded time interval, and if α is left-continuous, then so is $\bar{\alpha}$ and then we do have $(\bar{\alpha})_l = \overline{\alpha_l}$. This assumption is always true in discrete time, and in most cases in practice.

1.2.4   Minimum Arrival Curve

Consider now a given flow $R(t)$, for which we would like to determine a minimal arrival curve. This problem arises, for example, when R is known from measurements. The following theorem says that there is indeed one minimal arrival curve.

Theorem 1.2.2 (Minimum Arrival Curve). *Consider a flow $R(t)_{t\geq0}$. Then*

- *function $R \oslash R$ is an arrival curve for the flow*

- *for any arrival curve α that constrains the flow, we have: $(R \oslash R) \leq \alpha$*

- *$R \oslash R$ is a "good" function*

Function $R \oslash R$ is called the minimum arrival curve *for flow R.*

The minimum arrival curve uses min-plus deconvolution, defined in Chapter 3. Figure 1.2.4 shows an example of $R \oslash R$ for a measured function R.

Proof: By definition of $\oslash$, we have $(R \oslash R)(t) = \sup_{v\geq0}\{R(t + v) - R(v)\}$, it follows that $(R \oslash R)$ is an arrival curve.

Now assume that some α is also an arrival curve for R. From Lemma 1.2.3, we have $R \leq R \otimes \alpha)$. From Rule 14 in Theorem 3.1.12 in Chapter 3, it follows that $R \oslash R \leq \alpha$, which shows that $R \oslash R$ is the minimal arrival curve for R. Lastly, $R \oslash R$ is a "good" function from Rule 15 in Theorem 3.1.12.   □

Consider a greedy source, with $R(t) = \alpha(t)$, where α is a "good" function. What is the minimum arrival curve ?[5] Lastly, the curious reader might wonder

---

[5]Answer: from the equivalence in Definition 1.2.4, the minimum arrival curve is α itself.

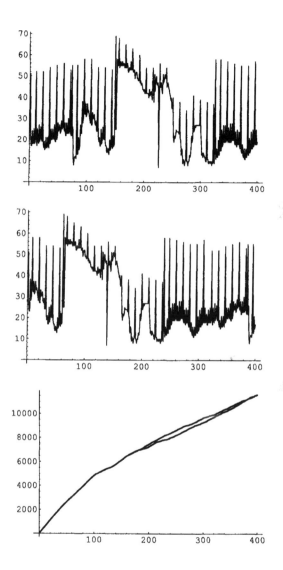

Figure 1.7: Example of minimum arrival curve. Time is discrete, one time unit is 40 ms. The top figures shows, for two similar traces, the number of packet arrivals at every time slot. Every packet is of constant size (416 bytes). The bottom figure shows the minimum arrival curve for the first trace (top curve) and the second trace (bottom curve). The large burst in the first trace comes earlier, therefore its minimum arrival curve is slightly larger.

whether $R \oslash R$ is left-continuous. The answer is as follows. Assume that R is either right or left-continuous. By lemma 1.2.1, the limit to the left $(R \oslash R)_l$ is also an arrival curve, and is bounded from above by $R \oslash R$. Since $R \oslash R$ is the minimum arrival curve, it follows that $(R \oslash R)_l = R \oslash R$, thus $R \oslash R$ is left-continuous (and is thus a "very good" function).

In many cases, one is interested not in the absolute minimum arrival curve as presented here, but in a minimum arrival curve within a family of arrival curves, for example, among all $\gamma_{r,b}$ functions. For a development along this line, see [54].

1.3 Service Curves

1.3.1 Definition of Service Curve

We have seen that one first principle in integrated services networks is to put arrival curve constraints on flows. In order to provide reservations, network nodes in return need to offer some guarantees to flows. This is done by packet schedulers [39]. The details of packet scheduling are abstracted using the concept of service curve, which we introduce and study in this section. Since the concept of service curve is more abstract than that of arrival curve, we introduce it on some examples.

A first, simple example of a scheduler is a Generalized Processor Sharing (GPS) node [56]. We define now a simple view of GPS; more details are given in Chapter 2. A GPS node serves several flows in parallel, and we can consider that every flow is allocated a given rate. The guarantee is that during a period of duration t, for which a flow has some backlog in the node, it receives an amount of service at least equal to rt, where r is its allocated rate. A GPS node is a theoretical concept, which is not really implementable, because it relies on a fluid model, while real networks use packets. We will see in Section 2.1 on page 83 how to account for the difference between a real implementation and GPS. Consider a input flow R, with output R^*, that is served in a GPS node, with allocated rate r. Let us also assume that the node buffer is large enough so that overflow is not possible. We will see in this section how to compute the buffer size required to satisfy this assumption. Lossy systems are the object of Chapter 9. Under these assumptions, for all time t, call t_0 the beginning of the last busy period for the flow up to time t. From the GPS assumption, we have

$$R^*(t) - R^*(t_0) \geq r(t - t_0)$$

Assume as usual that R is left-continuous; at time t_0 the backlog for the flow is 0, which is expressed by $R(t_0) - R^*(t_0) = 0$. Combining this with the previous equation, we obtain:

$$R^*(t) - R(t_0) \geq r(t - t_0)$$

We have thus shown that, for all time t: $R^*(t) \geq \inf_{0 \leq s \leq t}[R(s) + r(t - s)]$, which can be written as

$$R^* \geq R \otimes \gamma_{r,0} \tag{1.7}$$

Note that a limiting case of GPS node is the constant bit rate server with rate r, dedicated to serving a single flow. We will study GPS in more details in Chapter 2.

Consider now a second example. Assume that the only information we have about a network node is that the maximum delay for the bits of a given flow R is bounded by some fixed value T, and that the bits of the flow are served in first in, first out order. We will see in Section 1.5 that this is used with a family of schedulers called "earliest deadline first" (EDF). We can translate the assumption on the delay bound to $d(t) \leq T$ for all t. Now since R^* is always wide-sense increasing, it follows from the definition of $d(t)$ that $R^*(t + T) \geq R(t)$. Conversely, if $R^*(t + T) \geq R(t)$, then $d(t) \leq T$. In other words, our condition that the maximum delay is bounded by T is equivalent to $R^*(t + T) \geq R(t)$ for all t. This in turn can be re-written as

$$R^*(s) \geq R(s - T)$$

for all $s \geq T$. We have introduced in Chapter 3 the "impulse" function δ_T defined by $\delta_T(t) = 0$ if $0 \leq t \leq T$ and $\delta_T(t) = +\infty$ if $t > T$. It has the property that, for any wide-sense increasing function $x(t)$, defined for $t \leq 0$, $(x \otimes \delta_T)(t) = x(t - T)$ if $t \geq T$ and $(x \otimes \delta_T)(t) = x(0)$ otherwise. Our condition on the maximum delay can thus be written as

$$R^* \geq R \otimes \delta_T \tag{1.8}$$

For the two examples above, there is an input-output relationship of the same form (Equations (1.7) and (1.8)). This suggests the definition of service curve, which, as we see in the rest of this section, is indeed able to provide useful results.

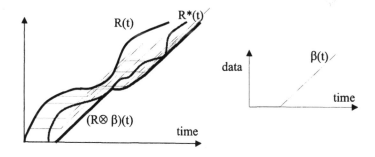

Figure 1.8: Definition of service curve. The output R^* must be above $R \otimes \beta$, which is the lower envelope of all curves $t \mapsto R(t_0) + \beta(t - t_0)$.

Definition 1.3.1 (Service Curve). *Consider a system S and a flow through S with input and output function R and R^*. We say that S offers to the flow a service curve β if and only if $\beta \in \mathcal{F}$ and $R^* \geq R \otimes \beta$*

Figure 1.8 illustrates the definition.

The definition means that β is a wide sense increasing function, with $\beta(0) = 0$, and that for all $t \geq 0$,

$$R^*(t) \geq \inf_{s \leq t} (R(s) + \beta(t - s))$$

In practice, we can avoid the use of an infimum if β is continuous. The following proposition is an immediate consequence of Theorem 3.1.8 on Page 139.

Proposition 1.3.1. *If β is continuous, the service curve property means that for all t we can find $t_0 \leq t$ such that*

$$R^*(t) \geq R_l(t_0) + \beta(t - t_0) \tag{1.9}$$

where $R_l(t_0) = \sup_{\{s < t_0\}} R(s)$ is the limit to the left of R at t_0. If R is left-continuous, then $R_l(t_0) = R(t_0)$.

For a constant rate server (and also for any *strict* service curve, the number t_0 in Equation (1.9) is the beginning of the busy period. For other cases, there is not such a simple definition. However, in some cases we can make sure that t_0 increases with t:

Proposition 1.3.2. *If the service curve β is convex, then we can find some wide sense increasing function $\tau(t)$ such that we can choose $t_0 = \tau(t)$ in Equation (1.9).*

Note that since a service curve is assumed to be wide-sense increasing, β, being convex, is necessarily continuous; thus we can apply Proposition 1.3.1.

Proof: We give the proof when R is left-continuous. The proof for the general case is essentially the same but involves some ϵ cutting. Consider some $t_1 < t_2$ and call τ_1 a value of t_0 as in Equation (1.9)) at $t = t_1$. Also consider any $t' \leq \tau_1$. From the definition of τ_1, we have

$$R^*(t') + \beta(t_1 - t') \geq R^*(\tau_1) + \beta(t_1 - \tau_1)$$

and thus

$$R^*(t') + \beta(t_2 - t') \geq R^*(\tau_1) + \beta(t_1 - \tau_1) - \beta(t_1 - t') + \beta(t_2 - t')$$

Now β is convex, thus for any four numbers a, b, c, d such that $a \leq c \leq b, a \leq d \leq b$ and $a + b = c + d$, we have

$$\beta(a) + \beta(b) \geq \beta(c) + \beta(d)$$

(the interested reader will be convinced by drawing a small figure). Applying this to $a = t_1 - \tau_1, b = t_2 - t', c = t_1 - t', d = t_2 - \tau_1$ gives

$$R^*(t') + \beta(t_2 - t') \geq R^*(\tau_1) + \beta(t_2 - \tau_1)$$

and the above equation holds for all $t' \leq \tau_1$. Consider now the minimum, for a fixed t_2, of $R^*(t') + \beta(t_2 - t')$ over all $t' \leq t_2$. The above equation shows that the minimum is reached for some $t' \geq \tau_1$. □

We will see in Section 1.4 that the combination of a service curve guarantee with an arrival curve constraint forms the basis for deterministic bounds used in integrated services networks. Before that, we give the fundamental service curve examples that are used in practice.

1.3.2 Classical Service Curve Examples

Guaranteed Delay Node The analysis of the second example in Section 1.3.1 can be rephrased as follows.

Proposition 1.3.3. *For a lossless bit processing system, saying that the delay for any bit is bounded by some fixed T is equivalent to saying that the system offers to the flow a service curve equal to δ_T.*

Non Preemptive Priority Node Consider a node that serves two flows, $R_H(t)$ and $R_L(t)$. The first flow has non-preemptive priority over the second one (Figure 1.9). This example explains the general framework used when some traffic classes have priority over some others, such as with the Internet differentiated services [6]. The rate of the server is constant, equal to C. Call $R_H^*(t)$ and $R_L^*(t)$ the outputs for the two flows. Consider first the high priority flow. Fix some time t and call s the

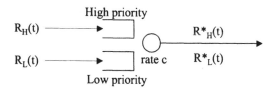

Figure 1.9: Two priority flows (H and L) served with a preemptive head of the line (HOL) service discipline. The high priority flow is constrained by arrival curve α.

beginning of the backlog period for high priority traffic. The service for high priority can be delayed by a low priority packet that arrived shortly before s', but as soon as this packet is served, the server is dedicated to high priority as long as there is some high priority traffic to serve. Over the interval $(s, t]$, the output is $C(t - s)$ Thus

$$R_H^*(t) - R_H^*(s) \geq C(t - s) - l_{max}^H$$

where l_{max}^L is the maximum size of a low priority packet. Now by definition of s: $R_H^*(s) = R_H(s)$ thus

$$R_H^*(t) \geq R_H(s) + C(t - s) - l_{\max}^L$$

Now we have also

$$R_H^*(t) - R_H(s) = R_H^*(t) - R_H^*(s) \geq 0$$

from which we derive

$$R_H^*(t) \geq R_H(s) + [C(t - s) - l_{\max}^L]^+$$

The function $u \to [Cu - l_{\max}^L]^+$ is called the rate-latency function with rate C and latency $\frac{l_{\max}^L}{C}$ [67] (in this book we note it $\beta_{C, \frac{l_{\max}^L}{C}}$, see also Figure 3.1 on page 130). Thus the high priority traffic receives this function as a service curve.

Now let us examine low priority traffic. In order to assure that it does not starve, we assume in such situations that the high priority flow is constrained by an arrival curve α_H. Consider again some arbitrary time t. Call s' the beginning of the server busy period (note that $s' \leq s$). At time s', the backlogs for both flows are empty, namely, $R_H^*(s') = R_H(s')$ and $R_L^*(s') = R_L(s')$. Over the interval $(s', t]$, the output is $C(t - s')$. Thus

$$R_L^*(t) - R_L^*(s') = C(t - s') - [R_H^*(t) - R_H^*(s')]$$

Now

$$R_H^*(t) - R_H^*(s') = R_H^*(t) - R_H(s') \leq R_H(t) - R_H(s') \leq \alpha_H(t - s')$$

and obviously $R_H^*(t) - R_H^*(s') \geq 0$ thus

$$R_L^*(t) - R_L(s') = R_L^*(t) - R_L^*(s') \geq S(t - s')$$

with $S(u) = (Cu - \alpha_H(u))^+$. Thus, if S is wide-sense increasing, the low-priority flow receives a service curve equal to function S. Assume further that $\alpha_H = \gamma_{r,b}$, namely, the high priority flow is constrained by one single leaky bucket or GCRA. In that case, the service curve $S(t)$ offered to the low-priority flow is equal to the rate-latency function $\beta_{R,T}(t)$, with $R = C - r$ and $T = \frac{b}{C-r}$.

We have thus shown the following.

Proposition 1.3.4. *Consider a constant bit rate server, with rate C, serving two flows, H and L, with non-preemptive priority given to flow H. Then the high priority flow is guaranteed a rate-latency service curve with rate C and latency $\frac{l_{\max}^L}{C}$ where $l_{\max}^L$ is the maximum packet size for the low priority flow.*

If in addition the high priority flow is $\gamma_{r,b}$-smooth, with $r < C$, then the low priority flow is guaranteed a rate-latency service curve with rate $C - r$ and latency $\frac{b}{C-r}$.

This example justifies the importance of the rate-latency service curve. We will also see in Chapter 2 (Theorem 2.1.1 on page 87) that all practical implementations of GPS offer a service curve of the rate-latency type.

Strict service curve An important class of network nodes fits in the following framework.

Definition 1.3.2 (Strict Service Curve). *We say that system S offers a strict service curve β to a flow if, during any backlogged period of duration u, the output of the flow is at least equal to $\beta(u)$.*

A GPS node is an example of node that offers a strict service curve of the form $\beta(t) = rt$. Using the same busy-period analysis as with the GPS example in the previous section, we can easily prove the following.

Proposition 1.3.5. *If a node offers β as a strict service curve to a flow, then it also offers β as a service curve to the flow.*

The strict service curve property offers a convenient way of visualizing the service curve concept: in that case, $\beta(u)$ is the minimum amount of service guaranteed during a busy period. Note however that the concept of service curve, as defined in Definition 1.3.1 is more general. A greedy shaper (Section 1.5.2) is an example of system that offers its shaping curve as a service curve, without satisfying the strict service curve property. In contrast, we will find later in the book some properties that hold only if a strict service curve applies. The framework for a general discussion of strict service curves is given in Chapter 7.

Variable Capacity Node Consider a network node that offers a variable service capacity to a flow. In some cases, it is possible to model the capacity by a cumulative function $M(t)$, where $M(t)$ is the total service capacity available to the flow between times 0 and t. For example, for an ATM system, think of $M(t)$ as the number of time slots between times 0 and t that are available for sending cells of the flow. Let us also assume that the node buffer is large enough so that overflow is not possible. The following proposition is obvious but important in practice

Proposition 1.3.6. *If the variable capacity satisfies a minimum guarantee of the form*

$$M(t) - M(s) \geq \beta(t - s) \qquad (1.10)$$

for some fixed function β and for all $0 \leq s \leq t$, then β is a strict service curve,

Thus β is also a service curve for that particular flow. The concept of variable capacity node is also a convenient way to establish service curve properties. For an application to real time systems (rather than communication networks) see [70].

We will show in Chapter 4 that the output of the variable capacity node is given by

$$R^*(t) = \inf_{0 \leq s \leq t} \{M(t) - M(s) + R(s)\}$$

Lastly, coming back to the priority node, we have:

Proposition 1.3.7. *The service curve properties in Proposition 1.3.4 are strict.*

The proof is left to the reader. It relies on the fact that constant rate server is a shaper.

1.4   Network Calculus Basics

In this section we see the main simple network calculus results. They are all bounds for lossless systems with service guarantees.

1.4.1   Three Bounds

The first theorem says that the backlog is bounded by the vertical deviation between the arrival and service curves:

Theorem 1.4.1 (Backlog Bound). *Assume a flow, constrained by arrival curve α, traverses a system that offers a service curve β. The backlog $R(t) - R^*(t)$ for all t satisfies:*

$$R(t) - R^*(t) \leq \sup_{s \geq 0}\{\alpha(s) - \beta(s)\}$$

Proof: The proof is a straightforward application of the definitions of service and arrival curves:

$$R(t) - R^*(t) \leq R(t) - \inf_{0 \leq s \leq t}[R(t - s) + \beta(s)]$$

Thus

$$R(t) - R^*(t) \leq \sup_{0 \leq s \leq t}[R(t) - R(t - s) + \beta(s)] \leq \sup_{0 \leq s \leq t}[\alpha(s) + \beta(t - s)]$$

$\square$

We now use the concept of horizontal deviation, defined in Chapter 3, Equation (3.21). The definition is a little complex, but is supported by the following intuition. Call

$$\delta(s) = \inf\{\tau \geq 0 : \alpha(s) \leq \beta(s + \tau)\}$$

From Definition 1.1.1, $\delta(s)$ is the virtual delay for a hypothetical system that would have α as input and β as output, assuming that such a system exists (in other words, assuming that ($\alpha \leq \beta$). Then, $h(\alpha, \beta)$ is the supremum of all values of $\delta(s)$. The second theorem gives a bound on delay for the general case.

Theorem 1.4.2 (Delay Bound). *Assume a flow, constrained by arrival curve α, traverses a system that offers a service curve of β. The virtual delay $d(t)$ for all t satisfies: $d(t) \leq h(\alpha, \beta)$.*

Proof: Consider some fixed $t \geq 0$; for all $\tau < d(t)$, we have, from the definition of virtual delay, $R(t) > R^*(t + \tau)$. Now the service curve property at time $t + \tau$ implies that there is some s_0 such that

$$R(t) > R(t + \tau - s_0) + \beta(s_0)$$

It follows from this latter equation that $t + \tau - s_0 < t$. Thus

$$\alpha(\tau - s_0) \geq [R(t) - R(t + \tau - s_0)] > \beta(s_0)$$

Thus $\tau \leq \delta(\tau - s_0) \leq h(\alpha, \beta)$. This is true for all $\tau < d(t)$ thus $d(t) \leq h(\alpha, \beta)$. □

Theorem 1.4.3 (Output Flow). *Assume a flow, constrained by arrival curve α, traverses a system that offers a service curve of β. The output flow is constrained by the arrival curve $\alpha^* = \alpha \oslash \beta$.*

The theorem uses min-plus deconvolution, introduced in Chapter 3, which we have already used in Theorem 1.2.2.

Proof: With the same notation as above, consider $R^*(t) - R^*(t - s)$, for $0 \leq t - s \leq t$. Consider the definition of the service curve, applied at time $t - s$. Assume for a second that the inf in the definition of $R \otimes \beta$ is a min, that is to say, there is some $u \geq 0$ such that $0 \leq t - s - u$ and

$$(R \otimes \beta)(t - s) = R(t - s - u) + \beta(u)$$

Thus

$$R^*(t - s) - R(t - s - u) \geq \beta(u)$$

and thus

$$R^*(t) - R^*(t - s) \leq R^*(t) - \beta(u) - R(t - s - u)$$

Now $R^*(t) \leq R(t)$, therefore

$$R^*(t) - R^*(t - s) \leq R(t) - R(t - s - u) - \beta(u) \leq \alpha(s + u) - \beta(u)$$

and the latter term is bounded by $(\alpha \oslash \beta)(s)$ by definition of the $\oslash$ operator.

Now relax the assumption that the the inf in the definition of $R \otimes \beta$ is a min. In this case, the proof is essentially the same with a minor complication. For all $\epsilon > 0$ there is some $u \geq 0$ such that $0 \leq t - s - u$ and

$$(R \otimes \beta)(t - s) \geq R(t - s - u) + \beta(u) - \epsilon$$

and the proof continues along the same line, leading to:

$$R^*(t) - R^*(t - s) \leq (\alpha \oslash \beta)(s) + \epsilon$$

This is true for all $\epsilon > 0$, which proves the result.   □

A simple Example and Interpretation of Leaky Bucket Consider a flow constrained by one leaky bucket, thus with an arrival curve of the form $\alpha = \gamma_{r,b}$, served in a node with the service curve guarantee $\beta_{R,T}$. The alert reader will enjoy applying the three bounds and finding the results shown in Figure 1.10.

Consider in particular the case $T = 0$, thus a flow constrained by one leaky bucket served at a constant rate R. If $R \geq r$ then the buffer required to serve the flow is b, otherwise, it is infinite. This gives us a common interpretation of the leaky bucket parameters r and b: r is the minimum rate required to serve the flow, and b is the buffer required to serve the flow at any constant rate $\geq r$.

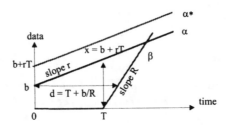

Figure 1.10: Computation of buffer, delay and output bounds for an input flow constrained by one leaky bucket, served in one node offered a rate-latency service curve. If $r \leq R$, then the buffer bound is $x = b + rT$, the delay bound is $d = T + \frac{b}{R}$ and the burstiness of the flow is increased by rT. If $r > R$, the bounds are infinite.

Example: VBR flow with rate-latency service curve Consider a VBR flow, defined by TSPEC (M, p, r, b). This means that the flow has $\alpha(t) = \min(M + pt, rt + b)$ as an arrival curve (Section 1.2). Assume that the flow is served in one node that guarantees a service curve equal to the rate-latency function $\beta = \beta_{R,T}$. This example is the standard model used in Intserv. Let us apply Theorems 1.4.1 and 1.4.2. Assume that $R \geq r$, that is, the reserved rate is as large as the sustainable rate of the flow.

From the convexity of the region between α and β (Figure 1.4.1), we see that the vertical deviation $v = \sup_{s \geq 0}[\alpha(s) - \beta(s)]$ is reached for at an angular point of either α or β. Thus

$$v = \max[\alpha(T), \alpha(\theta)]$$

with $\theta = \frac{b-M}{p-r}$. Similarly, the horizontal distance is reached an angular point. In the figure, it is either the distance markes as AA' or BB'. Thus, the bound on delay d is given by

$$d = \max\left(\frac{\alpha(\theta)}{R} + T - \theta, \frac{M}{R} + T\right)$$

After some max-plus algebra, we can re-arrange these results as follows.

Proposition 1.4.1 (Intserv model, buffer and delay bounds). *Consider a VBR flow, with TSPEC (M, p, r, b), served in a node that guarantees to the flow a service curve equal to the rate-latency function $\beta = \beta_{R,T}$. The buffer required for the flow is bounded by*

$$v = b + r \max\left(\frac{b - M}{p - r}, T\right)$$

The maximum delay for the flow is bounded by

$$d = \frac{M + \frac{b-M}{p-r}(p - R)^+}{R} + T$$

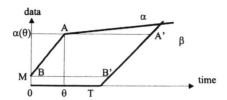

Figure 1.11: Computation of buffer and delay bound for one VBR flow served in one Intserv node.

We can also apply Theorem 1.4.3 and find an arrival curve α^* for the output flow. We have $\alpha^* = \alpha \oslash (\lambda_R \otimes \delta_T) = (\alpha \oslash \lambda_R) \oslash \delta_T$ from the properties of $\oslash$ (Chapter 3). Note that

$$(f \oslash \delta_T)(t) = f(t + T)$$

for all f (shift to the left).

The computation of $\alpha \oslash \lambda_R$ is explained in Theorem 3.1.14 on Page 152: it consists in inverting time, and smoothing. Here, we give however a direct derivation, which is possible since α is concave. Indeed, for a concave α, define t_0 as

$$t_0 = \inf\{t \geq 0 : \alpha'(t) \leq R\}$$

where α' is the left-derivative, and assume that $t_0 < +\infty$. A concave function always has a left-derivative, except maybe at the ends of the interval where it is defined. Then by studying the variations of the function $u \to \alpha(t + u) - Ru$ we find that $(\alpha \oslash \lambda_R)(s) = \alpha(s)$ if $s \geq t_0$, and $(\alpha \oslash \lambda_R)(s) = \alpha(t_0) + (s - t_0)R$ if $s < t_0$.

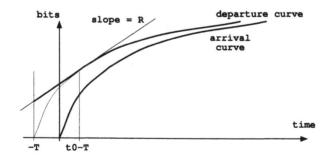

Figure 1.12: Derivation of arrival curve for the output of a flow served in a node with rate-latency service curve $\beta_{R,T}$.

Putting the pieces all together we see that the output function α^* is obtained from α by

- replacing α on $[0, t_0]$ by the linear function with slope R that has the same value as α for $t = t_0$, keeping the same values as α on $[t_0, +\infty[$,

- and shifting by T to the left.

Figure 1.12 illustrates the operation. Note that the two operations can be performed in any order since $\otimes$ is commutative. Check that the operation is equivalent to the construction in Theorem 3.1.14 on Page 152.

If we apply this to a VBR connection, we obtain the following result.

Proposition 1.4.2 (Intserv model, output bound). *With the same assumption as in Proposition 1.4.1, the output flow has an arrival curve α^* given by:*

$$\begin{cases} \text{if } \frac{b-M}{p-r} \leq T \text{ then } \alpha^*(t) = b + r(T + t) \\ \text{else } \alpha^*(t) = \min\left\{ (t + T)(p \wedge R) + M + \frac{b-M}{p-r}(p - R)^+, b + r(T + t) \right\} \end{cases}$$

An ATM Example Consider the example illustrated in Figure 1.13. The aggregate flow has as an arrival curve equal to the stair function $10v_{25,4}$. The figure illustrates that the required buffer is 18 ATM cells and the maximum delay is 10 time slots. We

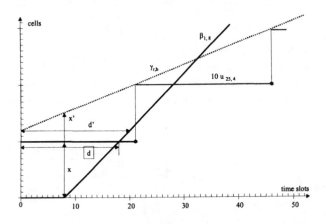

Figure 1.13: Computation of bounds for buffer x and delay d for an ATM example. An ATM node serves 10 ATM connections, each constrained with GCRA$(25, 4)$ (counted in time slots). The node offers to the aggregate flow a service curve $\beta_{R,T}$ with rate $R = 1$ cell per time slot and latency $T = 8$ time slots. The figure shows that approximating the stair function $10v_{25,4}$ by an affine function $\gamma_{r,b}$ results into an overestimation of the bounds.

know from Corollary 1.2.1 that a GCRA constraint is equivalent to a leaky bucket. Thus, each of the 10 connections is constrained by an affine arrival curve $\gamma_{r,b}$ with $r = \frac{1}{25} = 0.04$ and $b = 1 + \frac{4}{25} = 1.16$. However, if we take as an arrival curve for the aggregate flow the resulting affine function $10\gamma_{r,b}$, then we obtain a buffer bound of 11.6 and a delay bound of 19.6. The affine function overestimates the buffer and delay bounds. Remember that the equivalence between stair function and affine function is only for a flow where the packet size is equal to the value of the step, which is clearly not the case for an aggregate of several ATM connections.

A direct application of Theorem 1.4.3 shows that an arrival curve for the output flow is given by $\alpha_0^*(t) = \alpha(t + T) = v_{25,12}(t)$.

In Chapter 2, we give a slight improvement to the bounds if we know that the service curve is a strict service curve.

1.4.2   Are the Bounds Tight ?

We now examine how good the three bounds are. For the backlog and delay bounds, the answer is simple:

Theorem 1.4.4. *Consider the backlog and delay bounds in Theorems 1.4.1 and 1.4.2. Assume that*

- *α is a "good" function (that is, namely, is wide-sense increasing, sub-additive and $\alpha(0) = 0$)*

- *β is wide-sense increasing and $\beta(0) = 0$*

Then the bounds are tight. More precisely, there is one causal system with input flow $R(t)$ and output flow $R^*(t)$, such that the input is constrained by α, offering to the flow a service curve β, and which achieves both bounds.

A causal system means that $R(t) \leq R^*(t)$. The theorem means that the backlog bound in Theorem 1.4.1 is equal to $\sup_{t \geq 0}[R(t) - R^*(t)]$, and the delay bound in Theorem 1.4.1 is equal to $\sup_{t \geq 0} d(t)$. In the above, $d(t)$ is the virtual delay defined in Definition 1.1.1.

Proof: We build one such system R, R^* by defining $R = \alpha, R^* = \min(\alpha, \beta)$. The system is causal because $R^* \leq \alpha = R$. Now consider some arbitrary time t. If $\alpha(t) < \beta(t)$ then

$$R^*(t) = R(t) = R(t) + \beta(0)$$

Otherwise,

$$R^*(t) = \beta(t) = R(0) + \beta(t)$$

In all cases, for all t there is some $s \leq t$ such that $R^*(t) \geq R(t - s) + \beta(s)$, which shows the service curve property.   □

Of course, the bounds are as tight as the arrival and service curves are. We have seen that a source such that $R(t) = \alpha(t)$ is called *greedy*. Thus, the backlog and delay bounds are worst-case bounds that are achieved for greedy sources.

In practice, the output bound is also a worst-case bound, even though the detailed result is somehow less elegant.

Theorem 1.4.5. *Assume that*

1. *α is a "good" function (that is, is wide-sense increasing, sub-additive and $\alpha(0) = 0$)*

2. *α is left-continuous*

3. *β is wide-sense increasing and $\beta(0) = 0$*

4. *$\alpha\overline{\oslash}\alpha$ is not bounded from above.*

Then the output bound in Theorem 1.4.3 is tight. More precisely, there is one causal system with input flow $R(t)$ and output flow $R^*(t)$, such that the input is constrained by α, offering to the flow a service curve β, and α^* (given by Theorem 1.4.3) is the minimum arrival curve for R^*.

We know in particular from Section 1.2 that the first three conditions are not restrictive. Let us first discuss the meaning of the last condition. By definition of max-plus deconvolution:

$$(\alpha\overline{\oslash}\alpha)(t) = \inf_{s\geq 0}\{\alpha(t+s) - \alpha(s)\}$$

One interpretation of $\alpha\overline{\oslash}\alpha$ is as follows. Consider a greedy source, with $R(t) = \alpha(t)$; then $(\alpha\overline{\oslash}\alpha)(t)$ is the minimum number of bits arriving over an interval of duration t. Given that the function is wide-sense increasing, the last condition means that $\lim_{t\to+\infty}(\alpha\overline{\oslash}\alpha)(t) = +\infty$. For example, for a VBR source with T-SPEC (p, M, r, b) (Figure 1.5), we have $(\alpha\overline{\oslash}\alpha)(t) = rt$ and the condition is satisfied. The alert reader will easily be convinced that the condition is also true if the arrival curve is a stair function.

The proof of Theorem 1.4.5 is a little technical and is left at the end of this chapter.

We might wonder whether the output bound α^* is a "good" function. The answer is no, since $\alpha^*(0)$ is the backlog bound and is positive in reasonable cases. However, α^* is sub-additive (the proof is easy and left to the reader) thus the modified function $\delta_0 \wedge \alpha^*$ defined as $\alpha^*(t)$ for $t > 0$ and 0 otherwise is a "good" function. If α is left-continuous, $\delta_0 \wedge \alpha^*$ is even a "very good" function since we know from the proof of Theorem 1.4.5 that it is left-continuous.

1.4.3   Concatenation

So far we have considered elementary network parts. We now come to the main result used in the concatenation of network elements.

Theorem 1.4.6 (Concatenation of Nodes). *Assume a flow traverses systems S_1 and S_2 in sequence. Assume that S_i offers a service curve of β_i, $i = 1, 2$ to the flow. Then the concatenation of the two systems offers a service curve of $\beta_1 \otimes \beta_2$ to the flow.*

Proof: Call R_1 the output of node 1, which is also the input to node 2. The service curve property at node 1 gives

$$R_1 \geq R \otimes \beta_1$$

and at node 2

$$R^* \geq R_1 \otimes \beta_2 \geq (R \otimes \beta_1) \otimes \beta_2 = R \otimes (\beta_1 \otimes \beta_2)$$

$\square$

Examples: Consider two nodes offering each a rate-latency service curve β_{R_i,T_i}, $i = 1, 2$, as is commonly assumed with Intserv. A simple computation gives

$$\beta_{R_1,T_1} \otimes \beta_{R_1,T_1} = \beta_{\min(R_1,R_2),T_1+T_2}$$

Thus concatenating Intserv nodes amounts to adding the latency components and taking the minimum of the rates.

We are now also able to give another interpretation of the rate-latency service curve model. We know that $\beta_{R,T} = (\delta_T \otimes \lambda_R)(t)$; thus we can view a node offering a rate-latency service curve as the concatenation of a guaranteed delay node, with delay T and a constant bit rate or GPS node with rate R.

Pay Bursts Only Once The concatenation theorem allows us to understand a phenomenon known as "Pay Bursts Only Once". Consider the concatenation of two nodes offering each a rate-latency service curve β_{R_i,T_i}, $i = 1, 2$, as is commonly assumed with Intserv. Assume the fresh input is constrained by $\gamma_{r,b}$. Assume that $r < R_1$ and $r < R_2$. We are interested in the delay bound, which we know is a worst case. Let us compare the results obtained as follows.

1. by applying the network service curve;

2. by iterative application of the individual bounds on every node

The delay bound D_0 can be computed by applying Theorem 1.4.2:

$$D_0 = \frac{b}{R} + T_0$$

with $R = \min_i(R_i)$ and $T_0 = \sum_i T_i$ as seen above.

Now apply the second method. A bound on the delay at node 1 is (Theorem 1.4.2):

$$D_1 = \frac{b}{R_1} + T_1$$

The output of the first node is constrained by α^*, given by :

$$\alpha^*(t) = b + r \times (t + T_1)$$

A bound on the delay at the second buffer is:

$$D_2 = \frac{b + rT_1}{R_2} + T_2$$

And thus

$$D_1 + D_2 = \frac{b}{R_1} + \frac{b + rT_1}{R_2} + T_0$$

It is easy to see that $D_0 < D_1 + D_2$. In other words, the bounds obtained by considering the global service curve are better than the bounds obtained by considering every buffer in isolation.

Let us continue the comparison more closely. The delay through one node has the form $\frac{b}{R_1} + T_1$ (for the first node). The element $\frac{b}{R_1}$ is interpreted as the part of the delay due to the burstiness of the input flow, whereas T_1 is due to the delay component of the node. We see that $D_1 + D_2$ contains twice an element of the form $\frac{b}{R_i}$, whereas D_0 contains it only once. We sometimes say that "we pay bursts only once". Another difference between D_0 and $D_1 + D_2$ is the element $\frac{rT_1}{R_2}$: it is due to the increase of burstiness imposed by node 1. We see that this increase of burstiness does not result into an increase of the overall delay.

A corollary of Theorem 1.4.6 is also that the end-to-end delay bound does not depend on the order in which nodes are concatenated.

1.4.4   Improvement of Backlog Bounds

We give two cases where we can slightly improve the backlog bounds.

Theorem 1.4.7. *Assume that a lossless node offers a* strict *service curve β to a flow with arrival curve α. Assume that $\alpha(u_0) \leq \beta(u_0)$ for some $u_0 > 0$. Then the duration of the busy period is $\leq u_0$. Furthermore, for any time t, the backlog $R(t) - R^*(t)$ satisfies*

$$R(t) - R^*(t) \leq \sup_{u:0 \leq u < u_0} [R(t) - R(t-u) - \beta(u)] \leq \sup_{u:0 \leq u < u_0} [\alpha(u) - \beta(u)]$$

The theorem says that, for the computation of a buffer bound, it is sufficient to consider time intervals less than u_0. The idea is that the busy period duration is less than u_0.

Proof: Consider a given time t at which the buffer is not empty, and call s the last time instant before t at which the buffer was empty. Then, from the strict service curve property, we have

$$R^*(t) \geq R^*(s) + \beta(t-s) = x(s) + \beta(t-s)$$

Thus the buffer size $b(t) = R(t) - R^*(t)$ at time t satisfies

$$b(t) \leq R(t) - R(s) - \beta(t-s) \leq \alpha(t-s) - \beta(t-s)$$

Now if $t - s \geq u_0$, then there is a time $t' = s + u_0$, with $s + 1 \leq t' \leq t$ such that $b(t') = 0$. This contradicts the definition of s. Thus we can assume that $t - s < u_0$. □

Theorem 1.4.8. *Assume that a lossless node offers a service curve β to a flow with sub-additive arrival curve α. Assume that β is super-additive, and that $\alpha(u_0) \leq \beta(u_0)$ for some $u_0 > 0$. Then for any time t, the backlog $R(t) - R^*(t)$ satisfies*

$$R(t) - R^*(t) \leq \sup_{u:0 \leq u < u_0} [R(t) - R(t - u) - \beta(u)] \leq \sup_{u:0 \leq u < u_0} [\alpha(u) - \beta(u)]$$

Note that the condition that α is super-additive is not a restriction. In contrast, the condition that β is super-additive is a restriction. It applies in particular to rate-latency service curves. The theorem does not say anything about the duration of the busy period, which is consistent with the fact we do not assume here that the service curve is strict.

Proof: For an arbitrary time t the backlog at time t satisfies

$$b(t) \leq \sup_{u \geq 0} [R(t) - R(t - u) - \beta(u)]$$

For $s \leq t$ define $k = \lceil \frac{t-s}{u_0} \rceil$ and $s' = ku_0 + s$. We have $s \leq s' \leq t$ and

$$t - u_0 < s' \tag{1.11}$$

Now from the super-additivity of β:

$$R(t) - R(s) \leq [R(t) - R(s') - \beta(t - s')] + [R(s') - R(s) - \beta(s' - s)]$$

Note that for the second part we have

$$R(s') - R(s) - \beta(s' - s) \leq k [\alpha(u_0) - \beta(u_0)] \leq 0$$

thus

$$R(t) - R(s) \leq [R(t) - R(s') - \beta(t - s')]$$

which shows the theorem. □

1.5 Greedy Shapers

1.5.1 Definitions

We have seen with the definition of the leaky bucket and of the GCRA two examples of devices that enforce a general arrival curve. We call *policer* with curve σ a device that counts the bits arriving on an input flow and decides which bits conform with an arrival curve of σ. We call *shaper*, with shaping curve σ, a bit processing device that forces its output to have σ as an arrival curve. We call *greedy shaper* a shaper that delays the input bits in a buffer, whenever sending a bit would violate the constraint σ, but outputs them as soon as possible.

With ATM and sometimes with Intserv, traffic sent over one connection, or flow, is policed at the network boundary. Policing is performed in order to guarantee that users do not send more than specified by the contract of the connection. Traffic in excess is either discarded, or marked with a low priority for loss in the case of ATM, or passed as best effort traffic in the case of Intserv. In the latter case, with IPv4, there is no marking mechanism, so it is necessary for each router along the path of the flow to perform the policing function again.

Policing devices inside the network are normally buffered, they are thus shapers. Shaping is also often needed because the output of a buffer normally does not conform any more with the traffic contract specified at the input.

1.5.2   Input-Output Characterization of Greedy Shapers

The main result with greedy shapers is the following.

Theorem 1.5.1 (Input-Output Characterization of Greedy Shapers). *Consider a greedy shaper with shaping curve σ. Assume that the shaper buffer is empty at time 0, and that it is is large enough so that there is no data loss. For an input flow R, the output R^* is given by*

$$R^* = R \otimes \bar{\sigma} \tag{1.12}$$

where $\bar{\sigma}$ is the sub-additive closure of σ.

Proof: Remember first that if σ is sub-additive and $\sigma(0) = 0$, then $\bar{\sigma} = \sigma$. In general, we know that we can replace σ by $\bar{\sigma}$ without changing the definition of the shaper. We thus assume without loss of generality that $\bar{\sigma} = \sigma$.

The proof of the theorem is an application of min-plus algebra. First, let us consider a virtual system that would take R as input and have an output S satisfying the constraints:

$$\begin{cases} S \le R \\ S \le S \otimes \sigma \end{cases} \tag{1.13}$$

Such a system would behave as a buffer (the first equation says that the output is derived from the input) and its output would satisfy the arrival curve constraint σ. However, such a system is not necessarily a greedy shaper; we could have for example a lazy shaper with $S(t) = 0$ for all $t \ge 0$! For this system to be a greedy shaper, it has to output the bits as soon as possible. Now there is a general result about systems satisfying conditions 1.13.

Lemma 1.5.1 (A min-plus linear system). *Assume that σ is a "good" function (that is, is sub-additive and $\sigma(0) = 0$). Among all functions $S(t)$ satisfying conditions 1.13 for some fixed function R, there is one that is an upper bound for all. It is equal to $R \otimes \sigma$*

Proof of the lemma: The lemma is a special case of a general result in Chapter 4. However, it is also possible to give a very simple proof, as follows.

Define $S^* = R \otimes \sigma$. Since σ is a "good" function, it follows immediately that S^* is a solution to System (1.13). Now, let S' be some other solution. We have $S' \leq R$ and thus

$$S' \leq S_0 \otimes \sigma = S^*$$

Therefore S^* is the maximal solution. □

Note that the lemma proves the existence of a maximal solution to System (1.13). Note also that, in the lemma, function R need not be wide-sense increasing.

Now we can use the lemma by showing that $R^* = S^*$. Function R is wide-sense increasing, thus so is S^*. Obviously, R^* is a solution of System (1.13), thus $R^*(t) \leq S^*(t)$ for all t. Now if there would be some t such that $R^*(t) \neq S^*(t)$, then this would contradict the condition that the greedy shaper attempts to send the bits out as early as possible. □

The following corollary derives immediately.

Corollary 1.5.1 (Service Curve offered by a Greedy Shaper). *Consider a greedy shaper with shaping curve σ. Assume that σ is sub-additive and $\sigma(0) = 0$. This system offers to the flow a service curve equal to σ.*

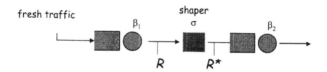

Figure 1.14: Reshaping example.

Example: Buffer Sizing at a Re-shaper Re-shaping is often introduced because the output of a buffer normally does not conform any more with the traffic contract specified at the input. For example, consider a flow with the arrival curve $\sigma(t) = \min(pt + M, rt + b)$ that traverses a sequence of nodes, which offer a service curve $\beta_1 = \beta_{R,T}$. A greedy shaper, with shaping curve σ, is placed after the sequence of nodes (Figure 1.14). The input to the shaper (R in the figure) has an arrival curve α^*, given by Proposition 1.4.2. Corollary 1.5.1 gives a service curve property for the greedy shaper, thus the buffer B required at the greedy shaper is the vertical distance $v(\alpha^*, \sigma)$. After some algebra, we obtain:

$$B = \begin{cases} \text{if } \frac{b-M}{p-r} < T & \text{then } b + Tr \\ \text{if } \frac{b-M}{p-r} \geq T \text{ and } p > R & \text{then } M + \frac{(b-M)(p-R)}{p-r} + TR \\ \text{else} & M + Tp \end{cases} \quad (1.14)$$

Corollary 1.5.2 (Buffer Occupancy at a Greedy Shaper). *Consider a greedy shaper with shaping curve* σ*. Assume that* σ *is sub-additive and* $\sigma(0) = 0$*. Call* $R(t)$ *the input function. The buffer occupancy* $x(t)$ *at time t is given by*

$$x(t) = \sup_{0 \le s \le t} \{R(t) - R(s) - \sigma(t - s)\}$$

Proof: The backlog is defined by $x(t) = R(t) - R^*(t)$, where R^* is the output. We apply Theorem 1.5.1 and get:

$$x(t) = R(t) - \inf_{0 \le s \le t} \{R(s) + \sigma(t - s)\} = R(t) + \sup_{0 \le s \le t} \{-R(s) - \sigma(t - s)\}$$

$\square$

Note that Lemma 1.2.2 is a special case of this corollary.

In min-plus algebraic terms, we say that a system is linear and time invariant if its input-output characterization has the form $R^* = R \otimes \beta$ (where β is not necessarily sub-additive). We can thus say from the theorem that greedy shapers are min-plus linear and time invariant systems. There are min-plus linear and time invariant system that are not greedy shapers. For example, a node imposing a *constant* delay T is characterized by the input-output relationship

$$R^* = R \otimes \delta_T$$

Compare to the guaranteed delay node (namely, a node imposing a variable delay bounded by T), for which the input-output relationship is a service curve property :

$$R^* \ge R \otimes \delta_T$$

The rest of this Section illustrates similarly that the input-output characterization of greedy shapers $R^* = R \otimes \sigma$ is much stronger than the service curve property described in Corollary 1.5.1.

1.5.3   Properties of Greedy Shapers

Consider again Figure 1.14. We have seen in the previous section how we can compute the buffer size required at the greedy shaper. Now if greedy shapers are introduced along a path, then some bits may be delayed at the shaper, thus the end-to-end delay might increase. However, this is not true, as the following results state that, from a global viewpoint, "greedy shapers come for free".

Theorem 1.5.2 (Re-Shaping does not increase delay or buffer requirements). *Assume a flow, constrained by arrival curve* α*, is input to networks* S_1 *and* S_2 *in sequence. Assume a greedy shaper, with curve* $\sigma \ge \alpha$ *is inserted between* S_1 *and* S_2*. Then the backlog and delay bounds given by Theorem 1.4.2 for the system without shaper are also valid for the system with shaper.*

The condition $\sigma \ge \alpha$ means that re-shaping maybe only partial.

Proof: Call β_i the service curve of $\mathcal{S}_i$. The backlog bound in Theorem 1.4.1 is given by

$$v(\alpha, \beta_1 \otimes \sigma \otimes \beta_2) = v(\alpha, \sigma \otimes \beta_1 \otimes \beta_2) \qquad (1.15)$$

Now the last expression is the backlog bound obtained if we put the shaper immediately at the entrance of the network. Clearly, this introduces no backlog, which shows that the overall backlog is not influenced by the shaper. The same reasoning applies to the delay bound. □

If you read carefully, you should not agree with the last paragraph. Indeed, there is a subtlety. The bounds in Section 1.4 are tight, but since we are using several bounds together, there is no guarantee that the resulting bound is tight. All we can say at this point is that the bound computed for the system with shaper is the same if we put the shaper in front; we still need to show that the bound for such a system is the same bound as if there would be no shaper. This can be proven in a number of ways. We give here a computational one. The proof relies on Lemma 1.5.2, given below. □

Lemma 1.5.2. *Let α and σ be "good" functions. Assume $\alpha \leq \sigma$. Then for any function β, $v(\alpha, \sigma \otimes \beta) = v(\alpha, \beta)$ and $h(\alpha, \sigma \otimes \beta) = h(\alpha, \beta)$.*

Proof: We use the reduction to min-plus deconvolution explained in Section 3.1.11. We have:

$$v(\alpha, \sigma \otimes \beta) = [\alpha \oslash (\sigma \otimes \beta)](0)$$

Now from Theorem 3.1.12 on Page 148: $\alpha \oslash (\sigma \otimes \beta) = (\alpha \oslash \sigma) \oslash \beta$. Also, since $\sigma \geq \alpha$, we have $\alpha \oslash \sigma \leq \alpha \oslash \alpha$. Now $\alpha \oslash \alpha = \alpha$ because α is a "good" function, thus

$$\alpha \oslash (\sigma \otimes \beta) = \alpha \oslash \beta \qquad (1.16)$$

and finally $v(\alpha, \sigma \otimes \beta) = v(\alpha, \beta)$.

Similarly $h(\alpha, \beta) = \inf\{d$ such that $(\alpha \oslash \beta)(-d) \leq 0\}$ which, combined with Equation (1.16) proves that $h(\alpha, \sigma \otimes \beta) = h(\alpha, \beta)$. □

Consider again Figure 1.14. Assume that the first network element and the greedy shaper are placed in the same node. Theorem 1.5.2 says that the *total* buffer required for this combined node is the same as if there would be no greedy shaper at the output. Thus, if you can dynamically allocate buffer space from a common pool to the first network element and the greedy shaper, then the greedy shaper costs no memory. However, the greedy shaper does need some buffer space, as given in Equation (1.14). Similarly, the theorem says that there is no penalty for the worst-case delay.

In contrast, placing a greedy shaper has an obvious benefit. The burstiness of the flow admitted in the next network element is reduced, which also reduces the buffer required in that element. To be more concrete, consider the example "Pay Bursts Only Once" in Section 1.4.3. Assume that a re-shaper is introduced at the output of the first node. Then the input to the second node has the same arrival curve as the fresh input, namely, $\gamma_{r,b}$ instead of $\gamma_{r,b+rT_1}$. The buffer required for the flow at node 2 is then $b + rT_2$ instead of $b + r(T_1 + T_2)$.

The following result is another "physical" property of greedy shapers. It says that shaping cannot be undone by shaping.

Theorem 1.5.3 (Shaping Conserves Arrival Constraints). *Assume a flow with arrival curve α is input to a greedy shaper with shaping curve σ. Assume σ is a "good" function. Then the output flow is still constrained by the original arrival curve α.*

Proof:

$$R^* = R \otimes \sigma \leq (R \otimes \alpha) \otimes \sigma$$

since the condition $R \leq R \otimes \alpha$ expresses that α is an arrival curve. Thus

$$R^* \leq R \otimes \sigma \otimes \alpha = R^* \otimes \alpha$$

$\square$

The output of the greedy shaper has thus $\min(\alpha, \sigma)$ as an arrival curve. If α is also a "good" function, we know (Lemma 1.2.5) that the sub-additive closure of $\min(\alpha, \sigma)$ is $\alpha \otimes \sigma$.

Example (ATM Multiplexer):   Consider an ATM switch that receives 3 ATM connections, each constrained by GCRA(10, 0) (periodic connections). The switch serves the connection in any work conserving manner and outputs them on a link with rate 1 cell per time slot. What is a good arrival curve for the aggregate output ?

The aggregate input has an arrival curve $\alpha = 3v_{10,0}$. Now the server is a greedy shaper with shaping curve $\sigma = v_{1,0}$, thus it keeps arrival constraints. Thus the output is constrained by $3v_{10,0} \otimes v_{1,0}$, which is a "good" function. We have already met this example in Figure 1.6.

1.6   Maximum Service Curve, Variable and Fixed Delay

1.6.1   Maximum Service Curves

If we modify the sense of the inequation in the definition of service curve in Section 1.3, then we obtain a new concept, called *maximum service curve*, which is useful to (1) account for constant delays and (2) in some cases to establish a relationship between delay and backlog.

Definition 1.6.1 (Maximum Service Curve). *Consider a system S and a flow through S with input and output function R and R^*. We say that S offers to the flow a maximum service curve γ if and only if $\gamma \in \mathcal{F}$ and $R^* \leq R \otimes \gamma$*

Note that the definition is equivalent to saying that γ is wide-sense increasing and that

$$R^*(t) \leq R(s) + \gamma(t - s)$$

for all t and all $s \leq t$, or equivalently

$$R^*(t) - R^*(s) \leq B(s) + \gamma(t - s)$$

where $B(s)$ is the backlog at time s. A greedy shaper with shaping curve σ offers σ both as a service curve and a maximum service curve.

In general, the concept of maximum service curve is not as powerful as the concept of service curve. However, as we see below, it can be useful to account for maximum rates and for constant propagation delays. We also see in Chapter 6 that it allows us to find good bounds for aggregate multiplexing.

The following propositions give two special cases of interest. Their proof is easy and left to the reader.

Proposition 1.6.1 (Minimum Delay). *A lossless node offers a maximum service curve equal to δ_T if and only if it imposes a minimum virtual delay equal to T.*

Proposition 1.6.2 (Arrival Constraint on Output). *Assume the output of a lossless node is constrained by some arrival curve σ. Then the node offers σ as a maximum service curve.*

Like minimum service curves, maximum service curves can be concatenated:

Theorem 1.6.1 (Concatenation of Nodes). *Assume a flow traverses systems S_1 and S_2 in sequence. Assume that S_i offers a maximum service curve of γ_i, $i = 1, 2$ to the flow. Then the concatenation of the two systems offers a service curve of $\gamma_1 \otimes \gamma_2$ to the flow.*

Proof: The proof mimics the proof of Theorem 1.4.6   □

Application: Consider a node with a maximum output rate equal to c and with internal propagation delay equal to T. It follows from Theorem 1.6.1 and the two previous propositions that this node offers to any flow a maximum service curve equal to the rate-latency function $\beta_{c,T}(t) = [c(t - T)]^+$.

Maximum service curves do not allow us to derive as strong results as (ordinary) service curves. However, they can be used to reduce the output bound and, in some cases, to obtain a minimum delay bound. Indeed, we have the following two results.

Theorem 1.6.2 (Output Flow, generalization of Theorem 1.4.3). *Assume a flow, constrained by arrival curve α, traverses a system that offers a service curve β and a maximum service curve γ. The output flow is constrained by the arrival curve $\alpha^* = (\alpha \otimes \gamma) \oslash \beta$.*

Proof: Instead of a computational proof as with Theorem 1.4.3, it is simpler at this stage to use min-plus algebra. Call R and R^* the input and output functions, and consider $R^* \oslash R^*$, the minimum arrival curve for R^*. We have $R^* \leq R \otimes \gamma$ and $R^* \geq R \otimes \beta$, thus

$$R^* \oslash R^* \leq (R \otimes \gamma) \oslash (R \otimes \beta)$$

From Rule 12 in Chapter 3, Theorem 3.1.12, applied to $f = R \otimes \gamma$, $g = R$ and $h = \beta$, we derive

$$R^* \oslash R^* \leq \{(R \otimes \gamma) \oslash R\} \oslash \beta$$

Now from the commutativity of $\otimes$ and from Rule 13 in Theorem 3.1.12:

$$\{(R \otimes \gamma) \oslash R\} = \{(\gamma \otimes R) \oslash R\} \leq \{\gamma \otimes (R \oslash R)\}$$

Thus

$$R^* \oslash R^* \leq \{\gamma \otimes (R \oslash R)\} \oslash \beta \leq (\gamma \otimes \alpha) \oslash \beta$$

$\square$

Theorem 1.6.3 (Minimum Delay Bound). *Assume a flow, constrained by arrival curve α, traverses a system that offers a maximum service curve of γ. Assume that $\gamma(D) = 0$. The virtual delay $d(t)$ satisfies $d(t) \geq D$ for all t.*

Proof: We have $R^*(t) \leq R(t - D) + \gamma(D)$ thus $R^*(t) \leq R(t - D)$ $\square$

Note that the output bound is improved by the knowledge of the maximum service curve since in general we expect $\alpha \otimes \gamma$ to be less than α. In contrast, the minimum delay bound gives some new information only in the cases where there is a latency part in the maximum service curve, which is the case for the first example (Minimum Delay), but not in general for the second example (Arrival Constraint on Output).

Numerical Example: Consider again the example illustrated in Figure 1.13. Let us first apply Theorem 1.4.3 and compute an arrival curve α_0^* for the output. The details are as follows. We have

$$\alpha_0^* = 10v_{25,4} \oslash \beta_{1,8} = 10v_{25,4} \oslash (\lambda_1 \otimes \delta_8)$$

Now from Rule 15 in Chapter 3, we have

$$\alpha_0^* = (10v_{25,4} \oslash \delta_8) \oslash \lambda_1$$

Now $(10v_{25,4} \oslash \delta_8)(t) = 10v_{25,4}(t + 8) = 10v_{25,12}(t)$, and a straightforward application of the definition of $\oslash$ shows that finally $\alpha_0^* = v_{25,12}$.

Assume now that we have more information about the node, and that we can model is as node $\mathcal{S}_1$ defined as the concatenation of two schedulers and a fixed delay element (Figure 1.15). Each scheduler offers to the aggregate flow a service curve β_{R_0,T_0} with rate $R_0 = 1$ cell per time slot and latency $T_0 = 2$ time slots. The delay element is a link with maximum rate equal to 1 cell per time slot, and a fixed propagation and transmission delay equal to 4 time slots. The delay element is thus the combination of a greedy shaper with shaping curve $\lambda_1(t) = t$ and a fixed delay element δ_4. We can verify that the concatenation of the three elements in node 1 offers a service curve equal to $\beta_{1,2} \otimes \lambda_1 \otimes \delta_4 \otimes \beta_{1,2} = \beta_{1,8}$. Now, from the delay element allows us to say that, in addition, the node also offers to the aggregate flow a *maximum service curve* equal to $\beta_{1,4}$. We can apply Theorem 1.6.2 and derive from that the output is constrained by the arrival curve α_1^* given by

$$\alpha_1^* = (\alpha \otimes \beta_{1,4}) \oslash \beta_{1,8}$$

The computation is similar to that of α_0^* and involves the computation of $10v_{25,4} \otimes \lambda_1$, which is similar to the example illustrated in Figure 1.6. Finally, we have:

$$\alpha_1^*(t) = (10v_{25,4} \otimes \lambda_1)(t + 4)$$

Figure 1.15 shows that α_1^* is a better bound than the arrival curve α_0^* that we would obtain if we did not know the maximum service curve property.

Assume next that we change the order of the delay element in node $\mathcal{S}1$ and place it as the last element of the node. Call $\mathcal{S}_2$ the resulting node. Then the conclusion of the previous paragraph remains, since the bounds are insensitive to the order, due to the commutativity of min-plus convolution. Thus the output of system $\mathcal{S}_2$ also has α_1^* as an arrival curve. However, in that case, we can also model the delay element as the combination of a shaper, with shaping curve λ_1 (corresponding to a fixed rate of 1 cell per time slot), followed by a fixed delay element, with constant delay equal to 4 time slots. The input to the shaper has an arrival curve equal to $\alpha \oslash \beta_{1,4}$, where $\alpha = 10v_{25,4}$ is the fresh arrival curve. Thus, from the properties of shapers, the output of the shaper is constrained by

$$\alpha_2^* = (\alpha \oslash \beta_{1,4}) \otimes \lambda_1 = 10v_{25,8} \otimes \lambda_1$$

Since the fixed delay component does not alter the flow, the output of system $\mathcal{S}_2$ has α_2^* as an arrival curve. Figure 1.15 shows that α_2^* is a better bound than α_1^*.

This fact is true in general: whenever a network element can be modeled as a shaper, then this model provides stronger bounds than the maximum service.

1.6.2 Delay from Backlog

In general it is not possible to bound delay from backlog with the framework of service curves, except in one particular but important case.

Theorem 1.6.4. *Assume a lossless node offers to a flow a minimum service curve β and a maximum service curve γ, such that $\beta(t) = \gamma(t - v)$. Let f be the max-plus deconvolution $\gamma \overline{\oslash} \gamma$, that is,*

$$f(t) = \inf_{s \geq 0}[\gamma(s + t) - \gamma(s)]$$

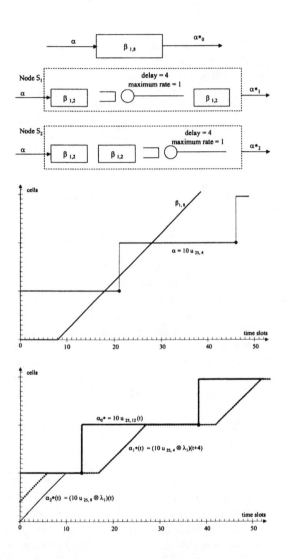

Figure 1.15: Use of maximum service curve to improve output bound. The figure is for the same example as Figure 1.15. Top: nodes S_1 and S_2, two possible implementations of a system offering the overall service curve $\beta_{1,8}$. Middle: arrival curve α and overall service curve $\beta_{1,8}$. Bottom: constraint for the output. α_0^* (top curve, thick, plain line) is obtained with the only knowledge that the service curve is $\beta_{1,8}$. α_1^* (middle curve, thick, dashed line) is obtained assuming the system is S_1. α_2^* (bottom curve, thin, plain line) is obtained assuming the system is S_2.

Then the backlog $B(t)$ and the virtual delay $d(t)$ satisfy

$$f(d(t) - v) \leq B(t)$$

If in addition γ is super-additive, then

$$\beta(d(t)) \leq B(t)$$

Proof: Fix some $t \geq 0$; we have $d(t) = \inf E_t$ where the set E_t is defined by

$$E_t = \{s \geq 0 : R^*(t + s) \geq R(t)\}$$

Since R^* and R are wide-sense increasing, E_t is an interval. Thus

$$d(t) = \sup\{s \geq 0 : R^*(t + s) < R(t)\}$$

We assume that R and R^* are left-continuous. It follows that

$$R^*(t + d(t)) \leq R(t)$$

For some arbitrary ϵ, we can find some s such that

$$R^*(t + d(t)) \geq R(s) + \beta(t - s + d(t)) - \epsilon$$

Now from the maximum service curve property

$$R^*(t) - R(s) \leq \gamma(t - s)$$

Combining the three gives

$$B(t) = R(t) - R^*(t) \geq \beta(t-s+d(t)) - \gamma(t-s) - \epsilon = \gamma(t-s+d(t)-v) - \gamma(t-s) - \epsilon$$

and thus

$$B(t) \geq \inf_{u \geq 0} [\gamma(d(t) - v + u) - \gamma(u)] \tag{1.17}$$

From the definition of f, the latter term is $f(d(t) - v)$. Finally, if γ is super-additive, then $\gamma \overline{\oslash} \gamma = \gamma$ □

We can apply the theorem to a practical case:

Corollary 1.6.1. *Assume a lossless node offers to a flow a minimum service curve $\beta = \beta_{r,v}$ and a maximum service curve $\gamma = \beta_{r,v'}$, with $v' \leq v$. The backlog $B(t)$ and the virtual delay $d(t)$ satisfy*

$$d(t) \leq \frac{B(t)}{r} + v$$

Proof: We apply the theorem and note that γ is super-additive, because it is convex.   □

1.6.3 Variable versus Fixed Delay

Some network elements impose fixed delays (propagation and transmission), whereas some other network elements impose variable delays (queueing). In a number of cases, it is important to evaluate separately the total delay and the variable part of the delay. The total delay is important, for example, for determining throughput and response time; the variable part is important for dimensioning playout buffers (see Section 1.1.3 for a simple example, and chapter 5 for a more general discussion). We have seen at the end of end of Section 1.5.2 that a node imposing a constant delay can be modeled as a min-plus linear system. Beyond this, the concept of maximum service curve is a tool for telling apart variable delay from fixed delay, as follows.

Consider a network, made of a series of network elements $1, ..., I$, each element being the combination of a fixed delay d_i and a variable delay. Assume the variable delay component offers a service curve β_i. A fixed delay component offers δ_{d_i} both as a service curve and as a maximum service curve. Define $\beta = \beta_1 \otimes ... \otimes \beta_I$; the network offers as end-to-end service curve $\beta \otimes \delta_{d_1+...+d_I}$, and as end-to-end maximum service curve $\delta_{d_1+...+d_I}$. Assume the input flow is constrained by some arrival curve α; from Theorems 1.4.2 and 1.6.3, the end-to-delay $d(t)$ satisfies

$$d_1 + ... + d_I \leq d(t) \leq h(\alpha, \beta \otimes \delta_{d_1+...+d_I})$$

By simple inspection, $h(\alpha, \beta \otimes \delta_{d_1+...+d_I}) = d_1 + ... + d_I + h(\alpha, \beta)$, thus the end-to-end delay satisfies

$$0 \leq d(t) - [d_1 + ... + d_I] \leq h(\alpha, \beta)$$

In the formula, $d_1 + ... + d_I$ is the fixed part of the delay, and $h(\alpha, \beta)$ is the variable part. Thus, for the computation of the variable part of the delay, we can simply ignore fixed delay components.

Similarly, an arrival curve constraint for the output is

$$\alpha^* = (\alpha \otimes \delta_{d_1+...+d_I}) \oslash (\beta \otimes \delta_{d_1+...+d_I}) = \alpha \oslash \beta$$

thus the fixed delay can be ignored for the computation of the output bound.

For the determination of backlog, the alert reader can easily be convinced that fixed delays cannot be ignored. In summary:

Proposition 1.6.3.   *1. For the computation of backlog and fixed delay bounds, fixed or variable delay are modeled by introducing δ_T functions in the service curves. As a consequence of the commutativity of $\otimes$, such delays can be inserted in any order along a sequence of buffers, without altering the delay bounds.*

   2. For the computation of variable delay bounds, or for an arrival constraint on the output, fixed delays can be ignored.

1.7 Handling Variable Length Packets

All results in this chapter apply directly to ATM systems, using discrete time models. In contrast, for variable length packets (as is usually the case with IP services), there are additional subtleties, which we now study in detail. The main parts in this section is the definition of a packetizer, and a study of its effect on delay, burstiness and backlog bounds. We also revisit the notion of shaper in a variable length context. For the rest of this section, time is continuous.

Throughout the section, we will consider some wide sense increasing sequences of packet arrival times $T_i \geq 0$. We assume that for all t the set $\{i : T_i \leq t\}$ is finite.

1.7.1 An Example of Irregularity Introduced by Variable Length Packets

The problem comes from the fact that real packet switching systems normally output entire packets, rather than a continuous data flow. Consider the example illustrated in Figure 1.16. It shows the output of a constant bit rate trunk, with rate c, that receives as input a sequence of packets, of different sizes. Call l_i, T_i the size (in bits) and the arrival epoch for the ith packet, $i = 1, 2, \dots$. The input function is

$$R(t) = \sum_i l_i 1_{\{T_i \leq t\}} \tag{1.18}$$

In the formula, we used the indicator function $1_{\{expr\}}$ which is equal to 1 if $expr$ is true, and 0 otherwise.

We assume, as is usual in most systems, that we observe only entire packets delivered by the trunk. This is shown as $R'(t)$ in the figure, which results from the bit-by-bit output R^* by a packetization operation. The bit-by-bit output R^* is well understood; we know from Section 1.5 that $R^* = R \otimes \lambda_r$. However, what is the effect of packetization ? Do the results in Sections 1.4 and 1.5 still hold ?

Certainly, we should expect some modifications. For example, the bit-by-bit output R^* in the figure is the output of a greedy shaper with curve λ_c, thus it has λ_c as an arrival curve, but this is certainly not true for R'. Worse, we know that a greedy shaper keeps arrival constraints, thus if R is σ-smooth for some σ, then so is R^*. However, this is not true for R'. Consider the following example (which is originally from [29]). Assume that $\sigma(t) = l_{\max} + rt$ with $r < c$. Assume that the input flow $R(t)$ sends a first packet of size $l_1 = l_{\max}$ at time $T_1 = 0$, and a second packet of size l_2 at time $T_2 = \frac{l_2}{r}$. Thus the flow R is indeed σ-smooth. The departure time for the first packet is $T'_1 = \frac{l_{\max}}{c}$. Assume that the second packet l_2 is small, specifically, $l_2 < \frac{r}{c} l_{\max}$; then the two packets are sent back-to-back and thus the departure time for the second packet is $T'_2 = T'_1 + \frac{l_2}{c}$. Now the spacing $T'_2 - T'_1$ is less than $\frac{l_2}{r}$, thus the second packet is not conformant, in other words, R' is not σ-smooth. Note that this example is not possible if all packets are the same size.

We will see in this section that this example is quite general: packetizing variable length packets does introduce some additional irregularities. However, we are able

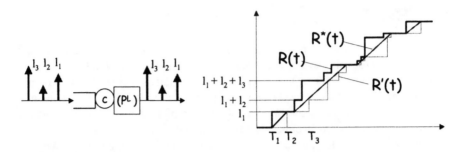

Figure 1.16: A real, variable length packet trunk of constant bit rate, viewed as the concatenation of a greedy shaper and a packetizer. The input is $R(t)$, the output of the greedy shaper is $R^*(t)$, the final output is the output of the packetizer is $R'(t)$.

to quantify them, and we will see that the irregularities are small (but may be larger than the order of a packet length). Most results are extracted from [45]

1.7.2 The Packetizer

We first need a few definitions.

Definition 1.7.1 (cumulative packet lengths). *A sequence L of cumulative packet lengths is a wide sense increasing sequence $(L(0) = 0, L(1), L(2), ...)$ such that*

$$l_{\max} = \sup_n \{L(n + 1) - L(n)\}$$

is finite

In this chapter, we interpret $L(n) - L(n - 1)$ as the length of the nth packet. We now introduce a new building block, which was introduced in [10].

Definition 1.7.2 (Function P^L [10]). *Consider a sequence of cumulative packet lengths L with $L(0) = 0$. For any real number x, define*

$$P^L(x) = \sup_{n \in \mathbb{N}} \{L(n)1_{\{L(n) \le x\}}\} \tag{1.19}$$

Figure 1.17 illustrates the definition. Intuitively, $P^L(x)$ is the largest cumulative packet length that is entirely contained in x. Function P^L is right-continuous; if R is right-continuous, then so is $P^L(R(t))$. For example, if all packets have unit length, then $L(n) = n$ and for $x > 0$: $P^L(x) = \lfloor x \rfloor$. An equivalent characterization of P^L is

$$P^L(x) = L(n) \iff L(n) \le x < L(n + 1) \tag{1.20}$$

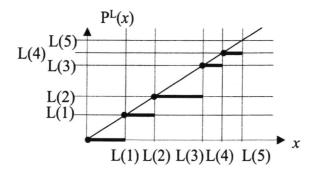

Figure 1.17: Definition of function P^L.

Definition 1.7.3 (Packetizer [10]). *Consider a sequence L of cumulative packet lengths. An L-packetizer is the system that transforms the input $R(t)$ into $P^L(R(t))$.*

For the example in Figure 1.16, we have $R'(t) = P^L(R^*(t))$ and the system can thus be interpreted as the concatenation of a greedy shaper and a packetizer.

The following equation follows immediately:

$$x - l_{\max} < P^L(x) \le x \tag{1.21}$$

Definition 1.7.4. *We say that a flow $R(t)$ is L-packetized if $P^L(R(t)) = R(t)$ for all t.*

The following properties are easily proven and left to the reader.

- (The packetizer is isotone) If $x \le y$ then $P^L(x) \le P^L(y)$ for all $x, y \in \mathbb{R}$.

- (P^L is idempotent) $P^L(P^L(x)) = P^L(x)$ for all $x \in \mathbb{R}$

- (Optimality of Packetizer) We can characterize a packetizer in a similar way as we did for a greedy shaper in Section 1.5. Among all flows $x(t)$ such that

$$\begin{cases} x \text{ is } L\text{-packetized} \\ x \le R \end{cases} \tag{1.22}$$

there is one that upper-bounds all, and it is $P^L(R(t))$.

The proof for this last item mimics that of Lemma 1.5.1; it relies on the property that P^L is idempotent.

We now study the effect of packetizers on the three bounds found in Section 1.4. We first introduce a definition.

Definition 1.7.5 (Per-packet delay). *Consider a system with L- packetized input and output. Call T_i, T_i' the arrival and departure time for the ith packet. Assume there is no packet loss. The per-packet delay is $\sup_i(T_i' - T_i)$*

Our main result in this section is the following theorem, illustrated in Figure 1.18.

Theorem 1.7.1 (Impact of packetizer). *Consider a system (bit-by-bit system) with L-packetized input R and bit-by-bit output R^*, which is then L-packetized to produce a final packetized output R'. We call combined system the system that maps R into R'. Assume both systems are first-in-first-out and lossless.*

1. *The per-packet delay for the combined system is the maximum virtual delay for the bit-by-bit system.*

2. *Call B^* the maximum backlog for the bit-by-bit system and B' the maximum backlog for the combined system. We have*

$$B^* \leq B' \leq B^* + l_{\max}$$

3. *Assume that the bit-by-bit system offers to the flow a maximum service curve γ and a minimum service curve β. The combined system offers to the flow a maximum service curve γ and a minimum service curve β' given by*

$$\beta'(t) = [\beta(t) - l_{\max}]^+$$

4. *If some flow $S(t)$ has $\alpha(t)$ as an arrival curve, then $P^L(S(t))$ has $\alpha(t) + l_{\max}1_{\{t>0\}}$ as an arrival curve.*

The proof of the theorem is given later in this section. Before, we discuss the implications. Item 1 says that appending a packetizer to a node does not increase

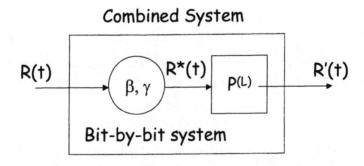

Figure 1.18: The scenario and notation in Theorem 1.7.1.

the packet delay at this node. However, as we see later, packetization does increase the end-to-end delay.

Consider again the example in Section 1.7.1. A simple look at the figure shows that the backlog (or required buffer) is increased by the packetization, as indicated by item 2. Item 4 tells us that the final output R' has $\sigma'(t) = \sigma(t) + l_{\max}1_{t>0}$ as an arrival curve, which is consistent with our observation in Section 1.7.1 that R' is not σ-smooth, even though R^* is. We will see in Section 1.7.4 that there is a stronger result, in relation with the concept of "packetized greedy shaper".

Item 3 is the most important practical result in this section. It shows that packetizing weakens the service curve guarantee by one maximum packet length. For example, if a system offers a rate-latency service curve with rate R, then appending a packetizer to the system has the effect of increasing the latency by $\frac{l_{\max}}{R}$.

Consider also the example in Figure 1.16. The combination of the trunk and the packetizer can be modeled as a system offering

- a minimum service curve $\beta_{c,\frac{l_{\max}}{c}}$

- a maximum service curve λ_c

Proof of Theorem 1.7.1

1. For some t such that $T_i \le t < T_{i+1}$ we have $R(t) = L(i)$ and thus

$$\sup_{t \in [T_i, T_{i+1})} d(t) = d(T_i)$$

now

$$d(T_i) = T'_i - T_i$$

Combining the two shows that

$$\sup_t d(t) = \sup_i (T'_i - T_i)$$

2. The proof is a direct consequence of Equation (1.21).

3. The result on maximum service curve γ follows immediately from Equation (1.21). Consider now the minimum service curve property. Fix some time t. For $T_i \le s < T_{i+1}$ we have $R(s) = R(T_i)$ and β is wide-sense increasing, thus

$$\inf_{T_i \le s < T_{i+1}} (R(s) + \beta(t-s)) = R(T_i) + \beta_r(t-T_i)$$

where $\beta_r(t-T_i) = \inf_{\epsilon>0}\{\beta[(t-T_i)+\epsilon]\}$ is the limit of β to the right. Thus

$$(R \otimes \beta)(t) = \inf_{i \text{ such that } T_i \le t} (R(T_i) + \beta_r(t-T_i))$$

For a fixed t there is only a finite number of i such that $T_i \le t$, thus the inf in the previous equation is a min and there is some j such that

$$(R \otimes \beta)(t) = R(T_j) + \beta_r(t-T_j)$$

By hypothesis, $R^*(t) \ge (R \otimes \beta)(t)$, thus

$$R'(t) \geq R^*(t) - l_{\max} \geq R(T_j) + \beta_r(t - T_j) - l_{\max}$$

On the other hand, $R^*(t) \geq R(T_j)$ and R is L-packetized, thus

$$R'(t) \geq R(T_j)$$

Combining the two shows that

$$
\begin{aligned}
R'(t) &\geq \max[R(T_j), R(T_j) + \beta_r(t - T_j) - l_{\max}] \\
&= R(T_j) + \max[\beta_r(t - T_j) - l_{\max}, 0] \\
&= R(T_j) + \beta'_r(t - T_j)
\end{aligned}
$$

from which we conclude that $R'(t) \geq \inf_{0 \leq s \leq t} (R(s) + \beta'(t - s))$

4. The proof is a direct consequence of Equation (1.21).

Example: concatenation of GPS nodes Consider the concatenation of the theoretical GPS node, with guaranteed rate R (see Section 1.3.1 on Page 22) and an
L-packetizer. Assume this system receives a flow of variable length packets. This
models a theoretical node that would work as a GPS node but is constrained to deliver entire packets. This is not very realistic, and we will see in Chapter 2 more
realistic implementations of GPS, but this example is sufficient to explain one important effect of packetizers.

By applying Theorem 1.7.1, we find that this node offers a rate-latency ser-
vice curve $\beta_{R, \frac{l_{\max}}{R}}$. Now concatenate m such identical nodes, as illustrated in Fig-

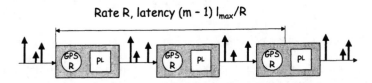

Rate R, latency (m − 1) l_{max}/R

Figure 1.19: The concatenation of several GPS fluid nodes with packetized
outputs

ure 1.19. The end-to-end service curve is the rate latency-function $\beta_{R,T}$ with

$$T = m\frac{l_{\max}}{R}$$

We see on this example that the additional latency introduced by one packetizer is
indeed of the order of one packet length; however, this effect is multiplied by the
number of hops.

For the computation of the end-to-end delay bound, we need to take into account
Theorem 1.7.1, which tells us that we can forget the last packetizer. Thus, a bound

on end-to-end delay is obtained by considering that the end-to-end path offers a
service curve equal to the latency-function β_{R,T_0} with

$$T_0 = (m - 1)\frac{l_{\max}}{R}$$

For example, if the original input flow is constrained by one leaky bucket of rate r
and bucket pool of size b, then an end-to-end delay bound is

$$\frac{b + (m - 1)l_{\max}}{R} \qquad (1.23)$$

The alert reader will easily show that this bound is a worst case bound. This illustrates that we should be careful in interpreting Theorem 1.7.1. It is only at the
last hop that the packetizer implies no delay increase. The interpretation is as follows. Packetization delays the first bits in a packet, which delays the processing at
downstream nodes. This effect is captured in Equation (1.23). In summary:

Remark 1.7.1. *Packetizers do not increase the maximum delay at the node where
they are appended. However, they generally increase the end-to-end delay.*

We will see in Chapter 2 that many practical schedulers can be modeled as the
concatenation of a node offering a service curve guarantee and a packetizer, and we
will give a practical generalization of Equation (1.23).

1.7.3 A Relation between Greedy Shaper and Packetizer

We have seen previously that appending a packetizer to a greedy shaper weakens
the arrival curve property of the output. There is however a case where this is not
true. This case is important for the results in Section 1.7.4, but also has practical
applications of its own. Figure 1.20 illustrates the theorem.

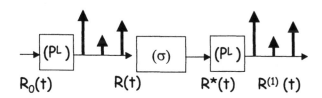

$$R_0(t) \qquad R(t) \qquad R^\star(t) \qquad R^{(1)}(t)$$

Figure 1.20: Theorem 1.7.2 says that $R^{(1)}$ is σ-smooth.

Theorem 1.7.2. *Consider a sequence L of cumulative packet lengths and call $\mathcal{P}_L$
the L-packetizer. Consider a "good" function σ and assume that*

$$\begin{cases} \text{There is a sub-additive function } \sigma_0 \text{ and a number } l \geq l_{\max} \text{ such that} \\ \sigma(t) = \sigma_0(t) + l1_{t>0} \end{cases} \qquad (1.24)$$

Call C_σ the greedy shaper with shaping curve σ. For any input, the output of the composition[6]$\mathcal{P}_L \circ C_\sigma \circ \mathcal{P}_L$ is σ-smooth.

In practical terms, the theorem is used as follows. Consider an L-packetized flow, pass it through a greedy shaper with shaping curve σ; and packetize the output; then the result is σ-smooth (assuming that σ satisfies condition in Equation (1.24) in the theorem).

Note that in general the output of $C_\sigma \circ \mathcal{P}_L$ is *not* L-packetized, even if σ satisfies the condition in the theorem (finding a counter-example is simple and is left to the reader for her enjoyment). Similarly, if the input to $\mathcal{P}_L \circ C_\sigma$ is not L-packetized, then the output is not σ-smooth, in general.

The theorem could also be rephrased by saying that, under condition in Equation (1.24)

$$\mathcal{P}_L \circ C_\sigma \circ \mathcal{P}_L = C_\sigma \circ \mathcal{P}_L \circ C_\sigma \circ \mathcal{P}_L$$

since the two above operators always produce the same output.

Discussion of Condition in Equation (1.24)   Condition Equation (1.24) is satisfied in practice if σ is concave and $\sigma_r(0) \geq l_{\max}$, where $\sigma_r(0) = \inf_{t>0} \sigma(t)$ is the limit to the right of σ at 0. This occurs for example if the shaping curve is defined by the conjunction of leaky buckets, all with bucket size at least as large as the maximum packet size.

This also sheds some light on the example in Figure 1.16: the problem occurs because the shaping curve λ_C does not satisfy the condition.

The alert reader will ask herself whether a sufficient condition for Equation (1.24) to hold is that σ is sub-additive and $\sigma_r(0) \geq l_{\max}$. Unfortunately, the answer is no. Consider for example the stair function $\sigma = l_{\max} v_T$. We have $\sigma_r(0) = l_{\max}$ but if we try to rewrite σ into $\sigma(t) = \sigma_0(t) + l 1_{t>0}$ we must have $l = l\max$ and $\sigma_0(t) = 0$ for $t \in (0, T]$; if we impose that σ_0 is sub-additive, the latter implies $\sigma_0 = 0$ which is not compatible with Equation (1.24).[7]

Proof of Theorem 1.7.2:   We use the notation in Figure 1.20. We want to show that $R^{(1)}$ is σ-smooth. We have $R^* = R \otimes \sigma$. Consider now some arbitrary s and t with $s < t$. From the definition of min-plus convolution, for all $\epsilon > 0$, there is some $u \leq s$ such that

$$(R \otimes \sigma)(s) \geq R(u) + \sigma(s - u) - \epsilon \tag{1.25}$$

Now consider the set E of $\epsilon > 0$ such that we can find one $u < s$ satisfying the above equation. Two cases are possible: either 0 is an accumulation point for E[8] (case 1) , or not (case 2).

Consider case 1; there is a sequence (ϵ_n, s_n), with $s_n < s$,

---

[6]We use the notation $\mathcal{P}_L \circ C_\sigma$ to denote the composition of the two operators, with C_σ applied first; see Section 4.1.3.

[7]The same conclusion unfortunately also holds if we replace sub-additive by "star-shaped" (Section 3.1).

[8]namely, there is a sequence of elements in E which converges to 0

$$\lim_{n \to +\infty} \epsilon_n = 0$$

and

$$(R \otimes \sigma)(s) \geq R(s_n) + \sigma(s - s_n) - \epsilon_n$$

Now since $s_n \leq t$:

$$(R \otimes \sigma)(t) \leq R(s_n) + \sigma(t - s_n)$$

Combining the two:

$$(R \otimes \sigma)(t) - (R \otimes \sigma)(s) \leq \sigma(t - s_n) - \sigma(s - s_n) + \epsilon_n$$

Now $t - s_n > 0$ and $s - s_n > 0$ thus

$$\sigma(t - s_n) - \sigma(s - s_n) = \sigma_0(t - s_n) - \sigma_0(s - s_n)$$

We have assumed that σ_0 is sub-additive. Now $t \geq s$ thus

$$\sigma_0(t - s_n) - \sigma_0(s - s_n) \leq \sigma_0(t - s)$$

we have thus shown that, for all n

$$(R \otimes \sigma)(t) - (R \otimes \sigma)(s) \leq \sigma_0(t - s) + \epsilon_n$$

and thus

$$(R \otimes \sigma)(t) - (R \otimes \sigma)(s) \leq \sigma_0(t - s)$$

Now from Equation (1.21), it follows that

$$R^{(1)}(t) - R^{(1)}(s) \leq \sigma_0(t - s) + l_{\max} \leq \sigma(t - s)$$

which ends the proof for case 1.

Now consider case 2. There is some ϵ_0 such that for $0 < \epsilon < \epsilon_0$, we have to take $u = s$ in Equation (1.25). This implies that

$$(R \otimes \sigma)(s) = R(s)$$

Now R is L-packetized by hypothesis. Thus

$$R^{(1)}(s) = P^L((R \otimes \sigma)(s)) = P^L(R(s)) = R(s) = (R \otimes \sigma)(s)$$

thus

$$\begin{aligned} R^{(1)}(t) - R^{(1)}(s) = \ & P^L((R \otimes \sigma)(t) - (R \otimes \sigma)(s) \\ \leq \ & (R \otimes \sigma)(t) - (R \otimes \sigma)(s) \end{aligned}$$

now $R \otimes \sigma$ has σ as an arrival curve thus

$$R^{(1)}(t) - R^{(1)}(s) \leq \sigma(t - s)$$

which ends the proof for case 2. □

Example: Buffered Leaky Bucket Controller based on Virtual Finish Times
Theorem 1.7.2 gives us a practical implementation for a packet based shaper. Consider that we want to build a device that ensures that a packet flow satisfies some concave, piecewise linear arrival curve (and is of course L- packetized). We can realize such a device as the concatenation of a buffered leaky bucket controller operating bit-by-bit and a packetizer. We compute the output time for the last bit of a packet (= finish time) under the bit-by-bit leaky bucket controller, and release the entire packet instantly at this finish time. If each bucket pool is at least as large as the maximum packet size then Theorem 1.7.2 tells us that the final output satisfies the leaky bucket constraints.

Counter-example   If we consider non-concave arrival curves, then we can find an arrival curve σ that does satisfy $\sigma(t) \geq l_{\max}$ for $t > 0$ but that does not satisfy Equation (1.24). In such a case, the conclusion of Theorem 1.7.2 may not hold in general. Figure 1.21 shows an example where the output $R^{(1)}$ is not σ-smooth, when σ is a stair function.

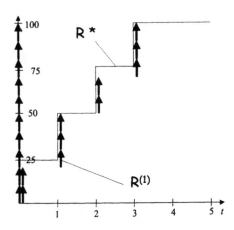

Figure 1.21: A counter example for Theorem 1.7.2. A burst of 10 packets of size equal to 10 data units arrive at time $t = 0$, and $\sigma = 25v_1$. The greedy shaper emits 25 data units at times 0 and 1, which forces the packetizer to create a burst of 3 packets at time 1, and thus $R^{(1)}$ is not σ-smooth.

1.7.4   Packetized Greedy Shaper

We can come back to the questions raised by the example in Figure 1.16 and give a more fundamental look at the issue of packetized shaping. Instead of synthesizing the concatenation of a greedy shaper and a packetizer as we did earlier, we define the following, consistent with Section 1.5.

Definition 1.7.6. *[Packetized Greedy Shaper] Consider an input sequence of packets, represented by the function $R(t)$ as in Equation (1.18). Call L the cumulative packet lengths. We call* packetized shaper, *with shaping curve σ, a system that forces its output to have σ as an arrival curve and be L-packetized. We call* packetized greedy shaper *a packetized shaper that delays the input packets in a buffer, whenever sending a packet would violate the constraint σ, but outputs them as soon as possible.*

Example: Buffered Leaky Bucket Controller based on Bucket Replenishment
The case $\sigma(t) = \min_{m=1,\ldots,M}(\gamma_{r_m,b_m}(t))$ can be implemented by a controller that observes a set of M fluid buckets, where the mth bucket is of size b_m and leaks at a constant rate r_m. Every bucket receives l_i units of fluid when packet i is released (l_i is the size of packet i). A packet is released as soon as the level of fluid in bucket m allows it, that is, has gone down below $b_m - l_i$, for all m. We say that now we have defined a buffered leaky bucket controller based on "bucket replenishment". It is clear that the output has σ as an arrival curve, is L-packetized and sends the packets as early as possible. Thus it implements the packetized greedy shaper. Note that this implementation differs from the buffered leaky bucket controller based on virtual finish times introduced in Section 1.7.3. In the latter, during a period where, say, bucket m only is full, fragments of a packet are virtually released at rate r_m, bucket m remains full, and the (virtual) fragments are then re-assembled in the packetizer; in the former, if a bucket becomes full, the controller waits until it empties by at least the size of the current packet. Thus we expect that the level of fluid in both systems is not the same, the former being an upper bound. We will see however in Corollary 1.7.1 that both implementations are equivalent.

In this example, if a bucket size is less than the maximum packet size, then it is never possible to output a packet: all packets remain stuck in the packet buffer, and the output is $\overline{R}(t) = 0$. In general, we can say that

Proposition 1.7.1. *If $\sigma_r(0) < l_{\max}$ then the the packetized greedy shaper blocks all packets for ever (namely, $\overline{R}(t) = 0$). Thus in this section, we assume that $\sigma(t) \geq l_{\max}$ for $t > 0$.*

Thus, for practical cases, we have to assume that the arrival curve σ has a discontinuity at the origin at least as large as one maximum packet size.

How does the packetized greedy shaper compare with the concatenation of a greedy shaper with shaping curve σ and a packetizer ? We know from the example in Figure 1.16 that the output has $\sigma'(t) = \sigma(t) + l_{\max} 1_{t>0}$ as an arrival curve, but not σ. Now, does the concatenation implement a packetized greedy shaper with shaping curve σ' ? Before giving a general answer, we study a fairly general consequence of Theorem 1.7.2.

Theorem 1.7.3 (Realization of packetized Greedy Shaper). *Consider a sequence L of cumulative packet lengths and a "good" function σ. Assume that σ satisfies the condition in Equation (1.24). Consider only inputs that are L packetized. Then the*

packetized greedy shaper for σ and L can be realized as the concatenation of the greedy shaper with shaping curve σ and the L-packetizer.

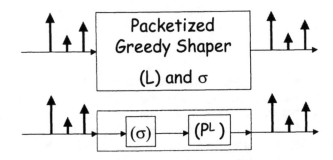

Figure 1.22: The packetized greedy shaper can be realized as a (bit-by-bit fluid shaper followed by a packetizer, assuming Equation (1.24) holds. In practice, this means that we can realize packetized greedy shaping by computing finish times in the virtual fluid system and release packets at their finish times.

Proof: Call $R(t)$ the packetized input; the output of the bit-by-bit greedy shaper followed by a packetizer is $R^{(1)}(t) = P^L(R \otimes \sigma)(t))$. Call $\overline{R}(t)$ the output of the packetized greedy shaper. We have $\overline{R} \leq R$ thus $\overline{R} \otimes \sigma \leq R \otimes \sigma$ and thus

$$P^L(\overline{R} \otimes \sigma) \leq P^L(R \otimes \sigma)$$

But $\overline{R}$ is σ-smooth, thus $\overline{R} \otimes \sigma = \overline{R}$, and is L-packetized, thus $P^L(\overline{R} \otimes \sigma) = \overline{R}$. Thus the former inequality can be rewritten as $\overline{R} \leq R^{(1)}$. Conversely, from Theorem 1.7.2, $R^{(1)}$ is also σ-smooth and L-packetized. The definition of the packetized greedy shaper implies that $\overline{R} \geq R^{(1)}$ (for a formal proof, see Lemma 1.7.1) thus finally $\overline{R} = R^{(1)}$.   □

We have seen that the condition in the theorem is satisfied in particular if σ is concave and $\sigma_r(0) \geq l_{\max}$, for example if the shaping curve is defined by the conjunction of leaky buckets, all with bucket size at least as large as the maximum packet size. This shows the following.

Corollary 1.7.1. *For L-packetized inputs, the implementations of buffered leaky bucket controllers based on bucket replenishment and virtual finish times are equivalent.*

If we relax Equation (1.24) then the construction of the packetized greedy shaper is more complex:

Theorem 1.7.4 (I/O characterisation of packetized greedy shapers). *Consider a packetized greedy shaper with shaping curve σ and cumulative packet length L. Assume that σ is a "good" function. The output $\overline{R}(t)$ of the packetized greedy shaper is given by*

$$\overline{R} = \inf \left\{ R^{(1)}, R^{(2)}, R^{(3)}, ... \right\} \tag{1.26}$$

with $R^{(1)}(t) = P^L((\sigma \otimes R)(t))$ and $R^{(i)}(t) = P^L((\sigma \otimes R^{(i-1)})(t))$ for $i \geq 2$.

Figure 1.23 illustrates the theorem, and shows the iterative construction of the output on one example. Note that this example is for a shaping function that does not satisfy Equation (1.24). Indeed, otherwise, we know from Theorem 1.7.3 that the iteration stops at the first step, namely, $\overline{R} = R^{(1)}$ in that case. We can also check for example that if $\sigma = \lambda_r$ (thus the condition in Proposition 1.7.1 is satisfied) then the result of Equation (1.26) is 0.

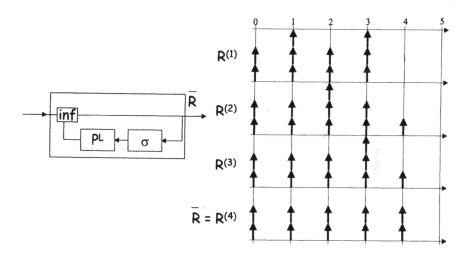

Figure 1.23: Representation of the output of the packetized greedy shaper (left) and example of output (right). The data are the same as with Figure 1.21.

Proof: The proof is a direct application of Lemma 1.7.1 (which itself is an application of the general method in Section 4.3 on Page 175). □

Lemma 1.7.1. *Consider a sequence L of cumulative packet lengths and a "good" function σ. Among all flows $x(t)$ such that*

$$\begin{cases} x \leq R \\ x \text{ is } L\text{-packetized} \\ x \text{ has } \sigma \text{ as an arrival curve} \end{cases} \tag{1.27}$$

there is one flow $\overline{R}(t)$ that upper-bounds all. It is given by Equation (1.26).

Proof: The lemma is a direct application of Theorem 4.3.1, as explained in Section 4.3.2. However, in order to make this chapter self-contained, we give an alternative, direct proof, which is quite short.

If x is a solution, then it is straightforward to show by induction on i that $x(t) \leq R^{(i)}(t)$ and thus $x \leq \overline{R}$. The difficult part is now to show that $\overline{R}$ is indeed a solution. We need to show that the three conditions in Equation (1.27) hold. Firstly, $R^{(1)} \leq R(t)$ and by induction on i, $R^{(i)} \leq R$ for all i; thus $\overline{R} \leq R$.

Secondly, consider some fixed t; $R^{(i)}(t)$ is L-packetized for all $i \geq 1$. Let $L(n_0) := R^{(1)}(t)$. Since $R^{(i)}(t) \leq R^{(1)}(t)$, $R^{(i)}(t)$ is in the set

$$\{L(0), L(1), L(2), ..., L(n_0)\}.$$

This set is finite, thus, $\overline{R}(t)$, which is the infimum of elements in this set, has to be one of the $L(k)$ for $k \leq n_0$. This shows that $\overline{R}(t)$ is L-packetized, and this is true for any time t.

Thirdly, we have, for all i

$$\overline{R}(t) \leq R^{(i+1)}(t) = P^L((\sigma \otimes R^{(i)})(t)) \leq (\sigma \otimes R^{(i)})(t)$$

thus

$$\overline{R} \leq \inf_i (\sigma \otimes R^{(i)})$$

Now convolution by a fixed function is upper-semi-continuous, which means that

$$\inf_i (\sigma \otimes R^{(i)}) = \sigma \otimes \overline{R}$$

This is a general result in Chapter 4 for any min-plus operator. An elementary proof is as follows.

$$
\begin{aligned}
\inf_i (\sigma \otimes R^{(i)})(t) &= \inf_{s \in [0,t], i \in \mathbb{N}} \left[\sigma(s) + R^{(i)}(t - s)\right] \\
&= \inf_{s \in [0,t]} \left\{\inf_{i \in \mathbb{N}} \left[(\sigma(s) + R^{(i)}(t - s)]\right\} \right. \\
&= \inf_{s \in [0,t]} \left\{\sigma(s) + \inf_{i \in \mathbb{N}} \left[R^{(i)}(t - s)]\right\} \right. \\
&= \inf_{s \in [0,t]} \left[\sigma(s) + \overline{R}(t - s)\right] \\
&= (\sigma \otimes \overline{R})(t)
\end{aligned}
$$

Thus

$$\overline{R} \leq \sigma \otimes \overline{R},$$

which shows the third condition. Note that $\overline{R}$ is wide-sense increasing.   □

Does a packetized greedy shaper keep arrival constraints ?   Figure 1.24 shows a counter-example, namely, a variable length packet flow that has lost its initial arrival curve constraint after traversing a packetized greedy shaper.

However, if arrival curves are defined by leaky buckets, we have a positive result.

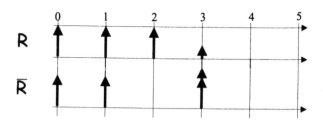

Figure 1.24: The input flow is shown above; it consists of 3 packets of size 10 data units and one of size 5 data units, spaced by one time unit. It is α-smooth with $\alpha = 10v_{1,0}$. The bottom flow is the output of the packetized greedy shaper with $\sigma = 25v_{3,0}$. The output has a burst of 15 data units packets at time 3. It is σ-smooth but *not* α-smooth.

Theorem 1.7.5 (Conservation of concave arrival constraints). *Assume an L-packetized flow with arrival curve α is input to a packetized greedy shaper with cumulative packet length L and shaping curve σ. Assume that α and σ are concave with $\alpha_r(0) \geq l_{\max}$ and $\sigma_r(0) \geq l_{\max}$. Then the output flow is still constrained by the original arrival curve α.*

Proof: Since σ satisfies Equation (1.24), it follows from Theorem 1.7.3 that $\overline{R} = P^L(\sigma \otimes R)$. Now R is α-smooth thus it is not modified by a bit-by-bit greedy shaper with shaping curve α, thus $R = \alpha \otimes R$. Combining the two and using the associativity of $\otimes$ gives $\overline{R} = P^L[(\sigma \otimes \alpha) \otimes R]$. From our hypothesis, $\sigma \otimes \alpha = \min(\sigma, \alpha)$ (see Theorem 3.1.6 on Page 136) and thus $\sigma \otimes \alpha$ satisfies Equation (1.24). Thus, by Theorem 1.7.2, $\overline{R}$ is $\sigma \otimes \alpha$-smooth, and thus α-smooth. □

Series decomposition of shapers

Theorem 1.7.6. *Consider a tandem of M packetized greedy shapers in series; assume that the shaping curve σ^m of the mth shaper is concave with $\sigma_r^m(0) \geq l_{\max}$. For L-packetized inputs, the tandem is equivalent to the packetized greedy shaper with shaping curve $\sigma = \min_m \sigma^m$.*

Proof: We do the proof for $M = 2$ as it extends without difficulty to larger values of M. Call $R(t)$ the packetized input, $R'(t)$ the output of the tandem of shapers, and $\overline{R}(t)$ the output of the packetized greedy shaper with input $R(t)$.

Firstly, by Theorem 1.7.3

$$R' = P^L[\sigma_2 \otimes P^L(\sigma^1 \otimes R)]$$

Now $\sigma^m \geq \sigma$ for all m thus

$$R' \geq P^L[\sigma \otimes P^L(\sigma \otimes R)]$$

Again by Theorem 1.7.3, we have $\overline{R} = P^L(\sigma \otimes R)$. Moreover $\overline{R}$ is L-packetized and σ-smooth, thus $\overline{R} = P^L(\overline{R})$ and $\overline{R} = \sigma \otimes \overline{R}$. Thus finally

$$R' \geq \overline{R} \tag{1.28}$$

Secondly, R' is L-packetized and by Theorem 1.7.5, it is σ-smooth. Thus the tandem is a packetized (possibly non greedy) shaper. Since $\overline{R}(t)$ is the output of the packetized greedy shaper, we must have $R' \leq \overline{R}$. Combining with Equation (1.28) ends the proof.   □

It follows that a shaper with shaping curve $\sigma(t) = \min_{m=1,\ldots,M}(r_m t + b_m)$, where $b_m \geq l_{\max}$ for all m, can be implemented by a tandem of M individual leaky buckets, in any order. Furthermore, by Corollary 1.7.1, every individual leaky bucket may independently be based either on virtual finish times or on bucket replenishment.

If the condition in the theorem is not satisfied, then the conclusion may not hold. Indeed, for the example in Figure 1.24, the tandem of packetized greedy shapers with curves α and σ does not have an α-smooth output, therefore it cannot be equivalent to the packetized greedy shaper with curve $\min(\alpha, \sigma)$.

Unfortunately, the other shaper properties seen in Section 1.5 do not generally hold. For shaping curves that satisfy Equation (1.24), and when a packetized greedy shaper is introduced, we need to compute the end-to-end service curve by applying Theorem 1.7.1.

1.8 Lossless Effective Bandwidth and Equivalent Capacity

1.8.1 Effective Bandwidth of a Flow

We can apply the results in this chapter to define a function of a flow called the effective bandwidth. This function characterizes the bit rate required for a given flow. More precisely, consider a flow with cumulative function R; for a fixed, but arbitrary delay D, we define the *effective bandwidth* $e_D(R)$ of the flow as the bit rate required to serve the flow in a work conserving manner, with a virtual delay $\leq D$.

Proposition 1.8.1. *The effective bandwidth of a flow is given by*

$$e_D(R) = \sup_{0 \leq s \leq t} \frac{R(t) - R(s)}{t - s + D} \tag{1.29}$$

For an arrival curve α we define the effective bandwidth $e_D(\alpha)$ as the effective bandwidth of the greedy flow $R = \alpha$. By a simple manipulation of Equation 1.29, the following comes.

Proposition 1.8.2. *The effective bandwidth of a "good" arrival curve is given by*

$$e_D(\alpha) = \sup_{0 \leq s} \frac{\alpha(s)}{s + D} \qquad (1.30)$$

The alert reader will check that the effective bandwidth of a flow R is also the effective bandwidth of its minimum arrival curve $R \oslash R$. For example, for a flow with T-SPEC (p, M, r, b), the effective bandwidth is the maximum of r and the slopes of lines (QA_0) and (QA_1) in Figure 1.25; it is thus equal to:

$$e_D = \max \left\{ \frac{M}{D}, r, p \left(1 - \frac{D - \frac{M}{p}}{\frac{b-M}{p-r} + D} \right) \right\} \qquad (1.31)$$

Assume α is sub-additive. We define the sustainable rate m as $m = \liminf_{s \to +\infty} \frac{\alpha(s)}{s}$

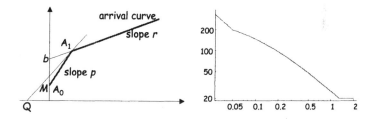

Figure 1.25: Computation of Effective Bandwidth for a VBR flow (left); example for $r = 20$ packets/second, $M = 10$ packets, $p = 200$ packets per second and $b = 26$ packets (right).

and the peak rate by $p = \sup_{s>0} \frac{\alpha(s)}{s}$. Then $m \leq e_D(\alpha) \leq p$ for all D. Moreover, if α is concave, then $\lim_{D \to +\infty} e_D(\alpha) = m$. If α is differentiable, $e(D)$ is the slope of the tangent to the arrival curve, drawn from the time axis at $t = -D$ (Figure 1.26). It follows also directly from the definition in (1.29) that

$$e_D(\sum_i \alpha_i) \leq \sum_i e_D(\alpha_i) \qquad (1.32)$$

In other words, the effective bandwidth for an aggregate flow is less than or equal to the sum of effective bandwidths. If the flows have all *identical* arrival curves, then the aggregate effective bandwidth is simply $I \times e_D(\alpha_1)$. It is this latter relation that is the origin of the term "effective bandwidth". The difference $\sum_i e_D(\alpha_i) - e_D(\sum_i \alpha_i)$ is a buffering gain; it tells us how much capacity is saved by sharing a buffer between the flows.

1.8.2 Equivalent Capacity

Similar results hold if we replace delay constraints by the requirement that a fixed buffer size is not exceeded. Indeed, the queue with constant rate C, guarantees a maximum backlog of B (in bits) for a flow R if $C \geq f_B(R)$, with

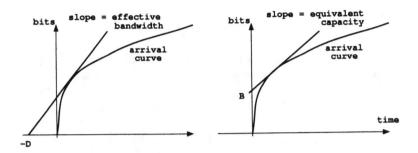

Figure 1.26: Effective Bandwidth for a delay constraint D and Equivalent Capacity for a buffer size B

$$f_B(R) = \sup_{0 \le s < t} \frac{R(t) - R(s) - B}{t - s} \qquad (1.33)$$

Similarly, for a "good" function α, we have:

$$f_B(\alpha) = \sup_{s > 0} \frac{\alpha(s) - B}{s} \qquad (1.34)$$

We call $f_B(\alpha)$ the *equivalent capacity*, by analogy to [42]. Similar to effective bandwidth, the equivalent capacity of a heterogeneous mix of flows is less than or equal to the sum of equivalent capacities of the flows, provided that the buffers are also added up; in other words, $f_B(\alpha) \le \sum_i f_{B_i}(\alpha_i)$, with $\alpha = \sum_i \alpha_i$ and $B = \sum_i B_i$. Figure 1.26 gives a graphical interpretation.

For example, for a flow with T-SPEC (p, M, r, b), using the same method as above, we find the following equivalent capacity:

$$f_B = \begin{cases} \text{if } B < M \text{ then } +\infty \\ \text{else } r + \frac{(p-r)(b-B)^+}{b-M} \end{cases} \qquad (1.35)$$

An immediate computation shows that $f_b(\gamma_{r,b}) = r$. In other words, if we allocate to a flow, constrained by an affine function $\gamma_{r,b}$, a capacity equal to its sustainable rate r, then a buffer equal to its burst tolerance b is sufficient to ensure loss-free operation.

Consider now a mixture of Intserv flows (or VBR connections), with T-SPECs (M_i, p_i, r_i, b_i). If we allocate to this aggregate of flows the sum of their sustainable rates $\sum_i r_i$, then the buffer requirement is the sum of the burst tolerances $\sum_i b_i$, regardless of other parameters such as peak rate. Conversely, Equation 1.35 also illustrates that there is no point allocating more buffer than the burst tolerance: if $B > b$, then the equivalent capacity is still r.

The above has illustrated that it is possible to reduce the required buffer or delay by allocating a rate larger than the sustainable rate. In Section 2.2, we described how this may be done with a protocol such as RSVP.

Note that formulas (1.29) or (1.33), or both, can be used to estimate the capacity required for a flow, based on a measured arrival curve. We can view them as low-pass filters on the flow function R.

1.8.3 Example: Acceptance Region for a FIFO Multiplexer

Consider a node multiplexing n_1 flows of type 1 and n_2 flows of type 2, where every flow is defined by a T-SPEC (p_i, M_i, r_i, b_i). The node has a constant output rate C. We wonder how many flows the node can accept.

If the only condition for flow acceptance is that the delay for all flows is bounded by some value D, then the set of acceptable values of (n_1, n_2) is defined by

$$e_D(n_1\alpha_1 + n_2\alpha_2) \leq C$$

We can use the same convexity arguments as for the derivation of formula (1.31), applied to the function $n_1\alpha_1 + n_2\alpha_2$. Define $\theta_i = \frac{b_i - M}{p_i - r_i}$ and assume $\theta_1 \leq \theta_2$. The result is:

$$e_D(n_1\alpha_1 + n_2\alpha_2) = \max \begin{cases} \frac{n_1 M_1 + n_2 M_2}{D}, \\ \frac{n_1 M_1 + n_2 M_2 + (n_1 p_1 + n_2 p_2)\theta_1}{\theta_1 + D}, \\ \frac{n_1 b_1 + n_2 M_2 + (n_1 r_1 + n_2 p_2)\theta_2}{\theta_2 + D}, \\ n_1 r_1 + n_2 r_2 \end{cases}$$

The set of feasible (n_1, n_2) derives directly from the previous equation; it is the convex part shown in Figure 1.27. The alert reader will enjoy performing the computation of the equivalent capacity for the case where the acceptance condition bears on a buffer size B.

i	p_i	M_i	r_i	b_i	θ_i
1	20'000 packets/s	1 packet	500 packets/s	26 packets	1.3 ms
2	5'000 packets/s	1 packet	500 packets/s	251 packets	55.5 ms

Figure 1.27: Acceptance region for a mix of type 1 and type 2 flows. Maximum delay $D = xx$. The parameters for types 1 and 2 are shown in the table, together with the resulting values of θ_i.

Coming back to equation 1.32, we can state in more general terms that the effective bandwidth is a convex function of function α, namely:

$$e_D(a\alpha_1 + (1 - a)\alpha_2) \leq ae_D(\alpha_1) + (1 - a)e_D(\alpha_2)$$

for all $a \in [0, 1]$. The same is true for the equivalent capacity function.

Consider now a call acceptance criterion based solely on a delay bound, or based on a maximum buffer constraint, or both. Consider further that there are I types of connections, and define the acceptance region $\mathcal{A}$ as the set of values $(n_1, \ldots, n_I)$ that satisfy the call acceptance criterion, where n_i is the number of connections of class i. From the convexity of the effective bandwidth and equivalent capacity functions, it follows that the acceptance region $\mathcal{A}$ is *convex*. In chapter 9 we compare this to acceptance regions for systems with some positive loss probability.

Sustainable Rate Allocation   If we are interested only in course results, then we can reconsider the previous solution and take into account only the sustainable rate of the connection mix. The aggregate flow is constrained (among others) by $\alpha(s) = b + rs$, with $b = \sum_i n_i b_i$ and $r = \sum_i n_i r_i$. Theorem 1.4.1 shows that the maximum aggregate buffer occupancy is bounded by b as long as $C \geq r$. In other words, allocating the sustainable rate guarantees a loss-free operation, as long as the total buffer is equal to the burstiness.

In a more general setting, assume an aggregate flow has α as minimum arrival curve, and assume that some parameters r and b are such that

$$\lim_{s \to +\infty} \alpha(s) - rs - b = 0$$

so that the sustainable rate r with burstiness b is a tight bound. It can easily be shown that if we allocate a rate $C = r$, then the maximum buffer occupancy is b.

Consider now multiplexing a number of VBR connections. If no buffer is available, then it is necessary for a loss-free operation to allocate the sum of the peak rates. In contrast, using a buffer of size b makes it possible to allocate only the sustainable rate. This is what we call the *buffering gain*, namely, the gain on the peak rate obtained by adding some buffer. The buffering gain comes at the expense of increased delay, as can easily be seen from Theorem 1.4.2.

1.9   Proof of Theorem 1.4.5

Step 1:   Consider a fixed time t_0 and assume, in this step, that there is some time u_0 that achieves the supremum in the definition of $\alpha \oslash \beta$. We construct some input and output functions R and R^* such that R is constrained by α, the system (R, R^*) is causal, and $\alpha^*(t_0) = (R^* \oslash R^*)(t_0)$. R and R^* are given by (Figure 1.28)

$$\begin{cases} R(t) = \alpha(t) \text{ if } t < u_0 + t_0 \\ R(t) = \alpha(u_0 + t_0) \text{ if } t \geq u_0 + t_0 \\ R^*(t) = \inf[\alpha(t), \beta(t)] \text{ if } t < u_0 + t_0 \\ R^*(t) = R(t) \text{ if } t \geq u_0 + t_0 \end{cases}$$

It is easy to see, as in the proof of Theorem 1.4.4 that R and R^* are wide-sense increasing, that $R^* \leq R$ and that β is a service curve for the flow. Now

$$R^*(u_0 + t_0) - R^*(u_0) = \alpha(u_0 + t_0) - R^*(u_0) \geq \alpha(u_0 + t_0) - \beta(u_0) = \alpha^*(t_0)$$

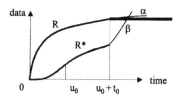

Figure 1.28: Step 1 of the proof of Theorem 1.4.5: a system that attains the output bound at one value t_0.

Step 2: Consider now a sequence of times $t_0, t_1, ..., t_n, ...$ (not necessarily increasing). Assume, in this step, that for all n there is a value u_n that achieves the supremum in the definition of $(\alpha \oslash \beta)(t_n)$. We prove that there are some functions R and R^* such that R is constrained by α, the system (R, R^*) is causal, has β as a service curve, and $\alpha^*(t_n) = (R^* \oslash R^*)(t_n)$ for all $n \geq 0$.

We build R and R^* by induction on a set of increasing intervals $[0, s_0], [0, s_1],...,[0, s_n]....$ The induction property is that the system restricted to time interval $[0, s_n]$ is causal, has α as an arrival curve for the input, has β as a service curve, and satisfies $\alpha^*(t_i) = (R^* \oslash R^*)(t_i)$ for $i \leq n$.

The first interval is defined by $s_0 = u_0 + t_0$; R and R^* are built on $[0, s_0]$ as in step 1 above. Clearly, the induction property is true for $n = 0$. Assume we have built the system on interval $[0, s_n]$. Define now $s_{n+1} = s_n + u_n + t_n + \delta_{n+1}$. We chose δ_{n+1} such that

$$\alpha(s + \delta_{n+1}) - \alpha(s) \geq R(s_n) \text{ for all } s \geq 0 \qquad (1.36)$$

This is possible from the last condition in the Theorem. The system is defined on $]s_n, s_{n+1}]$ by (Figure 1.29)

$$\begin{cases} R(t) = R^*(t) = R(s_n) \text{ for } s_n < t \leq s_n + \delta_{n+1} \\ R(t) = R(s_n) + \alpha(t - s_n - \delta_{n+1}) \text{ for } s_n + \delta_{n+1} < t \leq s_{n+1} \\ R^*(t) = R(s_n) + (\alpha \wedge \beta)(t - s_n - \delta_{n+1}) \text{ for } s_n + \delta_{n+1} < t < s_{n+1} \\ R^*(s_{n+1}) = R(s_{n+1}) \end{cases}$$

We show now that the arrival curve constraint is satisfied for the system defined on $[0, s_{n+1}]$. Consider $R(t) - R(v)$ for t and v in $[0, s_{n+1}]$. If both $t \leq s_n$ and $v \leq s_n$, or if both $t > s_n$ and $v > s_n$ then the arrival curve property holds from our construction and the induction property. We can thus assume that $t > s_n$ and $v \leq s_n$. Clearly, we can even assume that $t \geq s_n + \delta_{n+1}$, otherwise the property is trivially true. Let us rewrite $t = s_n + \delta_{n+1} + s$. We have, from our construction:

$$R(t) - R(v) = R(s_n + \delta_{n+1} + s) - R(v) = R(s_n) + \alpha(s) - R(v) \leq R(s_n) + \alpha(s)$$

Now from Equation (1.36), we have:

$$R(s_n) + \alpha(s) \leq \alpha(s + \delta_{n+1}) \leq \alpha(s + \delta_{n+1} + s_n - v) = \alpha(t - v)$$

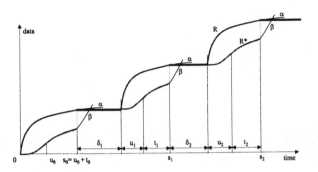

Figure 1.29: Step 2 of the proof of Theorem 1.4.5: a system that attains the output bound for all values t_n, $n \in \mathbb{N}$.

which shows the arrival curve property.

Using the same arguments as in step 1, it is simple to show that the system is causal, has β as a service curve, and that

$$R^*(u_{n+1} + t_{n+1}) - R^*(u_{n+1}) = \alpha^*(t_{n+1})$$

which ends the proof that the induction property is also true for $n + 1$.

Step 3: Consider, as in step 2, a sequence of times $t_0, t_1, ..., t_n, ...$ (not necessarily increasing). We now extend the result in step 2 to the case where the supremum in the definition of $\alpha^* = (\alpha \oslash \beta)(t_n)$ is not necessarily attained. Assume first that $\alpha^*(t_n)$ is finite for all n. For all n and all $m \in \mathbb{N}^*$ there is some $u_{m,n}$ such that

$$\alpha(t_n + u_{m,n}) - \beta(u_{m,n}) \geq \alpha^*(t_n) - \frac{1}{m} \qquad (1.37)$$

Now the set of all couples (m, n) is enumerable. Consider some numbering $(M(i), N(i))$, $i \in \mathbb{N}$ for that set. Using the same construction as in step 2, we can build by induction on i a sequence of increasing intervals $[0, s_i]$ and a system (R, R^*) that is causal, has α as an arrival curve for the input, has β as a service curve, and such that

$$R^*(s_i) - R^*(s_i - t_{N(i)}) \geq \alpha^*(t_{N(i)}) - \frac{1}{M(i)}$$

Now consider an arbitrary, but fixed n. By applying the previous equations to all i such that $N(i) = n$, we obtain

$$\begin{aligned}
(R^* \oslash R^*)(t_n) &\geq \sup_{i \text{ such that } N(i)=n} \left\{ \alpha^*(t_{N(i)}) - \frac{1}{M(i)} \right\} \\
&= \alpha^*(t_n) - \inf_{i \text{ such that } N(i)=n} \left\{ \frac{1}{M(i)} \right\}
\end{aligned}$$

Now the set of all $\frac{1}{M(i)}$ for i such that $N(i) = n$ is $\mathbb{N}^*$, thus

$$\inf_{i \text{ such that } N(i)=n} \left\{ \frac{1}{M(i)} \right\} = 0$$

and thus $(R^* \oslash R^*)(t_n) = \alpha^*(t_n)$, which ends the proof of step 3 in the case where $\alpha^*(t_n)$ is finite for all n.

A similar reasoning can be used if $\alpha^*(t_n)$ is infinite for some t_n. In that case replace Equation (1.37) by $\alpha(t_n + u_{m,n}) - \beta(u_{m,n}) \geq m$.

Step 4: Now we conclude the proof. If time is discrete, then step 3 proves the theorem. Otherwise we use a density argument. The set of nonnegative rational numbers $\mathbb{Q}^+$ is enumerable; we can thus apply step 3 to the sequence of all elements of $\mathbb{Q}^+$, and obtain system (R, R^*), with

$$(R^* \oslash R^*)(q) = \alpha^*(q) \text{ for all } q \in \mathbb{Q}^+$$

Function R^* is right-continuous, thus, from the discussion at the end of Theorem 1.2.2, it follows that $R^* \oslash R^*$ is left-continuous. We now show that α^* is also left-continuous. For all $t \geq 0$ we have:

$$\sup_{s<t} \alpha^*(s) = \sup_{(s,v) \text{ such that } s<t \text{ and } v \geq 0} \{\alpha(s+v)-\beta(v)\} = \sup_{v \geq 0}\{\sup_{s<t}[\alpha(s+v)-\beta(v)]\}$$

Now

$$\sup_{s<t} \alpha(s+v) = \alpha(t+v)$$

because α is left-continuous. Thus

$$\sup_{s<t} \alpha^*(s) = \sup_{v \geq 0}\{\alpha(t+v) - \beta(v)]\} = \alpha^*(t)$$

which shows that α is left-continuous.

Back to the main argument of step 4, consider some arbitrary $t \geq 0$. The set $\mathbb{Q}^+$ is dense in the set of nonnegative real numbers, thus there is a sequence of rational numbers $q_n \in \mathbb{Q}^+$, with $n \in \mathbb{N}$, such that $q_n \leq t$ and $\lim_{n \to +\infty} q_n = t$. From the left-continuity of $R^* \oslash R^*$ and α^* we have:

$$(R^* \oslash R^*)(t) = \lim_{n \to +\infty} (R^* \oslash R^*)(q_n) = \lim_{n \to +\infty} \alpha^*(q_n) = \alpha^*(t)$$

$\square$

1.10 Bibliographic Notes

Network calculus as has been applied to dimensioning ATM switches in [53]. A practical algorithm for the determination of the minimum arrival curve for ATM system is described in [54]. It uses the burstiness function of a flow, defined in [51] as follows. For any r, $B(r)$ is the minimum b such that the flow is $\gamma_{r,b}$-smooth, and is thus the required buffer if the flow is served at a constant rate r. Note that $B(r)$ is the Legendre transform of the minimum arrival curve σ of the flow, namely, $B(r) = \sup_{t \geq 0}(\sigma(t) - rt)$ [54] gives a fast algorithm for computing $B(r)$. Interestingly, the concept is applied also to the distribution of symbols in a text.

In [70], the concepts of arrival and service curve are used to analyze real time processing systems. It is shown that the service curve for a variable capacity node must be super-additive, and conversely, any super-additive function is a service curve for a variable capacity node. Compare to greedy shapers, which have a sub-additive service curve. This shows that, except for constant bit rate trunks, a greedy shaper cannot be modeled as a variable capacity node, and conversely.

In [8], the authors consider a crossbar switch, and call $r_{i,j}$ the rate assigned to the traffic from input port i to output port j. Assume that $\sum_i r_{i,j} \leq 1$ for all j and $\sum_j r_{i,j} \leq 1$ for all i. Using properties of doubly-stochastic matrices (such as $(r_{i,j})$ is), they give a simple scheduling algorithm that guarantees that the flow from port i to port j is allocated a variable capacity C satisfying $C_{i,j}(t) - C_{i,j}(s) \geq r_{i,j}(t - s) - s_{i,j}$ for some $s_{i,j}$ defined by the algorithm. Thus, the node offers a service curve equal to the rate-latency function $\beta_{r_{i,j}, s_{i,j}}$.

A dual approach to account for variable length packets is introduced in [10]. It consists in replacing the definition of arrival curve (or σ-smoothness) by the concept of g-regularity. Consider a flow of variable length packets, with cumulative packet length L and call T_i the arrival epoch for the ith packet. The flow is said to be g-regular if $T(j) - T(i) \geq g(L(j) - L(i))$ for all packet numbers $i \leq j$. A theory is then developed with concepts similar to the greedy shaper. The theory uses max-plus convolution instead of min-plus convolution. The (b, r) regulator originally introduced by Cruz [18] is a shaper in this theory, whose output is g-regular, with $g(x) = \frac{(x-b)^+}{r}$. This theory does not exactly correspond to the usual concept of leaky bucket controllers. More specifically, there is not an exact correspondence between the set of flows that are g-regular on one hand, and that are σ-smooth on the other. We explain why with an example. Consider the set of flows that are g-regular, with $g(x) = \frac{x}{r}$. The minimum arrival curve we can put on this set of flows is $\sigma(t) = rt + l_{\max}$ [10]. But conversely, if a flow is σ-smooth, we cannot guarantee that it is g-regular. Indeed, the following sequence of packets is a flow that is σ-smooth but not g-regular: the flow has a short packet (length $l_1 < l_{\max}$) at time $T_1 = 0$, followed by a packet of maximum size $l_{\max}$ at time $T_2 = \frac{l_1}{r}$. In fact, if a flow is σ-smooth, then it is g'-regular, with $g'(x) = \frac{(x - l_{\max})^+}{r}$.

The strict service curve in Definition 1.3.2 is called "strong" service curve in [41].

1.11 Exercises

Exercise 1.1. *Compute the maximum buffer size X for a system that is initially empty, and where the input function is $R(t) = \int_0^t r(s)ds$, for the following cases.*

1. if $r(t) = a$ (constant)

2. *one on-off connection with peak rate 1 Mb/s, on period 1 sec, off period τ seconds, and trunk bit rate $c = 0.5$ Mb/s.*

3. *if $r(t) = c + c \sin \omega t$, with trunk bit rate $c > 0$.*

Exercise 1.2. *You have a fixed buffer of size X, that receives a data input $r(t)$. Determine the output rate c that is required to avoid buffer overflow given that the buffer is initially empty.*

Exercise 1.3. *1. For a flow with constant bit rate c, give some possible arrival curves.*

2. *Consider a flow with an arrival curve given by: $\alpha(t) = B$, where B is constant. What does this mean for the flow ?*

Exercise 1.4. *We say that a flow is (P, B) constrained if it has $\gamma_{P,B}$ as an arrival curve.*

A trunk system has a buffer size of B and a trunk bitrate of P. Fill in the dots: (1) there is no loss if the input is $(.,.)$ constrained (2) the output is $(.,.)$ constrained.

2. *A (P, B) constrained flow is fed into an infinite buffer served at a rate of c. What is the maximum delay ?*

Exercise 1.5 (On-Off flows). *1. Assume a data flow is periodical, with period T, and satisfies the following: $r(t) = p$ for $0 \le t < T_0$, and $r(t) = 0$ for $T_0 \le t < T$.*

(a) *Draw $R(t) = \int_0^t r(s) ds$*

(b) *Find an arrival curve for the flow. Find the minimum arrival curve for the flow.*

(c) *Find the minimum (r, b) such that the flow is (r, b) constrained.*

2. *A traffic flow uses a link with bitrate P (bits/s). Data is sent as packets of variable length. The flow is controlled by a leaky bucket (r, b). What is the maximum packet size ? What is the minimum time interval between packets of maximum size ?*

Application: $P = 2$ Mb/s, $r = 0.2$ Mb/s; what is the required burst tolerance b if the packet length is 2 Kbytes ? What is then the minimum spacing between packets ?

Exercise 1.6. *Consider the following alternative definition of the GCRA:*

Definition 1.11.1. *The GCRA (T, τ) is a controller that takes as input a cell arrival time t and returns* result. *It has internal (static) variables X (bucket level) and LCT (last conformance time).*

- *initially, X = 0 and LCT = 0*

- *when a cell arrives at time* t, *then*

```
if (X - t + LCT > tau)
    result = NON-CONFORMANT;
else {
    X = max (X - t + LCT, 0) + T;
    LCT = t;
    result = CONFORMANT;
    }
```

Show that the two definitions of GCRA are equivalent.

Exercise 1.7.   *1. For the following flows and a GCRA(10, 2), give the conformant and non-conformant cells. Times are in cell slots at the link rate. Draw the leaky bucket behaviour assuming instantaneous cell arrivals.*

(a) *0, 10, 18, 28, 38*

(b) *0, 10, 15, 25, 35*

(c) *0, 10, 18, 26, 36*

(d) *0, 10, 11, 18, 28*

2. *What is the maximum number of cells that can flow back to back with GCRA(T, CDVT) (maximum "clump" size) ?*

Exercise 1.8.   *1. For the following flows and a GCRA(100, 500), give the conformant and non-conformant cells. Times are in cell slots at the link rate.*

(a) *0, 100, 110, 12, 130, 140, 150, 160, 170, 180, 1000, 1010*

(b) *0, 100, 130, 160, 190, 220, 250, 280, 310, 1000, 1030*

(c) *0, 10, 20, 300, 310, 320, 600, 610, 620, 800, 810, 820, 1000, 1010, 1020, 1200, 1210, 1220, 1400, 1410, 1420, 1600, 1610, 1620*

2. *Assume that a cell flow has a minimum spacing of γ time units between cell emission times (γ is the minimum time between the beginnings of two cell transmissions). What is the maximum burst size for GCRA(T, τ) ? What is the minimum time between bursts of maximum size ?*

3. *Assume that a cell flow has a minimum spacing between cells of γ time units, and a minimum spacing between bursts of T_1. What is the maximum burst size ?*

Exercise 1.9. *For a CBR connection, here are some values from an ATM operator:*

peak cell rate (cells/s)	100	1000	10000	100000
CDVT (microseconds)	2900	1200	400	135

1. *What are the (P, B) parameters in b/s and bits for each case ? How does T compare to τ ?*

2. *If a connection requires a peak cell rate of 1000 cells per second and a cell delay variation of 1400 microseconds, what can be done ?*

3. *Assume the operator allocates the peak rate to every connection at one buffer. What is the amount of buffer required to assure absence of loss ? Numerical Application for each of the following cases, where a number N of identical connections with peak cell rate P is multiplexed.*

```
case                        1      2      3      4
nb of connnections        3000    300    30      3
peak cell rate (c/s)       100   1000  10000 100000
```

Exercise 1.10. *The two questions in this problem are independent.*

1. *An ATM source is constrained by GCRA($T = 30$ slots, $\tau = 60$ slots), where time is counted in slots. One slot is the time it takes to transmit one cell on the link. The source sends cells according to the following algorithm.*

   - *In a first phase, cells are sent at times $t(1) = 0$, $t(2) = 15$, $t(3) = 30, \ldots, t(n) = 15(n - 1)$ as long as all cells are conformant. In other words, the number n is the largest integer such that all cells sent at times $t(i) = 15(i - 1)$, $i \leq n$ are conformant. The sending of cell n at time $t(n)$ ends the first phase.*

   - *Then the source enters the second phase. The subsequent cell $n + 1$ is sent at the earliest time after $t(n)$ at which a conformant cell can be sent, and the same is repeated for ever. In other words, call $t(k)$ the sending time for cell k, with $k > n$; we have then: $t(k)$ is the earliest time after $t(k - 1)$ at which a conformant cell can be sent.*

   How many cells were sent by the source in time interval $[0, 151]$?

2. *A network node can be modeled as a single buffer with a constant output rate c (in cells per second). It receives I ATM connections labeled $1, \ldots, I$. Each ATM connection has a peak cell rate p_i (in cells per second) and a cell delay variation tolerance τ_i (in seconds) for $1 \leq i \leq I$. The total input rate into the buffer is at least as large as $\sum_{i=1}^{I} p_i$ (which is equivalent to saying that it is unlimited). What is the buffer size (in cells) required for a loss-free operation ?*

Exercise 1.11. *In this problem, time is counted in slots. One slot is the duration to transmit one ATM cell on the link.*

1. *An ATM source S_1 is constrained by GCRA($T = 50$ slots, $\tau = 500$ slots), The source sends cells according to the following algorithm.*

- In a first phase, cells are sent at times $t(1) = 0$, $t(2) = 10$, $t(3) = 20, \ldots, t(n) = 10(n - 1)$ as long as all cells are conformant. In other words, the number n is the largest integer such that all cells sent at times $t(i) = 10(i - 1)$, $i \leq n$ are conformant. The sending of cell n at time $t(n)$ ends the first phase.

- Then the source enters the second phase. The subsequent cell $n + 1$ is sent at the earliest time after $t(n)$ at which a conformant cell can be sent, and the same is repeated for ever. In other words, call $t(k)$ the sending time for cell k, with $k > n$; we have then: $t(k)$ is the earliest time after $t(k - 1)$ at which a conformant cell can be sent.

How many cells were sent by the source in time interval $[0, 401]$?

2. An ATM source S_2 is constrained by both GCRA($T = 10$ slots, $\tau = 2$ slots) and GCRA($T = 50$ slots, $\tau = 500$ slots). The source starts at time 0, and has an infinite supply of cells to send. The source sends its cells as soon as it is permitted by the combination of the GCRAs. We call $t(n)$ the time at which the source sends the nth cell, with $t(1) = 0$. What is the value of $t(15)$?

Exercise 1.12. *Consider a flow $R(t)$ receiving a minimum service curve guarantee β. Assume that*

- *β is concave and wide-sense increasing*

- *the inf in $R \otimes \beta$ is a min*

For all t, call $\tau(t)$ a number such that

$$(R \otimes \beta)(t) = R(\tau(t)) + \beta(t - \tau(t))$$

Show that it is possible to choose τ such that if $t_1 \leq t_2$ then $\tau(t_1) \leq \tau(t_2)$.

Exercise 1.13.   *1. Find the maximum backlog and maximum delay for an ATM CBR connection with peak rate P and cell delay variation τ, assuming the service curve is $c(t) = r(t - T_0)^+$*

2. *Find the maximum backlog and maximum delay for an ATM VBR connection with peak rate P, cell delay variation τ, sustainable cell rate M and burst tolerance τ_B (in seconds), assuming the service curve is $c(t) = r(t - T_0)^+$*

Exercise 1.14. *Show the following statements:*

1. *Consider a (P, B) constrained flow, served at a rate $c \geq P$. The output is also (P, B) constrained.*

2. *Assume $a()$ has a bounded right-handside derivative. Then the output for a flow constrained by $a()$, served in a buffer at a constant rate $c \geq \sup_{t \geq 0} a'(t)$, is also constrained by $a()$.*

Exercise 1.15. *1. Find the the arrival curve constraining the output for an ATM CBR connection with peak rate P and cell delay variation τ, assuming the service curve is $c(t) = r(t - T_0)^+$*

2. Find the arrival curve constraining the output for an ATM VBR connection with peak rate P, cell delay variation τ, sustainable cell rate M and burst tolerance τ_B (in seconds), assuming the service curve is $c(t) = r(t - T_0)^+$

Exercise 1.16. *Consider the figure "Derivation of arrival curve for the output of a flow served in a node with rate-latency service curve $\beta_{R,T}$". What can be said if t_0 in the Figure is infinite, namely, if $a'(t) > r$ for all t ?*

Exercise 1.17. *Consider a series of guaranteed service nodes with service curves $c_i(t) = r_i(t - T_i)^+$. What is the maximum delay through this system for a flow constrained by (m, b) ?*

Exercise 1.18. *A flow with T-SPEC (p, M, r, b) traverses nodes 1 and 2. Node i offers a service curve $c_i(t) = R_i(t - T_i)^+$. What buffer size is required for the flow at node 2 ?*

Exercise 1.19. *A flow with T-SPEC (p, M, r, b) traverses nodes 1 and 2. Node i offers a service curve $c_i(t) = R_i(t - T_i)^+$. A shaper is placed between nodes 1 and 2. The shaper forces the flow to the arrival curve $z(t) = \min(R_2 t, bt + m)$.*

1. What buffer size is required for the flow at the shaper ?

2. What buffer size is required at node 2 ? What value do you find if $T_1 = T_2$?

3. Compare the sum of the preceding buffer sizes to the size that would be required if no re-shaping is performed.

4. Give an arrival curve for the output of node 2.

Exercise 1.20. *Prove the formula giving of paragraph "Buffer Sizing at a Re-shaper"*

Exercise 1.21. *Is Theorem "Input-Output Characterization of Greedy Shapers" a stronger result than Corollary "Service Curve offered by a Greedy Shaper" ?*

Exercise 1.22. *1. Explain what is meant by "we pay bursts only once".*

2. Give a summary in at most 15 lines of the main properties of shapers

3. Define the following concepts by using the $\otimes$ operator: Service Curve, Arrival Curve, Shaper

4. What is a greedy source ?

Exercise 1.23. *1. Show that for a constant bit rate trunk with rate c, the backlog at time t is given by*

$$W(t) = \sup_{s \le t} \{R(t) - R^*(s) - c(t - s)\}$$

2. What does the formula become if we assume only that, instead a constant bit rate trunk, the node is a scheduler offering β as a service curve ?

Exercise 1.24. Is it true that offering a service curve β implies that, during any busy period of length t, the amount of service received rate is at least $\beta(t)$?

Exercise 1.25. A flow $S(t)$ is constrained by an arrival curve α. The flow is fed into a shaper, with shaping curve σ. We assume that

$$\alpha(s) = \min(m + ps, b + rs)$$

and

$$\sigma(s) = \min(Ps, B + Rs)$$

We assume that $p > r$, $m \le b$ and $P \ge R$.

The shaper has a fixed buffer size equal to $X \ge m$. We require that the buffer never overflows.

1. Assume that $B = +\infty$. Find the smallest of P which guarantees that there is no buffer overflow. Let P_0 be this value.

2. We do not assume that $B = +\infty$ any more, but we assume that P is set to the value P_0 computed in the previous question. Find the value (B_0, R_0) of (B, R) which guarantees that there is no buffer overflow and minimizes the cost function $c(B, R) = aB + R$, where a is a positive constant.

   What is the maximum virtual delay if $(P, B, R) = (P_0, B_0, R_0)$?

Exercise 1.26. We consider a buffer of size X cells, served at a constant rate of c cells per second. We put N identical connections into the buffer; each of the N connections is constrained both by GCRA(T_1, τ_1) and GCRA(T_2, τ_2). What is the maximum value of N which is possible if we want to guarantee that there is no cell loss at all ?

Give the numerical application for $T_1 = 0.5$ ms, $\tau_1 = 4.5$ ms, $T_2 = 5$ ms, $\tau_2 = 495$ ms, $c = 10^6$ cells/second, $X = 10^4$ cells

Exercise 1.27. We consider a flow defined by its function $R(t)$, with $R(t) = $ the number of bits observed since time $t = 0$.

1. The flow is fed into a buffer, served at a rate r. Call $q(t)$ the buffer content at time t. We do the same assumptions as in the lecture, namely, the buffer is large enough, and is initially empty. What is the expression of $q(t)$ assuming we know $R(t)$?

   We assume now that, unlike what we saw in the lecture, the initial buffer content (at time $t = 0$) is not 0, but some value $q_0 \ge 0$. What is now the expression for $q(t)$?

2. *The flow is put into a leaky bucket policer, with rate r and bucket size b. This is a policer, not a shaper, so nonconformant bits are discarded. We assume that the bucket is large enough, and is initially empty. What is the condition on R which ensures that no bit is discarded by the policer (in other words, that the flow is conformant) ?*

    We assume now that, unlike what we saw in the lecture, the initial bucket content (at time $t = 0$) is not 0, but some value $b_0 \geq 0$. What is now the condition on R which ensures that no bit is discarded by the policer (in other words, that the flow is conformant) ?

Exercise 1.28. *Consider a variable capacity network node, with capacity curve $M(t)$. Show that there is one maximum function $S^*(t)$ such that for all $0 \leq s \leq t$, we have*

$$M(t) - M(s) \geq S^*(t - s)$$

Show that S^* is super-additive.

   Conversely, if a function β is super-additive, show that there is a variable capacity network node, with capacity curve $M(t)$, such that for all $0 \leq s \leq t$, we have $M(t) - M(s) \geq S^*(t - s)$.

   Show that, with a notable exception, a shaper cannot be modeled as a variable capacity node.

Exercise 1.29. *1. Consider a packetized greedy shaper with shaping curve $\sigma(t) = rt$ for $t \geq 0$. Assume that $L(k) = kM$ where M is fixed. Assume that the input is given by $R(t) = 10M$ for $t > 0$ and $R(0) = 0$. Compute the sequence $R^{(i)}(t)$ used in the representation of the output of the packetized greedy shaper, for $i = 1, 2, 3, \ldots$.*

2. *Same question if $sigma(t) = (rt + 2M)1_{\{t > 0\}}$.*

Exercise 1.30. *Consider a source given by the function*

$$\begin{cases} R(t) = B \text{ for } t > 0 \\ R(t) = 0 \text{ for } t \leq 0 \end{cases}$$

Thus the flow consists of an instantaneous burst of B bits.

1. *What is the minimum arrival curve for the flow ?*

2. *Assume that the flow is served in one node that offers a minimum service curve of the rate latency type, with rate r and latency Δ. What is the maximum delay for the last bit of the flow ?*

3. *We assume now that the flow goes through a series of two nodes, $\mathcal{N}_1$ and $\mathcal{N}_2$, where $\mathcal{N}_i$ offers to the flow a minimum service curve of the rate latency type, with rate r_i and latency Δ_i, for $i = 1, 2$. What is the the maximum delay for the last bit of the flow through the series of two nodes ?*

4. With the same assumption as in the previous item, call $R_1(t)$ the function describing the flow at the output of node $\mathcal{N}_1$ (thus at the input of node $\mathcal{N}_2$). What is the worst case minimum arrival curve for R_1 ?

5. We assume that we insert between $\mathcal{N}_1$ and $\mathcal{N}_2$ a "reformatter" S. The input to S is $R_1(t)$. We call $R_1'(t)$ the output of S. Thus $R_1'(t)$ is now the input to $\mathcal{N}_2$. The function of the "reformatter"S is to delay the flow R_1 in order to output a flow R_1' that is a delayed version of R. In other words, we must have $R_1'(t) = R(t - d)$ for some d. We assume that the reformatter S is optimal in the sense that it chooses the smallest possible d. In the worst case, what is this optimal value of d ?

6. With the same assumptions as in the previous item, what is the worst case end-to-end delay through the series of nodes $\mathcal{N}_1, S, \mathcal{N}_2$? Is the reformatter transparent ?

Exercise 1.31. Let σ be a good function. Consider the concatenation of a bit-by-bit greedy shaper, with curve σ, and an L-packetizer. Assume that $\sigma(0^+) = 0$. Consider only inputs that are L-packetized

1. Is this system a packetized shaper for σ ?

2. Is it a packetized shaper for $\sigma + l_{\max}$?

3. Is it a packetized greedy shaper for $\sigma + l_{\max}$?

Exercise 1.32. Assume that σ is a good function and $\sigma = \sigma_0 + l u_0$ where u_0 is the step function with a step at $t = 0$. Can we conclude that σ_0 is sub-additive ?

Exercise 1.33. Is the operator (P^L) upper-semi-continuous ?

Exercise 1.34.   1. Consider the concatenation of an L-packetizer and a network element with minimum service curve β and maximum service curve γ. Can we say that the combined system offer a minimum service curve $(\beta(t) - l_{\max})^+$ and a maximum service curve γ, as in the case where the concatenation would be in the reverse order ? .

2. Consider the concatenation of a GPS node offering a guarantee λ_{r_1}, an L-packetizer, and a second GPS node offering a guarantee λ_{r_2}. Show that the combined system offers a rate-latency service curve with rate $R = \min(r_1, r_2)$ and latency$E = \frac{l_{\max}}{\max(r_1, r_2)}$.

Exercise 1.35. Consider a node that offers to a flow $R(t)$ a rate-latency service curve $\beta = S_{R,L}$. Assume that $R(t)$ is L-packetized, with packet arrival times called $T_1, T_2, \ldots$ (and is left-continuous, as usual)

Show that $(R \otimes \beta)(t) = \min_{T_i \in [0,t]} [R(T_i) + \beta(t - T_i)]$ (and thus, the inf is attained).

Exercise 1.36. *1. Assume K connections, each with peak rate p, sustainable rate m and burst tolerance b, are offered to a trunk with constant service rate P and FIFO buffer of capacity X. Find the conditions on K for the system to be loss-free.*

2. If $Km = P$, what is the condition on X for K connections to be accepted ?

3. What is the maximum number of connection if $p = 2$ Mb/s, $m = 0.2$ Mb/s, $X = 10MBytes$, $b = 1Mbyte$ and $P = 0.1, 1, 2$ or 10 Mb/s ?

4. For a fixed buffer size X, draw the acceptance region when K and P are the variables.

Exercise 1.37. *Show the formulas giving the expressions for $f_B(R)$ and $f_B(\alpha)$.*

Exercise 1.38. *1. What is the effective bandwith for a connection with $p = 2$ Mb/s, $m = 0.2$ Mb/s, $b = 100$ Kbytes when $D = 1msec$, 10 msec, 100 msec, $1s$?*

2. Plot the effective bandwidth e as a function of the delay constraint in the general case of a connection with parameters p, m, b.

Exercise 1.39. *1. Compute the effective bandwidth for a mix of VBR connections $1, \ldots, I$.*

2. Show how the homogeneous case can be derived from your formula

3. Assume K connections, each with peak rate p, sustainable rate m and burst tolerance b, are offered to a trunk with constant service rate P and FIFO buffer of capacity X. Find the conditions on K for the system to be loss-free.

4. Assume that there are two classes of connections, with K_i connections in class i, $i = 1, 2$, offered to a trunk with constant service rate P and FIFO buffer of infinite capacity X. The connections are accepted as long as their queuing delay does not exceed some value D. Draw the acceptance region, that is, the set of (K_1, K_2) that are accepted by CAC2. Is the acceptance region convex ? Is the complementary of the acceptance region in the positive orthant convex ? Does this generalize to more than two classes ?

Chapter 2

Application of Network Calculus to the Internet

In this chapter we apply the concepts of Chapter 1 and explain the theoretical underpinnings of integrated and differentiated services. Integrated services define how reservations can be made for flows. We explain in detail how this framework was deeply influenced by GPS. In particular, we will see that it assumes that every router can be modeled as a node offering a minimum service curve that is a rate-latency function. We explain how this is used in a protocol such as RSVP. We also analyze the more efficient framework based on service curve scheduling. This allows us to address in a simple way the complex issue of schedulability.

Differentiated services differ radically, in that reservations are made per class of service, rather than per flow. We show how the bounding results in Chapter 1 can be applied to find delay and backlog bounds. We also introduce the "damper", which is a way of enforcing a maximum service curve, and show how it can radically reduce the delay bounds.

2.1 GPS and Guaranteed Rate Schedulers

In this section we describe GPS and its derivatives; they form the basis on which the Internet guaranteed model was defined.

2.1.1 Packet Scheduling

A guaranteed service network offers delay and throughput guarantees to flows, provided that the flows satisfy some arrival curve constraints (Section 2.2). This requires that network nodes implement some form of packet scheduling, also called service discipline. Packet scheduling is defined as the function that decides, at every buffer inside a network node, the service order for different packets.

A simple form of packet scheduling is FIFO: packets are served in the order of arrival. The delay bound, and the required buffer, depend on the minimum arrival curve of the aggregate flow (Section 1.8 on page 64). If one flow sends a large amount of traffic, then the delay increases for all flows, and packet loss may occur. Thus FIFO scheduling requires that arrival curve constraints on all flows be strictly enforced at all points in the network. Also, with FIFO scheduling, the delay bound is the same for all flows. We study FIFO scheduling in more detail in Section 6.

An alternative [21, 39] is to use per flow queuing, in order to (1) provide isolation to flows and (2) offer different guarantees. We consider first the ideal form of per flow queuing called "Generalized Processor Sharing" (GPS) [56], which was already mentioned in Chapter 1.

2.1.2 GPS and a Practical Implementation (PGPS)

A GPS node serves several flows in parallel, and has a total output rate equal to c b/s. A flow i is allocated a given weight, say ϕ_i. Call $R_i(t), R_i^*(t)$ the input and output functions for flow i. The guarantee is that at any time t, the service rate offered to flow i is 0 is flow i has no backlog (namely, if $R_i(t) = R_i^*(t)$), and otherwise is equal to $\frac{\phi_i}{\sum_{j \in B(t)} \phi_j} c$, where $B(t)$ is the set of backlogged flows at time t. Thus

$$R_i^*(t) = \int_0^t \frac{\phi_i}{\sum_{j \in B(s)} \phi_j} 1_{\{i \in B(s)\}} ds$$

In the formula, we used the indicator function $1_{\{expr\}}$, which is equal to 1 if $expr$ is true, and 0 otherwise.

It follows immediately that the GPS node offers to flow i a service curve equal to $\lambda_{r_i c}$, with $r_i = \frac{\phi_i C}{\sum_j \phi_j}$. It is shown in [57] that a better service curve can be obtained for every flow if we know some arrival curve properties for all flows; however the simple property is sufficient to understand the integrated service model.

GPS satisfies the requirement of isolating flows and providing differentiated guarantees. We can compute the delay bound and buffer requirements for every flow if we know its arrival curve, using the results of Chapter 1. However, a GPS node is a theoretical concept, which is not really implementable, because it relies on a fluid model, and assumes that packets are infinitely divisible. How can we make a practical implementation of GPS ? One simple solution would be to use the virtual finish times as we did for the buffered leaky bucket controller in Section 1.7.3: for every packet we would compute its finish time θ under GPS, then at time θ present the packet to a multiplexer that serves packets at a rate c. Figure 2.1 (left) shows the finish times on an example. It also illustrates the main drawback that this method would have: at times 3 and 5, the multiplexer would be idle, whereas at time 6 it would have a burst of 5 packets to serve. In particular, such a scheduler would not be work conserving.

This is what motivated researchers to find other practical implementations of GPS. We study here one such implementation of GPS, called packet by packet generalized processor sharing (PGPS) [56]. Other implementations of GPS are discussed in Section 2.1.3.

PGPS emulates GPS as follows. There is one FIFO queue per flow. The scheduler handles packets one at a time, until it is fully transmitted, at the system rate c. For every packet, we compute the finish time that it would have under GPS (we call this the "GPS-finish-time"). Then, whenever a packet is finished transmitting, the next packet selected for transmission is the one with the earliest GPS-finish-time, among all packets present. Figure 2.1 shows one example. We see that, unlike the simple solution discussed earlier, PGPS is work conserving, but does so at the expense of maybe scheduling a packet *before* its finish time under GPS.

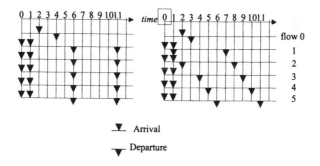

Figure 2.1: Scheduling with GPS (left) and PGPS (right). Flow 0 has weight 0.5, flows 1 to 5 have weight 0.1. All packets have the same transmission time equal to 1 time unit.

We can quantify the difference between PGPS and GPS in the following proposition. In Section 2.1.3, we will see how to derive a service curve property.

Proposition 2.1.1 ([56]). *The finish time for PGPS is at most the finish time of GPS plus $\frac{L}{c}$, where c is the total rate and L is the maximum packet size.*

Proof: Call $D(n)$ the finish time of the nth packet for the aggregate input flow under PGPS, in the order of departure, and $\theta(n)$ under GPS. Call n_0 the number of the packet that started the busy period in which packet n departs. Note that PGPS and GPS have the same busy periods, since if we observe only the aggregate flows, there is no difference between PGPS and GPS.

There may be some packets that depart before packet n in PGPS, but that nonetheless have a later departure time under GPS. Call $m_0 \geq n_0$ the largest packet number for which this occurs, if any; otherwise let $m_0 = n_0 - 1$. In this proposition, we call $l(m)$ the length in bits of packet m. Under PGPS, packet m_0 started service at $D(m_0) - \frac{l(m_0)}{c}$, which must be earlier than the arrival times of packets $m = m_0 + 1, ..., n$. Indeed, otherwise, by definition of PGPS, the PGPS scheduler would have scheduled packets $m = m_0 + 1, ..., n$ before packet m_0. Now let us observe the GPS system. Packets $m = m_0 + 1, ..., n$ depart no later than packet n, by definition of m_0; they have arrived after $D(m_0) - \frac{l(m_0)}{c}$. By expressing the amount of service in the interval $[D(m_0) - \frac{l(m_0)}{c}, \theta(n)]$ we find thus

$$\sum_{m=m_0+1}^{n} l(m) \leq c \left(\theta(n) - D(m_0) + \frac{l(m_0)}{c} \right)$$

Now since packets $m_0, ..., n$ are in the same busy period, we have

$$D(n) = D(m_0) + \frac{\sum_{m=m_0+1}^{n} l(m)}{c}$$

By combining the two equations above we find $D(n) \leq \theta(n) + \frac{l(m_0)}{c}$, which shows the proposition in the case where $m_0 \leq n_0$.

If $m_0 = n_0 - 1$, then all packets $n_0, ..., n$ depart before packet n under GPS and thus the same reasoning shows that

$$\sum_{m=n_0}^{n} l(m) \leq c \left(\theta(n) - t_0 \right)$$

where t_0 is the beginning of the busy period, and that

$$D(n) = t_0 + \frac{\sum_{m=n_0}^{n} l(m)}{c}$$

Thus $D(n) \leq \theta(n)$ in that case.   □

2.1.3   Guaranteed Rate Schedulers

A large number of practical implementations of GPS, other than PGSP, have been proposed in the literature; let us mention: virtual clock scheduling [43], packet by packet generalized processor sharing [56] and self-clocked fair queuing [35](see also [26]). For a thorough discussion of practical implementations of GPS, see [73, 26]). These implementations differ in their implementation complexity and in the bounds that can be obtained. It is shown in [27] that all of these implementations fit in the following framework, called "Guaranteed Rate" (GR) scheduling, which we define in a few lines.

The definition relies on a max-plus representation of the server with constant bit rate c, with packet inputs. Such a system can be modeled as the concatenation of the greedy shaper with curve λ_r and a packetizer, but we use a different representation.

Proposition 2.1.2 (Max-plus representation of CBR server). *Consider a FIFO server with constant bit rate r, which serves a flow of packets numbered $i = 1, 2, ...$ Call A_i, T_i', l_i the arrival time, departure time, and length in bits for packet i. Assume $A_1 \geq 0$. Then T_i' is defined by the following recursion.*

$$\begin{cases} T'_0 = 0 \\ T'_i = \max\left\{A_i, T'_{i-1}\right\} + \frac{l_i}{r} \quad \text{for all } i \geq 1 \end{cases} \tag{2.1}$$

Proof: The FIFO property implies that packet i starts its service at $\max\left\{A_i, T'_{i-1}\right\}$.
$\Box$

Definition 2.1.1 ([27]). *A scheduling policy is of the* guaranteed rate *type, with rate r and delay v for a given flow, if it guarantees that the departure time D_i for packet i ($i \geq 1$) satisfies $D_i \leq T'_i + v$, where T'_i is defined by Equation (2.1).*

The variables T'_i are called "Guaranteed Rate Clocks". It follows immediately from Proposition 2.1.1 that PGPS is a GR scheduler for every flow i, with rate $r_i = \frac{\phi_i C}{\sum_j \phi_j}$ and delay $v = \frac{L}{c}$.

Consider now a GR scheduler with rate r and delay v. Assume the input $R(t)$ is L-packetized. Call $R'(t)$ the output. The constant bit rate server, shifted by time v, can be expressed as the concatenation of a greedy shaper, shifted by v, and a packetizer. We can thus rewrite Definition 2.1.1 as

$$R'(t) \geq P^L[(\beta_{r,v} \otimes R)(t)] \tag{2.2}$$

This property is sufficient to obtain bounds such as Corollary 2.1.1 and Equation (2.5). However, for the sake of elegance, we give a slightly stronger result, at the expense of some technicalities.

Theorem 2.1.1. *Consider a GR scheduler with rate r and delay v. Assume the input R(t) is L-packetized. The node is the concatenation of a service curve element, with service curve equal to the rate-latency function $\beta_{r,v}$, and an L-packetizer.*

The theorem means that we can find some $S \in \mathcal{F}$ satisfying $R'(t) = P^L(S(t))$ and $S \geq \beta_{r,v} \otimes R$. Note that this obviously implies Equation (2.2), but the converse is not obvious.

Proof: Consider the virtual system S whose output $S(t)$ is defined by

$$\text{if } D_{i-1} < t \leq D_i \\ \text{then } S(t) = \min\{R(t), \max[L(i-1), L(i) - r(D_i - t)]\} \tag{2.3}$$

See Figure 2.2 for an illustration. It follows immediately that $R'(t) = P^L(S(t))$.
Also consider the virtual system S^0 whose output is

$$S^0(t) = (\beta_{r,v} \otimes R)(t)$$

S^0 is the constant rate server, delayed by v. Our goal is now to show that $S \geq S^0$.

Call D_i^0 the departure time of the last bit of packet i in S_0 (see Figure 2.2 for an example with $i = 2$). Let $u = D_i^0 - D_i$. The definition of GR scheduling means that $u \geq 0$. Now since S_0 is a shifted constant rate server, we have:

$$\text{if } D_i^0 - \frac{l_i}{r} < s < D_i^0 \text{ then } S^0(s) = L(i) - r(D_i^0 - s)$$

Also $D_{i-1}^0 \leq D_i^0 - \frac{l_i}{r}$ thus $S^0(D_i^0 - \frac{l_i}{r}) = L(i-1)$ and

$$\text{if } s \leq D_i^0 - \frac{l_i}{r} \text{ then } S^0(s) \leq L(i-1)$$

It follows that

$$\text{if } D_{i-1} + u < s < D_i^0 \text{ then } S^0(s) \leq \max[L(i-1), L(i) - r(D_i^0 - s)] \quad (2.4)$$

Consider now some $t \in (D_{i-1}, D_i]$ and let $s = t + u$. If $S(t) = R(t)$, since $R \geq S^0$, we then obviously have $S(t) \geq S^0(t)$. Else, from Equation (2.1), $S(t) = \max[L(i-1), L(i) - r(D_i - t)]$. We have $D_i^0 - s = D_i - t$ and thus, combining with Equation (2.4), we derive that $S^0(s) \leq S(t)$. Now $s \geq t$, thus finally $S^0(t) \leq S(t)$. $\qquad \square$

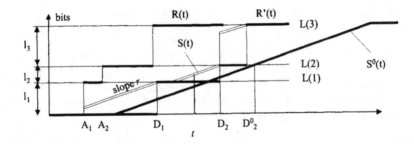

Figure 2.2: Arrival and departure functions for GR scheduling. The virtual system output is $S(t)$.

By applying Theorem 1.7.1, we obtain

Corollary 2.1.1. *A GR scheduler offers a minimum service curve* $\beta_{r,v+\frac{l_{\max}}{r}}$

Consider now a concatenation of GR schedulers with rates r_m and delay v_m, $m = 1, ..., M$. By Theorem 1.7.1, we know that for the computation of the end-to-end delay, we may ignore the last packetizer. Thus, we can consider the end-to-end service curve given by the rate-latency function with rate $r = \min_{m=1,...M} r_m$ and latency $\sum_{m=1}^{M} v_m + l_{\max} \sum_{m=1}^{M-1} \frac{1}{r_m}$. If the flow is constrained by one leaky bucket with parameter (ρ, σ), then, by applying Theorem 1.4.2, we find that for $\rho \leq r$, a bound on the end-to-end delay is [27]

$$B = \sum_{m=1}^{M} v_m + l_{\max} \sum_{m=1}^{M-1} \frac{1}{r_m} + \frac{\sigma}{\min_m r_m} \quad (2.5)$$

The above equation is a generalization of Equation (1.23).

2.2 The Integrated Services Model of the IETF

2.2.1 The Guaranteed Service

The Internet supports different reservation principles. Two services are defined: the "guaranteed" service, and the " controlled load" service. They differ in that the former provides real guarantees, while the latter provides only approximate guarantees. We outline the differences in the rest of this section. In both cases, the principle is based on "admission control", which operates as follows.

- In order to receive the guaranteed or controlled load service, a flow must first perform a reservation during a flow setup phase.

- A flow must confirm to an arrival curve of the form $\alpha(t) = \min(M + pt, rt + b)$, which is called the T-SPEC (see Section 1.2.2 on page 16). The T-SPEC is declared during the reservation phase.

- All routers along the path accept or reject the reservation. With the guaranteed service, routers accept the reservation only if they are able to provide a service curve guarantee and enough buffer for loss-free operation. The service curve is expressed during the reservation phase, as explained below.

  For the controlled load service, there is no strict definition of what accepting a reservation means. Most likely, it means that the router has an estimation module that says that, with good probability, the reservation can be accepted and little loss will occur; there is no service curve or delay guarantee.

In the rest of this chapter we focus on the guaranteed service. Provision of the controlled load service relies on models with loss, which are discussed in Chapter 9.

2.2.2 The Integrated Services Model for Internet Routers

The reservation phase assumes that all routers can export their characteristics using a very simple model. The model is based on the view that an integrated services router implements a practical approximation of GPS, such as PGPS, or more generally, a GR scheduler. We have shown in Section 2.1.3 that the service curve offered to a flow by a router implementing GR is a rate-latency function, with rate R and latency T connected by the relationship

$$T = \frac{C}{R} + D \qquad (2.6)$$

with C = the maximum packet size for the flow and $D = \frac{L}{c}$, where L is the maximum packet size in the router across all flows, and c the total rate of the scheduler. This is the model defined for an Internet node [67].

Fact 2.2.1. *The Integrated Services model for a router is that the service curve offered to a flow is always a rate-latency function, with parameters related by a relation of the form (2.6).*

The values of C and D depend on the specific implementation of a router, see Corollary 2.1.1 in the case of GR schedulers. Note that a router does not necessarily implement a scheduling method that approximates GPS. In fact, we discuss in Section 2.3 a family of schedulers that has many advantages above GPS. If a router implements a method that largely differs from GPS, then we must find a service curve that lower-bounds the best service curve guarantee offered by the router. In some cases, this may mean loosing important information about the router. For example, it is *not* possible to implement a network offering constant delay to flows by means of a system like SCED+, discussed in Section 2.4.4, with the Integrated Services router model.

2.2.3 Reservation Setup with RSVP

Consider a flow defined by TSPEC (M, p, r, b), that traverses nodes $1, \ldots, N$. Usually, nodes 1 and N are end-systems while nodes n for $1 < n < N$ are routers. The Integrated Services model assumes that node n on the path of the flow offers a rate latency service curve β_{R_n, T_n}, and further assumes that T_n has the form

$$T_n = \frac{C_n}{R} + D_n$$

where C_n and D_n are constants that depend on the characteristics of node n.

The reservation is actually put in place by means of a flow setup procedure such as the resource reservation protocol (RSVP). At the end of the procedure, node n on the path has allocated to the flow a value $R_n \geq r$. This is equivalent to allocating a service curve β_{R_n, T_n}. From Theorem 1.4.6 on page 34, the end-to-end service curve offered to the flow is the rate-latency function with rate R and latency T given by

$$\begin{cases} R = \min_{n=1\ldots N} R_n \\ T = \sum_{n=1}^{N} \left(\frac{C_n}{R_n} + D_n \right) \end{cases}$$

Let $C_{\text{tot}} = \sum_{n=1}^{N} C_n$ and $D_{\text{tot}} = \sum_{n=1}^{N} D_n$. We can re-write the last equation as

$$T = \frac{C_{\text{tot}}}{R} + D_{\text{tot}} - \sum_{n=1}^{N} S_n \tag{2.7}$$

with

$$S_n = C_n \left(\frac{1}{R} - \frac{1}{R_n} \right) \tag{2.8}$$

The term S_n is called the "local slack" term at node n.

From Proposition 1.4.1 we deduce immediately:

Proposition 2.2.1. *If $R \geq r$, the bound on the end-to-end delay, under the conditions described above is*

$$\frac{b - M}{R} \left(\frac{p - R}{p - r} \right)^{+} + \frac{M + C_{\text{tot}}}{R} + D_{\text{tot}} - \sum_{n=1}^{N} S_n \tag{2.9}$$

We can now describe the reservation setup with RSVP. Some details of flow setup with RSVP are illustrated on Figure 2.3. It shows that two RSVP flows are involved: an advertisement (PATH) flow and a reservation (RESV) flow. We describe first the point-to-point case.

- A PATH message is sent by the source; it contains the T-SPEC of the flow (source T-SPEC), which is not modified in transit, and another field, the AD-SPEC, which is accumulated along the path. At a destination, the ADSPEC field contains, among others, the values of C_{tot}, D_{tot} used in Equation 2.9. PATH messages do not cause any reservation to be made.

- RESV messages are sent by the destination and cause the actual reservations to be made. They follow the reverse path marked by PATH messages. The RESV message contains a value, R', (as part of the so-called R-SPEC), which is a lower bound on the rate parameters R_n that routers along the path will have to reserve. The value of R' is determined by the destination based on the end-to-end delay objective d_{obj}, following the procedure described below. It is normally not changed by the intermediate nodes.

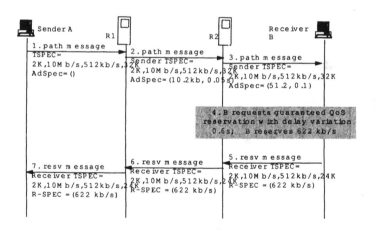

Figure 2.3: Setup of Reservations, showing the PATH and RESV flows

Define function f by

$$f(R') := \frac{b-M}{R'}\left(\frac{p-R'}{p-r}\right)^+ + \frac{M+C_{tot}}{R'} + D_{tot}$$

In other words, f is the function that defines the end-to-end delay bound, assuming all nodes along the path would reserve $R_n = R'$. The destination computes R' as the smallest value $\geq r$ for which $f(R') \leq d_{obj}$. Such a value exists only if $D_{tot} < d_{obj}$.

In the figure, the destination requires a delay variation objective of 600 ms, which imposes a minimum value of $R' = 622$ kb/s. The value of R' is sent to the next upstream node in the R-SPEC field of the PATH message. The intermediate nodes do not know the complete values C_{tot} and D_{tot}, nor do they know the total delay variation objective. Consider the simple case where all intermediate nodes are true PGPS schedulers. Node n simply checks whether it is able to reserve $R_n = R'$ to the flow; this involves verifying that the sum of reserved rates is less than the scheduler total rate, and that there is enough buffer available (see below). If so, it passes the RESV message upstream, up to the destination if all intermediate nodes accept the reservation. If the reservation is rejected, then the node discards it and normally informs the source. In this simple case, all nodes should set their rate to $R_n = R'$ thus $R = R'$, and Equation (2.9) guarantees that the end-to-end delay bound is guaranteed.

In practice, there is a small additional element (use of the slack term), due to the fact that the designers of RSVP also wanted to support other schedulers. It works as follows.

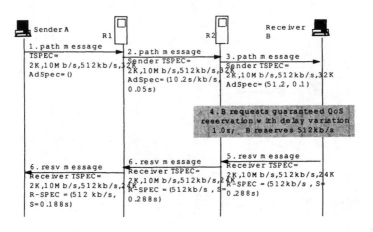

Figure 2.4: Use of the slack term

There is another term in the R-SPEC, called the *slack* term. Its use is illustrated on Figure 2.4. In the figure, we see that the end-to-end delay variation requirement, set by the destination, is 1000 ms. In that case, the destination reserves the minimum rate, namely, 512 kb/s. Even so, the delay variation objective D_{obj} is larger than the bound D_{max} given by Formula (2.9). The difference $D_{obj} - D_{max}$ is written in the slack term S and passed to the upstream node in the RESV message. The upstream node is not able to compute Formula (2.9) because it does not have the value of the end-to-end parameters. However, it can use the slack term to increase its internal delay objective, on top of what it had advertised. For example, a guaranteed rate scheduler may increase its value of v (Theorem 2.1.1) and thus reduce the internal resources required to perform the reservation. The figure shows that R1 reduces the slack term by 100 ms. This is equivalent to increasing the D_{tot} parameter by $100ms$, but without modifying the advertised D_{tot}.

The delays considered here are the total (fixed plus variable) delays. RSVP also contains a field used for advertising the fixed delay part, which can be used to compute the end-to-end fixed delay. The variable part of the delay (called delay jitter) is then obtained by subtraction.

2.2.4 A Flow Setup Algorithm

There are many different ways for nodes to decide which parameter they should allocate. We present here one possible algorithm. A destination computes the worst case delay variation, obtained if all nodes reserve the sustainable rate r. If the resulting delay variation is acceptable, then the destination sets $R = r$ and the resulting slack may be used by intermediate nodes to add a local delay on top of their advertised delay variation defined by C and D. Otherwise, the destination sets R to the minimum value R_{min} that supports the end-to-end delay variation objective and sets the slack to 0. As a result, all nodes along the path have to reserve R_{min}. As in the previous cases, nodes may allocate a rate larger than the value of R they pass upstream, as a means to reduce their buffer requirement.

Definition 2.2.1 (A Flow Setup Algorithm). • *At a destination system I, compute*

$$D_{max} = f_T(r) + \frac{C_{tot}}{r} + D_{tot}$$

If $D_{obj} > D_{max}$ then assign to the flow a rate $R_I = r$ and an additional delay variation $d_I \le D_{obj} - D_{max}$; set $S_I = D_{obj} - D_{max} - d_I$ and send reservation request R_I, S_I to station $I - 1$.

Else ($D_{obj} \le D_{max}$) find the minimum R_{min} such that $f_T(R_{min}) + \frac{C_{tot}}{R_{min}} \le D_{obj} - D_{tot}$, if it exists. Send reservation request $R_I = R_{min}, S_I = 0$ to station $I - 1$. If R_{min} does not exist, reject the reservation or increase the delay variation objective D_{obj}.

• *At an intermediate system i: receive from i+1 a reservation request R_{i+1}, S_{i+1}.*

If $S_i = 0$, then perform reservation for rate R_{i+1} and if successful, send reservation request $R_i = R_{i+1}, S_i = 0$ to station $i - 1$.

Else ($S_i > 0$), perform a reservation for rate R_{i+1} with some additional delay variation $d_i \le S_{i+1}$. if successful, send reservation request $R_i = R_{i+1}, S_i = S_{i+1} - d_i$ to station $i - 1$.

The algorithm ensures a constant reservation rate. It is easy to check that the end to end delay variation is bounded by D_{obj}.

2.2.5   Multicast Flows

Consider now a multicast situation. A source S sends to a number of destinations, along a multicast tree. PATH messages are forwarded along the tree, they are duplicated at splitting points; at the same points, RESV messages are merged. Consider such a point, call it node i, and assume it receives reservation requests for the same T-SPEC but with respective parameters R'_{in}, S'_{in} and R''_{in}, S''_{in}. The node performs reservations internally, using the semantics of algorithm 3. Then it has to merge the reservation requests it will send to node $i - 1$. Merging uses the following rules:

R-SPEC Merging Rules   The merged reservation R, S is given by

$$R = \max(R', R'')$$

$$S = \min(S', S'')$$

Let us consider now a tree where algorithm 3 is applied. We want to show that the end-to-end delay bounds at all destinations are respected.

The rate along the path from a destination to a source cannot decrease with this algorithm. Thus the minimum rate along the tree towards the destination is the rate set at the destination, which proves the result.

A few more features of RSVP are:

- states in nodes need to be refreshed; if they are not refreshed, the reservation is released ("soft states").

- routing is not coordinated with the reservation of the flow

We have so far looked only at the delay constraints. Buffer requirements can be computed using the values in Proposition 1.4.1.

2.2.6   Flow Setup with ATM

With ATM, there are the following differences:

- The path is determined at the flow setup time only. Different connections may follow different routes depending on their requirements, and once setup, a connection always uses the same path.

- With standard ATM signaling, connection setup is initiated at the source and is confirmed by the destination and all intermediate systems.

2.3   Schedulability

So far, we have considered one flow in isolation and assumed that a node is able to offer some scheduling, or service curve guarantee. In this section we address the global problem of resource allocation.

When a node performs a reservation, it is necessary to check whether local resources are sufficient. In general, the method for this consists in breaking the node down into a network of building blocks such as schedulers, shapers, and delay elements. There are mainly two resources to account for: bit rate (called "bandwidth") and buffer. The main difficulty is the allocation of bit rate. Following [31], we will see in this section that allocating a rate amounts to allocating a service curve. It is also equivalent to the concept of schedulability.

Consider the simple case of a PGPS scheduler, with outgoing rate C. If we want to allocate rate r_i to flow i, for every i, then we can allocate to flow i the GPS weight $\phi_i = \frac{r_i}{C}$. Assume that

$$\sum_i r_i \leq C \tag{2.10}$$

Then we know from Proposition 2.1.1 and Corollary 2.1.1 that every flow i is guaranteed the rate-latency service curve with rate r_i and latency $\frac{L}{C}$. In other words, the schedulability condition for PGPS is simply Equation (2.10). However, we will see now that a schedulability conditions are not always as simple. Note also that the end-to-end delay depends not only on the service curve allocated to the flow, but also on its arrival curve constraints.

Many schedulers have been proposed, and some of them do not fit in the GR framework. The most general framework in the context of guaranteed service is given by SCED (Service Curve Earliest Deadline first) [31],which we describe now. We give the theory for constant size packets and slotted time; some aspects of the general theory for variable length packets are known [10], some others remain to be done. We assume without loss of generality that every packet is of size 1 data unit.

2.3.1 EDF Schedulers

As the name indicates, SCED is based on the concept of Earliest Deadline First (EDF) scheduler. An EDF scheduler assigns a deadline D_i^n to the nth packet of flow i, according to some method. We assume that deadlines are wide-sense increasing within a flow. At every time slot, the scheduler picks at one of the packets with the smallest deadline among all packets present. There is a wide variety of methods for computing deadlines. The "delay based" schedulers [49] set $D_i^n = A^n + d_i$ where A^n is the arrival time for the nth packet for flow i, and d_i is the delay budget allocated to flow i. If d_i is independent of i, then we have a FIFO scheduler. We will see that those are special cases of SCED, which we view as a very general method for computing deadlines.

An EDF scheduler is work conserving, that is, it cannot be idle if there is at least one packet present in the system. A consequence of this is that packets from different flows are not necessarily served in the order of their deadlines. Consider for example a delay based scheduler, and assume that flow 1 has a lrage delay budget d_1, while flow 2 has a small delay budget d_2. It may be that a packet of flow 1 arriving at t_1 is served before a packet of flow 2 arriving at t_2, even though the deadline of packet 1, $t_1 + d_1$ is larger than the deadline of packet 2.

We will now derive a general schedulability criterion for EDF schedulers. Call $R_i(t)$, $t \in \mathbb{N}$, the arrival function for flow i. Call $Z_i(t)$ the number of packets of flow i that have deadlines $\leq t$. For example, for a delay based scheduler, $Z_i(t) = R_i(t - d_i)$. The following is a modified version of [10].

Proposition 2.3.1. *Consider an EDF scheduler with I flows and outgoing rate C. A necessary condition for all packets to be served within their deadlines is*

$$\text{for all } s \leq t : \quad \sum_{i=1}^{I} Z_i(t) - R_i(s) \leq C(t - s) \qquad (2.11)$$

A sufficient condition is

$$\text{for all } s \leq t : \quad \sum_{i=1}^{I} [Z_i(t) - R_i(s)]^+ \leq C(t - s) \qquad (2.12)$$

Proof: We first prove the necessary condition. Call R_i' the output for flow i. Since the scheduler is work conserving, we have $\sum_{i=1}^{I} R_i' = \lambda_C \otimes (\sum_{i=1}^{I} R_i)$. Now $R_i' \geq Z_i$ by hypothesis. Thus

$$\sum_{i=1}^{I} Z_i(t) \leq \inf_{s \in [0,t]} C(t - s) + \sum_{i=1}^{I} R_i(s)$$

which is equivalent to Equation (2.11)

Now we prove the sufficient condition, by contradiction. Assume that at some t a packet with deadline t is not yet served. In time slot t, the packet served has a deadline $\leq t$, otherwise our packet would have been chosen instead. Define s_0 such that the time interval $[s_0 + 1, t]$ is the maximum time interval ending at t that is within a busy period and for which all packets served have deadlines $\leq t$.

Now call S the set of flows that have a packet with deadline $\leq t$ present in the system at some point in the interval $[s_0 + 1, t]$. We show that if

$$\text{if } i \in S \text{ then } R_i'(s_0) = R_i(s_0) \qquad (2.13)$$

that is, flow i is not backlogged at the end of time slot s_0. Indeed, if $s_0 + 1$ is the beginning of the busy period, then the property is true for any flow. Otherwise, we proceed by contradiction. Assume that $i \in S$ and that i would have some backlog at the end of time slot s_0. At time s_0 some packet with deadline $> t$ was served; thus the deadline of all packets remaining in the queue at the end of time slot s_0 must have a deadline $> t$. Since deadlines are assumed wide-sense increasing within a flow, all deadlines of flow i packets that are in the queue at time s_0, or will arrive later, have deadline $> t$, which contradicts that $i \in S$.

Further, it follows from the last argument that if $i \in S$, then all packets served before or at t must have a deadline $\leq t$. Thus

$$\text{if } i \in \mathcal{S} \text{ then } R_i'(t) \leq Z_i(t)$$

Now since there is at least one packet with deadline $\leq t$ not served at t, the previous inequality is strict for at least one i in $\mathcal{S}$. Thus

$$\sum_{i \in \mathcal{S}} R_i'(t) < \sum_{i \in \mathcal{S}} Z_i(t) \tag{2.14}$$

Observe that all packets served in $[s_0 + 1, t]$ must be from flows in $\mathcal{S}$. Thus

$$\sum_{i=1}^{I} (R_i'(t) - R_i'(s_0)) = \sum_{i \in \mathcal{S}} (R_i'(t) - R_i'(s_0))$$

Combining with Equation (2.13) and Equation (2.14) gives

$$\sum_{i=1}^{I} (R_i'(t) - R_i'(s_0)) < \sum_{i \in \mathcal{S}} (Z_i(t) - R_i(s_0))$$

Now $[s_0 + 1, t]$ is entirely in a busy period thus $\sum_{i=1}^{I} (R_i'(t) - R_i'(s_0)) = C(t - s_0)$; thus

$$C(t - s_0) < \sum_{i \in \mathcal{S}} (Z_i(t) - R_i(s_0)) = \sum_{i \in \mathcal{S}} (Z_i(t) - R_i(s_0))^+ \leq \sum_{i=1}^{I} (Z_i(t) - R_i(s_0))^+$$

which contradicts Equation (2.12). $\qquad\qquad\square$

A consequence of the proposition that if a set of flows is schedulable for some deadline allocation algorithm, then it is also schedulable for any other deadline allocation method that produces later or equal deadlines. Other consequences, of immediate practical importance, are drawn in the next section.

2.3.2 SCED Schedulers [65]

Given, for all i, a function β_i, SCED defines a deadline allocation algorithm that guarantees, under some conditions, that flow i does have β_i as a minimum service curve[1]. Roughly speaking, SCED sets $Z_i(t)$, the number of packets with deadline up to t, to $(R_i \otimes \beta_i)(t)$.

Definition 2.3.1 (SCED). *Call A_i^n the arrival time for packet n of flow i. Define functions R_i^n by:*

$$R_i^n(t) = \inf_{s \in [0, A_i^n]} [R_i(s) + \beta_i(t - s)]$$

With SCED, the deadline for packet n of flow i is defined by

$$D_i^n = (R_i^n)^{-1}(n) = \min\{t \in \mathbb{N} : R_i^n(t) \geq n\}$$

Function β_i is called the "target service curve" for flow i.

---

[1]We use the original work in [65], which is called there "SCED-B". For simplicity, we call it SCED.

Function R_i^n is similar to the min-plus convolution $R_i \otimes \beta_i$, but the minimum is computed over all times up to A_i^n. This allows to compute a packet deadline as soon as the packet arrives; thus SCED can be implemented in real time. The deadline is obtained by applying the pseudo-inverse of R_i^n, as illustrated on Figure 2.5. If $\beta_i = \delta_{d_i}$, then it is easy to see that $D_i^n = A_i^n + d_i$, namely, SCED is the delay based scheduler in that case. The following proposition is the main property of SCED. It

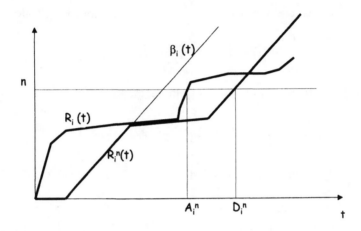

Figure 2.5: Definition of SCED. Packet n of flow i arrives at time A_i^n. Its deadline is D_i^n.

shows that SCED implements a deadline allocation method based on service curves.

Proposition 2.3.2. *For the SCED scheduler, the number of packets with deadline $\leq t$ is given by $Z_i(t) = \lfloor (R_i \otimes \beta_i)(t) \rfloor$*

Proof: We drop index i in this demonstration. First, we show that $Z(t) \geq \lfloor (R \otimes \beta)(t) \rfloor$. Let $n = \lfloor (R \otimes \beta)(t) \rfloor$. Since $R \otimes \beta \leq R$ and R takes integer values, we must have $R(t) \geq n$ and thus $A^n \leq t$. Now $R^n(t) \geq (R \otimes \beta)(t)$ thus

$$R^n(t) \geq (R \otimes \beta)(t) \geq n$$

By definition of SCED, D^n this implies that $D^n \leq t$ which is equivalent to $Z(t) \geq n$.

Conversely, for some fixed but arbitrary t, let now $n = Z(t)$. Packet n has a deadline $\leq t$, which implies that $A^n \leq t$ and for all $s \in [0, A^n]$:

$$R(s) + \beta(t - s) \geq n \qquad (2.15)$$

Now for $s \in [A^n, t]$ we have $R(s) \geq n$ thus $R(s) + \beta(t - s) \geq n$. Thus Equation (2.15) is true for all $s \in [0, t]$, which means that $(R \otimes \beta)(t) \geq n$.   □

Theorem 2.3.1 (Schedulability of SCED, ATM). *Consider a SCED scheduler with I flows, total outgoing rate C, and target service curve β_i for flow i.*

1. *If*

$$\sum_{i=1}^{I} \beta_i(t) \leq Ct \text{ for all } t \geq 0 \qquad (2.16)$$

   then every packet is served before or at its deadline and every flow i receives $\lfloor \beta_i \rfloor$ as a service curve.

2. *Assume that in addition we know that every flow i is constrained by an arrival curve α_i. If*

$$\sum_{i=1}^{I} (\alpha_i \otimes \beta_i)(t) \leq Ct \text{ for all } t \geq 0 \qquad (2.17)$$

   then the same conclusion holds

Proof:

1. Proposition 2.3.2 implies that $Z_i(t) \leq R_i(s) + \beta_i(t - s)$ for $0 \leq s \leq t$. Thus $Z_i(t) - R_i(s) \leq \beta_i(t - s)$. Now $0 \leq \beta_i(t - s)$ thus

$$[Z_i(t) - R_i(s)]^+ = \max[Z_i(t) - R_i(s), 0] \leq \beta_i(t - s)$$

   By hypothesis, $\sum_{i=1}^{I} \beta_i(t - s) \leq C(t - s)$ thus by application of Proposition 2.3.1, we know that every packet is served before or at its deadline. Thus $R_i' \geq Z_i$ and from Proposition 2.3.2:

$$R_i' \geq Z_i = \lfloor \beta_i \otimes R_i \rfloor$$

   Now R_i takes only integer values thus $\lfloor \beta_i \otimes R_i \rfloor = \lfloor \beta_i \rfloor \otimes R_i$.

2. By hypothesis, $R_i = \alpha_i \otimes R_i$ thus $Z_i = \lfloor \alpha_i \otimes \beta_i \otimes R_i \rfloor$ and we can apply the same argument, with $\alpha_i \otimes \beta_i$ instead of β_i. □

Schedulability of delay based schedulers A delay based scheduler assigns a delay objective d_i to all packets of flow i. A direct application of Theorem 2.3.1 gives the following schedulability condition.

Theorem 2.3.2 ([49]). *Consider a delay based scheduler that serves I flows, with delay d_i assigned to flow i. All packets have the same size and time is slotted. Assume flow i is α_i-smooth, where α_i is sub-additive. Call C the total outgoing bit rate. Any mix of flows satisfying these assumptions is schedulable if*

$$\sum_i \alpha_i(t - d_i) \leq Ct$$

If $\alpha_i(t) \in \mathbb{N}$ then the condition is necessary.

Proof: A delay based scheduler is a special case of SCED, with target service curve $\beta_i = \delta_{d_i}$. This shows that the condition in the theorem is sufficient. Conversely, consider the greedy flows given by $R_i(t) = \alpha_i(t)$. This is possible because α_i is assumed to be sub-additive. Flow R_i must be schedulable, thus the output R'_i satisfies $R'_i(t) \geq \alpha_i(i - d_i)$. Now $\sum_i R'_i(t) \leq ct$, which proves that the condition must hold.   □

It is shown in [49] that a delay based scheduler has the largest schedulability region among all schedulers, given arrival curves and delay budgets for every flow. Note however that in a network setting, we are interested in the end-to-end delay bound, and we know (Section 1.4.3) that it is generally less than the sum of per hop bounds.

The schedulability of delay based schedulers requires that an arrival curve is known and enforced at every node in the network. Because arrival curves are modified by network nodes, this motivates the principle of Rate Controlled Service Disciplines (RCSDs) [38, 74, 26], which implement in every node a packet shaper followed by a delay based scheduler. The packet shaper guarantees that an arrival curve is known for every flow. Note that such a combination is not work conserving.

Because of the "pay bursts only once" phenomenon, RCSD might provide end-to-end delay bounds that are worse than guaranteed rate schedulers. However, it is possible to avoid this by aggressively reshaping flows in every node, which, from Theorem 2.3.2, allows us to set smaller deadlines. If the arrival curves constraints on all flows are defined by a single leaky bucket, then it is shown in [59, 58] that one should reshape a flow to its sustained rate at every node in order to achieve the same end-to-end delay bounds as GR schedulers would.

Schedulability of GR Schedulers Consider the family of GR schedulers, applied to the ATM case. We cannot give a general schedulability condition, since the fact that a scheduler is of the GR type does not tell us exactly how the scheduler operates. However, we show that for any rate r and delay v we can implement a GR scheduler with SCED.

Theorem 2.3.3 (GR scheduler as SCED, ATM case). *Consider the SCED scheduler with I flows and outgoing rate C. Let the target service curve for flow i be equal to the rate-latency service curve with rate r_i and latency v_i. If*

$$\sum_{i=1}^{I} r_i \leq C$$

then the scheduler is a GR scheduler for each flow i, with rate r_i and delay v_i.

Proof: From Proposition 2.3.2:

$$Z_i(t) = \lfloor (R_i \otimes \lambda_{r_i})(t - v_i) \rfloor$$

thus Z_i is the output of the constant rate server, with rate r_i, delayed by v_i. Now from Theorem 2.3.1 the condition in the theorem guarantees that $R'_i \geq Z_i$, thus the

delay for any packet of flow i is bounded by the delay of the constant rate server
with rate r_i, plus v_i.   □

Note the fundamental difference between rate based and delay based schedulers.
For the former, schedulability is a condition on the sum of the rates; it is independent
of the input traffic. In contrast, for delay based schedulers, schedulability imposes a
condition on the arrival curves. Note however that in order to obtain a delay bound,
we need some arrival curves, even with delay based schedulers.

Better than Delay Based scheduler A scheduler need not be either rate based or
delay based. Rate based schedulers suffer from coupling between delay objective
and rate allocation: if we want a low delay, we may be forced to allocate a large
rate, which because of Theorem 2.3.3 will reduce the number of flows than can be
scheduled. Delay based schedulers avoid this drawback, but they require that flows
be reshaped at every hop. Now, with clever use of SCED, it is possible to obtain
the benefits of delay based schedulers without paying the price of implementing
shapers.

Assume that for every flow i we know an arrival curve α_i and we wish to obtain
an end-to-end delay bound d_i. Then the smallest network service curve that should
be allocated to the flow is $\alpha_i \otimes \delta_{d_i}$ (the proof is easy and left to the reader). Thus a
good thing to do is to build a scheduler by allocating to flow i the target service
curve $\alpha_i \otimes \delta_{d_i}$. The schedulability condition is the same as with a delay based
scheduler, however, there is a significant difference: the service curve is guaranteed
even if some flows are not conforming to their arrival curves. More precisely, if
some flows do not conform to the arrival curve constraint, then the service curve is
still guaranteed, but the delay bound is not.

This observation can be exploited to allocate service curves in a more flexible
way than what is done in Section 2.2 [17]. Assume flow i uses the sequence of
nodes $m = 1, ..., M$. Every node receives a part d_i^m of the delay budget d_i, with
$\sum_{m=1}^{M} d_i^m \leq d_i$. Then it is sufficient that every node implements SCED with a
target service curve $\beta_i^m = \delta_{d_i^m} \otimes \alpha_i$ for flow i. The schedulability condition at node
m is

$$\sum_{j \in E_m} \alpha_j(t - d_j^m) \leq C_m t$$

where E_m is the set of flows scheduled at node m and C_m is the outgoing rate of
node m. If it is satisfied, then flow i receives $\alpha_i \otimes \delta_{d_i}$ as end-to-end service curve
and therefore has a delay bounded by d_i. The schedulability condition is the same
as if we had implemented at node m the combination of a delay based scheduler
with delay budget d_i^m, and a reshaper with shaping curve α_i; but we do not have to
implement a reshaper. In particular, the delay bound for flow i at node m is larger
than d_i^m; we find again the fact that the end-to-end delay bound is less than the sum
of individual bounds.

In [65], it is explained how to allocate a service curves β_i^m to every network
element m on the path of the flow, such that $\beta_i^1 \otimes \beta_i^2 \otimes ... = \alpha_i \otimes \delta_i$, in order to

obtain a large schedulability set. This generalizes and improves the schedulability region of RCSD.

Extension to variable length packets   We can extend the previous results to variable length packets; we follow the ideas in [10]. The first step is to consider a fictitious preemptive EDF scheduler (system I), that allocates a deadline to every bit. We define $Z_i^I(t)$ as before, as the number of bits whose deadline is $\leq t$. A preemptive EDF scheduler serves the bits present in the system in order of their deadlines. It is preemptive (and fictitious) in that packets are not delivered entirely, but, in contrast, are likely to be interleaved. The results in the previous sections apply with no change to this system.

The second step is to modify system I by allocating to every bit a deadline equal to the deadline of the last bit in the packet. Call it system II. We have $Z_i^{II}(t) = P^{L_i}(Z_i^I(t))$ where P^{L_i} is the cumulative packet length (Section 1.7) for flow i. From the remarks following Proposition 2.3.1, it follows that if system I is schedulable, then so is system II. System II is made of a preemptive EDF scheduler followed by a packetizer.

The third step consists in defining "packet-EDF" scheduler (system III); this is derived from system II in the same way as PGSP is from GPS. More precisely, the packet EDF scheduler picks the next packet to serve among packets present in the system with minimum deadline. Then, when a packet is being served, it is not interrupted. We also say that system III is the non-preemptive EDF scheduler. Then the departure time of any packet in system III is bounded by its departure time in system II plus $\frac{l_{\max}}{C}$ where $l_{\max}$ is the maximum packet size across all flows and C is the total outgoing rate. The proof is similar to Proposition 2.1.1 and is left to the reader (it can also be found in [10]).

We can apply the three steps above to a SCED scheduler with variable size packets, called "Packet-SCED".

Definition 2.3.2 (Packet SCED). *A PSCED schedulers is a non-premptive EDF schedulers, where deadlines are allocated as follows. Call A_i^n the arrival time for packet n of flow i. Define functions R_i^n by:*

$$R_i^n(t) = \inf_{s \in [0, A_i^n]} [R_i(s) + \beta_i(t - s)]$$

With PSCED, the deadline for packet n of flow i is defined by

$$D_i^n = (R_i^n)^{-1}(L_i(n)) = \min\{t \in \mathbb{N} : R_i^n(t) \geq (L_i(n))\}$$

where L_i is the cumulative packet length for flow i. Function β_i is called the "target service curve" for flow i.

The following proposition follows from the discussion above.

Proposition 2.3.3. *[10] Consider a PSCED scheduler with I flows, total outgoing rate C, and target service curve β_i for flow i. Call $l_{\max}^i$ the maximum packet size for flow i and let $l_{\max} = \max_i l_{\max}^i$.*

1. If

$$\sum_{i=1}^{I} \beta_i(t) \leq Ct \text{ for all } t \geq 0 \tag{2.18}$$

then every packet is served before or at its deadline plus $\frac{l_{\max}}{C}$. A bound on packet delay is $h(\alpha_i, \beta_i) + \frac{l_{\max}}{C}$. Moreover, every flow i receives $[\beta_i(t - l^i_{\max}) - \frac{l_{\max}}{C}]^+$ as a service curve.

2. Assume that, in addition, we know that every flow i is constrained by an arrival curve α_i. If

$$\sum_{i=1}^{I} (\alpha_i \otimes \beta_i)(t) \leq Ct \text{ for all } t \geq 0 \tag{2.19}$$

then the same conclusion holds.

Note that the first part of the conclusion means that the maximum packet delay can be computed by assuming that flow i would receive β_i (not $\beta_i(t - l^i_{\max})$) as a service curve, and adding $\frac{\max}{C}$.

Proof: It follows from the three steps above that the PSCED scheduler can be broken down into a preemptive EDF scheduler, followed by a packetizer, followed by a delay element. The rest follows from the properties of packetizers and Theorem 2.3.1.

2.3.3 Buffer Requirements

As we mentioned at the beginning of this section, buffer requirements have to be computed in order to accept a reservation. The condition is simply $\sum_i X_i \leq X$ where X_i is the buffer required by flow i at this network element, and X is the total buffer allocated to the class of service. The computation of X_i is based on Theorem 1.4.1; it requires computing an arrival curve of every flow as it reaches the node. This is done using Theorem 1.4.2 and the flow setup algorithm, such as in Definition 2.2.1.

It is often advantageous to reshape flows at every node. Indeed, in the absence of reshaping, burstiness is increased linearly in the number of hops. But we know that reshaping to an initial constraint does not modify the end-to-end delay bound and does not increase the buffer requirement at the node where it is implemented. If reshaping is implemented per flow, then the burstiness remains the same at every node.

2.4 Application to Differentiated Services

2.4.1 Differentiated Services

In addition to the reservation based services we have studied in Section 2.2, the Internet also proposes differentiated services [6]. The major goal of differentiated services is to provide some form of better service while avoiding per flow state information as is required by integrated services. The idea to achieve this is based on the following principles.

- Traffic classes are defined; inside a network, all traffic belonging to the same class is treated as one single aggregate flow.

- At the network edge, individual flows (called "micro-flows") are assumed to conform to some arrival curve, as with integrated services.

If the aggregate flows receive appropriate service curves in the network, and if the total traffic on every aggregate flow is not too large, then we should expect some bounds on delay and loss. The condition on microflows is key to ensuring that the total aggregate traffic remains within some arrival curve constraints. A major difficulty however, as we will see, is to derive bounds for individual flows from characteristics of an aggregate.

Differentiated services is a framework that includes a number of different services. The main two services defined today are expedited forwarding (EF)[37] and assured forwarding (AF)[34]. The goal of EF is to provide to an aggregate some hard delay guarantees, and no loss. The goal of AF is to separate traffic between a small number of classes (4); inside each class, three levels of drop priorities are defined. One of the AF classes could be used to provide a low delay service with no loss, similar to EF.

In this chapter, we do not study in detail the implementations of EF or AF. We focus on the fundamental issue of how aggregate scheduling impacts delay and throughput guarantees. In the rest of this section, we use the network model shown on Figure 2.6. Our problem is to find bounds for end-to-end delay jitter on one hand, for backlog at all nodes on the other hand, under the assumptions mentioned above. Delay jitter is is the difference between maximum and minimum delay; its value decides the size if playout buffers (Section 1.1.3).

2.4.2 A Bounding Method for Aggregate Scheduling

Consider a node m. If all traffic entering the node is access traffic only (no transit traffic) then an arrival curve for the aggregate traffic entering the node is $\sum_{i \in F_m} \alpha_i$, where F_m is the set of flows that enter the network at this node. The aggregate flow is guaranteed a service curve S_m, thus, from Section 1.4.1, the total required buffer is bounded by $v(\sum_{i \in F_m} \alpha_i, S_m)$, and the delay by $v(\sum_{i \in F_m} \alpha_i, S_m)$.

In order to use Section 1.4.1 we need now to find an arrival curve for the traffic exiting node m. This in general requires more assumptions on the aggregate scheduler. We examine in Chapter 6 the properties of FIFO schedulers and will find there

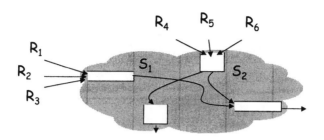

Figure 2.6: Network Model for Differentiated Services. Microflows $R_1, ... R_6$ are individually shaped and each conform to some arrival curve α_i. At node 1, microflows R_1 to R_3 are handled as one aggregate flow, which receives a service curve S_1. Upon leaving node 1, the different microflows take different paths and become part of other aggregates at other nodes.

some strong, but complex results. We have a simple result if the service curves are *strict*, as defined in Section 1.3.1; this applies to many practical cases, in particular to all variable capacity nodes and priority schedulers.

Theorem 2.4.1. *Consider a node serving two flows in an aggregate manner. Assume the aggregate is guaranteed a* strict *service curve β. Assume also that the second flow is α_2-smooth. Then the first flow is guaranteed a minimum service curve β_1^* given by*

$$\beta_1^*(t) = [\beta(t) - \alpha_2(t)]^+$$

Proof: Call R_i and R_i' the input and output, for $i = 1, 2$. Fix some arbitrary t and call s the beginning of the busy period (for the aggregate). Thus

$$R_1'(t) + R_2'(t) \geq R_1(s) + R_2(s) + \beta(t - s)$$

Now

$$R_2'(t) \leq R_2(t) \leq R_2(s) + \alpha_2(t - s)$$

thus

$$R_1'(t) \geq R_1(s) + \beta(t - s) - \alpha_2(t - s) \tag{2.20}$$

Since s is the beginning of the busy period, we have $R_1'(s) + R_2'(s) = R_1(s) + R_2(s)$ and therefore $R_1'(s) = R_1(s)$. Thus

$$R_1'(t) \geq R_1'(s) = R_1(s)$$

combining this with Equation (2.20), we find

$$R_1'(t) \geq R_1(s) + [\beta(t - s) - \alpha_2(t - s)]^+$$

which proves the service curve property.   □

If the arrival curves are affine, then the following corollary of Theorem 2.4.1 expresses the burstiness increase due to multiplexing.

Corollary 2.4.1. *Consider a node serving two flows in an aggregate manner. Assume the aggregate is guaranteed a* strict *service curve* $\beta_{R,T}$. *Assume also that flow i is constrained by one leaky bucket with parameters* (r_i, b_i). *The output of the first flow is constrained by a leaky bucket with parameters* (r_1, b_1^*) *with*

$$b_1^* = b_1 + r_1 T + r_1 \frac{b_2 + r_2 T}{R - r_2}$$

Note that the burstiness increase contains a term $r_1 T$ that is found even if there is no multiplexing; the second term $r_1 \frac{b_2 + r_2 T}{R - r_2}$ comes from multiplexing with flow 2. Note also that if we further assume that the node is FIFO, then we have a better bound (Chapter 6).

Proof: From Theorem 2.4.1, the first flow is guaranteed a service curve $\beta_{R',T'}$ with $R' = R - r_2$ and $T' = \frac{b_2 + T r_2}{R - r_2}$. The result follows from a direct application of Theorem 1.4.3.   □

We could think of using Corollary 2.4.1 to analyze the general network in Figure 2.6. However, this would work only in a *feed-forward* network, namely, a network where we can number nodes such that the sequence of node numbers followed by any flow is always increasing. Equivalently, this means that there is no cycle for the relation between nodes defined by $m \rightarrow m'$ iff among the flows entering m', at least one exits m. In a feed-forward, we can recursively apply Corollary 2.4.1 and find arrival curve constraints at all nodes, thus backlog and delay bounds.

However, feed-forward topologies are very restrictive, and most networks are not feedforward. We show now an analysis method that can be applied to non-feedforward networks.

Assumptions and notation   We consider in the rest of this subsection the case where all fresh arrival curves α_i have the form

$$\alpha_i = \gamma_{r_i, b_i}$$

In other words, the constraints are expressed by a single leaky bucket. To simplify the notation, we consider that the nodes are are constant rate, work conserving servers, with rate C_m for node m. We assume that there is no loop on the path followed by any flow. We use the notation $m \in i$ or $i \ni m$ to express that node m is on the path of flow i.

We call "utilization factor" at link l the ratio

$$\nu_l = \frac{\sum_{i \ni m} r_i}{C_l}$$

We also assume that the network is "sub-critical", that is, for all node m:

$$\nu_l < 1 \qquad (2.21)$$

We will illustrate the method on a specific example, shown on Figure 2.7.

In a non-feedforward network, we cannot directly apply Corollary 2.4.1. However, we can use the following trick, called the "time stopping method", which was introduced in [19]. The method has two steps. First, we assume that there is a finite burstiness bound for all flows; using Corollary 2.4.1 we obtain some equations for computing these bounds. Second, we use the same equations to show that, under some conditions, finite bounds exist.

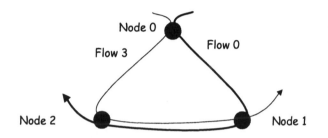

Figure 2.7: A simple example with aggregate scheduling, used to illustrate the bounding method. There are three nodes numbered $0, 1, 2$ and six flows, numbered $0, ..., 5$. For $i = 0, 1, 2$, the path of flow i is $i, (i + 1) \mod 3, (i + 2) \mod 3$ and the path of flow $i + 3$ is $i, (i + 2) \mod 3, (i + 1) \mod 3$. The fresh arrival curve is the same for all flows, and is given by $\alpha_i = \gamma_{\rho,\sigma}$. All nodes are constant rate, work conserving servers, with rate C. The utilization factor at all nodes is $6\frac{\rho}{C}$.

First step: inequations for the bounds   For any flow i and any node $m \in i$, define b_i^m as the maximum backlog that this flow would generate in a constant rate server with rate r_i. By convention, the fresh inputs are considered as the outputs of a virtual node numbered -1. In this first step, we assume that b_i^m is finite for all i and $m \in i$.

From Lemma 1.2.2 on Page 12, b_i^m is the smallest value such that the output of node m is constrained by the leaky bucket with parameters (r_i, b_i^m). By applying Corollary 2.4.1 we find that for all i and $m \in i$:

$$\begin{cases} b_i^0 \leq b_i \\ b_i^m = b_i^{\text{pred}_i(m)} + r_i \dfrac{\sum_{j \ni m, j \neq i} b_j^{\text{pred}_j(m)}}{C - \sum_{j \ni m, j \neq i} r_j} \end{cases} \qquad (2.22)$$

where $\text{pred}_i(m)$ is the predecessor of node m. If m is the first node on the path of flow i, we set by convention $\text{pred}_i(m) = -1$ and $b_i^{-1} = b_i$.

Now put all the b_i^m, for all (i, m) such that $m \in i$, into a vector $\vec{x}$ with one column and n rows, for some appropriate n. We can re-write Equation (2.22) as

$$\vec{x} \le A\vec{x} + \vec{a} \tag{2.23}$$

where A is an $n \times n$, non-negative matrix and $\vec{a}$ is a non-negative vector depending only on the known quantities b_i. The method now consists in assuming that the spectral radius of matrix A is less than 1. In that case the power series $I + A + A^2 + A^3 + \dots$ converges and is equal to $(I - A)^{-1}$, where I is the $n \times n$ identity matrix. Since A is non-negative, $(I - A)^{-1}$ is also non-negative; we can thus multiply Equation (2.22) to the left by $(I - A)^{-1}$ and obtain:

$$\vec{x} \le (I - A)^{-1}\vec{a} \tag{2.24}$$

which is the required result, since $\vec{x}$ describes the burstiness of all flows at all nodes. From there we can obtain bounds on delays and backlogs.

Let us apply this step to our network example. By symmetry, we have only two unknowns x and y, defined as the burstiness after one and two hops:

$$\begin{cases} x = b_0^0 = b_1^1 = b_2^2 = b_3^0 = b_4^2 = b_5^1 \\ y = b_0^1 = b_1^2 = b_2^0 = b_3^2 = b_4^1 = b_5^0 \end{cases}$$

Equation (2.22) becomes

$$\begin{cases} x \le \sigma + \frac{\rho}{C-5\rho}(\sigma + 2x + 2y) \\ y \le x + \frac{\rho}{C-5\rho}(2\sigma + x + 2y) \end{cases}$$

Define $\eta = \frac{\rho}{C-5\rho}$; from Equation (2.21) we conclude that $0 \le \eta < 1$. We can now write Equation (2.23) with

$$\vec{x} = \begin{pmatrix} x \\ y \end{pmatrix}, \ A = \begin{pmatrix} 2\eta & 2\eta \\ 1+\eta & 2\eta \end{pmatrix}, \ \vec{a} = \begin{pmatrix} \sigma(1+\eta) \\ 2\sigma\eta \end{pmatrix}$$

Some remnant from linear algebra, or a symbolic computation software, tells us that

$$(I - A)^{-1} = \begin{pmatrix} \frac{1-2\eta}{1-6\eta+2\eta^2} & \frac{2\eta}{1-6\eta+2\eta^2} \\ \frac{1+\eta}{1-6\eta+2\eta^2} & \frac{1-2\eta}{1-6\eta+2\eta^2} \end{pmatrix}$$

If $\eta < \frac{1}{2}(3 - \sqrt{7}) \approx 0.177$ then $(I - A)^{-1}$ is positive. This is the condition for the spectral radius of A to be less than 1. The corresponding condition on the utilization factor $\nu = \frac{6\rho}{C}$ is

$$\nu < 2\frac{8 - \sqrt{7}}{19} \approx 0.564 \tag{2.25}$$

Thus, for this specific example, if Equation (2.25) holds, and if the burstiness terms x and y are finite, then they are bounded as given in Equation (2.24), with $(I - A)^{-1}$ and $\vec{a}$ given above.

Second Step: time stopping We now prove that there is a finite bound if the spectral radius of A is less than 1. For any time $\tau > 0$, consider the virtual system made of the original network, where all sources are stopped at time τ. For this network the total number of bits in finite, thus we can apply the conclusion of step 1, and the burstiness terms are bounded by Equation (2.24). Since the right-handside Equation (2.24) is independent of τ, letting τ tend to $+\infty$ shows the following.

Proposition 2.4.1. *With the notation in this section, if the spectral radius of A is less than 1, then the burstiness terms b_i^m are bounded by the corresponding terms in Equation (2.24).*

Back to the example of Figure 2.7, we find that if the utilization factor ν is less than 0.564, then the burstiness terms x and y are bounded by

$$\begin{cases} x \leq 2\sigma \frac{18-33\nu+16\nu^2}{36-96\nu+57\nu^2} \\ y \leq 2\sigma \frac{18-18\nu+\nu^2}{36-96\nu+57\nu^2} \end{cases}$$

The aggregate traffic at any of the three nodes is $\gamma_{6\rho,b}$-smooth with $b = 2(\sigma+x+y)$. Thus a bound on delay is (see also Figure 2.8):

$$d = \frac{b}{C} = 2\frac{\sigma}{C}\frac{108 - 198\nu + 91\nu^2}{36 - 96\nu + 57\nu^2}$$

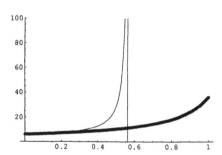

Figure 2.8: The bound d on delay at any node obtained by the method presented here for the network of Figure 2.7 (thin line). The graph shows d normalized by $\frac{\sigma}{C}$ (namely, $\frac{dC}{\sigma}$), plotted as a function of the utilization factor. The thick line is a delay bound obtained if every flow is re-shaped at every output.

What happens when the bound is infinite ? Call ν_0 the upper bound on utilization factors for which the method in Section 2.4.2 finds a finite bound. In the example, we found $\nu_0 \approx 0.564$, which is much less than 1. Does it mean that no finite bound exists when $\nu_0 < 1$? The answer to this question is not clear.

First, the ν_0 found with the method can be improved if we express more arrival constraints. Consider our particular example: we have not exploited the fact that the fraction of input traffic to node i that originates from another node has to be λ_C-smooth. If we do so, we will obtain better bounds. Second, if we know that nodes have additional properties, such as FIFO, then we may be able to find better bounds.

In general, the issue of stability, or existence of finite bounds, for a given network with aggregate multiplexing is still unresolved. The question of delay bounds for a network with aggregate scheduling was first raised in [7]. We will see in Chapter 6 that if the network is a ring of constant bit rate servers, then $\nu_0 = 1$, in other words, we can find a bound for any $\nu < 1$ [69]. However, the proof does not extend to general service curve guarantees, even strict service curves. In [3], the author exhibits an unstable network similar to ours, with $\nu = 1$ (a "critical" network), and claims that this also holds for some sub-critical networks, but the proof is not conclusive. In addition, a startling fact referred to as a "non-monotone property" of FIFO networks is described in [3], where it is shown that a network that is *stable* with a set of sessions with given rates may become *unstable* if the rates of some of these sessions are *reduced* for a period of time. On the other side of the spectrum, we will also see in Chapter 6 strong and explicit results [46, 13] with FIFO multiplexing.

The price for aggregate scheduling Consider again the example on Figure 2.7, but assume now that every flow is reshaped at every output. This is not possible with differentiated services, since there is no per-flow information at nodes other than access nodes. However, we use this scenario as a benchmark that illustrates the price we pay for aggregate scheduling.

With this assumption, every flow has the same arrival curve at every node. Thus we can compute a service curve β_1 for flow 1 (and thus for any flow) at every node, using Theorem 2.4.1; we find that β_1 is the rate-latency function with rate $(C - 5\rho)$ and latency $\frac{5\sigma}{C-5\rho}$. Thus a delay bound for flow at any node, including the re-shaper, is $h(\alpha_1, \alpha_1 \otimes \beta_1) = h(\alpha_1, \beta_1) = \frac{6C}{C-5\rho}$ for $\rho \leq \frac{C}{6}$. Figure 2.8 shows this delay bound, compared to the delay bound we found if no reshaper is used. As we already know, we see that with per-flow information, we are able to guarantee a delay bound for any utilization factor ≤ 1. However, note also that for relatively small utilization factors, the bounds are very close.

2.4.3 An Explicit Delay Bound for Differentiated Services Networks

We consider a low delay traffic class, as mentioned in Section 2.4.1, and find a closed form expression for the worst case delay, which is valid in any topology, in a lossless network. This bound is based on the method in the previous section.

Assumption and Notation We assume the following. Unlike with reservation services, we cannot assume here that we have detailed information about the path followed by every flow. In contrast, we have only aggregate parameters.

- All fresh arrival curves α_i have the form of single leaky bucket constraints:

$$\alpha_i = \gamma_{\rho_i, \sigma_i}$$

- The service curve provided to the aggregate of all low delay traffic at node m is a rate-latency function with rate r_m and latency e_m. The service curve guarantee need not be a strict service curve. Within an aggregate, packets are served in a FIFO manner. Let E be a bound on all e_m.

- The utilization factor for node m is defined as

$$\nu_m = \frac{\sum_{i \ni m} \rho_i}{r_m}$$

We assume that $\nu_m \leq \nu$ for all m. ν is the network-wide bound on utilization that is admissible for low delay traffic.

- For any node m let $\tau_m = \frac{1}{\sum_{i \ni m} \rho_i} \sum_{i \ni m} \sigma_i$, and let τ be a bound on all τ_m. τ is a time constant that, roughly speaking, gives the maximum packet delay variation for any micro-flow.

- The route of any flow in the network traverses at most h nodes (also referred to as hops).

- Let C_m denote a bound on the peak rate of all incoming low delay traffic traffic at node m. If we have no information about this peak rate, then $C_m = +\infty$. For a router with large internal speed and buffering only at the output, C_m is the sum of the bit rates of all incoming links. The delay bound is better for a smaller C_m.

- Let $u_m = \frac{C_m - r_m}{C_m - \nu r_m}$. Note that $0 < u_m \leq 1$, u_m increases with C_m, and if $C_m = +\infty$, then $u_m = 1$. Call $u = \max_m u_m$. The parameter u expresses how much we gain by knowing the maximum incoming rates C_m.

Theorem 2.4.2 (Closed form bound for delay and backlog [12]). *If $\nu < \nu_0 = \min_l \frac{C_m}{(C_m - r_m)(h-1) + r_m}$ then a bound on delay variation for low delay traffic is hD_1 with*

$$D_1 = \frac{E + u\tau\nu}{1 - (h-1)u\nu}$$

At node m, the buffer required for serving low delay traffic without loss is bounded by

$$B_{req} = r_m \nu \left[E + \tau + D_1(h-1) \right] - r_m \left\{ \nu(E + \tau) - D_1[1 - (h-1)\nu] \right\}^+ \leq r_m D_1$$

Proof We use the method in the previous section and show separately that (1) if a finite bound for delay exists, then the formula in the theorem is true, (2) that a finite bound exists then (3) we show the formula for backlog.

(Part 1) We assume that a finite bound exists. Call D' the worst case delay across any node. Consider a buffer at some node m. An arrival curve for the aggregate traffic at the input of is

$$\alpha(t) = \min\left(tC_m, \sum_{i \ni m} \alpha_i(t + (h - 1)D')\right)$$

The former part in the formula is because the total incoming bit rate is limited by C_m; the latter is because any flow reaching that node has undergone a delay bounded by $(h - 1)D'$. Thus

$$\alpha(t) \leq \alpha'(t) = \min\left(tC_m, t\nu r_m + b'\right)$$

with

$$b' = \nu r_m(\tau + (h - 1)D')$$

A bound on the delay at our node is given by the horizontal deviation between the arrival curve $\alpha'(t)$ and the service curve. After some algebra, this gives a bound on the delay as $e_m + \frac{u_m b'}{r_m}$. Now D' is the worst case delay; pick m to be a node where the worst case delay D' is attained. We must thus have

$$D' \leq e_m + \frac{u_m b'}{r_m}$$

from which we derive

$$D' \leq E + u\nu(\tau + (h - 1)u\nu D')$$

or equivalently

$$(1 - (h - 1)u\nu)\, D' \leq E + u\tau\nu \qquad (2.26)$$

The condition on ν means that $\nu < \frac{1}{(h-1)u}$. Equation (2.26) implies then that

$$D' \leq D_1 = \frac{E + u\tau\nu}{1 - (h - 1)u\nu}$$

The end-to-end delay is thus bounded by hD_1, which is the required formula.

(Part 2) We now prove that a finite bound exists, using the time-stopping method. For any time $t > 0$, consider the virtual system made of the original network, where all sources are stopped at time t. This network satisfies the assumptions of part 1, since there is only a finite number of bits at the input. Call $D'(t)$ the worst case delay across all nodes for the virtual network indexed by t. From the above derivation we see that $D'(t) \leq D_1$ for all t. Letting t tend to $+\infty$ shows that the worst case delay at any node remains bounded by D_1.

(Part 3) An arrival curve for the total incoming traffic at node m is $\min[C_m t, \alpha_1(t)]$, with

$$\alpha_1(t) = \nu r_m[t + \tau + (h-1)D_1]$$

A service curve is β_{E,r_m}. Thus a bound on backlog is obtained as $B_{req} = \sup_t\{\min[C_m t, \alpha_1(t)] - \beta_{E,r_m}(t)\}$. Define θ as the solution to $\alpha_1(\theta) = C_m\theta$. We have

$$B_{req} = \alpha_1(\max(E,\theta)) - \beta(\max(E,\theta)) = \alpha_1((\theta-E)^+ + E] - r_m(\theta-E)^+$$

Now

$$\theta = \frac{\nu}{1-\nu}(1-u)[\tau + (h-1)D_1]$$

After some algebra, this gives the desired result. $\qquad\square$

Discussion: If we have no information about the peak incoming rate C_l, then we set $C_l = +\infty$ and the theorem tells us that, for $\nu < \frac{1}{h-1}$, a bound on delay is $\frac{h}{1-(h-1)\nu}(E + \tau\nu)$.

For finite values of C_m, the delay bound is smaller. Figure 2.9 illustrates the value of our bound on one example

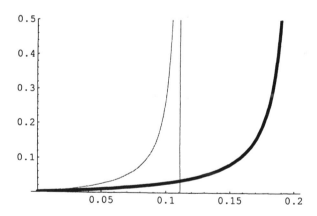

Figure 2.9: The bound D (in seconds) in Theorem 2.4.2 versus the utilization factor ν for $h = 10$, $E = 2\frac{1500B}{r_m}$, $\sigma_i = 100B$ and $\rho_i = 32\text{kb/s}$ for all flows, $r_m = 149.760\text{Mb/s}$, and $C_m = +\infty$ (thin line) or $C_m = 2r_m$ (thick line).

Our bound explodes when ν tends to $\nu_0 = \min_l \frac{C_m}{(C_m - r_m)(h-1)+r_m}$, which is similar to what we can see in Section 2.4.2. The same discussion applies here, that is to say, we do not know whether instability may occur or not, in general. In practice however, we should not expect the bound in Theorem 2.4.2 to be tight for values of ν close to ν_0. To see why, consider the example in Section 2.4.2. We can apply

Theorem 2.4.2 and find that $\nu_0 = 0.5$. However, we know a finite bound that is valid for $\nu < 0.564$, so explosion does not occur at ν_0. The value of Theorem 2.4.2 is to give an explicit, closed form bound, which is valid for small utilization factors. In Chapter 6, we find better bounds, at the expense of more restrictions on the routes and the rates. Such restrictions do not fit with the differentiated services framework. Note also that, for feed-forward networks, we know that there are finite bounds for $\nu < 1$. However we show now that the condition $\nu < \nu_0$ is optimal, in some sense.

Proposition 2.4.2. *[4, 12] With the assumptions of Theorem 2.4.2, if $\nu < \frac{1}{h-1}$, then for any $D' > 0$, there is a network in which the worst case delay is at least D'.*

In other words, the worst case queuing delay can be made arbitrarily large; thus if we want to go beyond Theorem 2.4.2, any bound for differentiated services must depend on the network topology or size, not only on the utilization factor and the number of hops.

Proof: We build a family of networks, out of which, for any D', we can exhibit an example where the queuing delay is at least D'.

The thinking behind the construction is as follows. All flows are low priority flows. We create a hierarchical network, where at the first level of the hierarchy we choose one "flow" for which its first packet happens to encounter just *one* packet of every other flow whose route it intersects, while its next packet does not encounter any queue at all. This causes the first two packets of the chosen flow to come back-to-back after several hops. We then construct the second level of the hierarchy by taking a new flow and making sure that its first packet encounters *two* back-to-back packets of each flow whose routes it intersects, where the two back-to-back packet bursts of all these flows come from the output of a sufficient number of networks constructed as described at the first level of the hierarchy. Repeating this process recursively sufficient number of times, for any chosen delay value D we can create deep enough hierarchy so that the queuing delay of the first packet of some flow encounters a queuing delay more than D (because it encounters a large enough back-to-back burst of packets of every other flow constructed in the previous iteration), while the second packet does not suffer any queuing delay at all. We now describe in detail how to construct such a hierarchical network (which is really a family of networks) such that utilization factor of any link does not exceed a given factor ν, and no flow traverses more than h hops.

Now let us describe the networks in detail. We consider a family of networks with a single traffic class and constant rate links, all with same bit rate C. The network is assumed to be made of infinitely fast switches, with one output buffer per link. Assume that sources are all leaky bucket constrained, but are served in an aggregate manner, first in first out. Leaky bucket constraints are implemented at the network entry; after that point, all flows are aggregated. Without loss of generality, we also assume that propagation delays can be set to 0; this is because we focus only on queuing delays. As a simplification, in this network, we also assume that all packets have a unit size. We show that for any fixed, but arbitrary delay budget D, we can build a network of that family where the worst case queueing delay is larger than D, while each flow traverses at most a specified number of hops.

A network in our family is called $\mathcal{N}(h, \nu, J)$ and has three parameters: h (maximum hop count for any flow), ν (utilization factor) and J (recursion depth). We focus on the cases where $h \geq 3$ and $\frac{1}{h-1} < \nu < 1$, which implies that we can always find some integer k such that

$$\nu > \frac{1}{h-1}\frac{kh+1}{kh-1} \tag{2.27}$$

Network $\mathcal{N}(h, \nu, J)$ is illustrated in Figures 2.10 and 2.11; it is a collection of identical building blocks, arranged in a tree structure of depth J. Every building block has one internal source of traffic (called "transit traffic"), $kh(h-1)$ inputs (called the "building block inputs"), $kh(h-1)$ data sinks, $h-1$ internal nodes, and one output. Each of the $h-1$ internal nodes receives traffic from kh building block inputs plus it receives transit traffic from the previous internal node, with the exception of the first one which is fed by the internal source. After traversing one internal node, traffic from the building block inputs dies in a data sink. In contrast, transit traffic is fed to the next internal node, except for the last one which feeds the building block output (Figure 2.10). Figure 2.11 illustrates that our network has the structure of a complete

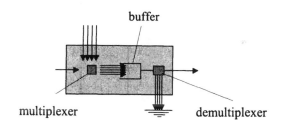

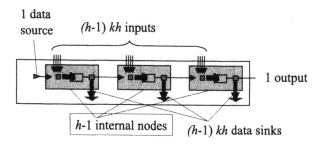

Figure 2.10: The internal node (top) and the building block (bottom) used in our network example.

tree, with depth J. The building blocks are organized in levels $j = 1, ..., J$. Each of the inputs of a level j building block ($j \geq 2$) is fed by the output of one level $j - 1$ building block. The inputs of level 1 building blocks are data sources. The output of one $j - 1$ building block feeds exactly one level j building block input. At level J, there is exactly one building block, thus at level $J - 1$ there are $kh(h - 1)$ building blocks, and at level 1 there are $(kh(h - 1))^{J-1}$ building blocks. All data sources

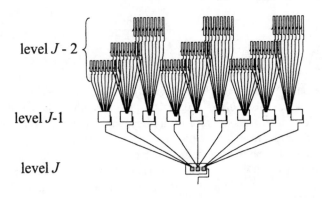

level J - 2

level J-1

level J

Figure 2.11: The network made of building blocks from Figure 2.10

have the same rate $r = \frac{\nu C}{kh+1}$ and burst tolerance $b = 1$ packet. In the rest of this section we take as a time unit the transmission time for one packet, so that $C = 1$. Thus any source may transmit one packet every $\theta = \frac{kh+1}{\nu}$ time units. Note that a source may refrain from sending packets, which is actually what causes the large delay jitter. The utilization factor on every link is ν, and every flow uses 1 or h hops.

Now consider the following scenario. Consider some arbitrary level 1 building block. At time t_0, assume that a packet fully arrives at each of the building block inputs of level 1, and at time $t_0 + 1$, let a packet fully arrive from each data source inside every level 1 building block (this is the first transit packet). The first transit packet is delayed by $hk - 1$ time units in the first internal node. Just one time unit before this packet leaves the first queue, let one packet fully arrive at each input of the second internal node. Our first transit packet will be delayed again by $hk - 1$ time units. If we repeat the scenario along all internal nodes inside the building block, we see that the first transit packet is delayed by $(h - 1)(hk - 1)$ time units. Now from Equation (2.27), $\theta < (h-1)(hk-1)$, so it is possible for the data source to send a second transit packet at time $(h - 1)(hk - 1)$. Let all sources mentioned so far be idle, except for the emissions already described. The second transit packet will catch up to the first one, so the output of any level 1 building block is a burst of two back-to-back packets. We can choose t_0 arbitrarily, so we have a mechanism for generating bursts of 2 packets.

Now we can iterate the scenario and use the same construction at level 2. The level-2 data source sends exactly three packets, spaced by θ. Since the internal node receives hk bursts of two packets originating from level 1, a judicious choice of the level 1 starting time lets the first level 2 transit packet find a queue of $2hk-1$ packets in the first internal node. With the same construction as in level 1, we end up with a total queuing delay of $(h-1)(2hk-1) > 2(h-1)(hk-1) > 2\theta$ for that packet. Now this delay is more than 2θ, and the first three level-2 transit packets are delayed by the same set of non-transit packets; as a result, the second and third level-2 transit packets will eventually catch up to the first one and the output of a level 2 block is a burst of three packets. This procedure easily generalizes to all levels up to J. In particular, the first transit packet at level J has an end-to-end delay of at least $J\theta$. Since all sources become idle after some time, we can easily create a last level J transit packet that finds an empty network and thus a zero queuing delay.

Thus there are two packets in network $\mathcal{N}(h, \nu, J)$, with one packet having a delay larger than $J\theta$, and the other packet has zero delay. This establishes that a bound on queuing delay, and thus on delay variation in network $\mathcal{N}(h, \nu, J)$ has to be at least as large as $J\theta$. □

2.4.4 Bounds for Aggregate Scheduling with Dampers

At the expense of some protocol complexity, the previous bounds can be improved without losing the feature of aggregate scheduling. It is even possible to avoid bound explosions at all, using the concepts of *damper*.Consider an EDF scheduler (for example a SCED scheduler) and assume that every packet sent on the outgoing link carries a field with the difference d between its deadline and its actual emission time, if it is positive, and 0 otherwise. A damper is a regulator in the next downstream node that picks for the packet an eligibility time that lies in the interval $[a+d-\Delta, a+d]$, where Δ is a constant of the damper, and a is the arrival time of the packet in the node where the damper resides. We call Δ the "damping tolerance". The packet is then withheld until its eligibility time [72, 17], see Figure 2.12. In addition, we assume that the damper operates in a FIFO manner; this means that the sequence of eligibility times for consecutive packets is wide-sense increasing.

Unlike the scheduler, the damper does not exist in isolation. It is associated with the next scheduler on the path of a packet. Its effect is to forbid scheduling the packet before the eligibility time chosen for the packet. Consider Figure 2.12. Scheduler m works as follows. When it has an opportunity to send a packet, say at time t, it picks a packet with the earliest deadline, among all packets that are present in node N, and whose eligibility date is $\geq t$. The timing information d shown in the figure is carried in a packet header, either as a link layer header information, or as an IP hop by hop header extension. At the end of a path, we assume that there is no damper at the destination node.

The following proposition is obvious, but important, and is given without proof.

Proposition 2.4.3. *Consider the combination S of a scheduler and its associated damper. If all packets are served by the scheduler before or at their deadlines, then S provides a bound on delay variation equal to Δ.*

It is possible to let $\Delta = 0$, in which case the delay is constant for all packets. A bound on the end-to-end delay variation is then the delay bound at the last scheduler

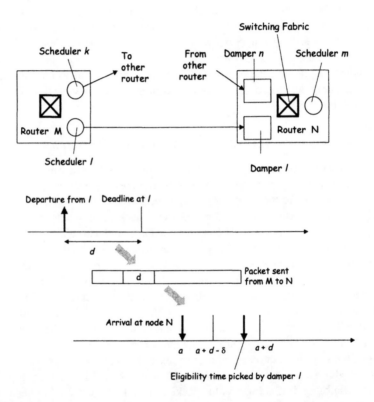

Figure 2.12: Dampers in a differentiated services context. The model shown here assumes that routers are made of infinitely fast switching fabrics and output schedulers. There is one logical damper for each upstream scheduler. The damper decides when an arriving packet becomes visible in the node.

using the combination of a scheduler and a damper (this is called "jitter EDD" in [72]). In practice, we consider $\Delta > 0$ for two reasons. Firstly, it is impractical to assume that we can write the field d with absolute accuracy. Secondly, having some slack in the delay variation objective provides better performance to low priority traffic [17].

There is no complicated feasibility condition for a damper, as there is for schedulers. The operation of a damper is always possible, as long as the there is enough buffer.

Proposition 2.4.4 (Buffer requirement for a damper). *If all packets are served by the scheduler before or at their deadlines, then the buffer requirement at the associated damper is bounded by the buffer requirement at the scheduler.*

Proof: Call $R_(t)$ the total input to the scheduler, and $R'(t)$ the amount of data with deadline $\leq t$. Call $R^*(t)$ the input to the damper, we have $R^*(t) \leq R(t)$. Packets do not stay in the damper longer than until their deadline in the scheduler, thus the output $R_1(t)$ of the damper satisfies $R_1(t) \geq R'(t)$. The buffer requirement at the scheduler at time t is $R(t) - R'(t)$; at the damper it is $R^*(t) - R_1(t) \geq R(t) - R'(t)$. □

Theorem 2.4.3 (Delay and backlog bounds with dampers). *Take the same assumptions as in Section 2.4.3, plus we assume that every scheduler m that is not an exit point is associated with a damper in the next downstream node, with damping tolerance Δ_m. Let Δ be a bound on all Δ_m.*

If $\nu \leq 1$, then a bound on the end-to-end delay jitter for low delay traffic is

$$D = E + (h-1)\Delta(1 + u\nu) + u\tau\nu$$

A bound on the queuing delay at any scheduler is

$$D_2 = E + u\nu[\tau + (h-1)\Delta]$$

The buffer required at scheduler m, for serving low delay traffic without loss is bounded by

$$B_{req} = r_m\nu[E + \tau + \Delta(h-1)] - r_m\{\nu[E + \tau + \Delta(h-1)] - D_2\}^+ \leq r_m D_2$$

A bound on the buffer required at damper m is the same as the buffer required at scheduler m.

Proof: The variable part of the delay between the input of a scheduler and the input of the next one is bounded by Δ. Now let us examine the last scheduler, say m, on the path of a packet. The delay between a source for a flow $i \ni m$ and scheduler m is a constant plus a variable part bounded by $(h-1)\Delta$. Thus an arrival curve for the aggregate low-delay traffic arriving at scheduler m is $\min C_m t, \alpha_2(t)$, with

$$\alpha_2(t) = \nu r_m(t + \tau + (h-1)\Delta)$$

By applying Theorem 1.4.2, a delay bound at scheduler m is given by

$$D_2 = E + u\nu[\tau + (h-1)\Delta]$$

A bound on end-to-end delay variation is $(h-1)\Delta + D_2$, which is the required formula.

The derivation of the backlog bound is similar to that in Theorem 2.4.2. □

The benefit of dampers is obvious: there is no explosion to the bound, it is finite (and small if Δ is small) for any utilization factor up to 1 (see Figure 2.13). Furthermore, the bound is dominated by $h\Delta$, across the whole range of utilization factors up to 1. A key factor in obtaining little delay variation is to have a small damping tolerance δ.

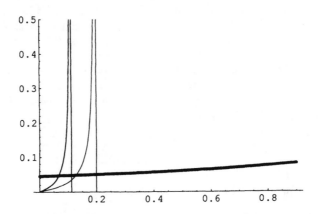

Figure 2.13: The bound D (in seconds) in Theorem 2.4.3 the same parameters as Figure 2.9, for a damping tolerance $\Delta = 5$ ms per damper, and $C_m = +\infty$ (thick line). The figure also shows the two curves of Figure 2.9, for comparison. The bound is very close to $h\Delta = 0.05$s, for all utilization factors up to 1.

There is a relation between a damper and a maximum service curve. Consider the combination of a scheduler with minimum service curve β and its associate damper with damping tolerance Δ. Call p the fixed delay on the link between the two. It follows immediately that the combination offers the maximum service curve $\beta \otimes \delta_{p-\Delta}$ and the minimum service curve $\beta \otimes \delta_p$. Thus a damper may be viewed as a way to implement maximum service curve guarantees. This is explored in detail in [17].

2.5 Exercises

Exercise 2.1. *Consider a guaranteed rate scheduler, with rate R and delay v, that receives a packet flow with cumulative packet length L. The (packetized) scheduler output is fed into a constant bit rate trunk with rate $c > R$ and propagation delay T.*

1. *Find a minimum service curve for the complete system.*

2. *Assume the flow of packets is (r, b)-constrained, with $b > l_{\max}$. Find a bound on the end-to-end delay and delay variation.*

Exercise 2.2. *Assume all nodes in a network are of the GR type. A flow with T-SPEC $\alpha(t) = \min(rt + b, M + pt)$ has performed a reservation with rate R across a sequence of H nodes. Assume no reshaping is done. What is the buffer requirement at the hth node along the path, for $h = 1, ...H$?*

Exercise 2.3. *Assume all nodes in a network are made of a shaper followed by a GR scheduler. A flow with T-SPEC $\alpha(t) = \min(rt + b, M + pt)$ has performed a reservation with rate R across a sequence of H nodes. Assume that the shaper at every node uses the shaping curve $\sigma = \gamma_{r,b}$. What is the buffer requirement at the hth node along the path, for $h = 1, ...H$?*

Exercise 2.4. *Assume all nodes in a network are made of a shaper followed by a FIFO multiplexer. Assume that flow I has T-SPEC, $\alpha_i(t) = \min(r_i t + b_i, M + p_i t)$, that the shaper at every node uses the shaping curve $\sigma_i = \gamma_{r_i, b_i}$ for flow i. Find the schedulability conditions for every node.*

Exercise 2.5. *A network consists of two nodes in tandem. There are n_1 flows of type 1 and n_2 flows of type 2. Flows of type i have arrival curve $\alpha_i(t) = r_i t + b_i$, $i = 1, 2$. All flows go through nodes 1 then 2. Every node is made of a shaper followed by an EDF scheduler. At both nodes, the shaping curve for flows of type i is some σ_i and the delay budget for flows of type i is d_i. Every flow of type i should have a end-to-end delay bounded by D_i. Our problem is to find good values of d_1 and d_2.*

1. *We assume that $\sigma_i = \alpha_i$. What are the conditions on d_1 and d_2 for the end-to-end delay bounds to be satisfied ? What is the set of (n_1, n_2) that are schedulable ?*

2. *Same question if we set $\sigma_i = \lambda_{r_i}$*

Exercise 2.6. *Consider the scheduler in Theorem 2.3.3. Find an efficient algorithm for computing the deadline of every packet.*

Exercise 2.7. *Consider a SCED scheduler with target service curve for flow i given by*

$$\beta_i = \gamma_{r_i, b_i} \otimes \delta_{d_i}$$

Find an efficient algorithm for computing the deadline of every packet.
Hint: use an interpretation as a leaky bucket.

Exercise 2.8. *Consider the example of Figure 2.7. Apply the method of Section 2.4.2 but express now that the fraction of input traffic to node i that originates from another node must have λ_C as an arrival curve. What is the upper-bound on utilization factors for which a bound is obtained ?*

Exercise 2.9. *Consider the delay bound in Theorem 2.4.2. Take the same assumptions but assume also that the network is feedforward. Which better bound can you give ?*

Part II

Mathematical Background

Chapter 3

Basic Min-plus and Max-plus Calculus

In this chapter we introduce the basic results from Min-plus that are needed for the next chapters. Max-plus algebra is dual to Min-plus algebra, with similar concepts and results when minimum is replaced by maximum, and infimum by supremum. As basic results of network calculus use more min-plus algebra than max-plus algebra, we present here in detail the fundamentals of min-plus calculus. We briefly discuss the care that should be used when max and min operations are mixed at the end of the chapter. A detailed treatment of Min- and Max-plus algebra is provided in [24], here we focus on the basic results that are needed for the remaining of the book. Many of the results below can also be found in [10] for the discrete-time setting.

3.1 Min-plus Calculus

In conventional algebra, the two most common operations on elements of $\mathbb{Z}$ or $\mathbb{R}$ are their addition and their multiplication. In fact, the set of integers or reals endowed with these two operations verify a number of well known axioms that define algebraic structures: $(\mathbb{Z}, +, \times)$ is a commutative ring, whereas $(\mathbb{R}, +, \times)$ is a field. Here we consider another algebra, where the operations are changed as follows: addition becomes computation of the minimum, multiplication becomes addition. We will see that this defines another algebraic structure, but let us first recall the notion of minimum and infimum.

3.1.1 Infimum and Minimum

Let S be a nonempty subset of $\mathbb{R}$. S is bounded from below if there is a number M such that $s \geq M$ for all $s \in S$. The completeness axiom states that every nonempty subset S of $\mathbb{R}$ that is bounded from below has a greatest lower bound. We will call it *infimum* of S, and denote it by $\inf S$. For example the closed and open intervals

$[a, b]$ and (a, b) have the same infimum, which is a. Now, if S contains an element that is smaller than all its other elements, this element is called *minimum* of S, and is denoted by $\min S$. Note that the minimum of a set does not always exist. For example, (a, b) has no minimum since $a \notin (a, b)$. On the other hand, if the minimum of a set S exists, it is identical to its infimum. For example, $\min[a, b] = \inf[a, b] = a$. One easily shows that every finite nonempty subset of $\mathbb{R}$ has a minimum. Finally, let us mention that we will often use the notation $\wedge$ to denote infimum (or, when it exists, the minimum). For example, $a \wedge b = \min\{a, b\}$. If S is empty, we adopt the convention that $\inf S = +\infty$.

If f is a function from S to $\mathbb{R}$, we denote by $f(S)$ its range:

$$f(S) = \{t \text{ such that } t = f(s) \text{ for some } s \in S\}.$$

We will denote the infimum of this set by the two equivalent notations

$$\inf f(S) = \inf_{s \in S}\{f(s)\}.$$

We will also often use the following property.

Theorem 3.1.1 ("Fubini" formula for infimum). *Let S be a nonempty subset of $\mathbb{R}$, and f be a function from S to $\mathbb{R}$. Let $\{S_n\}_{n \in \mathbb{N}}$ be a collection of subsets of S, whose union is S. Then*

$$\inf_{s \in S}\{f(s)\} = \inf_{n \in \mathbb{N}}\left\{\inf_{s \in S_n}\{f(s_n)\}\right\}.$$

Proof: By definition of an infimum, for any sets S_n,

$$\inf\left\{\bigcup_n S_n\right\} = \inf_n\{\inf S_n\}.$$

On the other hands, since $\cup_n S_n = S$,

$$f\left(\bigcup_{n \in \mathbb{N}} S_n\right) = \bigcup_{n \in \mathbb{N}} f(S_n)$$

so that

$$
\begin{aligned}
\inf_{s \in S}\{f(s)\} &= \inf f(S) = \inf f\left(\bigcup_{n \in \mathbb{N}} S_n\right) \\
&= \inf\left\{\bigcup_{n \in \mathbb{N}} f(S_n)\right\} = \inf_{n \in \mathbb{N}}\{\inf f(S_n)\} \\
&= \inf_{n \in \mathbb{N}}\left\{\inf_{s \in S_n}\{f(s)\}\right\}.
\end{aligned}
$$

□

3.1.2 Dioid $(\mathbb{R} \cup \{+\infty\}, \wedge, +)$

In traditional algebra, one is used to working with the algebraic structure $(\mathbb{R}, +, \times)$, that is, with the set of reals endowed with the two usual operations of addition and multiplication. These two operations possess a number of properties (associativity, commutativity, distributivity, etc) that make $(\mathbb{R}, +, \times)$ a commutative field. As mentioned above, in min-plus algebra, the operation of 'addition' becomes computation of the infimum (or of the minimum if it exists), whereas the one of 'multiplication' becomes the classical operation of addition. We will also include $+\infty$ in the set of elements on which min-operations are carried out, so that the structure of interest is now $(\mathbb{R} \cup \{+\infty\}, \wedge, +)$. Most axioms (but not all, as we will see later) defining a field still apply to this structure. For example, distribution of addition with respect to multiplication in conventional ('Plus-times') algebra

$$(3 + 4) \times 5 = (3 \times 5) + (4 \times 5) = 15 + 20 = 35$$

translates in min-plus algebra as

$$(3 \wedge 4) + 5 = (3 + 5) \wedge (4 + 5) = 8 \wedge 9 = 8.$$

In fact, one easily verifies that $\wedge$ and $+$ satisfy the following properties:

- **(Closure of $\wedge$)** For all $a, b \in \mathbb{R} \cup \{+\infty\}$, $a \wedge b \in \mathbb{R} \cup \{+\infty\}$.

- **(Associativity of $\wedge$)** For all $a, b, c \in \mathbb{R} \cup \{+\infty\}$, $(a \wedge b) \wedge c = a \wedge (b \wedge c)$.

- **(Existence of a zero element for $\wedge$)** There is some $e = +\infty \in \mathbb{R} \cup \{+\infty\}$ such that for all $a \in \mathbb{R} \cup \{+\infty\}$, $a \wedge e = a$.

- **(Idempotency of $\wedge$)** For all $a \in \mathbb{R} \cup \{+\infty\}$, $a \wedge a = a$.

- **(Commutativity of $\wedge$)** For all $a, b \in \mathbb{R} \cup \{+\infty\}$, $a \wedge b = b \wedge a$.

- **(Closure of $+$)** For all $a, b \in \mathbb{R} \cup \{+\infty\}$, $a + b \in \mathbb{R} \cup \{+\infty\}$.

- **(Associativity of $+$)** For all $a, b, c \in \mathbb{R} \cup \{+\infty\}$, $(a + b) + c = a + (b + c)$.

- **(The zero element for $\wedge$ is absorbing for $+$)** For all $a \in \mathbb{R} \cup \{+\infty\}$, $a + e = e = e + a$.

- **(Existence of a neutral element for $+$)** There is some $u = 0 \in \mathbb{R} \cup \{+\infty\}$ such that for all $a \in \mathbb{R} \cup \{+\infty\}$, $a + u = a = u + a$.

- **(Distributivity of $+$ with respect to $\wedge$)** For all $a, b, c \in \mathbb{R} \cup \{+\infty\}$, $(a \wedge b) + c = (a + c) \wedge (b + c) = c + (a \wedge b)$.

A set endowed with operations satisfying all the above axioms is called a *dioid*. Moreover as $+$ is also commutative (for all $a, b \in \mathbb{R} \cup \{+\infty\}$, $a + b = b + a$), the structure $(\mathbb{R} \cup \{+\infty\}, \wedge, +)$ is a commutative dioid. All the axioms defining a dioid are therefore the same axioms as the ones defining a ring, except one: the axiom of idempotency of the 'addition', which in dioids replaces the axiom of cancellation of 'addition' in rings (i.e. the existence of an element $(-a)$ that 'added' to a gives the zero element). We will encounter other dioids later on in this chapter.

3.1.3   A Catalog of Wide-sense Increasing Functions

A function f is wide-sense increasing if and only if $f(s) \leq f(t)$ for all $s \leq t$. We will denote by $\mathcal{G}$ the set of non-negative wide-sense increasing sequences or functions and by $\mathcal{F}$ denote the set of wide-sense increasing sequences or functions such that $f(t) = 0$ for $t < 0$. Parameter t can be continuous or discrete: in the latter case, $f = \{f(t), t \in \mathbb{Z}\}$ is called a sequence rather than a function. In the former case, we take the convention that the function $f = \{f(t), t \in \mathbb{R}\}$ is left-continuous. The range of functions or sequences of $\mathcal{F}$ and $\mathcal{G}$ is $\mathbb{R}^+ = [0, +\infty]$.

Notation $f + g$ (respectively $f \wedge g$) denotes the point-wise sum (resp. minimum) of functions f and g:

$$(f + g)(t) = f(t) + g(t)$$
$$(f \wedge g)(t) = f(t) \wedge g(t)$$

Notation $f \leq (=, \geq)g$ means that $f(t) \leq (=, \geq)g(t)$ for all t.

Some examples of functions belonging to $\mathcal{F}$ and of particular interest are the following ones. Notation $[x]^+$ denotes $\max\{x, 0\}$, $\lceil x \rceil$ denotes the smallest integer larger than or equal to x.

Definition 3.1.1 (Peak rate functions λ_R).

$$\lambda_R(t) = \begin{cases} Rt & \text{if } t > 0 \\ 0 & \text{otherwise} \end{cases}$$

for some $R \geq 0$ (the 'rate').

Definition 3.1.2 (Burst delay functions δ_T).

$$\delta_T(t) = \begin{cases} +\infty & \text{if } t > T \\ 0 & \text{otherwise} \end{cases}$$

for some $T \geq 0$ (the 'delay').

Definition 3.1.3 (Rate-latency functions $\beta_{R,T}$).

$$\beta_{R,T}(t) = R[t - T]^+ = \begin{cases} R(t - T) & \text{if } t > T \\ 0 & \text{otherwise} \end{cases}$$

for some $R \geq 0$ (the 'rate') and $T \geq 0$ (the 'delay').

Definition 3.1.4 (Affine functions $\gamma_{r,b}$).

$$\gamma_{r,b}(t) = \begin{cases} rt + b & \text{if } t > 0 \\ 0 & \text{otherwise} \end{cases}$$

for some $r \geq 0$ (the 'rate') and $b \geq 0$ (the 'burst').

Definition 3.1.5 (Step Function v_T).

$$v_T(t) = 1_{\{t>T\}} = \begin{cases} 1 & \text{if } t > T \\ 0 & \text{otherwise} \end{cases}$$

for some $T > 0$.

Definition 3.1.6 (Staircase Functions $u_{T,\tau}$).

$$u_{T,\tau}(t) = \begin{cases} \lceil \frac{t+\tau}{T} \rceil & \text{if } t > 0 \\ 0 & \text{otherwise} \end{cases}$$

for some $T > 0$ (the 'interval') and $0 \leq \tau \leq T$ (the 'tolerance').

These functions are also represented in Figure 3.1. By combining these basic functions, one obtains more general piecewise linear functions belonging to $\mathcal{F}$. For example, the two functions represented in Figure 3.2 are written using $\wedge$ and $+$ from affine functions and rate-latency functions as follows, with $r_1 > r_2 > \ldots > r_I$ and $b_1 < b_2 < \ldots < b_I$

$$f_1 = \gamma_{r_1,b_1} \wedge \gamma_{r_2,b_2} \wedge \ldots \gamma_{r_I,b_I} = \min_{1 \leq i \leq I} \{\gamma_{r_i,b_i}\} \tag{3.1}$$

$$f_2 = \lambda_R \wedge \{\beta_{R,2T} + RT\} \wedge \{\beta_{R,4T} + 2RT\} \wedge \ldots$$

$$= \inf_{i \geq 0} \{\beta_{R,2iT} + iRT\}. \tag{3.2}$$

We will encounter other functions later in the book, and obtain other representations with the min-plus convolution operator.

3.1.4 Pseudo-inverse of Wide-sense Increasing Functions

It is well known that any strictly increasing function is left-invertible. That is, if for any $t_1 < t_2$, $f(t_1) < f(t_2)$, then there is a function f^{-1} such that $f^{-1}(f(t)) = t$ for all t. Here we consider slightly more general functions, namely, wide-sense increasing functions, and we will see that a pseudo-inverse function can defined as follows.

Definition 3.1.7 (Pseudo-inverse). *Let f be a function or a sequence of $\mathcal{F}$. The pseudo-inverse of f is the function*

$$f^{-1}(x) = \inf \{t \text{ such that } f(t) \geq x\}. \tag{3.3}$$

For example, one can easily compute that the pseudo-inverses of the four functions of Definitions 3.1.1 to 3.1.4 are

$$\lambda_R^{-1} = \lambda_{1/R}$$
$$\delta_T^{-1} = \delta_0 \wedge T$$
$$\beta_{R,T}^{-1} = \gamma_{1/R,T}$$
$$\gamma_{r,b}^{-1} = \beta_{1/r,b}.$$

The pseudo-inverse enjoys the following properties:

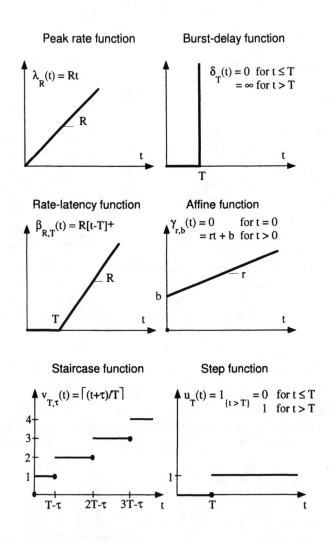

Figure 3.1: A catalog of functions of $\mathcal{F}$: Peak rate function (top left), burst-delay function (top right), rate-latency function (center left), affine function (center right), staircase function (bottom left) and step function (bottom right).

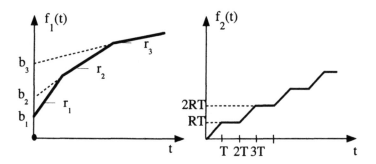

Figure 3.2: Two piecewise linear functions of $\mathcal{F}$ as defined by (3.1) (left) and (3.2) (right).

Theorem 3.1.2 (Properties of pseudo-inverse functions). *Let $f \in \mathcal{F}$, $x, t \geq 0$.*

- *(Closure)* $f^{-1} \in \mathcal{F}$ and $f^{-1}(0) = 0$.

- *(Pseudo-inversion)* We have that

$$f(t) \geq x \quad \Rightarrow \quad f^{-1}(x) \leq t \tag{3.4}$$
$$f^{-1}(x) < t \quad \Rightarrow \quad f(t) \geq x \tag{3.5}$$

- *(Equivalent definition)*

$$f^{-1}(x) = \sup \left\{ t \text{ such that } f(t) < x \right\}. \tag{3.6}$$

Proof: Define subset $S_x = \{t \text{ such that } f(t) \geq x\} \subseteq \mathbb{R}^+$. Then (3.3) becomes $f^{-1}(x) = \inf S_x$. (Closure) Clearly, from (3.3), $f^{-1}(x) = 0$ for $x \leq 0$ (and in particular $f^{-1}(0) = 0$). Now, let $0 \leq x_1 < x_2$. Then $S_{x_1} \supseteq S_{x_2}$, which implies that $\inf S_{x_1} \leq \inf S_{x_2}$ and hence that $f^{-1}(x_1) \leq f^{-1}(x_2)$. Therefore f^{-1} is wide-sense increasing. (Pseudo-inversion) Suppose first that $f(t) \geq x$. Then $t \in S_x$, and so is larger than the infimum of S_x, which is $f^{-1}(x)$: this proves (3.4). Suppose next that $f^{-1}(x) < t$. Then $t > \inf S_x$, which implies that $t \in S_x$, by definition of an infimum. This in turn yields that $f(t) \geq x$ and proves (3.5). (Equivalent definition) Define subset $\tilde{S}_x = \{t \text{ such that } f(t) < x\} \subseteq \mathbb{R}^+$. Pick $t \in S_x$ and $\tilde{t} \in \tilde{S}_x$. Then $f(\tilde{t}) < f(t)$, and since f is wide-sense increasing, it implies that $\tilde{t} \leq t$. This is true for any $t \in S_x$ and $\tilde{t} \in \tilde{S}_x$, hence $\sup \tilde{S}_x \leq \inf S_x$. As $\tilde{S}_x \cup S_x = \mathbb{R}^+$, we cannot have $\sup \tilde{S}_x < \inf S_x$. Therefore

$$\sup \tilde{S}_x = \inf S_x = f^{-1}(x).$$

$\square$

3.1.5   Concave, Convex and Star-shaped Functions

As an important class of functions in min-plus calculus are the convex and concave functions, it is useful to recall some of their properties.

Definition 3.1.8 (Convexity in $\mathbb{R}^n$). *Let u be any real such that $0 \leq u \leq 1$.*

- *Subset $S \subseteq \mathbb{R}^n$ is convex if and only if $ux + (1 - u)y \in S$ for all $x, y \in S$.*

- *Function f from a subset $D \subseteq \mathbb{R}^n$ to $\mathbb{R}$ is convex if and only if $f(ux + (1 - u)y) \leq uf(x) + (1 - u)f(y)$ for all $x, y \in D$.*

- *Function f from a subset $D \subseteq \mathbb{R}^n$ to $\mathbb{R}$ is concave if and only if $-f$ is convex.*

For example, the rate-latency function (Fig 3.1, center left) is convex, the piecewise linear function f_1 given by (3.1) is concave and the piecewise linear function f_2 given by (3.2) is neither convex nor concave.

There are a number of properties that convex sets and functions enjoy [68]. Here are a few that will be used in this chapter, and that are a direct consequence of Definition 3.1.8.

- The convex subsets of $\mathbb{R}$ are the intervals.

- If S_1 and S_2 are two convex subsets of $\mathbb{R}^n$, their sum

$$S = S_1 + S_2 = \{s \in \mathbb{R}^n \mid s = s_1 + s_2 \text{ for some } s_1 \in S_1 \text{ and } s_2 \in S_2\}$$

is also convex.

- Function f from an interval $[a, b]$ to $\mathbb{R}$ is convex (resp. concave) if and only if $f(ux + (1 - u)y) \leq$ (resp. $\geq$) $uf(x) + (1 - u)f(y)$ for all $x, y \in [a, b]$ and all $u \in [0.1]$.

- The pointwise maximum (resp. minimum) of any number of convex (resp. concave) functions is a convex (resp. concave) function.

- If S is a convex subset of $\mathbb{R}^{n+1}$, $n \geq 1$, the function from $\mathbb{R}^n$ to $\mathbb{R}$ defined by

$$f(x) = \inf\{\mu \in \mathbb{R} \text{ such that } (x, \mu) \in S\}$$

is convex.

- If f is a convex function from $\mathbb{R}^n$ to $\mathbb{R}$, the set S defined by

$$S = \{(x, \mu) \in \mathbb{R}^{n+1} \text{ such that } f(x) \leq \mu\}$$

is convex. This set is called the epigraph of f. It implies in the particular case where $n = 1$ that the line segment between $\{a, f(a)\}$ and $\{b, f(b)\}$ lies above the graph of the curve $y = f(x)$.

The proof of these properties is given in [68] and can be easily deduced from Definition 3.1.8, or even from a simple drawing. Chang [10] introduced *star-shaped* functions, which are defined as follows.

Definition 3.1.9 (Star-shaped function). *Function $f \in \mathcal{F}$ is star-shaped if and only if $f(t)/t$ is wide-sense decreasing for all $t > 0$.*

Star-shaped enjoy the following property:

Theorem 3.1.3 (Minimum of star-shaped functions). *Let f, g be two star-shaped functions. Then $h = f \wedge g$ is also star-shaped.*

Proof: Consider some $t \geq 0$. If $h(t) = f(t)$, then for all $s > t$, $h(t)/t = f(t)/t \geq f(s)/s \geq h(s)/s$. The same argument holds of course if $h(t) = g(t)$. Therefore $h(t)/t \geq h(s)/s$ for all $s > t$, which shows that h is star-shaped. □

We will see other properties of star-shaped functions in the next sections. Let us conclude this section with an important class of star-shaped functions.

Theorem 3.1.4. *Concave functions are star-shaped.*

Proof: Let f be a concave function. Then for any $u \in [0, 1]$ and $x, y \geq 0$, $f(ux + (1-u)y) \geq uf(x) + (1-u)f(y)$. Take $x = t, y = 0$ and $u = s/t$, with $0 < s \leq t$. Then the previous inequality becomes $f(s) \geq (s/t)f(t)$, which shows that $f(t)/t$ is a decreasing function of t. □

On the other hand, a star-shaped function is not necessarily a concave function. We will see one such example in Section 3.1.7.

3.1.6 Min-plus Convolution

Let $f(t)$ be a real-valued function, which is zero for $t \leq 0$. If $t \in \mathbb{R}$, the integral of this function in the conventional algebra $(\mathbb{R}, +, \times)$ is

$$\int_0^t f(s)ds$$

which becomes, for a sequence $f(t)$ where $t \in \mathbb{Z}$,

$$\sum_{s=0}^t f(s).$$

In the min-plus algebra $(\mathbb{R} \cup \{+\infty\}, \wedge, +)$, where the 'addition' is $\wedge$ and the 'multiplication' is $+$, an 'integral' of the function f becomes therefore

$$\inf_{s \in \mathbb{R} \text{ such that } 0 \leq s \leq t} \{f(s)\},$$

which becomes, for a sequence $f(t)$ where $t \in \mathbb{Z}$,

$$\min_{s \in \mathbb{Z} \text{ such that } 0 \le s \le t} \{f(s)\}.$$

We will often adopt a shorter notation for the two previous expressions, which is

$$\inf_{0 \le s \le t} \{f(s)\},$$

with $s \in \mathbb{Z}$ or $s \in \mathbb{R}$ depending on the domain of f.

A key operation in conventional linear system theory is the convolution between two functions, which is defined as

$$(f \otimes g)(t) = \int_{-\infty}^{+\infty} f(t-s)g(s)ds$$

and becomes, when $f(t)$ and $g(t)$ are two functions that are zero for $t < 0$,

$$(f \otimes g)(t) = \int_{0}^{t} f(t-s)g(s)ds.$$

In min-plus calculus, the operation of convolution is the natural extension of the previous definition:

Definition 3.1.10 (Min-plus convolution). *Let f and g be two functions or sequences of $\mathcal{F}$. The min-plus convolution of f and g is the function*

$$(f \otimes g)(t) = \inf_{0 \le s \le t} \{f(t-s) + g(s)\}. \tag{3.7}$$

(If $t < 0$, $(f \otimes g)(t) = 0$).

Example. Consider the two functions $\gamma_{r,b}$ and $\beta_{R,T}$, with $0 < r < R$, and let us compute their min-plus convolution. Let us first compute it for $0 \le t \le T$.

$$
\begin{aligned}
(\gamma_{r,b} \otimes \beta_{R,T})(t) &= \inf_{0 \le s \le t} \{\gamma_{r,b}(t-s) + R[s-T]^+\} \\
&= \inf_{0 \le s \le t} \{\gamma_{r,b}(t-s) + 0\} = \gamma_{r,b}(0) + 0 = 0 + 0 = 0
\end{aligned}
$$

Now, if $t > T$, one has

$$
\begin{aligned}
(\gamma_{r,b} &\otimes \beta_{R,T})(t) \\
&= \inf_{0 \le s \le t} \{\gamma_{r,b}(t-s) + R[s-T]^+\} \\
&= \inf_{0 \le s \le T} \{\gamma_{r,b}(t-s) + R[s-T]^+\} \wedge \inf_{T \le s < t} \{\gamma_{r,b}(t-s) + R[s-T]^+\} \\
&\quad \wedge \inf_{s=t} \{\gamma_{r,b}(t-s) + R[s-T]^+\} \\
&= \inf_{0 \le s \le T} \{b + r(t-s) + 0\} \wedge \inf_{T < s < t} \{b + r(t-s) + R(s-T)\} \\
&\quad \wedge \{0 + R(t-T)\} \\
&= \{b + r(t-T)\} \wedge \left\{b + rt - RT + \inf_{T < s < t} \{(R-r)s\}\right\} \wedge \{R(t-T)\} \\
&= \{b + r(t-T)\} \wedge \{b + r(t-T)\} \wedge \{R(t-T)\} \\
&= \{b + r(t-T)\} \wedge \{R(t-T)\}.
\end{aligned}
$$

The result is shown in Figure 3.3. Let us now derive some useful properties for the

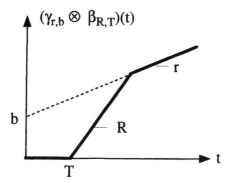

Figure 3.3: Function $\gamma_{r,b} \otimes \beta_{R,T}$ when $0 < r < R$.

computation of min-plus convolution.

Theorem 3.1.5 (General properties of $\otimes$). *Let* $f, g, h \in \mathcal{F}$.

- **Rule 1 (Closure of $\otimes$)** $(f \otimes g) \in \mathcal{F}$.

- **Rule 2 (Associativity of $\otimes$)** $(f \otimes g) \otimes h = f \otimes (g \otimes h)$.

- **Rule 3 (The zero element for $\wedge$ is absorbing for $\otimes$)** *The zero element for $\wedge$ belonging to $\mathcal{F}$ is the function ε, defined as $\varepsilon(t) = +\infty$ for all $t \geq 0$ and $\varepsilon(t) = 0$ for all $t < 0$. One has $f \otimes \varepsilon = \varepsilon$.*

- **Rule 4 (Existence of a neutral element for $\otimes$)** *The neutral element is δ_0, as $f \otimes \delta_0 = f$.*

- **Rule 5 (Commutativity of $\otimes$)** $f \otimes g = g \otimes f$.

- **Rule 6 (Distributivity of $\otimes$ with respect to $\wedge$)** $(f \wedge g) \otimes h = (f \otimes h) \wedge (g \otimes h)$.

- **Rule 7 (Addition of a constant)** *For any $K \in \mathbb{R}^+$, $(f + K) \otimes g = (f \otimes g) + K$.*

The proof of these rules is easy. We prove the two first rules, the proof of the five others are left to the reader.

Proof: (Rule 1) Since f is wide-sense increasing,

$$f(t_1 - s) + g(s) \leq f(t_2 - s) + g(s)$$

for all $0 \leq t_1 < t_2$ and all $s \in \mathbb{R}$. Therefore

$$\inf_{s \in \mathbb{R}} \{f(t_1 - s) + g(s)\} \le \inf_{s \in \mathbb{R}} \{f(t_2 - s) + g(s)\}$$

and as $f(t) = g(t) = 0$ when $t < 0$, this inequality is equivalent to

$$\inf_{0 \le s \le t_1} \{f(t_1 - s) + g(s)\} \le \inf_{0 \le s \le t_2} \{f(t_2 - s) + g(s)\},$$

which shows that $(f \otimes g)(t_1) \le (f \otimes g)(t_2)$ for all $0 \le t_1 < t_2$. (Rule 2) One has

$$
\begin{aligned}
((f \otimes g) \otimes h)(t) &= \inf_{0 \le s \le t} \left\{ \inf_{0 \le u \le t-s} \{f(t - s - u) + g(u)\} + h(s) \right\} \\
&= \inf_{0 \le s \le t} \left\{ \inf_{s \le u' \le t} \{f(t - u') + g(u' - s) + h(s)\} \right\} \\
&= \inf_{0 \le u' \le t} \left\{ \inf_{0 \le s \le u'} \{f(t - u') + g(u' - s) + h(s)\} \right\} \\
&= \inf_{0 \le u' \le t} \left\{ f(t - u') + \inf_{0 \le s \le u'} \{g(u' - s) + h(s)\} \right\} \\
&= \inf_{0 \le u' \le t} \{f(t - u') + (g \otimes h)(u')\} \\
&= (f \otimes (g \otimes h))(t).
\end{aligned}
$$

$\square$

Rules 1 to 6 establish a structure of a commutative dioid for $(\mathcal{F}, \wedge, \otimes)$, whereas Rules 6 and 7 show that $\otimes$ is a linear operation on $(\mathbb{R}^+, \wedge, +)$. Now let us also complete these results by two additional rules that are helpful in the case of concave or convex functions.

Theorem 3.1.6 (Properties of $\otimes$ for concave/convex functions). *Let $f, g \in \mathcal{F}$.*

- **Rule 8 (Functions passing through the origin)** *If $f(0) = g(0) = 0$ then $f \otimes g \le f \wedge g$. Moreover, if f and g are star-shaped, then $f \otimes g = f \wedge g$.*

- **Rule 9 (Convex functions)** *If f and g are convex then $f \otimes g$ is convex. In particular if f, g are convex and piecewise linear, $f \otimes g$ is obtained by putting end-to-end the different linear pieces of f and g, sorted by increasing slopes.*

Since concave functions are star-shaped, Rule 8 also implies that if f, g are concave with $f(0) = g(0) = 0$, then $f \otimes g = f \wedge g$.

Proof: (Rule 8) As $f(0) = g(0) = 0$,

$$(f \otimes g)(t) = g(t) \wedge \inf_{0 < s < t} \{f(t - s) + g(s)\} \wedge f(t) \le f(t) \wedge g(t). \qquad (3.8)$$

Suppose now that, in addition, f and g are star-shaped. Then for any $t > 0$ and $0 \le s \le t$ $f(t - s) \ge (1 - s/t)f(t)$ and $g(s) \ge (s/t)g(t)$, so that

$$f(t - s) + g(s) \ge f(t) + (s/t)(g(t) - f(t)).$$

Now, as $0 \leq s/t \leq 1$, $f(t) + (s/t)(g(t) - f(t)) \geq f(t) \wedge g(t)$ so that

$$f(t - s) + g(s) \geq f(t) \wedge g(t)$$

for all $0 \leq s \leq t$. Combining this inequality with (3.8), we obtain the desired result. (Rule 9) The proof uses properties of convex sets and functions listed in the previous subsection. The epigraphs of f and g are the sets

$$
\begin{aligned}
S_1 &= \{(s_1, \mu_1) \in \mathbb{R}^2 \text{ such that } f(s_1) \leq \mu_1\} \\
S_2 &= \{(s_2, \mu_2) \in \mathbb{R}^2 \text{ such that } g(s_2) \leq \mu_2\}
\end{aligned}
$$

Since f and g are convex, their epigraphs are also convex, and so is their sum $S = S_1 + S_2$, which can be expressed as

$$S = \{(t, \mu) \in \mathbb{R}^2 \mid \text{ for some } (s, \xi) \in [0, t] \times [0, \mu], f(t - s) \leq \mu - \xi, g(s) \leq \xi\}.$$

As S is convex, function $h(t) = \inf\{\mu \in \mathbb{R} \text{ such that } (t, \mu) \in S\}$ is also convex. Now h can be recast as

$$
\begin{aligned}
h(t) \\
&= \inf\{\mu \in \mathbb{R} \mid \text{ for some}(s, \xi) \in [0, t] \times [0, \mu], f(t - s) \leq \mu - \xi, g(s) \leq \xi\} \\
&= \inf\{\mu \in \mathbb{R} \mid \text{ for some } s \in [0, t], f(t - s) + g(s) \leq \mu\} \\
&= \inf\{f(t - s) + g(s), s \in [0, t]\} \\
&= (f \otimes g)(t),
\end{aligned}
$$

which proves that $(f \otimes g)$ is convex.

If f and g are piecewise linear, one can construct the set $S = S_1 + S_2$, which is the epigraph of $f \otimes g$, by putting end-to-end the different linear pieces of f and g, sorted by increasing slopes [20].

Indeed, let h' denote the function that results from this operation, and let us show that $h' = f \otimes g$. Suppose that there are a total of n linear pieces from f and g, and label them from 1 to n according to their increasing slopes: $0 \leq r_1 \leq r_2 \leq \ldots \leq r_n$. Figure 3.4 shows an example for $n = 5$. Let T_i denote the length of the projection of segment i onto the horizontal axis, for $1 \leq i \leq n$. Then the length of the projection of segment i onto the vertical axis is $r_i T_i$. Denote by S' the epigraph of h', which is convex, and by $\partial S'$ its boundary. Pick any point $(t, h'(t))$ on this boundary $\partial S'$. We will show that it can always be obtained by adding a point $(t - s, f(t - s))$ of the boundary ∂S_1 of S_1 and a point $(s, g(s))$ of the boundary ∂S_2 of S_2. Let k be the linear segment index to which $(t, h'(t))$ belongs, and assume, with no loss of generality, that this segment is a piece of f (that is, $k \subseteq \partial S_1$). We can express $h'(t)$ as

$$h'(t) = r_k(t - \sum_{i=1}^{k-1} T_i) + \sum_{i=1}^{k-1} r_i T_i. \tag{3.9}$$

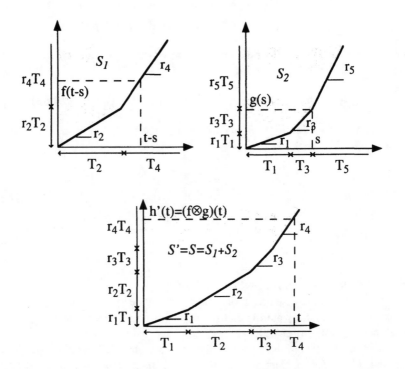

Figure 3.4: Convex, piecewise linear functions f (and its epigraph $\mathcal{S}_1$ (top left)), g (and its epigraph $\mathcal{S}_2$ (top right)), and $f \otimes g$ (and its epigraph $\mathcal{S} = \mathcal{S}_1 + \mathcal{S}_2$ (bottom)).

Now, let s be the sum of the lengths of the horizontal projections of the segments belonging to g and whose index is less than k, that is,

$$s = \sum_{i \subseteq \partial S_2, 1 \le i \le k-1} T_i.$$

Then we can compute that

$$t - s \;=\; t - \sum_{i=1}^{k-1} T_i + \sum_{i=1}^{k-1} T_i - \sum_{i \subseteq \partial S_2, 1 \le i \le k-1} T_i$$

$$=\; t - \sum_{i=1}^{k-1} T_i + \sum_{i \subseteq \partial S_1, 1 \le i \le k-1} T_i$$

and that

$$f(t - s) \;=\; r_k(t - \sum_{i=1}^{k-1} T_i) + \sum_{i \subseteq \partial S_1, 1 \le i \le k-1} r_i T_i$$

$$g(s) \;=\; \sum_{i \subseteq \partial S_2, 1 \le i \le k-1} r_i T_i.$$

The addition of the right hand sides of these two equations is equal to $h'(t)$, because of (3.9), and therefore $f(t - s) + g(s) = h'(t)$. This shows that any point of $\partial S'$ can be broken down into the sum of a point of ∂S_1 and of a point of ∂S_2, and hence that $\partial S' = \partial S_1 + \partial S_2$, which in turn implies that $S' = S_1 + S_2 = S$. Therefore $h' = f \otimes g$. □

The last rule is easy to prove, and states that $\otimes$ is isotone, namely:

Theorem 3.1.7 (Isotonicity of $\otimes$). *Let $f, g, f', g' \in \mathcal{F}$.*

- *Rule 10 (Isotonicity) If $f \le g$ and $f' \le g'$ then $f \otimes f' \le g \otimes g'$.*

We will use the following theorem:

Theorem 3.1.8. *For f and g in $\mathcal{F}$, if in addition g is continuous, then for any t there is some t_0 such that*

$$(f \otimes g)(t) = f_l(t_0) + g(t - t_0) \tag{3.10}$$

where $f_l(t_0) = \sup_{\{s < t_0\}} f(s)$ is the limit to the left of f at t_0. If f is left-continuous, then $f_l(t_0) = f(t_0)$.

Proof: Fix t. There is a sequence of times $0 \le s_n \le t$ such that

$$\inf_{t_0 \le t} (f(t_0) + g(t - t_0)) = \lim_{n \to \infty} (f(s_n) + g(t - s_n)) \tag{3.11}$$

Since $0 \le s_n \le t$, we can extract a sub-sequence that converges towards some value t_0. We take a notation shortcut and write $\lim_{n \to \infty} s_n = t_0$. If f is continuous, the right hand-side in 3.11 is equal to $f_l(t_0) + g(t - t_0)$ which shows the proposition. Otherwise f has a discontinuity at t_0. Define $\delta = f(t_0) - f_l(t_0)$. We show that we can again extract a subsequence such that $s_n < t_0$. Indeed, if this would not be true, we would have $s_n \geq t_0$ for all but a finite number of indices n. Thus for n large enough we would have

$$f(s_n) \geq f_l(t_0) + \delta$$

and by continuity of g:

$$g(t - s_n) \geq g(t - t_0) - \frac{\delta}{2}$$

thus

$$f(s_n) + g(t - s_n) \geq f_l(t_0) + g(t - t_0) + \frac{\delta}{2}$$

Now

$$f_l(t_0) + g(t - t_0) \geq \inf_{s \leq t} (f(s) + g(t - s))$$

thus

$$f(s_n) + g(t - s_n) \geq \inf_{s \leq t} (f(s) + g(t - s)) + \frac{\delta}{2}$$

which contradicts 3.11. Thus we can assume that $s_n \leq t_0$ for n large enough and thus $\lim_{n \to \infty} f(s_n) = f_l(t_0)$. □

Finally, let us mention that it will sometimes be useful to break down a somewhat complex function into the convolution of a number of simpler functions. For example, observe that the rate-latency function $\beta_{R,T}$ can be expressed as

$$\beta_{R,T} = \delta_T \otimes \lambda_R. \tag{3.12}$$

3.1.7 Sub-additive Functions

Another class of functions will be important in network calculus are sub-additive functions, which are defined as follows.

Definition 3.1.11 (Sub-additive function). *Let f be a function or a sequence of $\mathcal{F}$. Then f is sub-additive if and only if $f(t + s) \leq f(t) + f(s)$ for all $s, t \geq 0$.*

Note that this definition is equivalent to imposing that $f \leq f \otimes f$. If $f(0) = 0$, it is equivalent to imposing that $f \otimes f = f$.

We will see in the following theorem that concave functions passing through the origin are sub-additive. So the piecewise linear function f_1 given by (3.1), being concave and passing through the origin, is sub-additive.

The set of sub-additive functions is however larger than that of concave functions: the piecewise linear function f_2 given by (3.2) is not concave, yet one check that it verifies Definition 3.1.11 and hence is sub-additive.

Contrary to concave and convex functions, it is not always obvious, from a quick visual inspection of the graph of a function, to establish whether it is sub-additive or not. Consider the two functions $\beta_{R,T} + K'$ and $\beta_{R,T} + K''$, represented respectively on the left and right of Figure 3.5. Although they differ only by the constants K' and K'', which are chosen so that $0 < K'' < RT < K' < +\infty$, we will see $\beta_{R,T} + K'$ is sub-additive but not $\beta_{R,T} + K''$. Consider first $\beta_{R,T} + K'$. If $s + t \leq T$, then

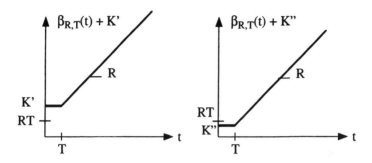

Figure 3.5: Functions $\beta_{R,T} + K'$ (left) and $\beta_{R,T} + K''$ (right). The only difference between them is the value of the constant: $K'' < RT < K'$.

$s, t \leq T$ and

$$\beta_{R,T}(s + t) + K' = K' < 2K' = (\beta_{R,T}(s) + K') + (\beta_{R,T}(t) + K').$$

On the other hand, if $s + t > T$, then, since $K' > RT$,

$$
\begin{aligned}
\beta_{R,T}(t + s) + K' &= R(t + s - T) + K' \\
&< R(s + t - T) + K' + (K' - RT) \\
&= (R(t - T) + K') + (R(s - T) + K') \\
&\leq (\beta_{R,T}(t) + K') + (\beta_{R,T}(s) + K'),
\end{aligned}
$$

which proves that $\beta_{R,T} + K'$ is sub-additive. Consider next $\beta_{R,T} + K''$. Pick $s = T$ and $t > T$. Then, since $K'' < RT$,

$$
\begin{aligned}
\beta_{R,T}(t + s) + K'' &= \\
\beta_{R,T}(t + T) + K'' &= Rt + K'' = R(t - T) + RT + K'' \\
&> R(t - T) + K'' + K'' = (\beta_{R,T}(t) + K'') + (\beta_{R,T}(s) + K''),
\end{aligned}
$$

which proves that $\beta_{R,T} + K''$ is not sub-additive.

Let us list now some properties of sub-additive functions.

Theorem 3.1.9 (Properties of sub-additive functions). *Let $f, g \in \mathcal{F}$.*

- *(Star-shaped functions passing through the origin) If f is star-shaped with $f(0) = 0$, then f is sub-additive.*

- *(Sum of sub-additive functions) If f and g are sub-additive, so is $(f + g)$.*

- **(Min-plus convolution of sub-additive functions)** If f and g are sub-additive, so is $(f \otimes g)$.

The first property also implies that concave functions passing through the origin are sub-additive. The proof of the second property is simple and left to the reader, we prove the two others.

Proof: (Star-shaped functions passing through the origin) Let $s, t \geq 0$ be given. If s or $t = 0$, one clearly has that $f(s+t) = f(s) + f(t)$. Assume next that $s, t > 0$. As f is star-shaped,

$$f(s) \geq \frac{s}{s+t} f(s+t)$$
$$f(t) \geq \frac{t}{s+t} f(s+t)$$

which sum up to give $f(s) + f(t) \geq f(s+t)$. (Min-plus convolution of sub-additive functions) Let $s, t \geq 0$ be given. Then

$$
\begin{aligned}
&(f \otimes g)(s) + (f \otimes g)(t) \\
&= \inf_{0 \leq u \leq s} \{f(s-u) + g(u)\} + \inf_{0 \leq v \leq t} \{f(t-v) + g(v)\} \\
&= \inf_{0 \leq u \leq s} \inf_{0 \leq v \leq t} \{f(s-u) + f(t-v) + g(u) + g(v)\} \\
&\geq \inf_{0 \leq u \leq s} \inf_{0 \leq v \leq t} \{f(s+t-(u+v)) + g(u+v)\} \\
&= \inf_{0 \leq u+v \leq s+t} \{f(s+t-(u+v)) + g(u+v)\} \\
&= (f \otimes g)(t+s).
\end{aligned}
$$

$\square$

The minimum of any number of star-shaped (resp. concave) functions is still a star-shaped (resp. concave) function. If one of them passes through the origin, it is therefore a sub-additive function: for example, as already mentioned earlier, the concave piecewise linear function f_1 given by (3.1) is sub-additive. On the other hand the minimum of two sub-additive functions is not, in general, sub-additive. Take for example the minimum between a rate latency function $\beta_{R',T}$ and function f_2 given by (3.2), when $R' = 2R/3$. with R, T as defined in (3.2). Both functions are sub-additive, but one can check that $\beta_{R',T} \wedge f_2$ is not.

The first property of the previous theorem tells us that all star-shaped functions are sub-additive. One can check for example that $\beta_{R,T} + K'$ is a star-shaped function (which is not concave), but not $\beta_{R,T} + K''$. One can also wonder if, conversely, all sub-additive functions are star-shaped. The answer is no: take again function f_2 given by (3.2), which is sub-additive. It is not star-shaped, because $f(2T)/2T = R/2 < 2R/3 = f(3T)/3T$.

3.1.8 Sub-additive Closure

Given a function $f \in \mathcal{F}$, if $f(0) = 0$, then $f \geq f \otimes f \geq 0$. By repeating this operation, we will get a sequence of functions that are each time smaller and converges to some limiting function that, as we will see, is the largest sub-additive function smaller than f and zero in $t = 0$, and is called sub-additive closure of f. The formal definition is as follows.

Definition 3.1.12 (Sub-additive closure). *Let f be a function or a sequence of $\mathcal{F}$. Denote $f^{(n)}$ the function obtained by repeating $(n-1)$ convolutions of f with itself. By convention, $f^{(0)} = \delta_0$, so that $f^{(1)} = f$, $f^{(2)} = f \otimes f$, etc. Then the sub-additive closure of f, denoted by $\overline{f}$, is defined by*

$$\overline{f} = \delta_0 \wedge f \wedge (f \otimes f) \wedge (f \otimes f \otimes f) \wedge \ldots = \inf_{n \geq 0} \left\{ f^{(n)} \right\}. \tag{3.13}$$

Example. Let us compute the sub-additive closure of the two functions $\beta_{R,T} + K'$ and $\beta_{R,T} + K''$, represented respectively on the left and right of Figure 3.5. Note first that Rule 7 of Theorem 3.1.5 and Rule 9 of Theorem 3.1.6 yield that for any $K > 0$,

$$(\beta_{R,T} + K) \otimes (\beta_{R,T} + K) = (\beta_{R,T} \otimes \beta_{R,T}) + 2K = \beta_{R,2T} + 2K.$$

Repeating this convolution n times yields that for all integers $n \geq 1$

$$(\beta_{R,T} + K)^{(n)} = \beta_{R,nT} + nK.$$

Now, if $K = K' > RT$ and $t \leq nT$,

$$\begin{aligned}
\beta_{R,nT} + nK' &= nK' > (n-1)RT + K' = R(nT - T) + K' \\
&\geq R[t - T]^+ + K' = \beta_{R,T} + K',
\end{aligned}$$

whereas if $t > nT$

$$\begin{aligned}
\beta_{R,nT} + nK' &= R(t - nT) + nK' = R(t - T) + (n-1)(K' - RT) + K' \\
&> R(t - T) + K' = \beta_{R,T} + K'
\end{aligned}$$

so that $(\beta_{R,T} + K')^{(n)} \geq \beta_{R,T} + K'$ for all $n \geq 1$. Therefore (3.13) becomes

$$\overline{\beta_{R,T} + K'} = \delta_0 \wedge \inf_{n \geq 1} \left\{ (\beta_{R,T} + K')^{(n)} \right\} = \delta_0 \wedge (\beta_{R,T} + K'),$$

and is shown on the left of Figure 3.6. On the other hand, if $K = K'' < RT$, the infimum in the previous equation is not reached in $n = 1$ for every $t > 0$, so that the sub-additive closure is now expressed by

$$\overline{\beta_{R,T} + K''} = \delta_0 \wedge \inf_{n \geq 1} \left\{ (\beta_{R,T} + K'')^{(n)} \right\} = \delta_0 \wedge \inf_{n \geq 1} \left\{ (\beta_{R,nT} + nK'') \right\},$$

and is shown on the right of Figure 3.6.

Among all the sub-additive functions that are smaller than f and that are zero in $t = 0$, there is one that is an upper bound for all others; it is equal to $\overline{f}$, as established by the following theorem.

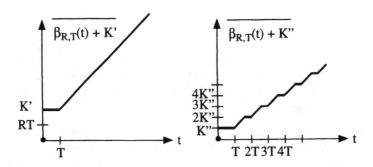

Figure 3.6: The sub-additive closure of functions $\beta_{R,T} + K'$ (left) and $\beta_{R,T} + K''$ (right), when $K'' < RT < K'$.

Theorem 3.1.10 (Sub-additive closure). *Let f be a function or a sequence of $\mathcal{F}$, and let $\overline{f}$ be its sub-additive closure. Then (i) $\overline{f} \le f$, $\overline{f} \in \mathcal{F}$ and $\overline{f}$ is sub-additive. (ii) if function $g \in \mathcal{F}$ is sub-additive, with $g(0) = 0$ and $g \le f$, then $g \le \overline{f}$.*

Proof: (i) It is obvious from Definition 3.1.12, that $\overline{f} \le f$. By repeating $(n-1)$ times Rule 1 of Theorem 3.1.5, one has that $f^{(n)} \in \mathcal{F}$ for all $n \ge 1$. As $f^{(0)} = \delta_0 \in \mathcal{F}$ too, $\overline{f} = \inf_{n \ge 0}\{f^{(n)}\} \in \mathcal{F}$. Let us show next that $\overline{f}$ is sub-additive. For any integers $n, m \ge 0$, and for any $s, t \ge 0$,

$$f^{(n+m)}(t+s) = (f^{(n)} \otimes f^{(m)})(t+s) = \inf_{0 \le u \le t+s}\{f^{(n)}(t+s-u) + f^{(m)}(u)\}$$
$$\le f^{(n)}(t) + f^{(m)}(s)$$

so that

$$\overline{f}(t+s) = \inf_{n+m \ge 0}\{f^{(n+m)}(t+s)\} = \inf_{n,m \ge 0}\{f^{(n+m)}(t+s)\}$$
$$\le \inf_{n,m \ge 0}\{f^{(n)}(t) + f^{(m)}(s)\}$$
$$= \inf_{n \ge 0}\{f^{(n)}(t)\} + \inf_{m \ge 0}\{f^{(m)}(s)\} = \overline{f}(t) + \overline{f}(s)$$

which shows that $\overline{f}$ is sub-additive. (ii) Next, suppose that $g \in \mathcal{F}$ is sub-additive, $g(0) = 0$ and $g \le f$. Suppose that for some $n \ge 1$, $f^{(n)} \ge g$. Clearly, this holds for $n = 0$ (because $g(0) = 0$ implies that $g \le \delta_0 = f^{(0)}$) and for $n = 1$. Now, this assumption and the sub-additivity of g yield that for any $0 \le s \le t$, $f^{(n)}(t-s) + f(s) \ge g(t-s) + g(s) \ge g(t)$ and hence that $f^{(n+1)}(t) \ge g(t)$. By recursion on n, $f^{(n)} \ge g$ for all $n \ge 0$, and therefore $\overline{f} = \inf_{n \ge 0}\{f^{(n)}\} \ge g$. $\qquad\square$

Corollary 3.1.1 (Sub-additive closure of a sub-additive function). *Let $f \in \mathcal{F}$. Then the three following statements are equivalent: (i) $f(0) = 0$ and f is sub-additive (ii) $f \otimes f = f$ (iii) $\overline{f} = f$.*

Proof: (i) $\Rightarrow$ (ii) follows immediately from from Definition 3.1.11. (ii) $\Rightarrow$ (iii): first note that $f \otimes f = f$ implies that $f^{(n)} = f$ for all $n \geq 1$. Second, note that $(f \otimes f)(0) = f(0) + f(0)$, which implies that $f(0) = 0$. Therefore $\overline{f} = \inf_{n \geq 0}\{f^{(n)}\} = \delta_0 \wedge f = f$. (iii) $\Rightarrow$ (i) follows from Theorem 3.1.10. $\square$

The following theorem establishes some additional useful properties of the sub-additive closure of a function.

Theorem 3.1.11 (Other properties of sub-additive closure). *Let $f, g \in \mathcal{F}$*

- *(Isotonicity) If $f \leq g$ then $\overline{f} \leq \overline{g}$.*

- *(Sub-additive closure of a minimum) $\overline{f \wedge g} = \overline{f} \otimes \overline{g}$.*

- *(Sub-additive closure of a convolution) $\overline{f \otimes g} \geq \overline{f} \otimes \overline{g}$. If $f(0) = g(0) = 0$ then $\overline{f \otimes g} = \overline{f} \otimes \overline{g}$.*

Proof: (Isotonocity) Suppose that we have shown that for some $n \geq 1$, $f^{(n)} \geq g^{(n)}$ (Clearly, this holds for $n = 0$ and for $n = 1$). Then applying Theorem 3.1.7 we get

$$f^{(n+1)} = f^{(n)} \otimes f \geq g^{(n)} \otimes g = g^{(n+1)},$$

which implies by recursion on n that $\overline{f} \leq \overline{g}$. (Sub-additive closure of a minimum) One easily shows, using Theorem 3.1.5, that

$$(f \wedge g)^{(2)} = (f \otimes f) \wedge (f \otimes g) \wedge (g \otimes g).$$

Suppose that we have shown that for some $n \geq 0$, the expansion of $(f \wedge g)^{(n)}$ is

$$(f \wedge g)^{(n)} =$$
$$f^{(n)} \wedge (f^{(n-1)} \otimes g) \wedge (f^{(n-2)} \otimes g^{(2)}) \wedge \ldots \wedge g^{(n)} =$$
$$\inf_{0 \leq k \leq n} \left\{ f^{(n-k)} \otimes g^{(k)} \right\}.$$

Then

$$
\begin{aligned}
(f \wedge g)^{(n+1)} &= (f \wedge g) \otimes (f \wedge g)^{(n)} = \left\{ f \otimes (f \wedge g)^{(n)} \right\} \wedge \left\{ g \otimes (f \wedge g)^{(n)} \right\} \\
&= \inf_{0 \leq k \leq n} \left\{ f^{(n+1-k)} \otimes g^{(k)} \right\} \wedge \inf_{0 \leq k \leq n} \left\{ f^{(n-k)} \otimes g^{(k+1)} \right\} \\
&= \inf_{0 \leq k \leq n} \left\{ f^{(n+1-k)} \otimes g^{(k)} \right\} \wedge \inf_{1 \leq k' \leq n+1} \left\{ f^{(n+1-k')} \otimes g^{(k')} \right\} \\
&= \inf_{0 \leq k \leq n+1} \left\{ f^{(n+1-k)} \otimes g^{(k)} \right\}
\end{aligned}
$$

which establishes the recursion for all $n \geq 0$. Therefore

$$\overline{f \wedge g} = \inf_{n \geq 0} \inf_{0 \leq k \leq n} \left\{ f^{(n-k)} \otimes g^{(k)} \right\} = \inf_{k \geq 0} \inf_{n \geq k} \left\{ f^{(n-k)} \otimes g^{(k)} \right\}$$

$$= \inf_{k \geq 0} \inf_{l \geq 0} \left\{ f^{(l)} \otimes g^{(k)} \right\} = \inf_{k \geq 0} \left\{ \inf_{l \geq 0} \{ f^{(l)} \} \otimes g^{(k)} \right\}$$

$$= \inf_{k \geq 0} \left\{ \overline{f} \otimes g^{(k)} \right\} = \overline{f} \otimes \inf_{k \geq 0} \{ g^{(k)} \} = \overline{f} \otimes \overline{g}.$$

(Sub-additive closure of a convolution) Using the same recurrence argument as above, one easily shows that $(f \otimes g)^{(n)} = f^{(n)} \otimes g^{(n)}$, and hence that

$$\overline{f \otimes g} = \inf_{n \geq 0} \left\{ (f \otimes g)^{(n)} \right\} = \inf_{n \geq 0} \left\{ f^{(n)} \otimes g^{(n)} \right\}$$

$$\geq \inf_{n,m \geq 0} \left\{ f^{(n)} \otimes g^{(m)} \right\}$$

$$= \left(\inf_{n \geq 0} \left\{ f^{(n)} \right\} \right) \otimes \left(\inf_{m \geq 0} \left\{ g^{(m)} \right\} \right) = \overline{f} \otimes \overline{g}. \qquad (3.14)$$

If $f(0) = g(0) = 0$, Rule 8 in Theorem 3.1.6 yields that $f \otimes g \leq f \wedge g$, and therefore that $\overline{f \otimes g} \leq \overline{f \wedge g}$. Now we have just shown above that $\overline{f \wedge g} = \overline{f} \otimes \overline{g}$, so that

$$\overline{f \otimes g} \leq \overline{f} \otimes \overline{g}.$$

Combining this result with (3.14), we get $\overline{f \otimes g} = \overline{f} \otimes \overline{g}$. $\square$

Let us conclude this section with an example illustrating the effect that a difference in taking t continuous or discrete may have. This example is the computation of the sub-additive closure of

$$f(t) = \begin{cases} t^2 & \text{if} \quad t > 0 \\ 0 & \text{if} \quad t \leq 0 \end{cases}$$

Suppose first that $t \in \mathbb{R}$. Then we compute that

$$(f \otimes f)(t) = \inf_{0 \leq s \leq t} \left\{ (t - s)^2 + s^2 \right\} = (t/2)^2 + (t/2)^2 = t^2/2$$

as the infimum is reached in $s = t/2$. By repeating this operation n times, we obtain

$$f^{(n)}(t) = \inf_{0 \leq s \leq t} \left\{ (t - s)^2 + (f^{(n-1)})^2(s) \right\} =$$

$$\inf_{0 \leq s \leq t} \left\{ (t - s)^2 + s^2/(n - 1) \right\} = t^2/n$$

as the infimum is reached in $s = t(1 - 1/n)$. Therefore

$$\overline{f}(t) = \inf_{n \geq 0} \{ t^2/n \} = \lim_{n \to \infty} t^2/n = 0.$$

Consequently, if $t \in \mathbb{R}$, the sub-additive closure of function f is

$$\overline{f} = 0,$$

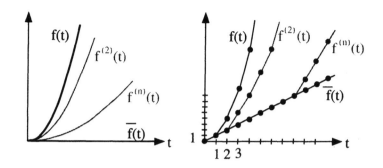

Figure 3.7: The sub-additive closure of $f(t) = t\lambda_1(t)$, when $t \in \mathbb{R}$ (left) and when $t \in \mathbb{Z}$ (right).

as shown on the left of Figure 3.7.

Now, if $t \in \mathbb{Z}$, the sequence $f(t)$ is convex and piecewise linear, as we can always connect the different successive points (t, t^2) for all $t = 0, 1, 2, 3, \ldots$: the resulting graph appears as a succession of segments of slopes equal to $(2t + 1)$ (the first segment in particular has slope 1), and of projections on the horizontal axis having a length equal to 1, as shown on the right of Figure 3.7. Therefore we can apply Rule 9 of Theorem 3.1.6, which yields that $f \otimes f$ is obtained by doubling the length of the different linear segments of f, and putting them end-to-end by increasing slopes. The analytical expression of the resulting sequence is

$$(f \otimes f)(t) = \min_{0 \leq s \leq t} \left\{ (t - s)^2 + s^2 \right\} = \lceil t^2/2 \rceil.$$

Sequence $f^{(2)} = f \otimes f$ is again convex and piecewise linear. Note the first segment has slope 1, but has now a double length. If we repeat n times this convolution, it will result in a convex, piecewise linear sequence $f^{(n)}(t)$ whose first segment has slope 1 and horizontal length n:

$$f^{(n)}(t) = t \quad \text{if } 0 \leq t \leq n,$$

as shown on the right of Figure 3.7. Consequently, the sub-additive closure of sequence f is obtained by letting $n \to \infty$, and is therefore $\overline{f}(t) = t$ for $t \geq 0$. Therefore, if $t \in \mathbb{Z}$,

$$\overline{f} = \lambda_1.$$

3.1.9 Min-plus Deconvolution

The dual operation (in a sense that will clarified later on) of the min-plus convolution is the min-plus deconvolution. Similar considerations as the ones of Subsection 3.1.1 can be made on the difference between a sup and a max. Notation $\vee$ stands for sup or, if it exists, for max: $a \vee b = \max\{a, b\}$.

Definition 3.1.13 (Min-plus deconvolution). *Let f and g be two functions or sequences of $\mathcal{F}$. The min-plus deconvolution of f by g is the function*

$$(f \oslash g)(t) = \sup_{u \geq 0} \{f(t + u) - g(u)\}. \tag{3.15}$$

If both $f(t)$ and $g(t)$ are infinite for some t, then Equation (3.15) is not defined. Contrary to min-plus convolution, function $(f \oslash g)(t)$ is not necessarily zero for $t \leq 0$, and hence this operation is not closed in $\mathcal{F}$, as shown by the following example.

Example. Consider again the two functions $\gamma_{r,b}$ and $\beta_{R,T}$, with $0 < r < R$, and let us compute the min-plus deconvolution of $\gamma_{r,b}$ by $\beta_{R,T}$. We have that

$$
\begin{aligned}
&(\gamma_{r,b} \oslash \beta_{R,T})(t) \\
&= \sup_{u \geq 0} \left\{ \gamma_{r,b}(t + u) - R[u - T]^+ \right\} \\
&= \sup_{0 \leq u \leq T} \left\{ \gamma_{r,b}(t + u) - R[u - T]^+ \right\} \vee \sup_{u > T} \left\{ \gamma_{r,b}(t + u) - R[u - T]^+ \right\} \\
&= \sup_{0 \leq u \leq T} \left\{ \gamma_{r,b}(t + u) \right\} \vee \sup_{u > T} \left\{ \gamma_{r,b}(t + u) - Ru + RT \right\} \\
&= \left\{ \gamma_{r,b}(t + T) \right\} \vee \sup_{u > T} \left\{ \gamma_{r,b}(t + u) - Ru + RT \right\}. \tag{3.16}
\end{aligned}
$$

Let us first compute this expression for $t \leq -T$. Then $\gamma_{r,b}(t + T) = 0$ and (3.16) becomes

$$
\begin{aligned}
&(\gamma_{r,b} \oslash \beta_{R,T})(t) \\
&= 0 \vee \sup_{T < u \leq -t} \left\{ \gamma_{r,b}(t + u) - Ru + RT \right\} \\
&\qquad \vee \sup_{u > -t} \left\{ \gamma_{r,b}(t + u) - Ru + RT \right\} \\
&= 0 \vee \sup_{T < u \leq -t} \left\{ 0 - Ru + RT \right\} \vee \sup_{u > -t} \left\{ b + r(t + u) - Ru + RT \right\} \\
&= 0 \vee 0 \vee \left\{ b + Rt + RT \right\} = [b + R(t + T)]^+.
\end{aligned}
$$

Let us next compute $(\gamma_{r,b} \oslash \beta_{R,T})(t)$ for $t > -T$. Then (3.16) becomes

$$
\begin{aligned}
(\gamma_{r,b} \oslash \beta_{R,T})(t) &= \left\{ b + r(t + T) \right\} \vee \sup_{u > T} \left\{ b + r(t + u) - Ru + RT \right\} \\
&= \left\{ b + r(t + T) \right\} \vee \left\{ b + r(t + T) \right\} = b + r(t + T).
\end{aligned}
$$

The result is shown in Figure 3.8.

Let us now state some properties of $\oslash$ (Other properties will be given in the next section).

Theorem 3.1.12 (Properties of $\oslash$). *Let $f, g, h \in \mathcal{F}$.*

- *Rule 11 (Isotonicity of $\oslash$) If $f \leq g$, then $f \oslash h \leq g \oslash h$ and $h \oslash f \geq h \oslash g$.*

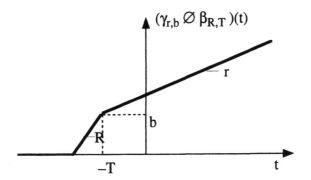

Figure 3.8: Function $\gamma_{r,b} \oslash \beta_{R,T}$ when $0 < r < R$.

- **Rule 12 (Composition of $\oslash$)** $(f \oslash g) \oslash h = f \oslash (g \otimes h)$.

- **Rule 13 (Composition of $\oslash$ and $\otimes$)** $(f \otimes g) \oslash g \leq f \otimes (g \oslash g)$.

- **Rule 14 (Duality between $\oslash$ and $\otimes$)** $f \oslash g \leq h$ if and only if $f \leq g \otimes h$.

- **Rule 15 (Self-deconvolution)** $(f \oslash f)$ is a sub-additive function of $\mathcal{F}$ such that $(f \oslash f)(0) = 0$.

Proof: (Rule 11) If $f \leq g$, then for any $h \in \mathcal{F}$

$$(f \oslash h)(t) = \sup_{u \geq 0} \{f(t+u) - h(u)\} \leq \sup_{u \geq 0} \{g(t+u) - h(u)\} = (g \oslash h)(t)$$

$$(h \oslash f)(t) = \sup_{u \geq 0} \{h(t+u) - f(u)\} \geq \sup_{u \geq 0} \{h(t+u) - g(u)\} = (h \oslash g)(t).$$

(Rule 12) One computes that

$$
\begin{aligned}
((f \oslash g) \oslash h)(t) &= \sup_{u \geq 0} \{(f \oslash g)(t+u) - h(u)\} \\
&= \sup_{u \geq 0} \left\{ \sup_{v \geq 0} \{f(t+u+v) - g(v)\} - h(u) \right\} \\
&= \sup_{u \geq 0} \left\{ \sup_{v' \geq u} \{f(t+v') - g(v'-u)\} - h(u) \right\} \\
&= \sup_{u \geq 0\, v' \geq u} \{f(t+v') - \{g(v'-u) + h(u)\}\} \\
&= \sup_{v' \geq 0\, 0 \leq u \leq v'} \{f(t+v') - \{g(v'-u) + h(u)\}\} \\
&= \sup_{v' \geq 0} \left\{ f(t+v') - \inf_{0 \leq u \leq v'} \{g(v'-u) + h(u)\} \right\} \\
&= \sup_{v' \geq 0} \{f(t+v') - (g \otimes h)(v')\} = (f \oslash (g \otimes h))(t).
\end{aligned}
$$

(Rule 13) One computes that

$$
\begin{aligned}
((f \otimes g) \oslash g)(t) &= \sup_{u \geq 0} \{(f \otimes g)(t + u) - g(u)\} \\
&= \sup_{u \geq 0} \inf_{0 \leq s \leq t+u} \{f(t + u - s) + g(s) - g(u)\} \\
&= \sup_{u \geq 0} \inf_{-u \leq s' \leq t} \{f(t - s') + g(s' + u) - g(u)\} \\
&\leq \sup_{u \geq 0} \inf_{0 \leq s' \leq t} \{f(t - s') + g(s' + u) - g(u)\} \\
&\leq \sup_{u \geq 0} \inf_{0 \leq s' \leq t} \left\{ f(t - s') + \sup_{v \geq 0} \{g(s' + v) - g(v)\} \right\} \\
&= \inf_{0 \leq s' \leq t} \left\{ f(t - s') + \sup_{v \geq 0} \{g(s' + v) - g(v)\} \right\} \\
&= \inf_{0 \leq s' \leq t} \{f(t - s') + (g \oslash g)(s')\} = (f \otimes (g \oslash g))(t).
\end{aligned}
$$

(Rule 14) Suppose first that $(f \oslash g)(s) \leq h(s)$ for all s. Take any $s, v \geq 0$. Then

$$
f(s + v) - g(v) \leq \sup_{u \geq 0} \{f(s + u) - g(u)\} = (f \oslash g)(s) \leq h(s)
$$

or equivalently,

$$
f(s + v) \leq g(v) + h(s).
$$

Let $t = s + v$. The former inequality can be written as

$$
f(t) \leq g(t - s) + h(s).
$$

As it is verified for all $t \geq s \geq 0$, it is also verified in particular for the value of s that achieves the infimum of the right-hand side of this inequality. Therefore it is equivalent to

$$
f(t) \leq \inf_{0 \leq s \leq t} \{g(t - s) + h(s)\} = (g \otimes h)(t)
$$

for all $t \geq 0$. Suppose now that for all v, $f(v) \leq (g \otimes h)(v)$. Pick any $t \in \mathbb{R}$. Then, since $g, h \in \mathcal{F}$,

$$
f(v) \leq \inf_{0 \leq s \leq v} \{g(v - s) + h(s)\} = \inf_{s \in \mathbb{R}} \{g(v - s) + h(s)\} \leq g(t - v) + h(t).
$$

Let $u = t - v$, the former inequality can be written as

$$
f(t + u) - g(u) \leq h(t).
$$

As this is true for all u, it is also verified in particular for the value of u that achieves the supremum of the left-hand side of this inequality. Therefore it is equivalent to

$$
\sup_{u \in \mathbb{R}} \{f(t + u) - g(u)\} \leq h(t).
$$

Now if $u < 0$, $g(u) = 0$, so that $\sup_{u<0}\{f(t+u) - g(u)\} = f(t)$ and the former inequality is identical to

$$\sup_{u \geq 0}\{f(t+u) - g(u)\} \leq h(t)$$

for all t. (Rule 15) It is immediate to check that $(f \oslash f)(0) = 0$ and that $f \oslash f$ is wide-sense increasing. Now,

$$
\begin{aligned}
&(f \oslash f)(s) + (f \oslash f)(t) \\
&= \sup_{u \geq 0}\{f(t+u) - f(u)\} + \sup_{v \geq 0}\{f(s+v) - f(v)\} \\
&= \sup_{u \geq 0}\{f(t+u) - f(u)\} + \sup_{w \geq -t}\{f(s+t+w) - f(t+w)\} \\
&\geq \sup_{w \geq 0}\left\{\sup_{u \geq 0}\{f(t+u) - f(u) + f(s+t+w) - f(t+w)\}\right\} \\
&\geq \sup_{w \geq 0}\{f(t+w) - f(w) + f(s+t+w) - f(t+w)\} \\
&= (f \oslash f)(s+t).
\end{aligned}
$$

$\square$

Let us conclude this section by a special property that applies to self-deconvolution of sub-additive functions.

Theorem 3.1.13 (Self-deconvolution of sub-additive functions). *Let $f \in \mathcal{F}$. Then $f(0) = 0$ and f is sub-additive if and only if $f \oslash f = f$.*

Proof: ($\Rightarrow$) If f is sub-additive, then for all $t, u \geq 0$, $f(t+u) - f(u) \leq f(t)$ and therefore for all $t \geq 0$,

$$(f \oslash f)(t) = \sup_{u \geq 0}\{f(t+u) - f(u)\} \leq f(t).$$

On the other hand, if $f(0) = 0$,

$$(f \oslash f)(t) = \sup_{u \geq 0}\{f(t+u) - f(u)\} \geq f(t) - f(0) = f(t).$$

Combining both equations, we get that $f \oslash f = f$. ($\Leftarrow$) Suppose now that $f \oslash f = f$. Then $f(0) = (f \oslash f)(0) = 0$ and for any $t, u \geq 0$, $f(t) = (f \oslash f)(t) \geq f(t+u) - f(u)$ so that $f(t) + f(u) \geq f(t+u)$, which shows that f is sub-additive. $\square$

3.1.10 Representation of Min-plus Deconvolution by Time Inversion

Min-plus deconvolution can be represented in the time inverted domain by min-plus convolution, for functions that have a finite lifetime. Function $g \in \mathcal{G}$ has a finite lifetime if there exist some finite T_0 and T such that $g(t) = 0$ if $t \leq T_0$ and $g(t) = g(T)$ for $t \geq T$. Call $\widehat{\mathcal{G}}$ the subset of $\mathcal{G}$, which contains functions having a finite lifetime. For function $g \in \widehat{\mathcal{G}}$, we use the notation $g(+\infty)$ as a shorthand for $\sup_{t \in \mathbb{R}}\{g(t)\} = \lim_{t \to +\infty} g(t)$.

Lemma 3.1.1. *Let* $f \in \mathcal{F}$ *be such that* $\lim_{t \to +\infty} f(t) = +\infty$. *For any* $g \in \widehat{\mathcal{G}}$, $g \oslash f$ *is also in* $\widehat{\mathcal{G}}$ *and* $(g \oslash f)(+\infty) = g(+\infty)$.

Proof: Define $L = g(+\infty)$ and call T a number such that $g(t) = L$ for $t \geq T$. $f(0) \geq 0$ implies that $g \oslash f \leq g(+\infty) = g(L)$. Thus

$$(g \oslash f)(t) \leq L \text{ for } t \geq T. \tag{3.17}$$

Now since $\lim_{t \to +\infty} f(t) = +\infty$, there is some $T_1 > T$ such that $f(t) \geq L$ for all $t > T_1$. Now let $t > 2T_1$. If $u > T_1$, then $f(u) \geq L$. Otherwise, $u \leq T_1$ thus $t - u \geq t - T_1 > T_1$ thus $g(t - u) \geq L$. Thus in all cases $f(u) + g(t - u) \geq L$. Thus we have shown that

$$(g \otimes f)(t) \geq L \text{ for } t > 2T_1. \tag{3.18}$$

Combining (3.17) and (3.18) shows the lemma.   □

Definition 3.1.14 (Time Inversion). *For a fixed* $T \in [0, +\infty[$, *the inversion operator* Φ_T *is defined on* $\widehat{\mathcal{G}}$ *by:*

$$\Phi_T(f)(g) = g(+\infty) - g(T - t)$$

Graphically, time inversion can be obtained by a rotation of $180°$ around the point $(\frac{T}{2}, \frac{g(+\infty)}{2})$. It is simple to check that $\Phi_T(g)$ is in $\widehat{\mathcal{G}}$, that time inversion is symmetrical ($\Phi_T(\Phi_T(g)) = g$) and preserves the total value ($\Phi_T(g)(+\infty) = g(+\infty)$). Lastly, for any α and T, α is an arrival curve for g if and only if α is an arrival curve for $\Phi_T(g)$.

Theorem 3.1.14 (Representation of Deconvolution by Time Inversion). *Let* $g \in \widehat{\mathcal{G}}$, *and let* T *be such that* $g(T) = g(+\infty)$. *Let* $f \in \mathcal{F}$ *be such that* $\lim_{t \to +\infty} f(t) = +\infty$. *Then*

$$g \oslash f = \Phi_T(\Phi_T(g) \otimes f) \tag{3.19}$$

The theorem says that $g \oslash f$ can be computed by first inverting time, then computing the min-plus convolution between f, and the time-inverted function g, and then inverting time again. Figure 3.9 shows a graphical illustration.

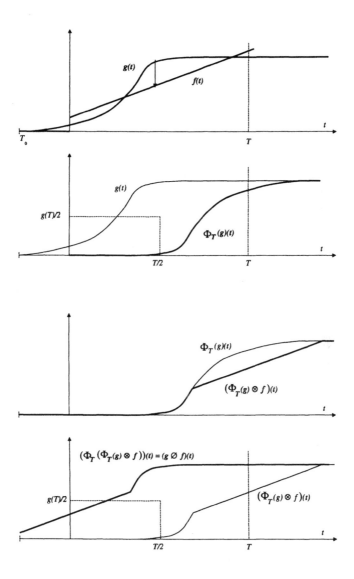

Figure 3.9: Representation of the min-plus deconvolution of g by $f = \gamma_{r,b}$ by time-inversion. From top to bottom: functions f and g, function $\Phi_T(g)$, function $\Phi_T(g) \otimes f$ and finally function $g \oslash f = \Phi_T(\Phi_T(g) \otimes f)$.

Proof: The proof consists in computing the right handside in Equation (3.19). Call $\hat{g} = \Phi_T(g)$. We have, by definition of the inversion

$$\Phi_T(\Phi_T(g) \otimes f) = \Phi_T(\hat{g} \otimes f) = (\hat{g} \otimes f)(+\infty) - (\hat{g} \otimes f)(T - t)$$

Now from Lemma 3.1.1 and the preservation of total value:

$$(\hat{g} \otimes f)(+\infty) = \hat{g}(+\infty) = g(+\infty)$$

Thus, the right-handside in Equation (3.19) is equal to

$$g(+\infty) - (\hat{g} \otimes f)(T - t) = g(+\infty) - \inf_{u \geq 0} \{\hat{g}(T - t - u) + f(u)\}$$

Again by definition of the inversion, it is equal to

$$g(+\infty) - \inf_{u \geq 0} \{g(+\infty) - g(t + u) + f(u)\} = \sup_{u \geq 0} \{g(t + u) - f(u)\}.$$

$$\square$$

3.1.11   Vertical and Horizontal Deviations

The deconvolution operator allows to easily express two very important quantities in network calculus, which are the maximal vertical and horizontal deviations between the graphs of two curves f and g of $\mathcal{F}$. The mathematical definition of these two quantities is as follows.

Definition 3.1.15 (Vertical and horizontal deviations). *Let f and g be two functions or sequences of $\mathcal{F}$. The vertical deviation $v(f, g)$ and horizontal deviation $h(f, g)$ are defined as*

$$v(f, g) = \sup_{t \geq 0} \{f(t) - g(t)\} \tag{3.20}$$

$$h(f, g) = \sup_{t \geq 0} \{\inf \{d \geq 0 \text{ such that } f(t) \leq g(t + d)\}\}. \tag{3.21}$$

Figure 3.10 illustrates these two quantities on an example.

Note that (3.20) can be recast as

$$v(f, g) = (f \oslash g)(0) \tag{3.22}$$

whereas (3.20) is equivalent to requiring that $h(f, g)$ is the smallest $d \geq 0$ such that for all $t \geq 0$, $f(t) \leq g(t + d)$ and can therefore be recast as

$$h(f, g) = \inf \{d \geq 0 \text{ such that } (f \oslash g)(-d) \leq 0\}.$$

Now the horizontal deviation can be more easily computed from the pseudo-inverse of g. Indeed, Definition 3.1.7 yields that

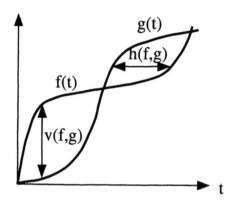

Figure 3.10: The horizontal and vertical deviations between functions f and g.

$$\begin{aligned}
g^{-1}(f(t)) &= \inf\{\Delta \text{ such that } g(\Delta) \geq f(t)\} \\
&= \inf\{d \geq 0 \text{ such that } g(t+d) \geq f(t)\} + t
\end{aligned}$$

so that (3.21) can be expressed as

$$h(f,g) = \sup_{t \geq 0}\{g^{-1}(f(t)) - t\} = (g^{-1}(f) \oslash \lambda_1)(0). \tag{3.23}$$

We have therefore the following expression of the horizontal deviation between f and g:

Proposition 3.1.1 (Horizontal deviation).

$$h(f,g) = \sup_{t \geq 0}\{g^{-1}(f(t)) - t\}.$$

3.2 Max-plus Calculus

Similar definitions, leading to similar properties, can be derived if we replace the infimum (or minimum, it is exists) by a supremum (or maximum, if it exists). We use the notation $\vee$ for denoting sup or max. In particular, one can show that $(\mathbb{R} \cup \{-\infty\}, \vee, +)$ is also a dioid, and construct a max-plus convolution and deconvolution, which are defined as follows.

3.2.1 Max-plus Convolution and Deconvolution

Definition 3.2.1 (Max-plus convolution). *Let f and g be two functions or sequences of $\mathcal{F}$. The max-plus convolution of f and g is the function*

$$(f \overline{\otimes} g)(t) = \sup_{0 \leq s \leq t}\{f(t-s) + g(s)\}. \tag{3.24}$$

(If $t < 0$, $(f \overline{\otimes} g)(t) = 0$).

Definition 3.2.2 (Max-plus deconvolution). *Let f and g be two functions or sequences of $\mathcal{F}$. The max-plus deconvolution of f by g is the function*

$$(f \overline{\oslash} g)(t) = \inf_{u \geq 0} \{f(t + u) - g(u)\}. \tag{3.25}$$

3.2.2   Linearity of Min-plus Deconvolution in Max-plus Algebra

Min-plus deconvolution is, in fact, an operation that is linear in $(\mathbb{R}^+, \vee, +)$. Indeed, one easily shows the following property.

Theorem 3.2.1 (Linearity of $\oslash$ in max-plus algebra). *Let $f, g, h \in \mathcal{F}$.*

- **Rule 16 (Distributivity of $\oslash$ with respect to $\vee$)** $(f \vee g) \oslash h = (f \oslash h) \vee (g \oslash h)$.

- **Rule 17 (Addition of a constant)** *For any $K \in \mathbb{R}^+$, $(f + K) \oslash g = (f \oslash g) + K$.*

Min-plus convolution is not, however, a linear operation in $(\mathbb{R}^+, \vee, +)$, because in general

$$(f \vee g) \otimes h \neq (f \otimes h) \vee (g \otimes h).$$

Indeed, take $f = \beta_{3R,T}$, $g = \lambda_R$ and $h = \lambda_{2R}$ for some $R, T > 0$. Then using Rule 9, one easily computes (see Figure 3.11) that

$$
\begin{aligned}
f \otimes h &= \beta_{3R,T} \otimes \lambda_{2R} = \beta_{2R,T} \\
g \otimes h &= \lambda_R \otimes \lambda_{2R} = \lambda_R \\
(f \vee g) \otimes h &= (\beta_{3R,T} \vee \lambda_R) \otimes \lambda_{2R} = \beta_{2R,3T/4} \vee \lambda_R \\
&\neq \beta_{2R,T} \vee \lambda_R = (f \otimes h) \vee (g \otimes h).
\end{aligned}
$$

Conversely, we have seen that min-plus convolution is a linear operation in $(\mathbb{R}^+, \wedge, +)$, and one easily shows that min–plus deconvolution is not linear in $(\mathbb{R}^+, \wedge, +)$. Finally, let us mention that one can also replace $+$ by $\wedge$, and show that $(\mathbb{R} \cup \{+\infty\} \cup \{-\infty\}, \vee, \wedge)$ is also a dioid. **Remark** *However, as we have seen above, as soon as the three operations $\wedge$, $\vee$ and $+$ are involved in a computation, one must be careful before applying any distribution.*

3.3   Exercises

Exercise 3.1.   *1. Compute $\alpha \otimes \delta$ for any function α*

2. Express the rate-latency function by means of δ and λ functions.

Exercise 3.2.   *1. Compute $\bigotimes_i \beta_i$ when β_i is a rate-latency function*

2. Compute $\beta_1 \otimes \beta_2$ with $\beta_1(t) = R(t - T)^+$ and $\beta_2(t) = (rt + b)1_{\{t>0\}}$

Exercise 3.3.   *1. Is $\otimes$ distributive with respect to the min operator ?*

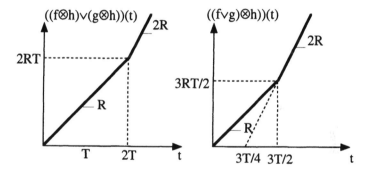

Figure 3.11: Function $(f \otimes h) \vee (g \otimes h)$ (left) and $(f \vee g) \otimes h$ (right) when $f = \beta_{3R,T}$, $g = \lambda_R$ and $h = \lambda_{2R}$ for some $R, T > 0$.

Chapter 4

Min-plus and Max-plus System Theory

In Chapter 3 we have introduced the basic operations to manipulate functions and sequences in Min-Plus or Max-Plus algebra. We have studied in detail the operations of convolution, deconvolution and sub-additive closure. These notions form the mathematical cornerstone on which a first course of network calculus has to be built.

In this chapter, we move one step further, and introduce the theoretical tools to solve more advanced problems in network calculus developed in the second half of the book. The core object in Chapter 3 were *functions and sequences* on which operations could be performed. We will now place ourselves at the level of *operators* mapping an input function (or sequence) to an output function or sequence. Max-plus system theory is developed in detail in [24], here we focus on the results that are needed for the remaining chapters of the book. As in Chapter 3, we focus here Min-Plus System Theory, as Max-Plus System Theory follows easily by replacing minimum by maximum, and infimum by supremum.

4.1 Min-plus and Max-plus Operators

4.1.1 Vector Notations

Up to now, we have only worked with scalar operations on scalar functions in $\mathcal{F}$ or $\mathcal{G}$. In this chapter, we will also work with vectors and matrices. The operations are extended in a straightforward manner.

Let J be a finite, positive integer. For vectors $\vec{z}, \vec{z'} \in \mathbb{R}^{+\,J}$, we define $\vec{z} \wedge \vec{z'}$ as the coordinate-wise minimum of $\vec{z}$ and $\vec{z'}$, and similarly for the $+$ operator. We write $\vec{z} \leq \vec{z'}$ with the meaning that $z_j \leq z'_j$ for $1 \leq j \leq J$. Note that the comparison so defined is not a total order, that is, we cannot guarantee that either $\vec{z} \leq \vec{z'}$ or

$\vec{z'} \leq \vec{z}$ holds. For a constant K, we note $\vec{z} + K$ the vector defined by adding K to *all* elements of $\vec{z}$.

We denote by $\mathcal{G}^J$ the set of J-dimensional wide-sense increasing real-valued functions or sequences of parameter t, and $\mathcal{F}^J$ the subset of functions that are zero for $t < 0$.

For sequences or functions $\vec{x}(t)$, we note similarly $(\vec{x} \wedge \vec{y})(t) = \vec{x}(t) \wedge \vec{y}(t)$ and $(\vec{x} + K)(t) = \vec{x}(t) + K$ for all $t \geq 0$, and write $\vec{x} \leq \vec{y}$ with the meaning that $\vec{x}(t) \leq \vec{y}(t)$ for all t.

For matrices $A, B \in \mathbb{R}^{+\ J} \times \mathbb{R}^{+\ J}$, we define $A \wedge B$ as the entry-wise minimum of A and B. For vector $\vec{z} \in \mathbb{R}^{+\ J}$, the 'multiplication' of vector $\vec{z} \in \mathbb{R}^{+\ J}$ by matrix A is – remember that in min-plus algebra, multiplication is the $+$ operation – by

$$A + \vec{z},$$

and has entries $\min_{1 \leq j \leq J}(a_{ij} + z_j)$. Likewise, the 'product' of two matrices A and B is denoted by $A + B$ and has entries $\min_{1 \leq j \leq J}(a_{ij} + b_{jk})$ for $1 \leq i, k \leq J$.

Here is an example of a 'multiplication' of a vector by a matrix, when $J = 2$

$$\begin{bmatrix} 5 & 3 \\ 1 & 3 \end{bmatrix} + \begin{bmatrix} 2 \\ 1 \end{bmatrix} = \begin{bmatrix} 4 \\ 3 \end{bmatrix}$$

and an example of a matrix 'multiplication' is

$$\begin{bmatrix} 5 & 3 \\ 1 & 3 \end{bmatrix} + \begin{bmatrix} 2 & 4 \\ 1 & 0 \end{bmatrix} = \begin{bmatrix} 4 & 3 \\ 3 & 3 \end{bmatrix}.$$

We denote by $\mathcal{F}^{J^2}$ the set of $J \times J$ matrices whose entries are functions or sequences of $\mathcal{F}$, and similarly for $\mathcal{G}^{J^2}$.

The min-plus convolution of a matrix $A \in \mathcal{F}^{J^2}$ by a vector $\vec{z} \in \mathcal{F}^J$ is the vector of $\mathcal{F}^J$ defined by

$$(A \otimes \vec{z})(t) = \inf_{0 \leq s \leq t} \{A(t - s) + \vec{z}(s)\}$$

and whose J coordinates are thus

$$\min_{1 \leq j \leq J} \{a_{ij} \otimes z_j\}(t) = \inf_{0 \leq s \leq t} \min_{1 \leq j \leq J} \{a_{ij}(t - s) + z_j(s)\}.$$

Likewise, $A \otimes B$ is defined by

$$(A \otimes B)(t) = \inf_{0 \leq s \leq t} \{A(t - s) + B(s)\}$$

and has entries $\min_{1 \leq j \leq J}(a_{ij} \otimes b_{jk})$ for $1 \leq i, k \leq J$.

For example, we have

$$\begin{bmatrix} \lambda_r & \infty \\ \infty & \delta_T \end{bmatrix} \otimes \begin{bmatrix} \gamma_{r/2,b} \\ \delta_{2T} \end{bmatrix} = \begin{bmatrix} \lambda_r \wedge \gamma_{r/2,b} \\ \delta_{3T} \end{bmatrix}$$

and

$$\left[\begin{array}{cc} \lambda_r & \infty \\ \infty & \delta_T \end{array} \right] \otimes \left[\begin{array}{cc} \gamma_{r/2,b} & \gamma_{r,b} \\ \delta_{2T} & \lambda_r \end{array} \right] = \left[\begin{array}{cc} \lambda_r \wedge \gamma_{r/2,b} & \lambda_r \\ \delta_{3T} & \beta_{r,T} \end{array} \right].$$

Finally, we will also need to extend the set of wide-sense increasing functions $\mathcal{G}$ to include non decreasing functions of two arguments. We adopt the following definition (a slightly different definition can be found in [10]).

Definition 4.1.1 (Bivariate wide-sense increasing functions). *We denote by $\tilde{\mathcal{G}}$ the set of bivariate functions (or sequences) such that for all $s' \le s$ and any $t \le t'$*

$$f(t,s) \le f(t,s')$$
$$f(t,s) \le f(t',s).$$

We call such functions bivariate wide-sense increasing functions.

In the multi-dimensional case, we denote by $\tilde{\mathcal{G}}^J$ the set of $J \times J$ matrices whose entries are wide-sense increasing bivariate functions. A matrix of $A(t) \in \mathcal{F}^{J^2}$ is a particular case of a matrix $H(t,s) \in \tilde{\mathcal{G}}^J$, with s set to a fixed value.

4.1.2 Operators

A system is an operator Π mapping an input function or sequence $\vec{x}$ onto an output function or sequence $\vec{y} = \Pi(\vec{x})$. We will always assume in this book that $\vec{x}, \vec{y} \in \mathcal{G}^J$, where J is a fixed, finite, positive integer. This means that each of the J coordinates $x_j(t), y_j(t), 1 \le j \le J$, is a wide-sense increasing function (or sequence) of t.

It is important to mention that Min-plus system theory applies to more general operators, taking $\mathbb{R}^J$ to $\mathbb{R}^J$, where neither the input nor the output functions are required to be wide-sense increasing. This requires minor modifications in the definitions and properties established in this chapter, see [24] for the theory described in a more general setting. In this book, to avoid the unnecessary overhead of new notations and definitions, we decided to expose min-plus system theory for operators taking $\mathcal{G}^J$ to $\mathcal{G}^J$.

Most often, the only operator whose output may not be in $\mathcal{F}^J$ is deconvolution, but all other operators we need will take $\mathcal{F}^J$ to $\mathcal{F}^J$.

Most of the time, the dimension of the input and output is $J = 1$, and the operator takes $\mathcal{F}$ to $\mathcal{F}$. We will speak of a *scalar* operator. In this case, we will drop the arrow on the input and output, and write $y = \Pi(x)$ instead.

We write $\Pi_1 \le \Pi_2$ with the meaning that $\Pi_1(\vec{x}) \le \Pi_2(\vec{x})$ for all $\vec{x}$, which in turn has the meaning that $\Pi_1(\vec{x})(t) \le \Pi_2(\vec{x})(t)$ for all t.

For a set of operators Π_s, indexed by s in some set S, we call $\inf_{s \in S} \Pi_s$ the operator defined by $[\inf_{s \in S} \Pi_s](x(t)) = \inf_{s \in S}[\Pi_s(x(t))]$. For $S = \{1,2\}$ we denote it with $\Pi_1 \wedge \Pi_2$.

We also denote by $\circ$ the composition of two operators:

$$(\Pi_1 \circ \Pi_2)(\vec{x}) = \Pi_1(\Pi_2(\vec{x})).$$

We leave it to the alert reader to check that $\inf_{s \in S} \Pi_s$ and $\Pi_1 \circ \Pi_2$ do map functions in $\mathcal{G}^J$ to functions in $\mathcal{G}^J$.

4.1.3   A Catalog of Operators

Let us mention a few examples of scalar operators of particular interest. The first two have already been studied in detail in Chapter 3, whereas the third was introduced in Section 1.7. The fact that these operators map $\mathcal{G}^J$ into $\mathcal{G}^J$ follows from Chapter 3.

Definition 4.1.2 (Min-plus convolution $\mathcal{C}_\sigma$).

$$\mathcal{C}_\sigma \quad : \quad \mathcal{F} \quad \rightarrow \quad \mathcal{F}$$
$$x(t) \quad \rightarrow \quad y(t) = \mathcal{C}_\sigma(x)(t) = (\sigma \otimes x)(t) = \inf_{0 \le s \le t} \{\sigma(t - s) + x(s)\},$$

for some $\sigma \in \mathcal{F}$.

Definition 4.1.3 (Min-plus deconvolution $\mathcal{D}_\sigma$).

$$\mathcal{D}_\sigma \quad : \quad \mathcal{F} \quad \rightarrow \quad \mathcal{G}$$
$$x(t) \quad \rightarrow \quad y(t) = \mathcal{D}_\sigma(x)(t) = (x \oslash \sigma)(t) = \sup_{u \ge 0} \{x(t + u) - \sigma(u)\},$$

for some $\sigma \in \mathcal{F}$.

Note that Min-plus deconvolution produces an output that does not always belong to $\mathcal{F}$.

Definition 4.1.4 (Packetization $\mathcal{P}_L$).

$$\mathcal{P}_L \quad : \quad \mathcal{F} \quad \rightarrow \quad \mathcal{F}$$
$$x(t) \quad \rightarrow \quad y(t) = \mathcal{P}_L(x)(t) = P^L(x(t)) = \inf_{i \in \mathsf{N}} \{L(i) 1_{L(i+1) > x}\},$$

for some wide-sense increasing sequence L (defined by Definition 1.7.1).

We will also need later on the following operator, whose name will be justified later in this chapter.

Definition 4.1.5 (Linear idempotent operator h_σ).

$$h_\sigma \quad : \quad \mathcal{F} \quad \rightarrow \quad \mathcal{F}$$
$$x(t) \quad \rightarrow \quad y(t) = h_\sigma(x)(t) = \inf_{0 \le s \le t} \{\sigma(t) - \sigma(s) + x(s)\},$$

for some $\sigma \in \mathcal{F}$.

The extension of the scalar operators to the vector case is straightforward. The vector extension of the convolution is for instance:

Definition 4.1.6 (Vector min-plus convolution $\mathcal{C}_\Sigma$).

$$\mathcal{C}_\Sigma \quad : \quad \mathcal{F}^J \quad \rightarrow \quad \mathcal{F}^J$$
$$\vec{x}(t) \quad \rightarrow \quad \vec{y}(t) = \mathcal{C}_\Sigma(\vec{x})(t) = (\Sigma \otimes \vec{x})(t) = \inf_{0 \le s \le t} \{\Sigma(t - s) + \vec{x}(s)\},$$

for some $\Sigma \in \mathcal{F}^{J^2}$.

If the (i, j)th entry of Σ is σ_{ij}, the ith component of $\vec{y}(t)$ reads therefore

$$y_i(t) = \inf_{0 \leq s \leq t} \min_{1 \leq j \leq J} \{\sigma_{ij}(t - s) + x_j(s)\}$$

Let us conclude with the shift operator, which we directly introduce in the vector setting:

Definition 4.1.7 (Shift operator $\mathcal{S}_T$).

$$\begin{aligned} \mathcal{S}_T \; : \quad & \mathcal{G}^J \quad \rightarrow \quad \mathcal{G}^J \\ & \vec{x}(t) \quad \rightarrow \quad \vec{y}(t) = \mathcal{S}_T(\vec{x})(t) = \vec{x}(t - T), \end{aligned}$$

for some $T \in \mathbb{R}$

Let us remark that $\mathcal{S}_0$ is the identity operator: $\mathcal{S}_0(\vec{x}) = \vec{x}$.

4.1.4 Upper and Lower Semi-continuous Operators

We now study a number of properties of min-plus linear operators. We begin with that of upper-semi continuity.

Definition 4.1.8 (Upper semi-continuous operator). *Operator Π is upper semi-continuous if for any (finite or infinite) set of functions or sequences $\{\vec{x}_n\}$, $\vec{x}_n \in \mathcal{G}^J$,*

$$\Pi\left(\inf_n\{\vec{x}_n\}\right) = \inf_n \{\Pi(\vec{x}_n)\}. \tag{4.1}$$

We can check that $\mathcal{C}_\sigma, \mathcal{C}_\Sigma, h_\sigma$ and $\mathcal{S}_T$ are upper semi-continuous. For example, for $\mathcal{C}_\Sigma$, we check indeed that

$$\begin{aligned} \mathcal{C}_\Sigma\left(\inf_n\{\vec{x}_n\}\right)(t) &= \inf_{0 \leq s \leq t} \left\{\Sigma(t - s) + \inf_n\{\vec{x}_n(s)\}\right\} \\ &= \inf_{0 \leq s \leq t} \inf_n \{\Sigma(t - s) + \vec{x}_n(s)\} \\ &= \inf_n \inf_{0 \leq s \leq t} \{\Sigma(t - s) + \vec{x}_n(s)\} \\ &= \inf_n \{\mathcal{C}_\Sigma(\vec{x}_n)(t)\}. \end{aligned}$$

Likewise, noting that $L(i + 1) \leq \inf_{n \in \mathbb{N}}\{x_n\}$ if and only if $L(i + 1) \leq x_n$ for all $n \in \mathbb{N}$, we get that

$$1_{\{L(i+1) \leq \inf_{n \in \mathbb{N}}\{x_n\}\}} = \inf_{n \in \mathbb{N}} 1_{\{L(i+1) \leq x_n\}}$$

and thus we get that $\mathcal{P}_L$ is upper semi-continuous:

$$
\begin{aligned}
\mathcal{P}_L\left(\inf_n\{x_n\}\right) &= \inf_{i\in\mathbb{N}}\left\{L(i)1_{\{L(i+1)>\inf_n\{x_n\}\}}\right\} \\
&= \sup_{i\in\mathbb{N}}\left\{L(i)1_{\{L(i+1)\leq\inf_n\{x_n\}\}}\right\} \\
&= \sup_{i\in\mathbb{N}}\left\{\inf_n\left\{L(i)1_{\{L(i+1)\leq x_n\}}\right\}\right\} \\
&= \inf_{i\in\mathbb{N}}\left\{\inf_n\left\{L(i)1_{\{L(i+1)>x_n\}}\right\}\right\} \\
&= \inf_n\left\{\inf_{i\in\mathbb{N}}\left\{L(i)1_{\{L(i+1)>x_n\}}\right\}\right\} \\
&= \inf_n\left\{\mathcal{P}_L(x_n)\right\}.
\end{aligned}
$$

On the other hand, $\mathcal{D}_\sigma$ is not upper semi-continuous, because its application to an inf would involve the three operations sup, inf and $+$, which do not commute, as we have seen at the end of the previous chapter.

It is easy to show that if Π_1 and Π_2 are upper semi-continuous, so are $\Pi_1 \wedge \Pi_2$ and $\Pi_1 \circ \Pi_2$.

The dual definition of upper semi-continuity is that of lower semi-continuity, which is defined as follows.

Definition 4.1.9 (Lower semi-continuous operator). *Operator Π is lower semi-continuous if for any (finite or infinite) set of functions or sequences $\{\vec{x}_n\}$, $\vec{x}_n \in \mathcal{G}^J$,*

$$
\Pi\left(\sup_n\{\vec{x}_n\}\right) = \sup_n\left\{\Pi(\vec{x}_n)\right\}. \tag{4.2}
$$

It is easy to check that $\mathcal{D}_\sigma$ is lower semi-continuous, unlike other operators, except $\mathcal{S}_T$ which is also lower semi-continuous.

4.1.5   Isotone Operators

Definition 4.1.10 (Isotone operator). *Operator Π is isotone if $\vec{x}_1 \leq \vec{x}_2$ always implies $\Pi(\vec{x}_1) \leq \Pi(\vec{x}_2)$.*

All upper semi-continuous operators are isotone. Indeed, if $\vec{x}_1 \leq \vec{x}_2$, then $\vec{x}_1 \wedge \vec{x}_2 = \vec{x}_1$ and since Π is upper semi-continuous,

$$
\Pi(\vec{x}_1) = \Pi(\vec{x}_1 \wedge \vec{x}_2) = \Pi(\vec{x}_1) \wedge \Pi(\vec{x}_2) \leq \Pi(\vec{x}_2).
$$

Likewise, all lower semi-continuous operators are isotone. Indeed, if $\vec{x}_1 \leq \vec{x}_2$, then $\vec{x}_1 \vee \vec{x}_2 = \vec{x}_2$ and since Π is lower semi-continuous,

$$
\Pi(\vec{x}_1) \leq \Pi(\vec{x}_1) \vee \Pi(\vec{x}_2) = \Pi(\vec{x}_1 \vee \vec{x}_2) = \Pi(\vec{x}_2).
$$

4.1.6 Linear Operators

In classical system theory on $(\mathbb{R}, +, \times)$, a system Π is linear if its output to a linear combination of inputs is the linear combination of the outputs to each particular input. In other words, Π is linear if for any (finite or infinite) set of inputs $\{x_i\}$, and for any constant $k \in \mathbb{R}$,

$$\Pi\left(\sum_i x_i\right) = \sum_i \Pi(x_i)$$

and for any input x and any constant $k \in \mathbb{R}$,

$$\Pi(k \cdot x) = k \cdot \Pi(x).$$

The extension to min-plus system theory is straightforward. The first property being replaced by that of upper semi-continuity, a min-plus linear operator is thus defined as an upper semi-continuous operator that has the following property ("multiplication" by a constant):

Definition 4.1.11 (Min-plus linear operator). *Operator Π is min-plus linear if it is upper semi-continuous and if for any $\vec{x} \in \mathcal{G}^J$ and for any $k \geq 0$,*

$$\Pi(\vec{x} + k) = \Pi(\vec{x}) + k. \tag{4.3}$$

One can easily check that $\mathcal{C}_\sigma$, $\mathcal{C}_\Sigma$, h_σ and $\mathcal{S}_T$ are min-plus linear, unlike $\mathcal{D}_\sigma$ and $\mathcal{P}_L$. $\mathcal{D}_\sigma$ is not linear because it is not upper semi-continuous, and $\mathcal{P}_L$ is not linear because it fails to verify (4.3).

In classical linear theory, a linear system is represented by its impulse response $h(t, s)$, which is defined as the output of the system when the input is the Dirac function. The output of such a system can be expressed as

$$\Pi(x)(t) = \int_{-\infty}^{\infty} h(t, s)x(s)ds$$

Its straightforward extension in Min-plus system theory is provided by the following theorem [24]. To prove this theorem in the vector case, we need first to extend the burst delay function introduced in Definition 3.1.2, to allow negative values of the delay, namely, the value T in

$$\delta_T(t) = \begin{cases} 0 & \text{if } t \leq T \\ \infty & \text{if } t > T, \end{cases}$$

is now taking values in $\mathbb{R}$. We also introduce the following matrix $D_T \in \mathcal{G}^J \times \mathcal{G}^J$.

Definition 4.1.12 (Shift matrix). *The shift matrix is defined by*

$$D_T(t) = \begin{bmatrix} \delta_T(t) & \infty & \infty & \cdots & \infty \\ \infty & \delta_T(t) & \infty & & \\ \infty & \infty & \delta_T(t) & \ddots & \vdots \\ \vdots & \vdots & & \ddots & \infty \\ \infty & \cdots & & \infty & \delta_T(t) \end{bmatrix}$$

for some $T \in \mathbb{R}$

Theorem 4.1.1 (Min-plus impulse response). Π *is a min-plus linear operator if and only if there is a unique matrix $H \in \tilde{\mathcal{G}}^J$ (called the* impulse response*), such that for any $\vec{x} \in \mathcal{G}^J$ and any $t \in \mathbb{R}$,*

$$\Pi(\vec{x})(t) = \inf_{s \in \mathbb{R}} \{H(t, s) + \vec{x}(s)\}. \tag{4.4}$$

Proof: If (4.4) holds, one immediately sees that Π is upper semi-continuous and verifies (4.3), and therefore is min-plus linear. Π maps $\mathcal{G}^J$ to $\mathcal{G}^J$ because $H \in \tilde{\mathcal{G}}^J$.

Suppose next that Π is min-plus linear, and let us prove that there is a unique matrix $H(t, s) \in \tilde{\mathcal{G}}^J$ such that (4.4) holds.

Let us first note that $D_s(t) + \vec{x}(s) = \vec{x}(s)$ for any $s \geq t$. Since $\vec{x} \in \mathcal{G}^J$, we have

$$\inf_{s \geq t} \{D_s(t) + \vec{x}(s)\} = \inf_{s \geq t} \{\vec{x}(s)\} = \vec{x}(t).$$

On the other hand, all entries of $D_s(t)$ are infinite for $s < t$. We have therefore that

$$\inf_{s < t} \{D_s(t) + \vec{x}(s)\} = \infty$$

We can combine these two expressions as

$$\vec{x}(t) = \inf_{s \in \mathbb{R}} \{D_s(t) + \vec{x}(s)\},$$

or, dropping explicit dependence on t,

$$\vec{x} = \inf_{s \in \mathbb{R}} \{D_s + \vec{x}(s)\}.$$

Let $\vec{d}_{s,j}$ denote the jth column of D_s:

$$\vec{d}_{s,j} = \begin{bmatrix} \infty \\ \vdots \\ \infty \\ \delta_s \\ \infty \\ \vdots \\ \infty \end{bmatrix}$$

where δ_s is located at the jth position in this vector. Using repeatedly the fact Π is min-plus linear, we get that

$$
\begin{aligned}
\Pi(\vec{x}) &= \Pi\left(\inf_{s\in\mathbb{R}}\{D_s + \vec{x}(s)\}\right) \\
&= \inf_{s\in\mathbb{R}}\{\Pi(D_s + \vec{x}(s))\} \\
&= \inf_{s\in\mathbb{R}}\left\{\Pi\left(\min_{1\le j\le J}\{\vec{d}_{s,j} + x_j(s)\}\right)\right\} \\
&= \inf_{s\in\mathbb{R}}\left\{\min_{1\le j\le J}\{\Pi(\vec{d}_{s,j} + x_j(s))\}\right\} \\
&= \inf_{s\in\mathbb{R}}\left\{\min_{1\le j\le J}\{\Pi(\vec{d}_{s,j}) + x_j(s)\}\right\}.
\end{aligned}
$$

Defining

$$
H(t,s) = \begin{bmatrix}\vec{h}_1(t,s) & \dots & \vec{h}_j(t,s) & \dots & \vec{h}_J(t,s)\end{bmatrix} \tag{4.5}
$$

where

$$
\vec{h}_j(t,s) = \Pi\left(\vec{d}_{s,j}\right)(t) \tag{4.6}
$$

for all $t \in \mathbb{R}$, we obtain therefore that

$$
\Pi(\vec{x})(t) = \inf_{s\in\mathbb{R}}\left\{\min_{1\le j\le J}\{\vec{h}_j(t,s) + x_j(s)\}\right\} = \inf_{s\in\mathbb{R}}\{H(t,s) + \vec{x}(s)\}.
$$

We still have to check that $H(t,s) \in \tilde{\mathcal{G}}^J$. Since for any fixed s, $\Pi\left(\vec{d}_{s,j}\right) \in \mathcal{G}^J$, we have that for any $t \le t'$

$$
\vec{h}_j(t,s) = \Pi\left(\vec{d}_{s,j}\right)(t) \le \Pi\left(\vec{d}_{s,j}\right)(t') = \vec{h}_j(t',s),
$$

hence $H(t,s) \le H(t',s)$. On the other hand, if $s' \le s$, one easily check that $\vec{d}_{s,j} \le \vec{d}_{s',j}$. Therefore, since Π is isotone (because it is linear and thus upper semicontinuous),

$$
\vec{h}_j(t,s) = \Pi\left(\vec{d}_{s,j}\right)(t) \le \Pi\left(\vec{d}_{s',j}\right)(t) = \vec{h}_j(t,s')
$$

and therefore $H(t,s) \le H(t,s')$ for any $s \ge s'$. This shows that $H(t,s) \in \tilde{\mathcal{G}}^J$.

To prove uniqueness, suppose that there is another matrix $H' \in \tilde{\mathcal{G}}^J$ that satisfies (4.4), and let $\vec{h}'_j$ denote its jth column. Then for any $u \in \mathbb{R}$ and any $1 \le j \le J$, taking $\vec{x} = \vec{d}_{u,j}$ as the input, we get from (4.6) that for $t \in \mathbb{R}$

$$
\begin{aligned}
\vec{h}_j(t,u) &= \Pi\left(\vec{d}_{u,j}\right)(t) = \inf_{s\in\mathbb{R}}\{H'(t,s) + \vec{d}_{u,j}(s)\} \\
&= \inf_{s\in\mathbb{R}}\{\vec{h}'_j(t,s) + \delta_u(s)\} = \inf_{s\le u}\{\vec{h}'_j(t,s)\} = \vec{h}'_j(t,u).
\end{aligned}
$$

Therefore $H' = H$. $\qquad\square$

We will denote a general min-plus linear operator whose impulse response is H by $\mathcal{L}_H$. In other words, we have that

$$\mathcal{L}_H(\vec{x})(t) = \inf_{s \in \mathbb{R}} \{H(t,s) + \vec{x}(s)\}.$$

One can compute that the impulse response corresponding to $\mathcal{C}_\Sigma$ is

$$H(t,s) = \begin{cases} \Sigma(t-s) & \text{if } s \le t \\ \Sigma(0) & \text{if } s > t \end{cases},$$

to h_σ is

$$H(t,s) = \begin{cases} \sigma(t) - \sigma(s) & \text{if } s \le t \\ 0 & \text{if } s > t \end{cases},$$

and to $\mathcal{S}_T$ is

$$H(t,s) = D_T(t-s).$$

In fact the introduction of the shift matrix allows us to write the shift operator as a min-plus convolution: $\mathcal{S}_T = \mathcal{C}_{D_T}$ if $T \ge 0$.

Let us now compute the impulse response of the compostion of two min-plus linear operators.

Theorem 4.1.2 (Composition of min-plus linear operators). *Let $\mathcal{L}_H$ and $\mathcal{L}_{H'}$ be two min-plus linear operators. Then their composition $\mathcal{L}_H \circ \mathcal{L}_{H'}$ is also min-plus linear, and its impulse repsonse denoted by $H \circ H'$ is given by*

$$(H \circ H')(t,s) = \inf_{u \in \mathbb{R}} \{H(t,u) + H'(u,s)\}.$$

Proof: The composition $\mathcal{L}_H \circ \mathcal{L}_{H'}$ applied to some $\vec{x} \in \mathcal{G}^J$ is

$$\begin{aligned} \mathcal{L}_H(\mathcal{L}_{H'}(\vec{x}))(t) &= \inf_u \left\{ H(t,u) + \inf_s \{H'(u,s) + \vec{x}(s)\} \right\} \\ &= \inf_u \inf_s \{H(t,u) + H'(u,s) + \vec{x}(s)\} \\ &= \inf_s \left\{ \inf_u \{H(t,s) + H'(u,s)\} + \vec{x}(s) \right\}. \end{aligned}$$

□

We can therefore write

$$\mathcal{L}_H \circ \mathcal{L}_{H'} = \mathcal{L}_{H \circ H'}.$$

Likewise, one easily shows that

$$\mathcal{L}_H \wedge \mathcal{L}_{H'} = \mathcal{L}_{H \wedge H'}.$$

Finally, let us mention the dual definition of a max-plus linear operator.

Definition 4.1.13 (Max-plus linear operator). *Operator Π is max-plus linear if it is lower semi-continuous and if for any $\vec{x} \in \mathcal{G}^J$ and for any $k \ge 0$,*

$$\Pi(\vec{x} + k) = \Pi(\vec{x}) + k. \tag{4.7}$$

Max-plus linear operators can also be represented by their impulse response.

Theorem 4.1.3 (Max-plus impulse response). Π *is a max-plus linear operator if and only if there is a unique matrix* $H \in \tilde{\mathcal{G}}^J$ *(called the* impulse response*), such that for any* $\vec{x} \in \mathcal{G}^J$ *and any* $t \in \mathbb{R}$,

$$\Pi(\vec{x})(t) = \sup_{s \in \mathbb{R}} \{H(t, s) + \vec{x}(s)\}. \tag{4.8}$$

One can easily check that $\mathcal{D}_\sigma$ and $\mathcal{S}_T$ are max-plus linear, unlike $\mathcal{C}_\Sigma$, h_σ and $\mathcal{P}_L$.

For example, $\mathcal{D}_\sigma(x)(t)$ can be written as

$$\mathcal{D}_\sigma(x)(t) = \sup_{u \geq 0}\{x(t+u) - \sigma(u)\} = \sup_{s \geq t}\{x(s) - \sigma(s-t)\} = \sup_{s \in \mathbb{R}}\{x(s) - \sigma(s-t)\}$$

which has the form (4.8) if $H(t, s) = -\sigma(s - t)$.

Likewise, $\mathcal{S}_T(x)(t)$ can be written as

$$\mathcal{S}_T(\vec{x})(t) = \vec{x}(t - T) = \sup_{s \in \mathbb{R}}\{\vec{x}(s) - D_{-T}(s - t)\}$$

which has the form (4.8) if $H(t, s) = -D_{-T}(s - t)$.

4.1.7 Causal Operators

A system is causal if its output at time t only depends on its input before time t.

Definition 4.1.14 (Causal operator). *Operator* Π *is causal if for any* t, $\vec{x}_1(s) = \vec{x}_2(s)$ *for all* $s \leq t$ *always implies* $\Pi(\vec{x}_1)(t) = \Pi(\vec{x}_2)(t)$.

Theorem 4.1.4 (Min-plus causal linear operator). *A min-plus linear system with impulse response* H *is causal if* $H(t, s) = H(t, t)$ *for* $s > t$.

Proof: If $H(t, s) = 0$ for $s > t$ and if $\vec{x}_1(s) = \vec{x}_2(s)$ for all $s \leq t$ then since $\vec{x}_1, \vec{x}_2 \in \mathcal{G}^J$,

$$
\begin{aligned}
\mathcal{L}_H(\vec{x}_1)(t) &= \inf_{s \in \mathbb{R}}\{H(t, s) + \vec{x}_1(s)\} \\
&= \inf_{s \leq t}\{H(t, s) + \vec{x}_1(s)\} \wedge \inf_{s > t}\{H(t, s) + \vec{x}_1(s)\} \\
&= \inf_{s \leq t}\{H(t, s) + \vec{x}_1(s)\} \wedge \inf_{s > t}\{H(t, t) + \vec{x}_1(s)\} \\
&= \inf_{s \leq t}\{H(t, s) + \vec{x}_1(s)\} \\
&= \inf_{s \leq t}\{H(t, s) + \vec{x}_2(s)\} \\
&= \inf_{s \leq t}\{H(t, s) + \vec{x}_2(s)\} \wedge \inf_{s > t}\{H(t, t) + \vec{x}_2(s)\} \\
&= \inf_{s \leq t}\{H(t, s) + \vec{x}_2(s)\} \wedge \inf_{s > t}\{H(t, s) + \vec{x}_2(s)\} \\
&= \inf_{s \in \mathbb{R}}\{H(t, s) + \vec{x}_2(s)\} = \mathcal{L}_H(\vec{x}_2)(t).
\end{aligned}
$$

$\square$

$\mathcal{C}_\sigma$, $\mathcal{C}_\Sigma$, h_σ and $\mathcal{P}_L$ are causal. $\mathcal{S}_T$ is causal if and only if $T \geq 0$. $\mathcal{D}_\sigma$ is not causal. Indeed if $\vec{x}_1(s) = \vec{x}_2(s)$ for all $s \leq t$, but that $\vec{x}_1(s) \neq \vec{x}_2(s)$ for all $s > t$, then

$$
\begin{aligned}
\mathcal{D}_\sigma(\vec{x}_1)(t) &= \sup_{u \geq 0} \{\vec{x}_1(t + u) - \sigma(u)\} \\
&\neq \sup_{u \geq 0} \{\vec{x}_2(t + u) - \sigma(u)\} \\
&= \mathcal{D}_\sigma(\vec{x}_1)(t)
\end{aligned}
$$

4.1.8   Shift-invariant Operators

A system is shift-invariant, or time-invariant, if a shift of the input of T time units yields a shift of the output of T time units too.

Definition 4.1.15 (Shift-invariant operator). *Operator Π is shift-invariant if it commutes with all shift operators, i.e. if for any $\vec{x} \in \mathcal{G}$ and for any $T \in \mathbb{R}$*

$$
\Pi(\mathcal{S}_T(\vec{x})) = \mathcal{S}_T(\Pi(\vec{x})).
$$

Theorem 4.1.5 (Shift-invariant min-plus linear operator). *Let $\mathcal{L}_H$ and $\mathcal{L}_{H'}$ be two min-plus linear, shift-invariant operators.*

(i) A min-plus linear operator $\mathcal{L}_H$ is shift-invariant if and only if its impulse response $H(t, s)$ depends only on the difference $(t - s)$.

(ii) Two min-plus linear, shift-invariant operators $\mathcal{L}_H$ and $\mathcal{L}_{H'}$ commute. If they are also causal, the impulse response of their composition is

$$
(H \circ H')(t, s) = \inf_{0 \leq u \leq t - s} \{H(t - s - u) + H'(u)\} = (H \otimes H')(t - s).
$$

Proof: (i) Let $\vec{h}_j(t, s)$ and $\vec{d}_{s,j}(t)$ denote (respectively) the jth column of $H(t, s)$ and of $D_s(t)$. Note that $\vec{d}_{s,j}(t) = \mathcal{S}_s(\vec{d}_{0,j})(t)$. Then (4.6) yields that

$$
\begin{aligned}
\vec{h}_j(t, s) &= \Pi\left(\vec{d}_{s,j}\right)(t) = \Pi\left(\mathcal{S}_s(\vec{d}_{0,j})\right)(t) \\
&= \mathcal{S}_s\left(\Pi(\vec{d}_{0,j})\right)(t) = \left(\Pi(\vec{d}_{0,j})\right)(t - s) = \vec{h}_j(t - s, 0)
\end{aligned}
$$

Therefore $H(t, s)$ can be written as a function of a single variable $H(t - s)$.

(ii) Because of Theorem 4.1.2, the impulse response of $\mathcal{L}_H \circ \mathcal{L}_{H'}$ is

$$
(H \circ H')(t, s) = \inf_u \{H(t, u) + H'(u, s)\}.
$$

Since $H(t, u) = H(t - u)$ and $H'(u, s) = H'(u - s)$, and setting $v = u - s$, the latter can be written as

$$
(H \circ H')(t, s) = \inf_u \{H(t - u) + H'(u - s)\} = \inf_v \{H(t - s - v) + H'(v)\}.
$$

Similarly, the impulse response of $\mathcal{L}_{H'} \circ \mathcal{L}_H$ can be written as

$$(H' \circ H)(t, s) = \inf_u \{H'(t - u) + H(u - s)\} = \inf_v \{H(v) + H'(t - s - v)\}$$

where this time we have set $v = t - u$. Both impulse responses are identical, which shows that the two operators commute.

If they are causal, then their impulse response is infinite for $t > s$ and the two previous relations become

$$(H \circ H')(t, s) = (H' \circ H)(t, s) = \inf_{0 \le v \le t} \{H(t - s - v) + H'(v)\} = (H \otimes H')(t-s).$$

$\square$

Min-plus convolution $\mathcal{C}_\Sigma$ (including of course $\mathcal{C}_\sigma$ and $\mathcal{S}_T$) is therefore shift-invariant. In fact, it follows from this theorem that the only min-plus linear, causal and shift-invariant operator is min-plus convolution. Therefore h_σ is not shift-invariant.

Min-plus deconvolution is shift-invariant, as

$$\begin{aligned}
\mathcal{D}_\sigma(\mathcal{S}_T(x))(t) &= \sup_{u \ge 0}\{\mathcal{S}_T(x)(t + u) - \sigma(u)\} = \sup_{u \ge 0}\{x(t + u - T) - \sigma(u)\} \\
&= (x \oslash \sigma)(t - T) = \mathcal{D}_\sigma(x)(t - T) = \mathcal{S}_T(\mathcal{D}_\sigma)(x)(t).
\end{aligned}$$

Finally let us mention that $\mathcal{P}_L$ is not shift-invariant.

4.1.9 Idempotent Operators

An idempotent operator is an operator whose composition with itself produces the same operator.

Definition 4.1.16 (Idempotent operator). *Operator Π is idempotent if its self-composition is Π, i.e. if*

$$\Pi \circ \Pi = \Pi.$$

We can easily check that h_σ and $\mathcal{P}_L$ are idempotent. If σ is sub-additive, with $\sigma(0) = 0$, then $\mathcal{C}_\sigma \circ \mathcal{C}_\sigma = \mathcal{C}_\sigma$, which shows that in this case, $\mathcal{C}_\sigma$ is idempotent too. The same applies to $\mathcal{D}_\sigma$.

4.2 Closure of an Operator

By repeatedly composing a min-plus operator with itself, we obtain the closure of this operator. The formal definition is as follows.

Definition 4.2.1 (Sub-additive closure of an operator). *Let Π be a min-plus operator taking $\mathcal{G}^J \to \mathcal{G}^J$. Denote $\Pi^{(n)}$ the operator obtained by composing Π $(n - 1)$ times with itself. By convention, $\Pi^{(0)} = \mathcal{S}_0 = \mathcal{C}_{D_0}$, so $\Pi^{(1)} = \Pi$, $\Pi^{(2)} = \Pi \circ \Pi$, etc. Then the sub-additive closure of Π, denoted by $\overline{\Pi}$, is defined by*

$$\overline{\Pi} = \mathcal{S}_0 \wedge \Pi \wedge (\Pi \circ \Pi) \wedge (\Pi \circ \Pi \circ \Pi) \wedge \ldots = \inf_{n \ge 0} \left\{\Pi^{(n)}\right\}. \tag{4.9}$$

In other words,

$$\overline{\Pi}(\vec{x}) = \vec{x} \wedge \Pi(\vec{x}) \wedge \Pi(\Pi(\vec{x})) \wedge \dots$$

It is immediate to check that $\overline{\Pi}$ does map functions in $\mathcal{G}^J$ to functions in $\mathcal{G}^J$.

The next theorem provides the impulse response of the sub-additive closure of a min-plus linear operator. It follows immediately from applying recursively Theorem 4.1.2.

Theorem 4.2.1 (Sub-additive closure of a linear operator). *The impulse response of $\overline{\mathcal{L}}_H$ is*

$$\overline{H}(t,s) = \inf_{n \in \mathbb{N}} \inf_{u_n,\dots,u_2,u_1} \{H(t,u_1) + H(u_1,u_2) + \dots + H(u_n,s)\}. \quad (4.10)$$

and $\overline{\mathcal{L}}_H = \mathcal{L}_{\overline{H}}$.

For a min-plus linear, shift-invariant and causal operator, (4.10) becomes

$$\overline{H}(t-s)$$
$$= \inf_{n \in \mathbb{N}} \inf_{s \le u_n \le \dots \le u_2 \le u_1 \le t} \{H(t-u_1) + H(u_1-u_2) + \dots + H(u_n-s)\}$$
$$= \inf_{n \in \mathbb{N}} \inf_{0 \le v_n \le \dots \le v_2 \le v_1 \le t-s} \{H(t-s-v_1) + H(v_1-v_2) + \dots + H(v_n)\}$$
$$= \inf_{n \in \mathbb{N}} \{H^{(n)}\}(t-s) \quad (4.11)$$

where $H^{(n)} = H \otimes H \otimes \dots \otimes H$ (n times, $n \ge 1$) and $H^{(0)} = S_0$.

In particular, if all entries $\sigma_{ij}(t)$ of $\Sigma(t)$ are sub-additive functions, we find that

$$\overline{\mathcal{C}}_\Sigma = \mathcal{C}_\Sigma.$$

In the scalar case, the closure of the min-plus convolution operator $\mathcal{C}_\sigma$ reduces to the min-plus convolution of the sub-additive closure of σ:

$$\overline{\mathcal{C}}_\sigma = \mathcal{C}_{\overline{\sigma}}.$$

If σ is a "good" function (i.e., a sub-additive function with $\sigma(0) = 0$), then $\overline{\mathcal{C}}_\sigma = \mathcal{C}_\sigma$.

The sub-additive closure of the idempotent operators h_σ and $\mathcal{P}_L$ are easy to compute too. Indeed, since $h_\sigma(x) \le x$ and $\mathcal{P}_L(x) \le x$,

$$\overline{h_\sigma} = h_\sigma$$

and

$$\overline{\mathcal{P}}_L = \mathcal{P}_L.$$

The following result is easy to prove. We write $\Pi \le \Pi'$ to express that $\Pi(\vec{x}) \le \Pi'(\vec{x})$ for all $\vec{x} \in \mathcal{G}^J$.

Theorem 4.2.2 (Sub-additive closure of an isotone operator). *If Π and Π' are two isotone operators, and $\Pi \le \Pi'$, then $\overline{\Pi} \le \overline{\Pi'}$.*

Finally, let us conclude this section by computing the closure of the minimum between two operators.

Theorem 4.2.3 (Sub-additive closure of $\Pi_1 \wedge \Pi_2$). *Let Π_1, Π_2 be two isotone operators taking $\mathcal{G}^J \to \mathcal{G}^J$. Then*

$$\overline{\Pi_1 \wedge \Pi_2} = \overline{(\Pi_1 \wedge \mathcal{S}_0) \circ (\Pi_2 \wedge \mathcal{S}_0)}. \tag{4.12}$$

Proof: (i) Since $\mathcal{S}_0$ is the identity operator,

$$
\begin{aligned}
\Pi_1 \wedge \Pi_2 &= (\Pi_1 \circ \mathcal{S}_0) \wedge (\mathcal{S}_0 \circ \Pi_2) \\
&\geq ((\Pi_1 \wedge \mathcal{S}_0) \circ \mathcal{S}_0) \wedge (\mathcal{S}_0 \circ (\Pi_2 \wedge \mathcal{S}_0)) \\
&\geq ((\Pi_1 \wedge \mathcal{S}_0) \circ (\Pi_2 \wedge \mathcal{S}_0)) \wedge ((\Pi_1 \wedge \mathcal{S}_0) \circ (\Pi_2 \wedge \mathcal{S}_0)) \\
&= (\Pi_1 \wedge \mathcal{S}_0) \circ (\Pi_2 \wedge \mathcal{S}_0).
\end{aligned}
$$

Since Π_1 and Π_2 are isotone, so are $\Pi_1 \wedge \Pi_2$ and $(\Pi_1 \wedge \mathcal{S}_0) \circ (\Pi_2 \wedge \mathcal{S}_0)$. Consequently, Theorem 4.2.2 yields that

$$\overline{\Pi_1 \wedge \Pi_2} \geq \overline{(\Pi_1 \wedge \mathcal{S}_0) \circ (\Pi_1 \wedge \mathcal{S}_0)}. \tag{4.13}$$

(ii) Combining the two inequalities

$$
\begin{aligned}
\Pi_1 \wedge \mathcal{S}_0 &\geq \Pi_1 \wedge \Pi_2 \wedge \mathcal{S}_0 \\
\Pi_2 \wedge \mathcal{S}_0 &\geq \Pi_1 \wedge \Pi_2 \wedge \mathcal{S}_0
\end{aligned}
$$

we get that

$$\overline{(\Pi_1 \wedge \mathcal{S}_0) \circ (\Pi_1 \wedge \mathcal{S}_0)} \geq \overline{(\Pi_1 \wedge \Pi_2 \wedge \mathcal{S}_0) \circ (\Pi_1 \wedge \Pi_2 \wedge \mathcal{S}_0)}. \tag{4.14}$$

Let us show by induction that

$$((\Pi_1 \wedge \Pi_2) \wedge \mathcal{S}_0)^{(n)} = \min_{0 \leq k \leq n} \left\{ (\Pi_1 \wedge \Pi_2)^{(k)} \right\}.$$

Clearly, the claim holds for $n = 0, 1$. Suppose it is true up to some $n \in \mathbb{N}$. Then

$$((\Pi_1 \wedge \Pi_2) \wedge \mathcal{S}_0)^{(n+1)}$$

$$= ((\Pi_1 \wedge \Pi_2) \wedge \mathcal{S}_0) \circ ((\Pi_1 \wedge \Pi_2) \wedge \mathcal{S}_0)^{(n)}$$

$$= ((\Pi_1 \wedge \Pi_2) \wedge \mathcal{S}_0) \circ \left(\min_{0 \leq k \leq n} \left\{ (\Pi_1 \wedge \Pi_2)^{(k)} \right\} \right)$$

$$= \left((\Pi_1 \wedge \Pi_2) \circ \min_{0 \leq k \leq n} \left\{ (\Pi_1 \wedge \Pi_2)^{(k)} \right\} \right) \wedge \left(\mathcal{S}_0 \circ \min_{0 \leq k \leq n} \left\{ (\Pi_1 \wedge \Pi_2)^{(k)} \right\} \right)$$

$$= \min_{1 \leq k \leq n+1} \left\{ (\Pi_1 \wedge \Pi_2)^{(k)} \right\} \wedge \min_{0 \leq k \leq n} \left\{ (\Pi_1 \wedge \Pi_2)^{(k)} \right\}$$

$$= \min_{0 \leq k \leq n+1} \left\{ (\Pi_1 \wedge \Pi_2)^{(k)} \right\}.$$

Therefore the claim holds for all $n \in \mathbb{N}$, and

$$
\begin{aligned}
\left(\left((\Pi_1 \wedge \Pi_2) \wedge \mathcal{S}_0 \right) \circ \left((\Pi_1 \wedge \Pi_2) \wedge \mathcal{S}_0 \right) \right)^{(n)} &= \left((\Pi_1 \wedge \Pi_2) \wedge \mathcal{S}_0 \right)^{(2n)} \\
&= \min_{0 \leq k \leq 2n} \left\{ (\Pi_1 \wedge \Pi_2)^{(k)} \right\}.
\end{aligned}
$$

Consequently,

$$
\begin{aligned}
\overline{(\Pi_1 \wedge \Pi_2 \wedge \mathcal{S}_0) \circ (\Pi_1 \wedge \Pi_2 \wedge \mathcal{S}_0)} &= \inf_{n \in \mathbb{N}} \min_{0 \leq k \leq 2n} \left\{ (\Pi_1 \wedge \Pi_2)^{(k)} \right\} \\
&= \inf_{k \in \mathbb{N}} \left\{ (\Pi_1 \wedge \Pi_2)^{(k)} \right\} \\
&= \overline{\Pi_1 \wedge \Pi_2}
\end{aligned}
$$

and combining this result with (4.13) and (4.14), we get (4.12). □

If one of the two operators is an idempotent operator, we can simplify the previous result a bit more. We will use the following corollary in Chapter 9.

Corollary 4.2.1 (Sub-additive closure of $\Pi_1 \wedge h_M$). *Let Π_1 be an isotone operator taking $\mathcal{F} \to \mathcal{F}$, and let $M \in \mathcal{F}$. Then*

$$
\overline{\Pi_1 \wedge h_M} = \overline{(h_M \circ \Pi_1)} \circ h_M. \tag{4.15}
$$

Proof: Theorem 4.2.3 yields that

$$
\overline{\Pi_1 \wedge h_M} = \overline{(\Pi_1 \wedge \mathcal{S}_0)} \circ h_M \tag{4.16}
$$

because $h_M \leq \mathcal{S}_0$. The right hand side of (4.16) is the inf over all integers n of

$$
\left(\{ \Pi_1 \wedge \mathcal{S}_0 \} \circ h_M \right)^{(n)}
$$

which we can expand as

$$
\{ \Pi_1 \wedge \mathcal{S}_0 \} \circ h_M \circ \{ \Pi_1 \wedge \mathcal{S}_0 \} \circ h_M \circ \ldots \circ \{ \Pi_1 \wedge \mathcal{S}_0 \} \circ h_M.
$$

Since

$$
\begin{aligned}
h_M \circ \{ \Pi_1 \wedge \mathcal{S}_0 \} \circ h_M &= \{ h_M \circ \Pi_1 \circ h_M \} \wedge h_M \\
&= \left(\{ h_M \circ \Pi_1 \} \wedge \mathcal{S}_0 \right) \circ h_M \\
&= \min_{0 \leq q \leq 1} \left\{ (h_M \circ \Pi_1)^{(q)} \right\} \circ h_M,
\end{aligned}
$$

the previous expression is equal to

$$
\min_{0 \leq q \leq n} \left\{ (h_M \circ \Pi_1)^{(q)} \right\} \circ h_M.
$$

Therefore we can rewrite the right hand side of (4.16) as

$$\overline{(\Pi_1 \wedge \mathcal{S}_0) \circ h_M} = \inf_{n \in \mathbb{N}} \left\{ \min_{0 \leq q \leq n} \left\{ (h_M \circ \Pi_1)^{(q)} \right\} \circ h_M \right\}$$

$$= \inf_{q \in \mathbb{N}} \left\{ (h_M \circ \Pi_1)^{(q)} \right\} \circ h_M = \overline{(h_M \circ \Pi_1)} \circ h_M,$$

which establishes (4.15).

Therefore we can rewrite the right hand side of (4.16) as

$$\overline{(\Pi_1 \wedge \mathcal{S}_0) \circ h_M} = \inf_{n \in \mathbb{N}} \left\{ \min_{0 \leq q \leq n} \left\{ (h_M \circ \Pi_1)^{(q)} \right\} \circ h_M \right\}$$

$$= h_M \circ \inf_{q \in \mathbb{N}} \left\{ (h_M \circ \Pi_1)^{(q)} \right\} \circ h_M = h_M \circ \overline{(h_M \circ \Pi_1)} \circ h_M,$$

which establishes (4.15). □

The dual of super-additive closure is that of super-additive closure, defined as follows.

Definition 4.2.2 (Super-additive closure of an operator). *Let* Π *be an operator taking* $\mathcal{G}^J \rightarrow \mathcal{G}^J$. *The super-additive closure of* Π, *denoted by* $\underline{\Pi}$, *is defined by*

$$\underline{\Pi} = \mathcal{S}_0 \vee \Pi \vee (\Pi \circ \Pi) \vee (\Pi \circ \Pi \circ \Pi) \vee \ldots = \sup_{n \geq 0} \left\{ \Pi^{(n)} \right\}. \tag{4.17}$$

4.3 Fixed Point Equation (Space Method)

4.3.1 Main Theorem

We now have the tools to solve an important problem of network calculus, which has some analogy with ordinary differential equations in conventional system theory.

The latter problem reads as follows: let Π be an operator from $\mathbb{R}^J$ to $\mathbb{R}^J$, and let $\vec{a} \in \mathbb{R}^J$. What is then the solution $\vec{x}(t)$ to the differential equation

$$\frac{d\vec{x}}{dt}(t) = \Pi(\vec{x})(t) \tag{4.18}$$

with the inital condition

$$\vec{x}(0) = \vec{a}. \tag{4.19}$$

Here Π is an operator taking $\mathcal{G}^J \rightarrow \mathcal{G}^J$, and $\vec{a} \in \mathcal{G}^J$. The problem is now to find the largest function $\vec{x}(t) \in \mathcal{G}^J$, which verifies the recursive inequality

$$\vec{x}(t) \leq \Pi(\vec{x})(t) \tag{4.20}$$

and the initial condition

$$\vec{x}(t) \leq \vec{a}(t). \tag{4.21}$$

The differences are however important: first we have inequalities instead of equalities, and second, contrary to (4.18), (4.20) does not describe the evolution of the trajectory $\vec{x}(t)$ with time t, starting from a fixed point $\vec{a}$, but the successive iteration of Π on the whole trajectory $\vec{x}(t)$, starting from a fixed, given function $\vec{a}(t) \in \mathcal{G}^J$.

The following theorem provides the solution this problem, under weak, technical assumptions that are almost always met.

Theorem 4.3.1 (Space method). *Let Π be an upper semi-continuous operator taking $\mathcal{G}^J \to \mathcal{G}^J$. For any fixed function $\vec{a} \in \mathcal{G}^J$, the problem*

$$\vec{x} \leq \vec{a} \wedge \Pi(\vec{x}) \tag{4.22}$$

has one maximum solution in $\mathcal{G}^J$, given by $\vec{x}^\star = \overline{\Pi}(\vec{a})$.

The theorem is proven in [24]. We give here a direct proof that does not have the pre-requisites in [24]. It is based on a fixed point argument. We call the application of this theorem "Space method", because the iterated variable is not time t (as in the "Time method" described shortly later) but the full sequence $\vec{x}$ itself. The theorem applies therefore indifferently whether $t \in \mathbb{Z}$ or $t \in \mathbb{R}$.

Proof: (i) Let us first show that $\overline{\Pi}(\vec{a})$ is a solution of (4.22). Consider the sequence $\{\vec{x}^n\}$ of decreasing sequences defined by

$$\begin{aligned} \vec{x}_0 &= \vec{a} \\ \vec{x}_{n+1} &= \vec{x}_n \wedge \Pi(\vec{x}_n), \qquad n \geq 0. \end{aligned}$$

Then one checks that

$$\vec{x}^\star = \inf_{n \geq 0} \{\vec{x}_n\}$$

is a solution to (4.22) because $\vec{x}^\star \leq \vec{x}_0 = \vec{a}$ and because Π is upper-semi-continuous so that

$$\Pi(\vec{x}^\star) = \Pi(\inf_{n \geq 0} \{\vec{x}_n\}) = \inf_{n \geq 0} \{\Pi(\vec{x}_n)\} \geq \inf_{n \geq 0} \{\vec{x}_{n+1}\} \geq \inf_{n \geq 0} \{\vec{x}_n\} = \vec{x}^\star.$$

Now, one easily checks that $\vec{x}_n = \inf_{0 \leq m \leq n} \{\Pi^{(m)}(\vec{a})\}$, so

$$\vec{x}^\star = \inf_{n \geq 0} \{\vec{x}_n\} = \inf_{n \geq 0} \inf_{0 \leq m \leq n} \{\Pi^{(m)}(\vec{a})\} = \inf_{n \geq 0} \{\Pi^{(n)}(\vec{a})\} = \overline{\Pi}(\vec{a}).$$

This also shows that $\vec{x}^\star \in \mathcal{G}^J$.

(ii) Let $\vec{x}$ be a solution of (4.22). Then $\vec{x} \leq \vec{a}$ and since Π is isotone, $\Pi(\vec{x}) \leq \Pi(\vec{a})$. From (4.22), $\vec{x} \leq \Pi(\vec{x})$, so that $\vec{x} \leq \Pi(\vec{a})$. Suppose that for some $n \geq 1$, we have shown that $\vec{x} \leq \Pi^{(n-1)}(\vec{a})$. Then as $\vec{x} \leq \Pi(\vec{x})$ and as Π is isotone, it yields that $\vec{x} \leq \Pi^{(n)}(\vec{a})$. Therefore $\vec{x} \leq \inf_{n \geq 0} \{\Pi^{(n)}(\vec{a})\} = \overline{\Pi}(\vec{a})$, which shows that $\vec{x}^\star = \overline{\Pi}(\vec{a})$ is the maximal solution. $\square$

Similarly, we have the following result in Max-plus algebra.

Theorem 4.3.2 (Dual space method). *Let Π be a lower semi-continuous operator taking $\mathcal{G}^J \to \mathcal{G}^J$. For any fixed function $\vec{a} \in \mathcal{G}^J$, the problem*

$$\vec{x} \geq \vec{a} \vee \Pi(\vec{x}) \tag{4.23}$$

has one minimum solution, given by $\vec{x}^\star = \underline{\Pi}(\vec{a})$.

4.3.2 Examples of Application

Let us now apply this theorem to five particular examples. We will first revisit the input-output characterization of the greedy shaper of Section 1.5.2, and of the variable capacity node described at the end of Section 1.3.2. Next we will apply it to two window flow control problems (with a fixed length window). Finally, we will revisit the variable length packet greedy shaper of Section 1.7.4.

Input-Output Characterization of Greedy Shapers

Remember that a greedy shaper is a system that delays input bits in a buffer, whenever sending a bit would violate the constraint σ, but outputs them as soon as possible otherwise. If R is the input flow, the output is thus the maximal function $x \in \mathcal{F}$ satisfying the set of inequalities (1.13), which we can recast as

$$x \leq R \wedge C_\sigma(x).$$

It is thus given by $R^* = \overline{C_\sigma}(x) = C_{\overline{\sigma}}(x) = \overline{\sigma} \otimes x$. If σ is a "good" function, one therefore retrieves the main result of Theorem 1.5.1.

Input-Output Characterization of Variable Capacity Nodes

The variable capacity node was introduced at the end of Section 1.3.2, where the variable capacity is modeled by a cumulative function $M(t)$, where $M(t)$ is the total capacity available to the flow between times 0 and t. If $m(t)$ is the instantaneous capacity available to the flow at time t, then $M(t)$ is the primitive of this function. In other words, if $t \in \mathbb{R}$,

$$M(t) = \int_0^t m(s)ds \qquad (4.24)$$

and if $t \in \mathbb{Z}$ the integral is replaced by a sum on s. If R is the input flow and x is the output flow of the variable capacity node, then the variable capacity constraint imposes that for all $0 \leq s \leq t$

$$x(t) - x(s) \leq M(t) - M(s),$$

which we can recast using the idempotent operator h_M as

$$x \leq h_M(x). \qquad (4.25)$$

On the other hand, the system is causal, so that

$$x \leq R. \qquad (4.26)$$

The output of the variable capacity node is therefore the maximal solution of system (4.25) and (4.26). It is thus given by

$$R^*(t) = \overline{h}_M(R)(t) = h_M(R)(t) = \inf_{0 \leq s \leq t} \{M(t) - M(s) + R(s)\}$$

because the sub-additive closure of an idempotent operator is the operator itself, as we have seen in the previous section.

Static window flow control – example 1

Let us now consider an example of a feedback system. This example is found independently in [9] and [60, 2]. A data flow $a(t)$ is fed via a window flow controller to a network offering a service curve β. The window flow controller limits the amount of data admitted into the network in such a way that the total backlog is less than or equal to W, where $W > 0$ (the window size) is a fixed number (Figure 4.1).

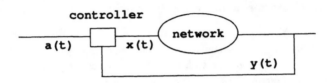

Figure 4.1: Static window flow control, from [9] or [60]

Call $x(t)$ the flow admitted to the network, and $y(t)$ the output. The definition of the controller means that $x(t)$ is the maximum solution to

$$\begin{cases} x(t) \leq a(t) \\ x(t) \leq y(t) + W \end{cases} \tag{4.27}$$

We do not know the mapping $\Pi : x \to y = \Pi(x)$, but we assume that Π is isotone, and we assume that $y(t) \geq (\beta \otimes x)(t)$, which can be recast as

$$\Pi(x) \geq \mathcal{C}_\beta(x). \tag{4.28}$$

We also recast System (4.27) as

$$x \leq a \wedge \{\Pi(x) + W\}, \tag{4.29}$$

and direclty apply Theorem 4.3.1 to derive that the maximum solution is

$$x = \overline{(\Pi + W)}(a).$$

Since Π is isotone, so is $\Pi + W$. Therefore, because of (4.28) and applying Theorem 4.2.2, we get that

$$x = \overline{(\Pi + W)}(a) \geq \overline{(\mathcal{C}_\beta + W)}(a). \tag{4.30}$$

Because of Theorem 4.2.1,

$$\overline{(\mathcal{C}_\beta + W)}(a) = \overline{\mathcal{C}}_{\beta + W}(a) = \mathcal{C}_{\overline{\beta + W}}(a) = \overline{(\beta + W)} \otimes a.$$

Combining this relationship with (4.30) we have that

$$y \geq \beta \otimes x \geq \beta \otimes \left(\overline{(\beta + W)} \otimes a\right) = \left(\beta \otimes \overline{(\beta + W)}\right)(a),$$

which shows that the complete, closed-loop system of Figure 4.1 offers to flow a a service curve [9]

$$\beta_{\text{wfc1}} = \beta \otimes \overline{(\beta + W)}. \tag{4.31}$$

For example, if $\beta = \beta_{R,T}$ then the service curve of the closed-loop system is the function represented on Figure 4.2. When $RT \leq W$, the window does not add any restriction on the service guarantee offered by the open-loop system, as in this case $\beta_{\text{wfc1}} = \beta$. If $RT > W$ on the other hand, the service curve is smaller than the open-loop service curve.

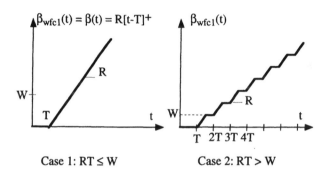

Case 1: RT ≤ W   Case 2: RT > W

Figure 4.2: The service curve β_{wfc1} of the closed-loop system with static window flow control, when the service curve of the open loop system is $\beta_{R,T}$ with $RT \leq W$ (left) and $RT > W$ (right).

Static window flow control – example 2

Let us extend the window flow control model to account for the existence of background traffic, which constraints the input traffic rate at time t, $dx/dt(t)$ (if $t \in \mathbb{R}$) or $x(t) - x(t-1)$ (if $t \in \mathbb{Z}$), to be less that some given rate $m(t)$. Let $M(t)$ denote the primitive of this prescribed rate function. Then the rate constraint on x becomes (4.25). Function $M(t)$ is not known, but we assume that there is some function $\gamma \in \mathcal{F}$ such that

$$M(t) - M(s) \geq \gamma(t-s)$$

for any $0 \leq s \leq t$, which we can recast as

$$h_M \geq \mathcal{C}_\gamma. \tag{4.32}$$

This is used in [41] to derive a service curve offered by the complete system to the incoming flow x, which we shall also compute now by applying Theorem 4.3.1.

With the additional constraint (4.25), one has to compute the maximal solution of

$$x \le a \wedge \{\Pi(x) + W\} \wedge h_M(x), \qquad (4.33)$$

which is

$$x = \overline{(\{\Pi + W\} \wedge h_M)}(a). \qquad (4.34)$$

As in the previous subsection, we do not know Π but we assume that it is isotone and that $\Pi \ge \mathcal{C}_\beta$. We also know that $h_M \ge \mathcal{C}_\gamma$. A first approach to get a service curve for y, is to compute a lower bound of the right hand side of (4.34) by time-invariant linear operators, which commute as we have seen earlier in this chapter. We get

$$\{\Pi + W\} \wedge h_M \ge \{\mathcal{C}_\beta + W\} \wedge \mathcal{C}_\gamma = \mathcal{C}_{\{\beta+W\}\wedge\gamma},$$

and therefore (4.34) becomes

$$x \ge \overline{\mathcal{C}}_{\{\beta+W\}\wedge\gamma}(a) = \mathcal{C}_{\overline{\{\beta+W\}\wedge\gamma}}(a) = \overline{(\{\beta + W\} \wedge \gamma)} \otimes a.$$

Because of Theorem 3.1.11,

$$\overline{\{\beta + W\} \wedge \gamma} = \overline{(\beta + W) \otimes \bar{\gamma}}$$

so that

$$y \ge \beta \otimes x \ge \left(\beta \otimes \overline{(\beta + W)} \otimes \bar{\gamma}\right) \otimes a$$

and thus a service curve for flow a is

$$\beta \otimes \overline{(\beta + W)} \otimes \bar{\gamma}. \qquad (4.35)$$

Unfortunately, this service curve can be quite useless. For example, if for some $T > 0$, $\gamma(t) = 0$ for $0 \le t \le T$, then $\bar{\gamma}(t) = 0$ for all $t \ge 0$, and so the service curve is zero.

A better bound is obtained by differing the lower bounding of h_M by the time-invariant operator $\mathcal{C}_\gamma$ after having used the idempotency property in the computation of the sub-additive closure of the right hand side of (4.34), via Corollary 4.2.1. Indeed, this corollary allows us to replace (4.34) by

$$x = \left(\overline{(h_M \circ (\Pi + W))} \circ h_M\right)(a).$$

Now we can bound h_M below by $\mathcal{C}_\gamma$ to obtain

$$
\begin{aligned}
\overline{(h_M \circ (\Pi + W))} \circ h_M &\ge \overline{(\mathcal{C}_\gamma \circ \mathcal{C}_{\beta+W})} \circ \mathcal{C}_\gamma \\
&= \overline{\mathcal{C}}_{\gamma\otimes(\beta+W)} \circ \mathcal{C}_\gamma \\
&= \mathcal{C}_{\overline{\beta\otimes\gamma+W}} \circ \mathcal{C}_\gamma \\
&= \mathcal{C}_{\gamma\otimes\overline{(\beta\otimes\gamma+W)}}.
\end{aligned}
$$

We obtain a better service curve than by our initial approach, where we had directly replaced h_M by $\mathcal{C}_\gamma$:

$$\beta_{\text{wfc2}} = \beta \otimes \gamma \otimes \overline{(\beta \otimes \gamma + W)}. \qquad (4.36)$$

is a better service curve than (4.35).

For example, if $\beta = \beta_{R,T}$ and $\gamma = \beta_{R',T'}$, with $R > R'$ and $W < R'(T + T')$, then the service curve of the closed-loop system is the function represented on Figure 4.3.

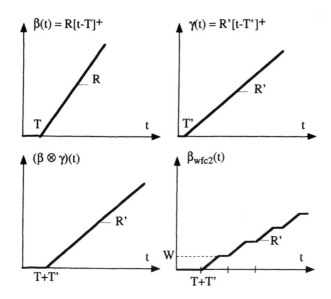

Figure 4.3: The service curve β_{wfc2} of the closed-loop system with window flow control (bottom right), when the service curve of the open loop system is $\beta = \beta_{R,T}$ (top left) and when $\gamma = \beta_{R',T'}$ (top right), with $R > R'$ and $W < R'(T + T')$.

Packetized greedy shaper

Our last example in this chapter is the packetized greedy shaper introduced in Section 1.7.4. It amounts to computing the maximum solution to the problem

$$x \le R \wedge \mathcal{P}_L(x) \wedge \mathcal{C}_\sigma(x)$$

where R is the input flow, σ is a "good" function and L is a given sequence of cumulative packet lengths.

We can apply Theorem 4.3.1 and next Theorem 4.2.2 to obtain

$$x = \overline{\mathcal{P}_L \wedge \mathcal{C}_\sigma}(R) = \overline{\mathcal{P}_L \circ \mathcal{C}_\sigma}(R)$$

which is precisely the result of Theorem 1.7.4.

4.4 Fixed Point Equation (Time Method)

We conclude this chapter by another version of Theorem 4.3.1 that applies only to the discrete-time setting. It amounts to compute the maximum solution $\vec{x} = \overline{\Pi}(\vec{a})$ of (4.22) by iterating on time t instead of interatively applying operator Π to the full trajectory $\vec{a}(t)$. We call this method the "time method" (see also [10]). It is valid

Operator	C_σ	D_σ	S_T	h_σ	P_L
Upper semi-continuous	yes	no	yes	yes	yes
Lower semi-continuous	no	yes	yes	no	no
Isotone	yes	yes	yes	yes	yes
Min-plus linear	yes	no	yes	yes	no
Max-plus linear	no	yes	yes	no	no
Causal	yes	no	yes (1)	yes	yes
Shift-invariant	yes	yes	yes	no	no
Idempotent	no (2)	no (2)	no (3)	yes	yes

(1) (if $T \geq 0$)
(2) (unless σ is a 'good' function)
(3) (unless $T = 0$)

Table 4.1: A summary of properties of some common operators

under stronger assumptions than the space method, as we require here that operator Π be min-plus linear.

Theorem 4.4.1. *Let $\Pi = \mathcal{L}_H$ be a min-plus linear operator taking $\mathcal{F}^J \to \mathcal{F}^J$, with impulse response $H \in \tilde{\mathcal{G}}^J$. For any fixed function $\vec{a} \in \mathcal{F}^J$, the problem*

$$\vec{x} \leq \vec{a} \wedge \mathcal{L}_H(\vec{x}) \tag{4.37}$$

has one maximum solution, given by

$$\vec{x}^\star(0) = \vec{a}(0)$$
$$\vec{x}^\star(t) = \vec{a}(0) \wedge \inf_{0 \leq u \leq t-1} \{H(t, u) + \vec{x}^\star(u)\}.$$

Proof: Note that the existence of a maximum solution is given by Theorem 4.3.1. Define $\vec{x}^\star$ by the recursion in the Theorem. As $H \in \tilde{\mathcal{G}}^J$ it follows easily by induction that $\vec{x}^\star$ is a solution to problem (4.37). Conversely, for any solution $\vec{x}$, $\vec{x}(0) \leq a(0) = \vec{x}^\star(0)$ and if $\vec{x}(u) \leq \vec{x}^\star(u)$ for all $0 \leq u \leq t-1$, it follows that $\vec{x}(t) \leq \vec{x}^\star(t)$ which shows that $\vec{x}^\star$ is the maximal solution.   □

4.5 Conclusion

This chapter has introduced min-plus and max-plus operators, and discussed their properties, which are summarized in Table 4.5. The central result of this chapter, which will be applied in the next chapters, is Theorem 4.3.1, which enables us to compute the maximal solution of a set of inqualities involving the iterative application of an upper semi-continuous operator.

Part III

A Second Course in Network Calculus

Chapter 5

Optimal Multimedia Smoothing

In this chapter we apply network calculus to smooth multimedia data over a network offering reservation based services, such as ATM or RSVP/IP, for which we know one minimal service curve. One approach to stream video is to act on the quantization levels at the encoder output: this is called rate control, see e.g. [22]. Another approach is to smooth the video stream, using a smoother fed by the encoder, see e.g. [61, 64, 52]. In this chapter, we deal with this second approach.

A number of smoothing algorithms have been proposed to optimize various performance metrics, such as peak bandwidth requirements, variability of transmission rates, number of rate changes, client buffer size [25]. With network calculus, we are able to compute the minimal client buffer size required given a maximal peak rate, or even a more complex (VBR) smoothing curve. We can also compute the minimal peak rate required given a given client buffer size. We will see that the scheduling algorithm that must be implemented to reach these bounds is not unique, and we will determine the full set of video transmission schedules that minimize these resources and achieve these optimal bounds.

5.1 Problem Setting

A video stream stored on the server disk is directly delivered to the client, through the network, as shown on Figure 5.1. At the sender side, a smoothing device reads the encoded video stream $R(t)$ and sends a stream $x(t)$ that must conform to an arrival curve σ, which we assume to be a 'good' function, i.e. is sub-additive and such that $\sigma(0) = 0$. The simplest and most popular smoothing curve in practice is a constant rate curve (or equivalently, a peak rate constraint) $\sigma = \lambda_r$ for some $r > 0$.

We take the transmission start as origin of time: this implies that $x(t) = 0$ for $t \leq 0$.

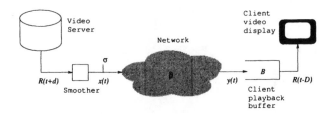

Figure 5.1: Video smoothing over a single network.

At the receiver side, the video stream R will be played back after D units of times, the *playback delay*: the output of the decoding buffer B must therefore be $R(t - D)$.

The network offers a guaranteed service to the flow x. If y denotes the output flow, it is not possible, in general, to express y as a function of x. However we assume that the service guarantee can be expressed by a service curve β. For example, as we have seen in Chapter 1, the IETF assumes that RSVP routers offer a rate-latency service curve β of the form $\beta_{L,C}(t) = C[t - L]^+ = \max\{0, C(t - L)\}$. Another example is a network which is completely transparent to the flow (i.e. which does not incur any jitter to the flow nor rate limitation, even if it can introduce a fixed delay, which we ignore in this chapter as we can always take it into account separately). We speak of a *null network*. It offers a service curve $\beta(t) = \delta_0(t)$.

To keep mathematical manipulations simple, we assume that the encoding buffer size is large enough to contain the full data stream. On the other hand, the receiver (decoding) buffer is a much more scarce resource. Its finite size is denoted by B.

As the stream is pre-recorded and stored in the video server, it allows the smoother to prefetch and send some of the data before schedule. We suppose that the smoother is able to look ahead data for up to d time units ahead. This *look-ahead delay* can take values ranging from zero (in the most restrictive case where no prefetching is possible) up to the length of the full stream. The sum of the look-ahead delay and playback delay is called the *total delay*, and is denoted by T: $T = D + d$.

These constraints are described more mathematically in Section 5.2.

We will then apply Theorem 4.3.1 to solve the following problems:

(i) we first compute, in Section 5.3, the minimal requirements on the playback delay D, on the look-ahead delay d, and on the client buffer size B guaranteeing a lossless transmission for given smoothing and service curves σ and β.

(ii) we then compute, in Section 5.4, all scheduling strategies at the smoother that will achieve transmission in the parameter setting computed in Section 5.3. We call the resulting scheduling "optimal smoothing".

(iii) in the CBR case ($\sigma = \lambda_r$), for a given rate r and for a rate-latency service curve ($\beta = \beta_{L,C}$), we will obtain, in Section 5.5, closed-form expressions of the minimal values of D, $T = D + d$ and B required for lossless smoothing. We will also solve the dual problem of computing the minimal rate r needed to deliver video for a given playback delay D, look-ahead delay d and client buffer size B.

We will then compare optimal smoothing with greedy shaping in Section 5.6 and with separate delay equalization in Section 5.7. Finally, we will repeat problems (i) and (iii) when intermediate caching is allowed between a backbone network and an access network.

5.2 Constraints Imposed by Lossless Smoothing

We can now formalize the constraints that completely define the smoothing problem illustrated on Figure 5.1).

- **Flow** $x \in \mathcal{F}$: As mentioned above, the chosen origin of time is such that $x(t) = 0$ for $t \le 0$, or equivalently

$$x(t) \le \delta_0(t). \tag{5.1}$$

- **Smoothness constraint**: Flow x is constrained by an arrival curve $\sigma(\cdot)$. This means that for all $t \ge 0$

$$x(t) \le (x \otimes \sigma)(t) = \mathcal{C}_\sigma(x)(t). \tag{5.2}$$

- **Playback delay constraint (no playback buffer underflow)**: The data is read out from the playback buffer after D unit of times at a rate given by $R(t - D)$. This implies that $y(t) \ge R(t - D)$. However we do not know the exact expression of y as a function of x. All we know is that the network guarantees a service curve β, namely that $y(t) \ge (x \otimes \beta)(t)$. The output flow may therefore be as low as $(x \otimes \beta)(t)$, and hence we can replace y in the previous inequality to obtain $(x \otimes \beta)(t) \ge R(t - D)$. Using Rule 14 in Theorem 3.1.12, we can recast this latter inequality as

$$x(t) \ge (R \oslash \beta)(t - D) = \mathcal{D}_\beta(R)(t - D) \tag{5.3}$$

for all $t \ge 0$.

- **Playback buffer constraint (no playback buffer overflow)**: The size of the playback buffer is limited to B, and to prevent any overflow of the buffer, we must impose that $y(t) - R(t - D) \le B$ for all $t \ge 0$. Again, we do not know the exact value of y, but we know that it can be as high as x, but not higher, because the network is a causal system. Therefore the constraint becomes, for all $t \ge 0$,

$$x(t) \le R(t - D) + B. \tag{5.4}$$

- **Look-ahead delay constraint**: We suppose that the encoder can prefetch data from the server up to d time units ahead, which translates in the following inequality:

$$x(t) \le R(t + d). \tag{5.5}$$

5.3   Minimal Requirements on Delays and Playback Buffer

Inequalities (5.1) to (5.5) can be recast as two sets of inequalities as follows:

$$x(t) \leq \delta_0(t) \wedge R(t+d) \wedge \{R(t-D) + B\} \wedge C_\sigma(x)(t) \qquad (5.6)$$
$$x(t) \geq (R \oslash \beta)(t-D). \qquad (5.7)$$

There is a solution x to the smoothing problem if and only if it simultaneously verifies (5.6) and (5.7). This is equivalent to requiring that the maximal solution of (5.6) is larger than the right hand side of (5.7) for all t.

Let us first compute the maximal solution of (5.6). Inequality (5.6) has the form

$$x \leq a \wedge C_\sigma(x) \qquad (5.8)$$

where

$$a(t) = \delta_0(t) \wedge R(t+d) \wedge \{R(t-D) + B\}. \qquad (5.9)$$

We can thus apply Theorem 4.3.1 to compute the unique maximal solution of (5.8), which is $x_{\max} = C_\sigma(a) = \sigma \otimes a$ because σ is a 'good' function. Replacing a by its expression in (5.9), we compute that the maximal solution of (5.6) is

$$x_{\max}(t) = \sigma(t) \wedge \{(\sigma \otimes R)(t+d)\} \wedge \{(\sigma \otimes R)(t-D) + B\}. \qquad (5.10)$$

We are now able to compute the smallest values of the playback delay D, of the total delay T and of the playback buffer B ensuring the existence of a solution to the smoothing problem, thanks to following theorem. The requirement on d for reaching the smallest value of D is therefore $d = T - D$.

Theorem 5.3.1 (Requirements for optimal smoothing). *The smallest values of D, T and B ensuring a lossless smoothing to a 'good' curve σ through a network offering a service curve β are*

$$D_{\min} = h(R, (\beta \otimes \sigma)) = \inf\{t \geq 0 : (R \oslash (\beta \otimes \sigma))(-t) \leq 0\} \quad (5.11)$$
$$T_{\min} = h((R \oslash R), (\beta \otimes \sigma)) \qquad (5.12)$$
$$= \inf\{t \geq 0 : ((R \oslash R) \oslash (\beta \otimes \sigma))(-t) \leq 0\}$$
$$B_{\min} = v((R \oslash R), (\beta \otimes \sigma)) = ((R \oslash R) \oslash (\beta \otimes \sigma))(0). \qquad (5.13)$$

where h and v denote respectively the horizontal and vertical distances given by Definition 3.1.15.

Proof: The set of inequalities (5.6) and (5.7) has a solution if, and only if, the maximal solution of (5.6) is larger or equal to the right hand side of (5.7) at all times. This amounts to impose that for all $t \in \mathbb{R}$

$$(R \oslash \beta)(t - D) - \sigma(t) \leq 0$$
$$(R \oslash \beta)(t - D) - (\sigma \otimes R)(t + d) \leq 0$$
$$(R \oslash \beta)(t - D) - (\sigma \otimes R)(t - D) \leq B.$$

Using the deconvolution operator and its properties, the latter three inequalities can be recast as

$$(R \oslash (\beta \otimes \sigma))(-D) \leq 0$$
$$((R \oslash R) \oslash (\beta \otimes \sigma))(-T) \leq 0$$
$$((R \oslash R) \oslash (\beta \otimes \sigma))(0) \leq B.$$

The minimal values of D, T and B satisfying these three inequalities are given by (5.11), (5.12) and (5.13). These three inequalities are therefore the necessary and sufficient conditions ensuring the existence of a solution to the smoothing problem. □

5.4 Optimal Smoothing Strategies

An optimal smoothing strategy is a solution $x(t)$ to the lossless smoothing problem where D, $T = D + d$ and B take their minimal value given by Theorem 5.3.1. The previous section shows that there exists at least one optimal solution, namely (5.10). It is however not the only one, as we will see in this section.

5.4.1 Maximal Solution

The maximal solution (5.10) requires only the evaluation of an infimum at time t over the past values of R and over the future values of R up to time $t + d_{\min}$, with $d_{\min} = T_{\min} - D_{\min}$. Of course, we need the knowledge of the traffic trace $R(t)$ to dimension $D_{\min}$, $d_{\min}$ and $B_{\min}$. However, once we have these values, we do not need the full stream for the computation of the smoothed input to the network.

5.4.2 Minimal Solution

To compute the minimal solution, we reformulate the lossless smoothing problem slightly differently. Because of Rule 14 of Theorem 3.1.12, an inequality equivalent to (5.2) is

$$x(t) \geq (x \oslash \sigma)(t) = \mathcal{D}_\sigma(x)(t). \tag{5.14}$$

We use this equivalence to replace the set of inequalities (5.6) and (5.7) by the equivalent set

$$x(t) \leq \delta_0(t) \wedge R(t + d) \wedge \{R(t - D) + B\}$$
$$\tag{5.15}$$
$$x(t) \geq (R \oslash \beta)(t - D) \vee \mathcal{D}_\sigma(x)(t). \tag{5.16}$$

One can then apply Theorem 4.3.2 to compute the *minimal* solution of (5.16), which is $x_{\min} = \mathcal{D}_\sigma(b) = b \oslash \sigma$ where $b(t) = \delta_0(t) \wedge R(t+d) \wedge \{R(t-D) + B\}$, because σ is a 'good' function. Eliminating b from these expressions, we compute that the minimal solution is

$$x_{\min}(t) = (R \oslash (\beta \otimes \sigma))(t - D), \qquad (5.17)$$

and compute the constraints on d, D and B ensuring that it verifies (5.15): one would get the very same values of $D_{\min}$, $T_{\min}$ and $B_{\min}$ given by (5.11) (5.12) and (5.13).

It does achieve the values of $D_{\min}$ and $B_{\min}$ given by (5.11) and (5.13), but requires nevertheless the evaluation, at time t, of a supremum over all values of R up to the end of the trace, contrary to the maximal solution (5.10). Min-plus deconvolution can however be represented in the time inverted domain by a min-plus convolution, as we have seen in Section 3.1.10. As the duration of the pre-recorded stream is usually known, the complexity of computing a min-plus deconvolution can thus be reduced to that of computing a convolution.

5.4.3 Set of Optimal Solutions

Any function $x \in \mathcal{F}$ such that

$$x_{\min} \leq x \leq x_{\max}$$

and

$$x \leq x \otimes \sigma$$

is therefore also a solution to the lossless smoothing problem, for the same minimal values of the playback delay, look-ahead delay and client buffer size. This gives the set of all solutions. A particular solution among these can be selected to further minimize another metric, such as the ones discussed in [25], e.g. number of rate changes or rate variability.

The top of Figure 5.2 shows, for a synthetic trace $R(t)$, the maximal solution (5.10) for a CBR smoothing curve $\sigma(t) = \lambda_r(t)$ and a service curve $\beta(t) = \delta_0(t)$, whereas the bottom shows the minimal solution (5.17). Figure 5.3 shows the same solutions on a single plot, for the MPEG trace $R(t)$ of the top of Figure 1.2.4 representing the number of packet arrivals per time slot of 40 ms corresponding to a MPEG-2 encoded video when the packet size is 416 bytes for each packet.

An example of VBR smoothing on the same MPEG trace is shown on Figure 5.4, with a smoothing curve derived from the T-SPEC field, which is given by $\sigma = \gamma_{P,M} \wedge \gamma_{r,b}$, where M is the maximum packet size (here $M = 416$ Bytes), P the peak rate, r the sustainable rate and b the burst tolerance. Here we roughly have $P = 560$ kBytes/sec, $r = 330$ kBytes/sec and $b = 140$ kBytes The service curve is a rate-latency curve $\beta_{L,C}$ with $L = 1$ second and $r = 370$ kBytes/sec. The two traces have the same envelope, thus the same minimum buffer requirement (here, 928kBytes). However the second trace has its bursts later, thus, has a smaller minimum playback delay ($D_2 = 2.05$s versus $D_1 = 2.81$s).

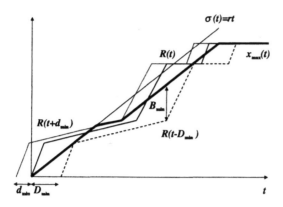

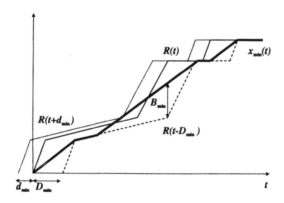

Figure 5.2: In bold, the maximal solution (top figure) and minimal solution (bottom figure) to the CBR smoothing problem with a null network.

5.5 Optimal Constant Rate Smoothing

Let us compute the above values in the case of a constant rate (CBR) smoothing curve $\sigma(t) = \lambda_r(t) = rt$ (with $t \geq 0$) and a rate-latency service curve of the network $\beta(t) = \beta_{L,C}(t) = C[t - L]^+$. We assume that $r < C$, the less interesting case where $r \geq C$ being handled similarly. We will often use the decomposition of a rate-latency function as the min-plus convolution of a pure delay function, with a constant rate function: $\beta_{L,C} = \delta_L \otimes \lambda_C$. We will also use the following lemma.

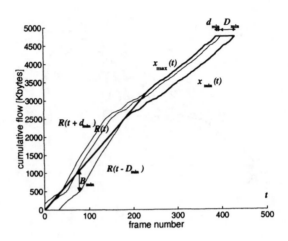

Figure 5.3: In bold, the maximal and minimal solutions to the CBR smoothing problem of an MPEG trace with a null network. A frame is generated every 40 msec.

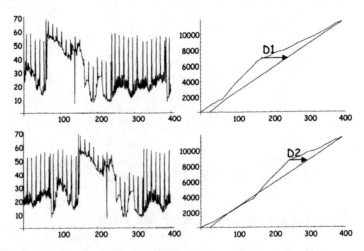

Figure 5.4: Two MPEG traces with the same arrival curve (left). The corresponding playback delays D_1 and D_2 are the horizontal deviations between the cumulative flows $R(t)$ and function $\sigma \otimes \beta$ (right).

Lemma 5.5.1. *If $f \in \mathcal{F}$,*

$$h(f, \beta_{L,C}) = L + \frac{1}{C}(f \oslash \lambda_C)(0). \tag{5.18}$$

Proof: As $f(t) = 0$ for $t \le 0$ and as $\beta_{L,C} = \delta_L \otimes \lambda_C$, we can write for any $t \ge 0$

$$
\begin{aligned}
(f \oslash \beta_{L,C})(-t) &= \sup_{u \ge 0}\{f(u - t) - (\delta_L \otimes \lambda_C)(u)\} \\
&= \sup_{u \ge 0}\{f(u - t) - \lambda_C(u - L)\} \\
&= \sup_{v \ge -t}\{f(v) - \lambda_C(v + t - L)\} \\
&= \sup_{v \ge 0}\{f(v) - \lambda_C(v + t - L)\} \\
&= \sup_{v \ge 0}\{f(v) - \lambda_C(v)\} - C(t - L) \\
&= (f \oslash \lambda_C)(0) - Ct + CL,
\end{aligned}
$$

from which we deduce the smallest value of t making the left-hand side of this equation non-positive is given by (5.18). $\qquad\square$

In the particular CBR case, the optimal values (5.11), (5.12) and (5.13) become the following ones.

Theorem 5.5.1 (Requirements for CBR optimal smoothing). *If $\sigma = \lambda_r$ and $\beta = \beta_{L,C}$ with $r < C$, the smallest values of D, of T and of B are*

$$
\begin{aligned}
D_{\min} &= L + \frac{1}{r}(R \oslash \lambda_r)(0) & (5.19) \\
T_{\min} &= L + \frac{1}{r}((R \oslash R) \oslash \lambda_r)(0) & (5.20) \\
B_{\min} &= ((R \oslash R) \oslash \lambda_r))(L) \le rT_{\min}. & (5.21)
\end{aligned}
$$

Proof: To establish (5.19) and (5.20), we note that R and $(R \oslash R) \in \mathcal{F}$. Since $r < C$

$$\beta \otimes \sigma = \beta_{L,C} \otimes \lambda_r = \delta_L \otimes \lambda_C \otimes \lambda_r = \delta_L \otimes \lambda_r = \beta_{L,r}$$

so that we can apply Lemma 5.5.1 with $f = R$ and $f = (R \oslash R)$, respectively.

To establish (5.21), we develop (5.13) as follows

$$
\begin{aligned}
((R \oslash R) \oslash (\beta \otimes \sigma))(0) &= ((R \oslash R) \oslash (\delta_L \otimes \lambda_r))(0) \\
&= \sup_{u \geq 0} \{(R \oslash R)(u) - \lambda_r(u - L)\} \\
&= ((R \oslash R) \oslash \lambda_r)(L) \\
&= \sup_{u \geq L} \{(R \oslash R)(u) - \lambda_r(u - L)\} \\
&= \sup_{u \geq L} \{(R \oslash R)(u) - \lambda_r(u)\} + rL \\
&\leq \sup_{u \geq 0} \{(R \oslash R)(u) - \lambda_r(u)\} + rL \\
&= ((R \oslash R) \oslash \lambda_r)(0) + rL = rT_{\min}.
\end{aligned}
$$

$\square$

This theorem provides the minimal values of playback delay $D_{\min}$ and buffer $B_{\min}$, as well as the minimal look-ahead delay $d_{\min} = T_{\min} - D_{\min}$ for a given constant smoothing rate $r < C$ and a given rate-latency service curve $\beta_{L,C}$. We can also solve the dual problem, namely compute for given values of playback delay D, of the look-ahead delay d, of the playback buffer B and for a given rate-latency service curve $\beta_{L,C}$, the minimal rate $r_{\min}$ which must be reserved on the network.

Theorem 5.5.2 (Optimal CBR smoothing rate). *If* $\sigma = \lambda_r$ *and* $\beta = \beta_{L,C}$ *with* $r < C$, *the smallest value of* r, *given* $D \geq L$, d *and* $B \geq (R \oslash R)(L)$, *is*

$$
r_{\min} = \sup_{t>0} \left\{ \frac{R(t)}{t + D - L} \right\} \vee \sup_{t>0} \left\{ \frac{(R \oslash R)(t)}{t + D + d - L} \right\}
$$
$$
\vee \sup_{t>0} \left\{ \frac{(R \oslash R)(t + L) - B}{t} \right\}. \tag{5.22}
$$

Proof: Let us first note that because of (5.19), there is no solution if $D < L$. On the other hand, if $D \geq L$, then (5.19) implies that the rate r must be such that for all $t > 0$

$$
D \geq L + \frac{1}{r}(R(t) - rt)
$$

or equivalently $r \geq R(t)/(t + D - L)$. The latter being true for all $t > 0$, we must have $r \geq \sup_{t \geq 0}\{R(t)/(t + D - L)\}$. Repeating the same argument with (5.20) and (5.21), we obtain the minimal rate (5.22). $\square$

In the particular case where $L = 0$ and $r < C$ the network is completely transparent to the flow, and can be considered as a null network: can replace $\beta(t)$ by $\delta_0(t)$. The values (5.19), (5.20) and (5.21) become, respectively,

$$
D_{\min} = \frac{1}{r}(R \oslash \lambda_r)(0) \tag{5.23}
$$

$$
T_{\min} = \frac{1}{r}((R \oslash R) \oslash \lambda_r)(0) \tag{5.24}
$$

$$
B_{\min} = ((R \oslash R) \oslash \lambda_r))(0) = rT_{\min}. \tag{5.25}
$$

It is interesting to compute these values on a real video trace, such as the first trace on top of Figure 1.2.4. Since $B_{\min}$ is directly proportional to $T_{\min}$ because of (5.25), we show only the graphs of the values of $D_{\min}$ and $d_{\min} = T_{\min} - D_{\min}$, as a function of the CBR smoothing rate r on Figure 5.5. We observe three qualitative ranges of rates: (i) the very low ones where the playback delay is very large, and where look-ahead does not help in reducing it; (ii) a middle range where the playback delay can be kept quite small, thanks to the use of look-ahead and (iii) the high rates above the peak rate of the stream, which do not require any playback nor lookahead of the stream. These three regions can be found on every MPEG trace [71], and depend on the location of the large burst in the trace. If it comes sufficiently late, then the use of look-ahead can become quite useful in keeping the playback delay small.

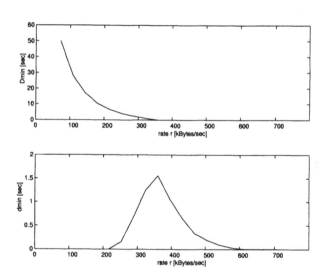

Figure 5.5: Minimum playback delay $D_{\min}$ and corresponding look-ahead delay $d_{\min}$ for a constant rate smoothing r of the MPEG-2 video trace shown on top of Figure 1.2.4.

5.6 Optimal Smoothing versus Greedy Shaping

An interesting question is to compare the requirements on D and B, due to the scheduling obtained in Section 5.4, which are minimal, with those that a simpler scheduling, namely the greedy shaper of Section 1.5, would create. As σ is a 'good' function, the solution of a greedy shaper is

$$x_{\text{shaper}}(t) = (\sigma \otimes R)(t). \tag{5.26}$$

To be a solution for the smoothing problem, it must satisfy all constraints listed in Section 5.2. It already satisfies (5.1), (5.2) and (5.5). Enforcing (5.3) is equivalent to impose that for all $t \in \mathbb{R}$

$$(R \oslash \beta)(t - D) \leq (\sigma \otimes R)(t),$$

which can be recast as

$$((R \oslash R) \oslash (\beta \otimes \sigma))(-D) \leq 0. \tag{5.27}$$

This implies that the minimal playback delay needed for a smoothing using a greedy shaping algorithm is equal to the minimal total delay $T_{\min}$, the sum of the playback and lookahead delays, for the optimal smoothing algorithm. It means that the only way an optimal smoother allows to decrease the playback delay is its ability to look ahead and send data in advance. If this look-ahead is not possible ($d = 0$) as for example for a live video transmission, the playback delay is the same for the greedy shaper and the optimal smoother.

The last constraint that must be verified is (5.4), which is equivalent to impose that for all $t \in \mathbb{R}$

$$(\sigma \otimes R)(t) \leq R(t - D) + B,$$

which can be recast as

$$((R \otimes \sigma) \oslash R)(D) \leq B. \tag{5.28}$$

Consequently, the minimal requirements on the playback delay and buffer using a greedy shaper instead of an optimal smoother are given by the following theorem.

Theorem 5.6.1 (Requirements for greedy shaper). *If σ is a 'good' function, then the smallest values of D and B for lossless smoothing of flow R by a greedy shaper are*

$$D_{shaper} = T_{\min} = h((R \oslash R), (\beta \otimes \sigma)) \tag{5.29}$$

$$B_{shaper} = ((R \otimes \sigma) \oslash R)(D_{shaper}) \in [B_{\min}, \sigma(D_{shaper})]. \tag{5.30}$$

Proof: The expressions of D_{shaper} and B_{shaper} follow immediately from (5.27) and (5.28). The only point that remains to be shown is that $B_{\text{shaper}} \leq \sigma(D_{\text{shaper}})$, which we do by picking $s = u$ in the inf below:

$$
\begin{aligned}
B_{\text{shaper}} &= (R \oslash (R \otimes \sigma))(D_{\text{shaper}}) \\
&= \sup_{u \geq 0} \left\{ \inf_{0 \leq s \leq u + D_{\text{shaper}}} \left\{ R(s) + \sigma(u + D_{\text{shaper}} - s) \right\} - R(u) \right\} \\
&\leq \sup_{u \geq 0} \left\{ R(u) + \sigma(u + D_{\text{shaper}} - u) - R(u) \right\} \\
&= \sigma(D_{\text{shaper}}).
\end{aligned}
$$

$\square$

Consequently, a greedy shaper does not minimize, in general, the playback buffer requirements, although it does minimize the playback delay when look-ahead is possible. Figure 5.6 shows the maximal solution x_{max} of the optimal shaper (top) and the solution x_{shaper} of the greedy shaper (bottom) when the shaping curve is a one leaky bucket affine curve $\sigma = \gamma_{r,b}$, when the look-ahead delay $d = 0$ (no look ahead possible) and for a null network ($\beta = \delta_0$). In this case the playback delays are identical, but not the playback buffers.

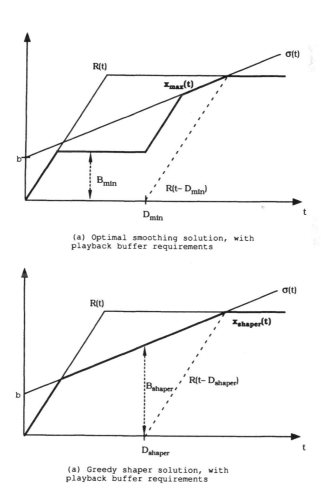

(a) Optimal smoothing solution, with playback buffer requirements

(a) Greedy shaper solution, with playback buffer requirements

Figure 5.6: In bold, the maximal solution (top figure) and minimal solution (bottom figure) to the smoothing problem with a null network, no look-ahead and an affine smoothing curve $\sigma = \gamma_{r,b}$.

Another example is shown on Figure 5.7 for the MPEG-2 video trace shown on top of Figure 1.2.4. Here the solution of the optimal smoother is the minimal solution x_{min}.

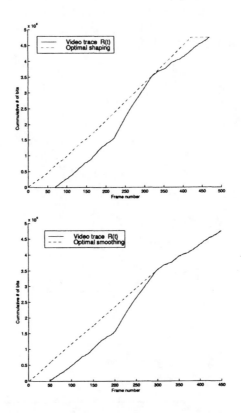

Figure 5.7: Example of optimal shaping versus optimal smoothing for the MPEG-2 video trace shown on top of Figure 1.2.4. The example is for a null network and a smoothing curve $\sigma = \gamma_{P,M} \wedge \gamma_{r,b}$ with $M = 416$ bytes, $P = 600$ kBytes/sec, $r = 300$ kBytes/sec and $b = 80$ kBytes. The figure shows the optimal shaper [resp. smoother] output and the original signal (video trace), shifted by the required playback delay. The playback delay is 2.76 sec for optimal shaping (top) and 1.92 sec for optimal smoothing (bottom).

There is however one case where a greedy shaper does minimize the playback buffer: a constant rate smoothing ($\sigma = \lambda_r$) over a null network ($\beta = \delta_0$). Indeed, in this case, (5.25) becomes

$$B_{min} = rT_{min} = rD_{shaper} = \sigma(D_{shaper}),$$

and therefore $B_{\text{shaper}} = B_{\min}$. Consequently, if no look-ahead is possible and if the network is transparent to the flow, greedy shaping is an optimal CBR smoothing strategy.

5.7 Comparison with Delay Equalization

A common method to implement a decoder is to first remove any delay jitter caused by the network, by delaying the arriving data in a delay equalization buffer, before using the playback buffer to compensate for fluctuations due to pre-fetching. Figure 5.8 shows such a system. If the delay equalization buffer is properly configured, its combination with the guaranteed service network results into a fixed delay network, which, from the viewpoint we take in this chapter, is equivalent to a null network. Compared to the original scenario in Figure 5.1, there are now two separate buffers for delay equalization and for compensation of prefetching. We would like to understand the impact of this separation on the minimum playback delay $D_{\min}$.

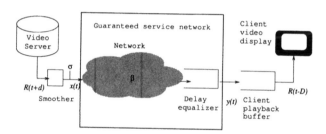

Figure 5.8: Delay equalization at the receiver.

The delay equalization buffer operates by delaying the first bit of data by an initial delay D_{eq}, equal to the worst case delay through the network. We assume that the network offers a rate-latency service curve $\beta_{L,C}$. Since the flow x is constainted by the arrival curve σ which is assumed to be a 'good' function, we know from Theorem 1.4.4, that the worst-case delay is

$$D_{eq} = h(\sigma, \beta_{L,C}).$$

On the other hand, the additional part of the playback delay to compensate for fluctuations due to pre-fetching, denoted by D_{pf}, is given by (5.11) with β replaced by δ_0:

$$D_{pf} = h(R, \delta_0 \otimes \sigma) = h(R, \sigma).$$

The sum of these two delays is, in general, larger than the optimal playback delay (without a separation between equalization and compensation for prefetching), $D_{\min}$, given by (5.11):

$$D_{\min} = h(R, \beta_{L,C} \otimes \sigma).$$

Consider the example of Figure 5.9, where $\sigma = \gamma_{r,b}$ with $r < C$. Then one easily computes the three delays D_{min}, D_{eq} and D_{pf}, knowing that

$$\begin{aligned}
\beta_{L,C} \otimes \sigma &= \delta_L \otimes \lambda_C \otimes \gamma_{r,b} = \delta_L \otimes (\lambda_C \wedge \gamma_{r,b}) \\
&= (\delta_L \otimes \lambda_C) \wedge (\delta_L \otimes \gamma_{r,b}) = \beta_{L,C} \wedge (\delta_L \otimes \gamma_{r,b}).
\end{aligned}$$

One clearly has $D_{min} < D_{eq} + D_{pf}$: separate delay equalization gives indeed a larger overall playback delay. In fact, looking carefully at the figure (or working out the computations), we can observe that the combination of delay equalization and compensation for prefetching in a single buffer accounts for the busrtiness of the (optimally) smoothed flow only once. This is another instance of the "pay bursts only once" phenomenon, which we have already met in Section 1.4.3.

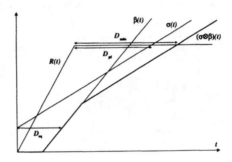

Figure 5.9: Delays D_{min}, D_{eq} and D_{pf} for a rate-latency service curve $\beta_{L,C}$ and an affine smoothing curve $\sigma = \gamma_{r,b}$.

We must however make – once again – an exception for a constant rate smoothing. Indeed, if $\sigma = \lambda_r$ (with $r < C$), then D_{pf} is given by (5.23) and D_{min} by (5.19), so that

$$\begin{aligned}
D_{eq} &= h(\lambda_r, \beta_{L,C}) = L \\
D_{pf} &= \frac{1}{r}(R \oslash \lambda_r)(0) \\
D_{min} &= L + \frac{1}{r}(R \oslash \lambda_r)(0)
\end{aligned}$$

and therefore $D_{min} = D_{eq} + D_{pf}$. In the CBR case, separate delay equalization is thus able to attain the optimal playback delay.

5.8 Lossless Smoothing over Two Networks

We now consider the more complex setting where two networks separate the video server from the client: the first one is a backbone network, offering a service curve β_1 to the flow, and the second one is a local access network, offering a service curve β_2 to the flow, as shown on Figure 5.10. This scenario models intelligent, dynamic caching often done at local network head-ends. We will compute the requirements on D, d, B and on the buffer X of this intermediate node in Subsection 5.8.1. Moreover, we will see in Subsection 5.8.2 that for constant rate shaping curves and rate-latency service curves, the size of the client buffer B can be reduced by implementing a particular smoothing strategy instead of FIFO scheduling at the intermediate node.

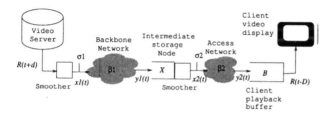

Figure 5.10: Smoothing over two networks with a local caching node.

Two flows need therefore to be computed: the first one $x_1(t)$ at the input of the backbone network, and the second one $x_2(t)$ at the input of the local access network, as shown on Figure 5.10.

The constraints on both flows are now as follows:

- **Causal flow** x_1: This constraint is the same as (5.1), but with x replaced by x_1:

$$x_1(t) \le \delta_0(t), \tag{5.31}$$

- **Smoothness constraint**: Both flows x_1 and x_2 are constrained by two arrival curves σ_1 and σ_2:

$$x_1(t) \le (x_1 \otimes \sigma_1)(t) \tag{5.32}$$
$$x_2(t) \le (x_2 \otimes \sigma_2)(t). \tag{5.33}$$

- **No playback and intermediate server buffers underflow**: The data is read out from the playback buffer after D unit of times at a rate given by $R(t - D)$, which implies that $y_2(t) \ge R(t - D)$. On the other hand, the data is retrieved from the intermediate server at a rate given by $x_2(t)$, which implies that $y_1(t) \ge x_2(t)$. As we do not know the expressions of the outputs of each network, but only a service curve β_1 and β_2 for each of them, we can replace y_1 by $x_1 \otimes \beta_1$ and y_2 by $x_2 \otimes \beta_2$, and reformulate these two constraints by

$$x_2(t) \leq (x_1 \otimes \beta_1)(t) \tag{5.34}$$

$$x_2(t) \geq (R \oslash \beta_2)(t - D). \tag{5.35}$$

- **No playback and intermediate server buffers overflow**: The size of the playback and cache buffers are limited to B and X, respectively, and to prevent any overflow of the buffer, we must impose that $y_1(t) - x_2(t) \leq X$ and $y_2(t) - R(t - D) \leq B$ for all $t \geq 0$. Again, we do not know the exact value of y_1 and y_2, but we know that they are bounded by x_1 and x_2, respectively, so that the constraints becomes, for all $t \geq 0$,

$$x_1(t) \leq x_2(t) + X \tag{5.36}$$

$$x_2(t) \leq R(t - D) + B. \tag{5.37}$$

- **Look-ahead delay constraint**: this constraint is the same as in the single network case:

$$x_1(t) \leq R(t + d). \tag{5.38}$$

5.8.1 Minimal Requirements on the Delays and Buffer Sizes for Two Networks

Inequalities (5.31) to (5.38) can be recast as three sets of inequalities as follows:

$$x_1(t) \leq \delta_0(t) \wedge R(t + d) \wedge (\sigma_1 \otimes x_1)(t) \wedge (x_2(t) + X) \tag{5.39}$$

$$x_2(t) \leq \{R(t - D) + B\} \wedge (\beta_1 \otimes x_1)(t) \wedge (\sigma_2 \otimes x_2)(t) \tag{5.40}$$

$$x_2(t) \geq (R \oslash \beta_2)(t - D). \tag{5.41}$$

We use the same technique for solving this problem sa in Section 5.3, except that now the dimension of the system J is 2 instead of 1.

With T denoting transposition, let us introduce the following notations:

$$\vec{x}(t) = [x_1(t) \quad x_2(t)]^T$$
$$\vec{a}(t) = [\delta_0(t) \wedge R(t + d) \quad R(t - D) + B]^T$$
$$\vec{b}(t) = [0 \quad (R \oslash \beta_2)(t - D)]^T$$

$$\Sigma(t) = \begin{bmatrix} \sigma_1(t) & \delta_0(t) + X \\ \beta_1(t) & \sigma_2(t) \end{bmatrix}.$$

With these notations, the set of inequalities (5.39), (5.40) and (5.41) can therefore be recast as

$$\vec{x} \leq \vec{a} \wedge (\Sigma \otimes \vec{x}) \tag{5.42}$$

$$\vec{x} \geq \vec{b}. \tag{5.43}$$

We will follow the same approach as in Section 5.3: we first compute the maximal solution of (5.42) and then derive the constraints on D, T (and hence d), X and B ensuring the existence of this solution. We apply thus Theorem 4.3.1 again, but this time in the two-dimensional case, to obtain an explicit formulation of the maximal solution of (5.42). We get

$$\vec{x}_{\max} = \overline{C}_\Sigma(\vec{a}) = (\overline{\Sigma} \otimes \vec{a}) \tag{5.44}$$

where $\overline{\Sigma}$ is the sub-additive closure of Σ, which is, as we know from Section 4.2,

$$\overline{\Sigma} = \inf_{n \in \mathbb{N}} \{\Sigma^{(n)}\} \tag{5.45}$$

where $\Sigma^{(0)} = D_0$ and $\Sigma^{(n)}$ denotes the nth self-convolution of Σ. Application of (5.45) to matrix Σ is straightforward, but involves a few manipulations which are skipped. Denoting

$$\begin{aligned}
\alpha &= \sigma_1 \otimes \sigma_2 \otimes \inf_{n \in \mathbb{N}} \left\{ \beta_1^{(n+1)} + nX \right\} \tag{5.46} \\
&= \sigma_1 \otimes \sigma_2 \otimes \beta_1 \otimes \overline{\beta_1 + X},
\end{aligned}$$

we find that

$$\overline{\Sigma} = \begin{bmatrix} \sigma_1 \wedge (\alpha + X) & (\sigma_1 \otimes \sigma_2 + X) \wedge (\alpha + 2X) \\ \alpha & \sigma_2 \wedge (\alpha + X) \end{bmatrix}$$

and therefore the two coordinates of the maximal solution of (5.42) are

$$\begin{aligned}
x_{1\,\max}(t) &= \sigma_1(t) \wedge \{\alpha(t) + X\} \wedge (\sigma_1 \otimes R)(t + d) \wedge \{(\alpha \otimes R)(t + d) + X\} \\
&\quad \wedge \{(\sigma_1 \otimes \sigma_2 \otimes R)(t - D) + B + X\} \\
&\quad \wedge \{(\alpha \otimes R)(t - D) + B + 2X\} \tag{5.47} \\
x_{2\,\max}(t) &= \alpha(t) \wedge (\alpha \otimes R)(t + d) \wedge \{(\sigma_2 \otimes R)(t - D) + B\} \\
&\quad \wedge \{(\alpha \otimes R)(t - D) + B + X\}. \tag{5.48}
\end{aligned}$$

Let us mention that an alternative (and computationally simpler) approach to obtain (5.47) and (5.48) would have been to first compte the maximal solution of (5.40), as a function of x_1, and next to replace x_2 in (5.39) by this latter value.

We can now express the constraints on X, B, D and d that will ensure that a solution exists by requiring that (5.48) be larger than (5.41). The result is stated in the following theorem, whose proof is similar to that of Theorem 5.3.1.

Theorem 5.8.1. *The lossless smoothing of a flow to (sub-additive) curves σ_1 and σ_2, respectively, over two networks offering service curves β_1 and β_2 has a solution if and only if the D, T, X and B verify the following set of inequalities, with α defined by (5.46):*

$$\begin{aligned}
(R \oslash (\alpha \otimes \beta_2))(-D) &\leq 0 \tag{5.49} \\
((R \oslash R) \oslash (\alpha \otimes \beta_2))(-T) &\leq 0 \tag{5.50} \\
((R \oslash R) \oslash (\sigma_2 \otimes \beta_2))(0) &\leq B \tag{5.51} \\
((R \oslash R) \oslash (\alpha \otimes \beta_2))(0) &\leq B + X. \tag{5.52}
\end{aligned}$$

5.8.2   Optimal Constant Rate Smoothing over Two Networks

Let us compute the values of Theorem 5.8.1 in the case of two constant rate (CBR) smoothing curves $\sigma_1 = \lambda_{r_1}$ and $\sigma_2 = \lambda_{r_2}$. We assume that each network offers a rate-latency service curve $\beta_i = \beta_{L_i, C_i}$, $i = 1, 2$. We assume that $r_i \leq C_i$ In this case the optimal values of D, T and B become the following ones, depending on the value of X.

Theorem 5.8.2. *Let* $r = r_1 \wedge r_2$. *Then we have the following three cases depending on* X:
(i) If $X \geq rL_1$, *then* $D_{\min}$, $T_{\min}$ *and* $B_{\min}$ *are given by*

$$D_{\min} = L_1 + L_2 + \frac{1}{r}(R \oslash \lambda_r)(0) \tag{5.53}$$

$$T_{\min} = L_1 + L_2 + \frac{1}{r}((R \oslash R) \oslash \lambda_r)(0) \tag{5.54}$$

$$B_{\min} = ((R \oslash R) \oslash \lambda_{r_2})(L_2) \vee \{((R \oslash R) \oslash \lambda_r)(L_1 + L_2) - X\}$$
$$\leq ((R \oslash R) \oslash \lambda_r)(L_2). \tag{5.55}$$

(ii) If $0 < X < rL_1$ *then* $D_{\min}$, $T_{\min}$ *and* $B_{\min}$ *are bounded by*

$$\frac{X}{r} + L_2 + \frac{L_1}{X}(R \oslash \lambda_{\frac{X}{L_1}})(0) \leq D_{\min}$$

$$\leq L_1 + L_2 + \frac{L_1}{X}(R \oslash \lambda_{\frac{X}{L_1}})(0) \tag{5.56}$$

$$\frac{X}{r} + L_2 + \frac{L_1}{X}((R \oslash R) \oslash \lambda_{\frac{X}{L_1}})(0) \leq T_{\min}$$

$$\leq L_1 + L_2 + \frac{L_1}{X}((R \oslash R) \oslash \lambda_{\frac{X}{L_1}})(0) \tag{5.57}$$

$$((R \oslash R) \oslash \lambda_{\frac{X}{L_1}})(L_1 + L_2) - r_2 L_1 \leq B_{\min}$$

$$\leq ((R \oslash R) \oslash \lambda_{\frac{X}{L_1}})(L_2) \tag{5.58}$$

(iii) Let K *be duration of the stream. If* $X = 0 < rL_1$ *then* $D_{\min} = K$.

Proof. One easily verifies that $\delta_{L_1}^{(n+1)} = \delta_{(n+1)L_1}$ and that $\lambda_{C_1}^{(n+1)} = \lambda_{C_1}$. Since $\beta_1 = \beta_{L_1, C_1} = \delta_{L_1} \otimes \lambda_{C_1}$, and since $r = r_1 \wedge r_2 \leq C_1$, (5.46) becomes

$$\alpha = \lambda_r \otimes \inf_{n \in \mathbb{N}} \{\delta_{(n+1)L_1} \otimes \lambda_{C_1} + nX\}$$

$$= \delta_{L_1} \otimes \inf_{n \in \mathbb{N}} \{\delta_{nL_1} \otimes \lambda_r + nX\}. \tag{5.59}$$

(i) If $X \geq rL_1$, then for $t \geq nL_1$

$$(\delta_{nL_1} \otimes \lambda_r)(t) + nX = \lambda_r(t - nL_1) + nX = rt + n(X - rL_1) \geq rt = \lambda_r(t)$$

whereas for $0 \leq t < nL_1$

$$(\delta_{nL_1} \otimes \lambda_r)(t) + nX = \lambda_r(t - nL_1) + nX = nX \geq nrL_1 > rt = \lambda_r(t).$$

Consequently, for all $t \geq 0$, $\alpha(t) \geq (\delta_{L_1} \otimes \lambda_r)(t)$. On the other hand, taking $n = 0$ in the infimum in (5.59) yields that $\alpha \leq \delta_{L_1} \otimes \lambda_r$. Combining these two inequalities, we get that

$$\alpha = \delta_{L_1} \otimes \lambda_r$$

and hence that

$$\alpha \otimes \beta_2 = \delta_{L_1} \otimes \lambda_r \otimes \delta_{L_2} \otimes \lambda_{r_2} = \delta_{L_1+L_2} \otimes \lambda_r = \beta_{L_1+L_2,r}. \qquad (5.60)$$

Inserting this last relation in (5.49) to (5.52), and using Lemma 5.5.1 we establish (5.53), (5.54) and the equality in (5.55). The inequality in (5.55) is obtained by noticing that $r_2 \geq r$ and that

$$
\begin{aligned}
((R \oslash R) \oslash \lambda_r)(L_1 + L_2) - X &= \sup_{u \geq 0}\{(R \oslash R)(u + L_1 + L_2) - ru\} - X \\
&= \sup_{v \geq L_1} \{(R \oslash R)(v + L_2) - r(v - L_1)\} - X \\
&\leq \sup_{v \geq 0}\{(R \oslash R)(v + L_2) - rv\} + (rL_1 - X) \\
&\leq ((R \oslash R) \oslash \lambda_r)(L_2).
\end{aligned}
$$

(ii) If $0 < X < rL_1$, the computation of α does not provide a rate-latency curve anymore, but a function that can be bounded below and above by the two following rate-latency curves: $\beta_{L_1, X/L_1} \leq \alpha \leq \beta_{X/r, X/L_1}$. Therefore, replacing (5.60) by

$$\delta_{L_1+L_2} \otimes \lambda_{\frac{X}{L_1}} \leq \alpha \otimes \beta_2 \leq \delta_{\frac{X}{r}+L_2} \otimes \lambda_{\frac{X}{L_1}},$$

and applying Lemma 5.5.1 to both bounding rate-latency curves $\beta_{L_1, X/L_1}$ and $\beta_{X/r, X/L_1}$, we get respectively the lower and upper bounds (5.56) to (5.58).

(iii) If $X = 0$ and $rL_1 > 0$ then (5.59) yields that $\alpha(t) = 0$ for all $t \geq 0$. In this case (5.49) becomes $\sup_{u \geq 0}\{R(u - D)\} \leq 0$. This is possible only if D is equal to the duration of the stream. $\qquad \square$

It is interesting to examine these results for two particular values of X.

The first one is $X = \infty$. If the intermediate server is a greedy shaper whose output is $x_2(t) = (\sigma_2 \otimes y_1)(t)$, one could have applied Theorem 5.5.1 with $\sigma_2 = \lambda_r$ and $\beta = \beta_1 \otimes \sigma_2 \otimes \beta_2 = \delta_{L_1+L_2} \otimes \lambda_{r_2} = \beta_{L_1+L_2,r_2}$ to find out that D and T are still given by (5.53) and (5.54) but that $B = ((R \oslash R) \oslash \lambda_r)(L_1 + L_2)$ is larger than (5.55). Using the caching scheduling (5.48) instead of a greedy shaping one allows therefore to decrease the playback buffer size, but not the delays. The buffer X of the intermediate node does not need to be infinite, but can be limited to rL_1.

The second one is $X = 0$. Then whatever the rate $r > 0$, if $L_1 > 0$, the playback delay is the length of the stream, which makes streaming impossible in practice. When $L_1 = L_2 = 0$ however (in which case we have two null networks) $X = rL_1 = 0$ is the optimal intermediate node buffer allocation. This was shown in [61](Lemma 5.3) using another approach. We see that when $L_1 > 0$, this is no longer the case.

5.9 Bibliographic Notes

The first application of network calculus to optimal smoohting is found in [48], for an unlimited value of the look-ahead delay. The minimal solution (5.17) is shown to be an optimal smoothing scheme. The computation of the minimum look-ahead delay, and of the maximal solution, is done in [71]. Network calculus allows to retrieve some results found using other methods, such as the optimal buffer allocation of the intermdiate node for two null networks computed in [61].

It also allows to extend these results, by computing the full set of optimal schedules and by taking into account non null networks, as well as by using more complex shaping curves σ than constant rate service curves. For example, with the Resource Reservation Protocol (RSVP), σ is derived from the T-SPEC field in messages used for setting up the reservation, and is given by $\sigma = \gamma_{P,M} \wedge \gamma_{r,b}$, where M is the maximum packet size, P the peak rate, r the sustainable rate and b the burst tolerance, as we have seen in Section 1.4.3.

The optimal T-SPEC field is computed in [48]. More precisely, the following problem is solved. As assumed by the Intserv model, every node offers a service of the form $\beta_{L,C}$ for some latency L and rate C, with the latency parameter L depending on the rate C according to $L = \frac{C_0}{\rho} + D_0$. The constants C_0 and D_0 depends on the route taken by the flow throughout the network. Destinations choose a target admissible network delay D_{net}. The choice of a specific service curve $\beta_{L,C}$ (or equivalently, of a rate parameter C) is done during the reservation phase and cannot be known exactly in advance. The algorithm developed in [48] computes the admissible choices of $\sigma = \gamma_{P,M} \wedge \gamma_{r,b}$ and of D_{net} in order to guarantee that the reservation that will subsequently be performed ensures a playback delay not exceeding a given value D.

Chapter 6

FIFO Systems and Aggregate Scheduling

6.1 Introduction

Aggregate scheduling arises naturally in many case. Let us just mention here the differentiated services framework (Section 2.4) and high speed switches with optical switching matrix and FIFO outputs.

The state of the art for aggregate multiplexing is surprisingly poor. We summarize this in the form of a conjecture in Section 6.3.1. In this chapter, we give a panorama of results, many of them are new. In Section 6.2, we give bounds for a service element in isolation that serves several flows in an aggregate. The particular service discipline is not known, but we assume that the aggregate receives a strict service curve guarantee. Then we are able to bound the service received by any sub-flow inside the aggregate. The bound corresponds actually to the worst case where a sub-flow receives the lowest priority.

Then in Section 6.3 we consider a global network using aggregate multiplexing; given constraints at the inputs of the network, can we obtain some bounds for backlog and delay ? An iterative application of Section 6.2 can be used as a solution; however, as illustrated in Section 2.4, it does not given very good bounds. We do not have a general answer, not even a general method. However, for the particular case of a unidirectional ring, we are able to obtain a closed form bound, which shows that the ring is always stable (for utilization factors less than 1).

Then we consider FIFO multiplexing. We expect to find better bounds, and we do. However, we find the same pattern as above. First, in Section 6.4, we find some bounds for FIFO network elements. If one of the flows is leaky-bucket constrained, we have simple closed form expressions, which improve on Section 6.2. However, their iterative application in a network setting does not give the best known bounds. Here too, we know little about global network effects. In Section 6.5, we analyze a particular case, where strong rate limitations at all sources have the effect of providing simple, closed form bounds (but the proof of such a result is extraordinarily complicate).

6.2 General Bounds for Aggregate Scheduling

Consider two flows multiplexed into the same service curve element; we are interested in the service received by one of the two flows, say flow 1. If we have no information about arbitration between the two flows, then a worst case is obtained by assuming that flow 2 receives low priority.

Theorem 6.2.1 (Blind multiplexing). *Consider a node serving two flows, 1 and 2, with some unknown arbitration between the two flows. Assume that the node guarantees a* strict *service curve β to the aggregate of the two flows. Assume that flow 2 is α_2-smooth. Define $\beta_1(t) := [\beta(t) - \alpha_2(t)]^+$. If β_1 is wide-sense increasing, then it is a service curve for flow 1.*

Proof: The proof is a straightforward extension of that of Proposition 1.3.4.   □

We have seen an example in Section 1.3.2: if $\beta(t) = Ct$ (constant rate server or GPS node) and $\alpha_2 = \gamma_{r,b}$ (constraint by one leaky bucket) then the service curve for flow 1 is the rate-latency service curve with rate $C - r$ and latency $\frac{b}{C-r}$.

Corollary 6.2.1 (Non preemptive priority node). *Consider a node serving two flows, H and L, with non-preemptive priority given to flow H. Assume that the node guarantees a* strict *service curve β to the aggregate of the two flows. Then the high priority flow is guaranteed a service curve $\beta_H(t) = [\beta(t) - l_{\max}^L]^+$ where $l_{\max}^L$ is the maximum packet size for the low priority flow.*

If in addition the high priority flow is α_H-smooth, then define β_L by $\beta_L(t) = [\beta(t) - \alpha_H]^+$. If β_L is wide-sense increasing, then it is a service curve for the low priority flow.

Proof: The first part is an immediate consequence of Theorem 6.2.1. The second part is proven in the same way as Proposition 1.3.4.   □

If we relax the assumption that the service curve property is strict, then the above results do not hold. A counter-example can be built as follows. All packets have the same size, 1 data unit, and input flows have a peak rate equal to 1. Flow 1 sends one packet at time 0, and then stops. The node delays this packet forever. With an obvious notation, we have, for $t \geq 0$:

$$R_1(t) = \min(t, 1) \text{ and } R'1(t) = 0$$

Flow 2 sends one packet every time unit, starting at time $t = 1$. The output is a continuous stream of packets, one per time unit, starting from time 1. Thus

$$R_2(t) = (t - 1)^+ \text{ and } R'2(t) = R_2(t)$$

The aggregate flows are, for $t \geq 0$:

$$R(t) = t \text{ and } R'(t) = (t-1)^t$$

In other words, the node offers to the aggregate flow a service curve δ_1. Obviously, Theorem 6.2.1 does not apply to flow 1: if it would, flow 1 would receive a service curve $(\delta_1 - \lambda_1)^+ = \delta_1$, which is not true since it receives 0 service. We can interpret this example in the light of Section 1.4.4 on Page 36: if the service curve property would be strict, then we could bound the duration of the busy period, which would give a minimum service guarantee to low priority traffic. We do not have such a bound on this example. In Section 6.4 we see that if we assume FIFO scheduling, then we do have a service curve guarantee.

6.3 Stability of a Network with Aggregate Scheduling

6.3.1 The Open Issue of Stability

In this section we consider the following global problem: Given a network with aggregate scheduling and arrival curve constraints at the input, can we find good bounds for delay and backlog ? As it turns out today, this problem is still open.

A first attempt at solving the problem is based on the previous section and the bounding method in Section 2.4.2. We have seen in Section 2.4.2 that finite bounds can be found with this method for small utilization factors. When the bounds are infinite, we do not know in general whether the delays can become arbitrarily large or not. In[3], the author exhibits networks of constant rate, FIFO queues, with leaky bucket constraint sources, and utilization factors less than 1 (a "critical" network), where the delay for some sources goes to infinity. However, the result is based on an incomplete proof. At the time of writing, it appears thus that the following conjecture is still open.

Assumption and Notation

- Consider a network with a fixed number I of flows, following fixed paths. A network node is modeled as a collection of output buffers, with no contention other than at the output buffers. Every buffer is associated with one unidirectional link that it feeds.

- Flow i is constrained by one leaky bucket of rate ρ_i and burstiness σ_i at the input.

- Inside the network, flows are treated as an aggregate by the network; within an aggregate, packets are served according to some unspecified arbitration policy. The only constraint we impose on the scheduling is that the aggregate of all flows receives a service curve at node m equal to the rate-latency function with rate r_m and latency $\frac{b_m}{r_m}$.

  This implies a form of work conservation. Note that we do not require that the service curve property be strict.

b_m accounts for the latency on the link that exits node m; it also account for delays due to the scheduler at node m.

- We write $i \ni m$ to express that node m is on the route of flow i. For any node m, define $\rho^{(m)} = \sum_{i \ni m} \rho_i$ and let $\nu = \min_m (r_m - \rho^{(m)})$.

- The bit rate of the link feeding node m is $C_m < +\infty$.

We say that such a network is *stable* if the backlog at any node remains bounded.

Conjecture 6.3.1 (Stability of sub-critical session oriented network). *We conjecture that, if $\nu > 0$ (the network is "subcritical"), any network satisfying the above assumptions is stable.*

[32] shows that, for constant rate servers, the problem can be reduced to the case where every source i sends a burst b_i instantly at time 0, then sends at a rate limited by ρ_i. In the next section we show that the conjecture is true for the case of a unidirectional ring.

6.3.2 The Ring is Stable

The result was initially obtained in [69] for the case of a ring of constant rate servers, with all servers having the same rate. We give here a more general, but simpler form.

Assumption and Notation   We take the same assumptions as in Section 6.3.1 and assume in addition that the network topology is a unidirectional ring. More precisely:

- The network is a unidirectional ring of M nodes, labelled $1, ..., M$. We use the notation $m \oplus k = (m + k - 1) \mod M + 1$ and $m \ominus k = (m - k - 1) \mod M + 1$, so that the successor of node m on the ring is node $m \oplus 1$ and its predecessor is node $m \ominus 1$.

- The route of flow i is $(0, i.\text{first}, i.\text{first} \oplus 1, ..., i.\text{first} \oplus (h_i - 1))$ where 0 is a virtual node representing the source of flow i, $i.\text{first}$ is the first hop of flow i, and h_i is the number of hops of flow i. At its last hop, flow i exits the network. We assume that a flow does not wrap, namely, $h_i \leq M$. If $h_i = M$, then the flow goes around the all ring, exiting at the same node it has entered.

- Let $b = \sum_m b_m$ reflect the total latency of the ring.

- For any node m let $\sigma^{(m)} = \sum_{i \ni m} \sigma_i$.

  Let $\sigma_{\max} = \max_{m=1}^{M} \sigma^{(m)}$ and $\sigma = \sum_i \sigma_i$. Note that $\sigma_{\max} \leq \sigma \leq M \sigma_{\max}$.

- Define $\nu = \min_m (r_m - \rho^{(m)})$.

- Let $\rho_0^{(m)} = \sum_{i.\text{first}=m} \rho_i$ and $\mu = \max_{m=0}^{M} \left[C_m - r_m + \rho^{(m)} \right]^+$. μ reflects the sum of the peak rate of transit links and the rates of fresh sources, minus the rate guaranteed to the aggregate of microflows. We expect high values of μ to give higher bounds.

Theorem 6.3.1. *If $\nu > 0$ (the network is "sub-critical") then the backlog at any node of the unidirectional ring is bounded by*

$$M \frac{\mu}{\nu} \left(M \sigma_{\max} + b \right) + \sigma + b$$

Proof: The proof relies on the concept of chain of busy periods, combined with the time stopping method in Section 2.4.2.

For a node m and a flow i, define $R_i^m(t)$ as the cumulative amount of data of flow i at the output of node m. For $m = 0$, this defines the input function. Also define

$$x_m(t) = \sum_{i \ni m} \left(R_i^0(t) - R_i^m(t) \right) \tag{6.1}$$

thus $x_m(t)$ is the total amount of data that is present in the network at time t and will go through node m at some time $> t$.

We also define the backlog at node m by

$$q_m(t) = \sum_{i \ni m, i.\text{first} \neq m} R_i^{m \ominus 1}(t) + \sum_{i.\text{first}=m} R_i^0(t) - \sum_{i \ni m} R_i^m(t)$$

Now obviously, for all time t and node m:

$$q_m(t) \leq x_m(t) \tag{6.2}$$

and

$$x_m(t) \leq \sum_{n=1}^{M} q_n(t) \tag{6.3}$$

(Step 1) Assume that a finite bound X exists. Consider a time t and a node m that achieves the bound: $x_m(t) = X$. We fix m and apply Lemma 6.3.1 to all nodes n. Call s_n the time called s in the lemma. Since $x_n(s_n) \leq X$, it follows from the first formula in the lemma that

$$(t - s_n)\nu \leq M \sigma_{\max} + b \tag{6.4}$$

By combining this with the second formula in the lemma we obtain

$$q_n(t) \leq \mu \frac{M \sigma_{\max} + b}{\nu} + b_n + \sigma_0^{(n)}$$

Now we apply Equation (6.3) and note that $\sum_{n=1}^{M} \sigma_0^{(n)} = \sigma$, from which we derive

$$X \leq M \frac{\mu}{\nu} (M\sigma_{\max} + b) + \sigma + b \qquad (6.5)$$

(Step 2) By applying the same reasoning as in Section 2.4.2, we find that Equation (6.5) is always true. The theorem follows from Equation (6.2).   □

Lemma 6.3.1. *For any nodes m, n (possibly with $m = n$), and for any time t there is some s such that*

$$\begin{cases} x_m(t) \leq x_n(s) - (t - s)\nu + M\sigma_{\max} + b \\ q_n(t) \leq (t - s)\mu + b_n + \sigma_0^{(n)} \end{cases}$$

with $\sigma_0^{(n)} = \sum_{i.\text{first}=n} \sigma_i$.

Proof: By definition of the service curve property at node m, there is some s_1 such that

$$\sum_{i \ni m} R_i^m(t) \geq \sum_{i \ni m, i.\text{first} \neq m} R_i^{m \ominus 1}(s_1) + \sum_{i.\text{first}=m} R_i^0(s_1) + r_m(t - s_1) - b_m$$

which we can rewrite as

$$\sum_{i \ni m} R_i^m(t) \geq -A + \sum_{i \ni m} R_i^0(s_1) + r_m(t - s_1) - b_m$$

with

$$A = \sum_{i \ni m, i.\text{first} \neq m} \left(R_i^0(s_1) - R_i^{m-1}(s_1) \right)$$

Now the condition $\{i \ni m, i.\text{first} \neq m\}$ implies that flow i passes through node $m - 1$, namely, $\{i \ni (m - 1)\}$. Furthermore, each element in the summation that constitutes A is nonnegative. Thus

$$A \leq \sum_{i \ni (m-1)} \left(R_i^0(s_1) - R_i^{m-1}(s_1) \right) = x_{m \ominus 1}(s_1)$$

Thus

$$\sum_{i \ni m} R_i^m(t) \geq -x_{m \ominus 1}(s_1) + \sum_{i \ni m} R_i^0(s_1) + r_m(t - s_1) - b_m \qquad (6.6)$$

Now combining this with the definition of $x_m(t)$ in Equation (6.1) gives:

$$x_m(t) \leq x_{m \ominus 1}(s_1) + \sum_{i \ni m} \left(R_i^0(t) - R_i^0(s_1) \right) - r_m(t - s_1) + b_m$$

From the arrival curve property applied to all micro-flows i in the summation, we derive:

$$x_m(t) \leq x_{m \ominus 1}(s_1) - (r_m - \rho^{(m)})(t - s_1) + \sigma^{(m)} + b_m$$

and since $r_m - \rho^{(m)} \geq \nu$ and $\sigma^{(m)} \leq \sigma_{\max}$ by definition of ν and $\sigma_{\max}$, we have

$$x_m(t) \leq x_{m\ominus1}(s_1) - (t - s_1)\nu + \sigma_{\max} + b_m$$

We apply the same reasoning to node $m \ominus 1$ and time s_1, and so on iteratively until we reach node n backwards from m. We thus build a sequence of times $s_0 = t, s_1, s_2, ..., s_j, ..., s_k$ such that

$$x_{m\ominus j}(s_j) \leq x_{m\ominus(j+1)}(s_{j+1}) - (t - s_{j+1})\nu + \sigma_{\max} + b_{m\ominus j} \qquad (6.7)$$

until we have $m \ominus k = n$. If $n = m$ we reach the same node again by a complete backwards rotation and $k = M$. In all cases, we have $k \leq M$. By summing Equation (6.7) for $j = 0$ to $k - 1$ we find the first part of the lemma.

Now we prove the second part. $s = s_k$ is obtained by applying the service curve property to node n and time s_{k-1}. Apply the service curve property to node n and time t. Since $t \geq s_{k-1}$, we know from Proposition 1.3.2 on Page 24 that we can find some $s' \geq s$ such that

$$\sum_{i\ni n} R_i^n(t) \geq \sum_{i\ni n, i.\text{first}\neq n} R_i^{n-1}(s') + \sum_{i.\text{first}=n} R_i^0(s') + r_n(t - s') - b_n$$

Thus

$$q_n(t) \leq \sum_{i\ni n, i.\text{first}\neq n} \left(R_i^{n\ominus1}(t) - R_i^{n\ominus1}(s')\right) +$$

$$\sum_{i.\text{first}=n} \left(R_i^0(t) - R_i^0(s')\right) - r_n(t - s') + b_n$$

$$\leq (C_n - r_n + \rho_0^{(n)})(t - s') + b_n + \sigma_0^{(n)} \leq (t - s')\mu + b_n + \sigma_0^{(n)}$$

the second part of the formula follows from $s \leq s'$. $\square$

Remark: A simpler, but weaker bound, is

$$M\frac{\mu}{\nu}(M\sigma + b) + \sigma + b$$

or

$$M\frac{\mu}{\nu}(M\sigma_{\max} + b) + M\sigma_{\max} + b \qquad (6.8)$$

The special case in [69]:   Under the assumption that all nodes are constant rate servers of rate equal to 1 (thus $C_m = r_m = 1$ and b_m is the latency of the link m), the following bound is found in [69]:

$$B_1 = \frac{Mb + M^2\sigma_{\max}}{\nu} + b \qquad (6.9)$$

In that case, we have $\mu \leq 1 - \nu$. By applying Equation (6.8), we obtain the bound

$$B_2 = \frac{M\mu b + [M^2\mu + M\nu]\sigma_{\max}}{\nu} + b$$

since

$$\mu \leq 1 - \nu \tag{6.10}$$

and $0 < \nu \leq 1$, $M \leq M^2$, we have $B_2 < B_1$, namely, our bound is better than that in [69]. If there is equality in Equation (6.10) (namely, if there is a node that receives no transit traffic), then both bounds are equivalent when $\nu \to 0$.

6.4 Bounds for a FIFO Service Curve Element

We give, in this section, the fundamental results for FIFO multiplexing; here, we assume that the node guarantees to the aggregate flow a minimum service curve. We find some explicit closed forms bounds for some simple cases. The results are valid for variable length packets as well as ATM.

Proposition 6.4.1 (FIFO Minimum Service Curves [17]). *Consider a lossless node serving two flows, 1 and 2, in FIFO order. Assume that packet arrivals are instantaneous. Assume that the node guarantees a minimum service curve β to the aggregate of the two flows. Assume that flow 2 is α_2-smooth. Define the family of functions β_θ^1 by*

$$\beta_\theta^1(t) = [\beta(t) - \alpha_2(t - \theta)]^+ 1_{\{t > \theta\}}$$

Call $R_1(t)$, $R_1'(t)$ the input and output for flow 1. Then for any $\theta \geq 0$

$$R_1' \geq R_1 \otimes \beta_\theta^1 \tag{6.11}$$

If β_θ^1 is wide-sense increasing, flow 1 is guaranteed the service curve β_θ^1

The assumption that packet arrivals are instantaneous means that we are either in a fluid system (one packet is one bit or one cell), or that the input to the node is packetized prior to being handled in FIFO order.

Proof: We give the proof for continuous time and assume that flow functions are left-continuous. All we need to show is Equation (6.11). Call R_i the flow i input, $R = R_1 + R_2$, and similarly R_i', R' the output flows.

Fix some arbitrary parameter θ and time t. Define

$$u := \sup\{v : R(v) \leq R'(t)\}$$

Note that $u \leq t$ and that

$$R(u) \leq R'(t) \text{ and } R(u^+) \geq R'(t) \tag{6.12}$$

where $R_r(u) = \inf_{v>u}[R(v)]$ is the limit to the right of R at u.

(Case 1) consider the case where $u = t$. It follows from the above and from $R' \leq R$ that $R_1'(t) = R_1(t)$. Thus for any θ, we have $R_1'(t) = R_1(t) + \beta_\theta^1(0)$ which shows that $R_1'(t) \geq (R_1 \otimes \beta_\theta^1)(t)$ in that case.

(Case 2), assume now that $u < t$. We claim that

$$R_1(u) \leq R_1'(t) \tag{6.13}$$

Indeed, if this is not true, namely, $R_1(u) > R_1'(t)$, it follows from the first part of Equation (6.12) that $R_2(u) < R_2'(t)$. Thus some bits from flow 2 arrived after time u and departed by time t, whereas all bits of flow 1 arrived up to time u have not yet departed at time t. This contradicts our assumption that the node is FIFO and that packets arrive instantaneously.

Similarly, we claim that

$$(R_2)_r(u) \geq R_2'(t) \tag{6.14}$$

Indeed, otherwise $x := R_2'(t) - (R_2)_r(u) > 0$ and there is some $v_0 \in (u, t]$ such that for any $v \in (u, v_0]$ we have $R_2(v) < R_2'(t) - \frac{x}{2}$. From Equation (6.12), we can find some $v_1 \in (u, v_0]$ such that if $v \in (u, v_1]$ then $R_1(v) + R_2(v) \geq R'(t) - \frac{x}{4}$. It follows that

$$R_1(v) \geq R_1'(t) + \frac{x}{4}$$

Thus we can find some v with $R_1(v) > R_1'(t)$ whereas $R_2(v) < R_2'(t)$, which contradicts the FIFO assumption.

Call s a time such that $R'(t) \geq R(s) + \beta(t - s)$. We have $R(s) \leq R'(t)$ thus $s \leq u$.

(Case 2a) Assume that $u < t - \theta$ thus also $t - s > \theta$. From Equation (6.14) we derive

$$R_1'(t) \geq R_1(s) + \beta(t-s) + R_2(s) - R_2'(t) \geq R_1(s) + \beta(t-s) + R_2(s) - (R_2)_r(u)$$

Now there exist some $\epsilon > 0$ such that $u + \epsilon \leq t - \theta$, thus $(R_2)_r(u) \leq R_2(t - \theta)$ and

$$R_1'(t) \geq R_1(s) + \beta(t - s) - \alpha_2(t - s - \theta)$$

It follows from Equation (6.13) that

$$R_1'(t) \geq R_1(s)$$

which shows that

$$R_1'(t) \geq R_1(s) + \beta_\theta^1(t - s)$$

(Case 2b) Assume that $u \geq t - \theta$. By Equation (6.13):

$$R_1'(t) \geq R_1(u) = R_1(u) + \beta_\theta^1(t - u)$$

□

We cannot conclude from Proposition 6.4.1 that $\inf_\theta \beta_\theta^1$ is a service curve. However, we can conclude something for the output.

Proposition 6.4.2 (Bound for Output with FIFO). *Consider a lossless node serving two flows, 1 and 2, in FIFO order. Assume that packet arrivals are instantaneous. Assume that the node guarantees to the aggregate of the two flows a minimum service curve β. Assume that flow 2 is α_2-smooth. Define the family of functions as in Proposition 6.4.1. Then the output of flow 1 is α_1^*-smooth, with*

$$\alpha_1^*(t) = \inf_{\theta \geq 0} \left(\alpha_1 \oslash \beta_\theta^1 \right)(t)$$

Proof: Observe first that the network calculus output bound holds even if β is not wide-sense increasing. Thus, from Proposition 6.4.1, we can conclude that $(\alpha_1 \otimes \gamma) \oslash \beta_\theta^1$ is an arrival curve for the output of flow 1. This is true for any θ.   □

We can apply the last proposition and obtain the following practical result.

Theorem 6.4.1 (Burstiness Increase due to FIFO). *Consider a node serving two flows, 1 and 2, in FIFO order. Assume that flow 1 is constrained by one leaky bucket with rate r_1 and burstiness b_1, and flow 2 is constrained by a sub-additive arrival curve α_2. Assume that the node guarantees to the aggregate of the two flows a rate latency service curve $\beta_{R,T}$. Call $r_2 := \inf_{t>0} \frac{1}{t}\alpha_2(t)$ the maximum sustainable rate for flow 2.*

If $r_1 + r_2 < R$, then at the output, flow 1 is constrained by one leaky bucket with rate r_1 and burstiness b_1^* with

$$b_1^* = b_1 + r_1 \left(T + \frac{\hat{B}}{R} \right)$$

and

$$\hat{B} = \sup_{t \geq 0} \left[\alpha_2(t) + r_1 t - Rt \right]$$

The bound is a worst case bound.

Proof: (Step 1) Define β_θ^1 as in Proposition 6.4.1. Define $B_2 = \sup_{t>0} [\alpha_2(t) - Rt]$. Thus B_2 is the buffer that would be required if the latency T would be 0. We first show the following

$$\text{if } \theta \geq \frac{B_2}{R} + T \text{ then for } t \geq \theta : \beta_\theta^1(t) = Rt - RT - \alpha_2(t - \theta) \quad (6.15)$$

To prove this, call $\phi(t)$ the right hand-side in Equation (6.15), namely, for $t \geq \theta$ define $\phi(t) = Rt - \alpha_2(t - \theta) - RT$. We have

$$\inf_{t > \theta} \phi(t) = \inf_{v > 0} \left[Rv - \alpha_2(v) - RT + R\theta \right]$$

From the definition of B_2:

$$\inf_{t > \theta} \phi(t) = -B_2 + R\theta - RT$$

If $\theta \geq \frac{B_2}{R} + T$ then $\phi(t) \geq 0$ for all $t > \theta$. The rest follows from the definition of β_θ^1.

(Step 2) We apply the second part of Proposition 6.4.1 with $\theta = \frac{\hat{B}}{R} + T$. An arrival curve for the output of flow 1 is given by

$$\alpha_1^* = \lambda_{r_1, b_1} \oslash \beta_\theta^1$$

We now compute α_1^*. First note that obviously $\hat{B} \leq B_2$, and therefore $\beta_\theta^1(t) = Rt - RT - \alpha_2(t - \theta)$ for $t \geq \theta$. α_1^* is thus defined for $t > 0$ by

$$\alpha_1^*(t) = \sup_{s \geq 0} \left[r_1 t + b_1 + r_1 s - \beta_\theta^1(s) \right] = r_1 t + b_1 + \sup_{s \geq 0} \left[r_1 s - \beta_\theta^1(s) \right]$$

Define $\psi(s) := r_1 s - \beta_\theta^1(s)$. Obviously:

$$\sup_{s \in [0,\theta]} [\psi(s)] = r_1 \theta$$

Now from Step 1, we have

$$
\begin{aligned}
\sup_{s > \theta}[\psi(s)] &= \sup_{s > \theta} \left[r_1 s - Rs + RT + \alpha_2(s - \theta) \right] \\
&= \sup_{v > 0} \left[r_1 v - Rv\alpha_2(v) \right] + (r_1 - R)\theta + RT
\end{aligned}
$$

From the definition of $\hat{B}$, the former is equal to

$$\sup_{s > \theta}[\psi(s)] = \hat{B} + (r_1 - R)\theta + RT = r_1 \theta$$

which shows the burstiness bound in the theorem.

(Step 3) We show that the bound is attained. There is a time a $\hat{\theta}$ such that $\hat{B} = (\alpha_2)_r(\hat{\theta}) - (R - r_1)\hat{\theta}$. Define flow 2 to be greedy up to time $\hat{\theta}$ and stop from there on:

$$
\begin{cases}
R_2(t) = \alpha_2(t) \text{ for } t \leq \hat{\theta} \\
R_2(t) = (R_2)_r(\hat{\theta}) \text{ for } t > \hat{\theta}
\end{cases}
$$

Flow 2 is α_2-smooth because α_2 is sub-additive. Define flow 1 by

$$
\begin{cases}
R_1(t) = r_1 t \text{ for } t \leq \hat{\theta} \\
R_1(t) = r_1 t + b_1 \text{ for } t > \hat{\theta}
\end{cases}
$$

Flow 1 is λ_{r_1, b_1}-smooth as required. Assume the server delays all bits by T at time 0, then after time T operates with a constant rate R, until time $\hat{\theta} + \theta$, when it becomes infinitely fast. Thus the server satisfies the required service curve property. The backlog just after time $\hat{\theta}$ is precisely $\hat{B} + RT$. Thus all flow-2 bits that arrive just after time $\hat{\theta}$ are delayed by $\frac{\hat{B}}{R} + T = \theta$. The output for flow 1 during the time interval $(\hat{\theta} + \theta, \hat{\theta} + \theta + t]$ is made of the bits that have arrived in $(\hat{\theta}, \hat{\theta} + t]$, thus there are $r_1 t + b_1^*$ such bits, for any t. □

The following corollary is an immediate consequence.

Corollary 6.4.1 (Burstiness Increase due to FIFO). *Consider a node serving two flows, 1 and 2, in FIFO order. Assume that flow i is constrained by one leaky bucket with rate r_i and burstiness b_i. Assume that the node guarantees to the aggregate of the two flows a rate latency service curve $\beta_{R,T}$. If $r_1 + r_2 < R$, then flow 1 has a service curve equal to the rate latency function with rate $R - r_2$ and latency $T + \frac{b_2}{R}$ and at the output, flow 1 is constrained by one leaky bucket with rate r_i and burstiness b_1^* with*

$$b_1^* = b_1 + r_1 \left(T + \frac{b_2}{R} \right)$$

Note that this bound is slightly better than the one we used in Corollary 2.4.1 onPage 106 (but the assumptions are slightly different). The bound is also better than if we apply Theorem 6.2.1. Indeed, in that case, we would obtain the rate-latency service curve with the same rate $R - r_2$ but with a larger latency: $T + \frac{b_2}{R-r_2}$ instead of $T + \frac{b_2}{R}$. The gain is due to the FIFO assumption.

6.5 Bounds for a Network of FIFO CBR Servers

When analyzing a global network, we can use the bounds in Section 6.4, using the same method as in Section 2.4. However, as illustrated in [36], the bounds so obtained are not optimal: indeed, even for a FIFO ring, the method does *not* find a finite bound for all utilization factors less than (although we know from Section 6.3.2 that such finite bounds exist).

In this section is Theorem 6.5.1, we show in Theorem 6.5.1 some partial result that goes beyond the per-node bounds in Section 6.4. The result was originally found in [13, 46, 75].

6.5.1 Closed Form Bounds for an ATM Network with Strong Source Rate Conditions

Consider an ATM network with the assumptions as in Section 6.3.1, with the following differences

- Every link has one origin node and one end node. We say that a link f is incident to link e if the origin node of link e is the destination node of link f. In general, a link has several incident links.

- All packets have the same size (called cell). All arrivals and departures occur at integer times (synchronized model). All links have the same bit rate, equal to 1 cell per time unit. The service time for one cell is 1 time unit. The propagation times are constant per link and integer.

- All links are FIFO.

Proposition 6.5.1. *For a network with the above assumption, the delay for a cell c arriving at node e over incident link i is bounded by the number of cells arriving on incident links $j \neq i$ during the busy period, and that will depart before c.*

Proof: Call $R'(t)$ (resp. $R_j(t)$, $R(t)$)the output flow (resp. input arriving on link j, total input flow). Call d the delay for a tagged cell arriving at time t on link i. Call A_j the number of cells arriving on link j up to time t that will depart before the tagged cell, and let $A = \sum_j A_j$. We have

$$d = A - R'(t) \leq A - R(s) - (t - s)$$

where s is the last time instant before the busy period at t. We can rewrite the previous equation as

$$d \leq \sum_{j \neq i}[A_j - R_j(s)] + [A_i(t) - R_i(s)] - (t - s)$$

Now the link rates are all equal to 1, thus $A_i - R_i(s) \leq t - s$ and

$$d \leq \sum_{j \neq i}[A_j - R_j(s)]$$

$\square$

An "Interference Unit" is defined as a set $(e, \{j, k\})$ where e is a link, $\{j, k\}$ is a set of two distinct flows that each have e on their paths, and that arrive at e over two different incident links (Figure 6.1). The Route Interference Number (RIN) of flow j is the number of interference units that contain j. It is thus the number of other flows that share a common sub-path, counted with multiplicity if some flows share several distinct sub-paths along the same path. The RIN is used to define a sufficient condition, under which we prove a strong bound.

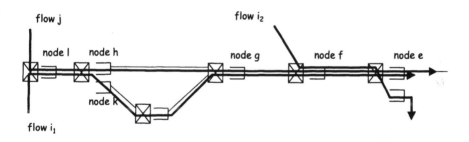

Figure 6.1: The network model and definition of an interference unit. Flows j and i_2 have an interference unit at node f. Flows j and i_1 have an interference unit at node l and one at node g.

Definition 6.5.1 (Source Rate Condition). *The fresh arrival curve constraint (at network boundary) for flow j is the stair function $v_{R+1,R+1}$, where R is the RIN of flow j.*

The source rate condition is equivalent to saying that a flow generates at most one cell in any time interval of duration RIN $+ 1$.

Theorem 6.5.1. *If the source rate condition holds at all sources, then*

1. The backlog at any node is bounded by $N - \max_i N_i$, where N_i is the number of flows entering the node via input link i, and $N = \sum_i N_i$.

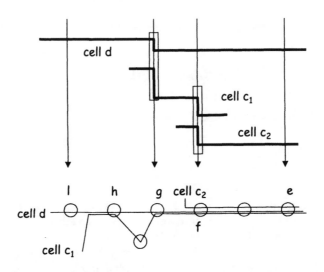

Figure 6.2: A time-space diagram illustrating the definitions of $d \preccurlyeq_g c_1$ and $c_1 \preccurlyeq_f c_2$. Time flows downwards. Rectangles illustrate busy periods.

> *2. The end-to-end queuing delay for a given flow is bounded by its RIN.*

> *3. There is at most one cell per flow present during any busy period.*

The proof of item 3 involves a complex analysis of chained busy periods, as does the proof of Theorem 6.3.1. It is given in Section 6.5.2. Item 3 gives an intuitive explanation of what happens: the source rate condition forces sources to leave enough spacing between cells, so that two cells of the same flow do not interfere, in some sense. The precise meaning of this is given in Section 6.5.2. Items 1 and 2 derive from item 3 by a classical network calculus method (Figure 6.4).

6.5.2   Proof of Theorem 6.5.1

As a simplification, we call "path of a cell" the path of the flow of the cell. Similarly, we use the phrase "interference unit of c" with the meaning of interference unit of the flow of c.

We define a busy period as a time interval during which the backlog for the flow at the node is always positive. We now introduce a definition (super-chain) that will be central in the proof. First we use the following relation:

Definition 6.5.2 ("Delay Chain" [13]). *For two cells c and d, and for some link e, we say that $c \preccurlyeq_e d$ if c and d are in the same busy period at e and c leaves e before d.*

Figure 6.2 illustrates the definition.

Definition 6.5.3 (Super-Chain [13]). *Consider a sequence of cells* $\underline{c} = (c_0, ..., c_i, ..., c_k)$ *and a sequence of nodes* $\underline{f} = (f_1, ..., f_k)$. *We say that* $(\underline{c}, \underline{f})$ *is a super-chain if*

- $f_1, ..., f_k$ *are all on the path P of cell c_0 (but not necessarily consecutive)*

- $c_{i-1} \preccurlyeq_{f_i} c_i$ *for $i = 1$ to k.*

- *the path of cell c_i from f_i to f_{i+1} is a sub-path of P*

We say that the sub-path of c_0 that spans from node f_1 to node f_k is the path of the super-chain.

Definition 6.5.4 (Segment Interfering with a Super-Chain). *For a given super-chain, we call "segment" a couple (d, P) where P is a sub-path of the path of the super-chain, d is a cell whose path also has P as a sub-path, and P is maximal (namely, we cannot extend P to be a common sub-path of both d and the super-chain). We say that the segment (d, P) is interfering with super-chain $(\underline{c}, \underline{f})$ if there is some i on P such that $d \preccurlyeq_{f_i} c_i$.*

Lemma 6.5.1. *Let $(\underline{c}, \underline{f})$ be a super-chain. Let s_0 be the arrival time of cell c_0 at link f_1 and s'_k the departure time of cell c_k from link f_k. Then $s'_k - s_0 \leq R_{1,k} + T_{1,k}$, where $R_{1,k}$ is the total number of segments interfering with $(\underline{c}, \underline{f})$ and $T_{1,k}$ is the total transmission and propagation time on the path of the super-chain.*

Proof: Consider first some node f_j on the super-chain. Let s_{j-1} (resp. t_j) be the arrival time of cell c_{j-1} (resp. c_j) at the node. Let t'_{j-1} (resp. s'_j) be the departure time of cell c_{j-1} (resp. c_j) (Figure 6.3). Let v_j be the last time slot before the busy period that t_j is in. By hypothesis, $v_j + 1 \leq s_{j-1}$. Also define $\mathcal{B}_j$ (resp. $\mathcal{B}^0_j$) as the

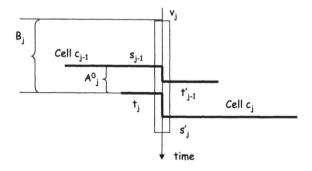

Figure 6.3: The notation used in the proof of Lemma 6.5.1.

set of segments (d, P) where d is a cell arriving at the node after time v_j on a link incident to the path of the super-chain (resp. on the path of the super-chain) and that will depart no later than cell c_j, and where P is the maximal common sub-path for d and the super-chain that f_j is in. Also define $\mathcal{A}_j^0$ as the subset of those segments in $\mathcal{B}_j^0$ for which the cell departs after c_{j-1}. Let B_j (resp. B_j^0, A_j^0) be the number of elements in $\mathcal{B}_j$ (resp. $\mathcal{B}_j^0$, $\mathcal{A}_j^0$), see Figure 6.3.

Since the rate of all incident links is 1, we have

$$B_j^0 - A_j^0 \le s_{j-1} - v_j$$

Also, since the rate of the node is 1, we have:

$$s_j' - v_j = B_j + B_j^0$$

Combining the two, we derive

$$s_j' - s_{j-1} = B_j + B_j^0 - (s_{j-1} - v_j) \le B_j + A_j^0 \qquad (6.16)$$

By iterative application of Equation (6.16) from $j = 1$ to k, we obtain

$$s_k' - s_0 \le \sum_{j=1}^{k} (B_j + A_j^0) + T_{1,k}$$

Now we show that all sets in the collection $\{\mathcal{B}_j, \mathcal{A}_j^0, \ j = 1 \text{ to } k\}$ are two-by-two disjoint. Firstly, if $(d, P) \in \mathcal{B}_j$ then f_j is the first node of P thus (d, P) cannot be in some other $\mathcal{B}_{j'}$ with $j \ne j'$. Thus the $\mathcal{B}_j$ are two-by-two disjoint. Second, assume $(d, P) \in \mathcal{B}_j$ and $(d, P) \in \mathcal{A}_{j'}^0$. It is obvious from their definitions that, for a fixed j, $\mathcal{B}_j$ and $\mathcal{A}_j^0$ are disjoint; thus $j \ne j'$. Since f_j is the first node of P and j' is on P, it follows that $j < j'$. Now d leaves f_j before c_j and leaves $f_{j'}$ after $c_{j'-1}$, which contradicts the FIFO assumption. Thus the $\mathcal{B}_j$ and $\mathcal{A}_{j'}^0$ are two-by-two disjoint. The same reasoning shows that it is not possible that $(d, P) \in \mathcal{A}_j \cap \mathcal{A}_{j'}$ with $j < j'$.

Now, by definition, every segment in either $\mathcal{B}_j$ or $\mathcal{A}_j^0$ is an interfering segment. Thus

$$\sum_{j=1}^{k} (B_j + A_j^0) \le R_{1,k}$$

$\square$

.

Proposition 6.5.2. *Assume the source rate condition holds. Let $(\underline{c}, \underline{f})$ be a super-chain.*

1. *For every interference unit of c_0 there is at most one cell interfering with the super-chain.*

2. *c_k does not belong to the same flow as c_0.*

Proof: Define the time of a super-chain as the exit time for the last cell c_k on the last node f_k. We use a recursion on the time t of the super-chain.

If $t = 1$, the proposition is true because any flow has at most one cell on a link in one time slot. Assume now that the proposition holds for any super-chain with time $\leq t - 1$ and consider a super-chain with time t.

First, we associate an interference unit to any segment (d, P) interfering with the sub-chain, as follows. The paths of d and c_0 may share several non contiguous sub-paths, and P is one of them. Call f the first node of P. To d we associate the interference unit $(f, \{j_0, j\})$, where j_0 (resp. j) is the flow of c_0 (resp. d).

We now show that this mapping is injective. Assume that another segment $(d', P') \neq (d, P)$ is associated with the same interference unit $(f, \{j_0, j\})$. Without loss of generality, we can assume that d was emitted before d'. d and d' belong to the same flow j, thus, since P and P' are maximal, we must have $P = P'$. By hypothesis, have an interference with the super-chain at a node on P. Let f_l be a node on the super-chain and on P such that $d \preccurlyeq_{f_l} c_l$. If d' leaves node f_l before c_l, then $d \preccurlyeq_{f_l} d'$, and thus $((d, d'), (f_l))$ is a super-chain. Since d' is an interfering cell, necessarily, it must leave node f_l before t, thus the proposition is true for super-chain $((d, d'), (f_l))$, which contradicts item 2. Thus d' must leave node f_l after cell c_l. But there is some other index $m \leq k$ such that $d \preccurlyeq_{f_m} c_m$, thus cell d' leaves node f_m before cell c_m. Define l' as the smallest index with $l < l' \leq m$ such that d' leaves node $f_{l'}$ after cell $c_{l'-1}$ and before $c_{l'}$. Then $((d, c_l, ..., c_{l'-1}, d'), (f_l, .., f_{l'}))$ is a super-chain with time $\leq t - 1$ which would again contradict item 2 in the proposition. Thus, in all cases we have a contradiction, the mapping is injective, and item 1 is shown for the super-chain.

Second, let us count a bound on the maximum queuing delay of cell c_0. Call u_0 its emission time, P_0 the sub-path of c_0 from its source up to, but excluding, node f_1, and T the total transmission and propagation time for the flow of c_0. The transmission and propagation time along P_0 is thus $T - T_{1,k}$. By Proposition 6.5.1, the queuing delay of c_0 at a node f on P_0 is bounded by the number of cells $d \preccurlyeq_f c_0$ that arrive on a link not on P_0. By the same reasoning as in the previous paragraph, there is at most one such cell d per interference unit of c_0 at f. Define R as the number of interference units of the flow of c_0 on P_1. We have thus

$$s_0 \leq u_0 + R + T - T_{1,k} \tag{6.17}$$

Similarly, from Lemma 6.5.1, we have

$$s'_k \leq s_0 + R_{1,k} + T_{1,k}$$

Call R' the number of interference units of the flow of c_0 on the path of the super-chain. It follows from the first part of the proof that $R_{1,k} \leq R'$, thus

$$s'_k \leq s_0 + R' + T_{1,k}$$

Combining with Equation (6.17) gives

$$s'_k \leq u_0 + R + R' + T \tag{6.18}$$

Now by the source condition, if c_k belongs to the flow of c_0, its emission time u' must satisfy

$$u' \geq u_0 + R + R' + 1$$

and thus

$$s'_k \geq u_0 + R + R' + 1 + T$$

which contradicts Equation (6.18). This shows that the second item of the proposition must hold for the super-chain. □

Proof of Theorem 6.5.1:   Item 3 follows from Proposition 6.5.2, since if there would be two cells d, d' of the same flow in the same busy period, then $((d, d'), (e))$ would be a super-chain.

Now we show how items 1 and 2 derive from item 3. Call $\alpha_i^*(t)$ the maximum number of cells that may ever arrive on incident link i during t time units inside a busy period. Since λ_1 is a service curve for node e, the backlog B at node e is bounded by

$$B \leq \sup_{t \geq 0} \left[\sum_{i=1}^{I} \alpha_i^*(t) - t \right]$$

Now by item 3, $\alpha_i^*(t) \leq N_i$ and thus

$$\alpha_i^*(t) \leq \alpha_i(t) := \min[N_i, t]$$

Thus

$$B \leq \sup_{t \geq 0} \left[\sum_{i=1}^{I} \alpha_i(t) - t \right]$$

Now define a renumbering of the N_i's such that $N_{(1)} \leq N_{(2)} \leq \dots \leq N_{(I)}$. The function $\sum_i \alpha_i(t) - t$ is continuous and has a derivative at all points except the $N_{(i)}$'s (Figure 6.4). The derivative changes its sign at $N_{(I)}$ ($=\max_{1 \leq i \leq I}(N_i)$) thus the maximum is at $N_{(I)}$ and its value is $N - N_{(I)}$, which shows item 1.

From Item 1, the delay at a node is bounded by the number of interference units of the flow at this node. This shows item 2. □

6.6   Bibliographic Notes

In [46], a stronger property is shown than Theorem 6.5.1: Consider a given link e and a subset A of m connections that use that link. Let n be a lower bound on the number of route interferences that any connection in the subset will encounter after this link. Then over any time interval of duration $m + n$, the number of cells belonging to A that leave link e is bounded by m.

It follows from item 1 in Theorem 6.5.1 that a better queuing delay bound for flow j is:

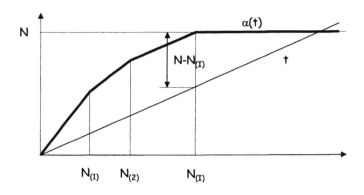

Figure 6.4: Derivation of a backlog bound.

$$\delta(j) = \sum_{e \text{ such that } e \in j} \left\{ \min_{i \text{ such that } 1 \leq i \leq I(e)} (N(e) - N_i(e)) \right\}$$

where $I(e)$ is the number of incident links at node e, $N_i(e)$ is the number of flows entering node e on link i, and $N = \sum_{i=1}^{I(e)} N_i(e)$. In other words, the end-to-end queuing delay is bounded by the sum of the minimum numbers of route interference units for all flows at all nodes along the path of a flow. For asymmetric cases, this is less than the RIN of the flow.

6.7 Exercises

Exercise 6.1. *Consider the same assumptions as in Section 6.3.2 but with a linear network instead of a ring. Thus node m feeds node m+1 for m = 1, ..., M−1; node 1 receives only fresh traffic, whereas all traffic exiting node M leaves the network. Assume that all service curves are strict. Find a bound which is finite for $\nu \leq 1$. Compare to Theorem 6.3.1.*

Exercise 6.2. *Consider the same assumptions as in Theorem 6.5.1. Show that the busy period duration is bounded by N.*

Chapter 7

Adaptive and Packet Scale Rate Guarantees

7.1 Introduction

In Chapter 1 we defined a number of service curve concepts: minimum service curve, maximum service curve and strict service curves. In this chapter we go beyond and define some concepts that more closely capture the properties of generalized processor sharing (GPS).

We start by a motivating section, in which we analyze some features of service curves that do not match GPS. Then we provide the theoretical framework of adaptive guarantees, which was first proposed in Okino's dissertation in [55] and by Agrawal, Cruz, Okino and Rajan in [1]. This framework is underlying the concept of packet scale rate guarantees, which is used in the definition of the Internet Expedited Forwarding service. We explain the relationship between the two and give practical applications.

In all of this chapter, we assume that flow functions are left-continuous, unless stated otherwise.

7.2 Adaptive Guarantee

7.2.1 Limitations of the Service Curve Abstraction

The definition of service curve introduced in Section 1.3 is an abstraction of nodes such as GPS and its practical implementations, as well as guaranteed delay nodes. This abstraction is used in many situations, described all along this book. However, it is not always sufficient.

Firstly, it does not provide a guarantee over any interval. Consider for example a node offering to a flow $R(t)$ the service curve λ_C. Assume $R(t) = B$ for $t > 0$, so the flow has a very large burst at time 0 and then stops. A possible output is illustrated on Figure 7.1. It is perfectly possible that there is no output during the time interval $(0, \frac{B-\epsilon}{C}]$, even though there is a large backlog. This is because the server gave a higher service than the minimum required during some interval of time, and the service property allows it to be lazy after that.

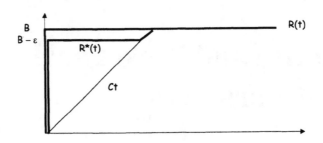

Figure 7.1: The service curve property is not sufficient.

Secondly, there are case where we would like to deduce a bound on the delay that a packet will suffer given the backlog that we can measure in the node. This is used for obtaining bounds in FIFO systems with aggregate scheduling. In Chapter 6 we use such a property for a constant delay server with rate C: given that the backlog at time t is Q, the last bit present at time t will depart before within a time of $\frac{Q}{C}$. If we assume instead that the server has a service curve λ_C, then we cannot draw such a conclusion. Consider for example Figure 7.1: at time $t > 0$, the backlog, ϵ, can be made arbitrily small, whereas the delay $\frac{B-\epsilon}{C} - t$ can be made arbitrarily large.

A possible fix is the use of *strict service curve*, as defined in Definition 1.3.2 on Page 27. Indeed, it follows from the next section (and can easily be shown independently) that if a FIFO node offers a strict service curve β, then the delay at time t is bounded by $\beta^{-1}(Q(t))$, where $Q(t)$ is the backlog at time t, and β^{-1} is the pseudo-inverse (Definition 3.1.7 on Page 129).

We know that the GPS node offers to a flow a strict service curve equal of the form λ_R. However, we cannot model delay nodes with a strict service curve. Consider for example a node with input $R(t) = \epsilon t$, which delays all bits by a constant time d. Any interval $[s, t]$ with $s \geq d$ is within a busy period, thus if the node offers a strict service curve β to the flow, we should have $\beta(t - s)\epsilon(t - s)$, and ϵ can be arbitrarily small. Thus, the strict service curve does not make much sense for a constant delay node.

7.2.2   Definition of Adaptive Guarantee

We know introduce a stronger concept, called *adaptive guarantee*, that better captures the properties of GPS [55, 1]. Before giving the formula, we motivate it on three examples.

Consider first a node offering a strict service curve β. Consider some fixed, but arbitrary times $s < t$. Assume that β is continuous. If $[s, t]$ is within a busy period, we must have

$$R^*(t) \geq R^*(s) + \beta(t - s)$$

Else, call u the beginning of the busy period at t. We have

$$R^*(t) \geq R(u) + \beta(t - u)$$

thus in all cases

$$R^*(t) \geq (R^*(s) + \beta(t - s)) \wedge \inf_{u \in [s,t]} (R(u) + \beta(t - u)) \qquad (7.1)$$

Second, consider a node that guarantees a virtual delay $\leq d$. If $t - s \leq d$ then trivially

$$R^*(t) \geq R^*(s) + \delta_d(t - s)$$

and if $t - s > d$ then the virtual delay property means that

$$R^*(t) \geq R(t - d) = \inf_{u \in [s,t]} (R(u) + \delta_d(t - u))$$

thus we have the same relation as in Equation (7.1) with $\beta = \delta_d$.

Thirdly, consider a greedy shaper with shaping function σ (assumed to be a good function). Then

$$R^*(t) = \inf_{u \leq t} [R(u) + \sigma(t - u)]$$

Breaking the inf into $u < s$ and $u \geq s$ gives

$$R^*(t) = \inf_{u < s} [R(u) + \sigma(t - u)] \wedge \inf_{u \in [s,t]} [R(u) + \sigma(t - u)] \qquad (7.2)$$

Define $\tilde{\sigma} := \sigma \overline{\oslash} \sigma$, namely,

$$\tilde{\sigma}(u) = \inf_t [\sigma(t + u) - \sigma(u)] \qquad (7.3)$$

For example, for a piecewise linear concave arrival curve (conjunction of leaky buckets), $\sigma(t) = \min_i(r_i u + b_i)$, we have $\tilde{\sigma}(u) = \min_i r_i u$. Back to Equation (7.2), we have

$$\sigma(t - u) \geq \sigma(s - u) + \tilde{\sigma}(t - s)$$

and finally

$$R^*(t) \geq (R^*(s) + \tilde{\sigma}(t - s)) \wedge \inf_{u \in [s,t]} (R(u) + \sigma(t - u)) \qquad (7.4)$$

We see that these three cases fall under a common model:

Definition 7.2.1 (Adaptive Service Curve). *Let $\tilde{\beta}, \beta$ be in $\mathcal{F}$. Consider a system S and a flow through S with input and output functions R and R^*. We say that S offers the adaptive guarantee $(\tilde{\beta}, \beta)$ if for any $s \leq t$ it holds:*

$$R^*(t) \geq \left(R^*(s) + \tilde{\beta}(t - s) \right) \wedge \inf_{u \in [s,t]} [R(u) + \beta(t - u)]$$

If $\tilde{\beta} = \beta$ we say that the node offers the adaptive guarantee β.

The following proposition summarizes the examples discussed above:

Proposition 7.2.1.   • *If S offers to a flow a strict service curve β, then it also offers the adaptive guarantee β.*

  • *If S guarantees a virtual delay bounded by d, then it also offers the adaptive guarantee δ_d*

  • *A greedy shaper with shaping curve σ, where σ is a good function, offers the adaptive guarantee $(\tilde{\sigma}, \sigma)$, with $\tilde{\sigma}$ defined in Equation (7.3).*

Similar to [55], we use the notation $R \to (\tilde{\beta}, \beta) \to R^*$ to express that Definition 7.2.1 holds. If $\tilde{\beta} = \beta$ we write $R \to (\beta) \to R^*$.

Assume that R is left-continuous and β is continuous. It follows from Theorem 3.1.8 on Page 139 that the adaptive guarantee is equivalent to saying that for all $s \leq t$, we have either

$$R^*(t) - R^*(s) \geq \tilde{\beta}(t - s)$$

or

$$R^*(t) \geq R(u) + \beta(t - u)$$

for some $u \in [s, t]$.

7.2.3   Properties of Adaptive Guarantees

Theorem 7.2.1. *Let $R \to (\tilde{\beta}, \beta) \to R^*$. If $\tilde{\beta} \leq \beta$ then β is a minimum service curve for the flow.*

Proof: Apply Definition 7.2.1 with $s = 0$ and use the fact that $\tilde{\beta} \leq \beta$.   □

Theorem 7.2.2 (Concatenation). *If $R \to (\tilde{\beta}_1, \beta_1) \to R_1$ and $R_1 \to (\tilde{\beta}_2, \beta_2) \to R^*$ then $R \to (\tilde{\beta}, \beta) \to R^*$ with*

$$\tilde{\beta} = \left(\tilde{\beta}_1 \otimes \beta_2 \right) \wedge \tilde{\beta}_2$$

and

$$\beta = \beta_1 \otimes \beta_2$$

Proof: Consider some fixed but arbitrary times $s \leq t$ and let $u \in [s, t]$. We have

$$R_1(u) \geq \left[R_1(s) + \tilde{\beta}(u - s)\right] \wedge \inf_{v \in [s,u]} [R(v) + \beta_1(u - v)]$$

thus

$$R_1(u) + \beta_2(t - u) \geq \left[R_1(s) + \tilde{\beta}(u - s) + \beta_2(t - u)\right] \wedge$$
$$\inf_{v \in [s,u]} [R(v) + \beta_1(u - v) + \beta_2(t - u)]$$

and

$$\inf_{u \in [s,t]} [R_1(u) + \beta_2(t - u)] \geq$$
$$\inf_{u \in [s,t]} \left[R_1(s) + \tilde{\beta}(u - s) + \beta_2(t - u)\right]$$
$$\wedge \inf_{u \in [s,t], v \in [s,u]} [R(v) + \beta_1(u - v) + \beta_2(t - u)]$$

After re-arranging the infima, we find

$$\inf_{u \in [s,t]} [R_1(u) + \beta_2(t - u)] \geq$$
$$\left(R_1(s) + \inf_{u \in [s,t]} \left[\tilde{\beta}(u - s) + \beta_2(t - u)\right]\right) \wedge$$
$$\inf_{v \in [s,t]} \left(R(v) + \inf_{u \in [v,t]} [\beta_1(u - v) + \beta_2(t - u)]\right)$$

which can be rewritten as

$$\inf_{u \in [s,t]} [R_1(u) + \beta_2(t - u)] \geq$$
$$\left(R_1(s) + (\tilde{\beta}_1 \otimes \beta_2)(t - s)\right) \wedge$$
$$\inf_{v \in [s,t]} [R(v) + \beta(t - v)]$$

Now by hypothesis we have

$$R^*(t) \geq \left(R^*(s) + \tilde{\beta}_2(t - s)\right) \wedge \inf_{u \in [s,t]} [R(u) + \beta_2(t - u)]$$

Combining the two gives

$$R^*(t) \geq$$
$$\left(R^*(s) + \tilde{\beta}_2(t - s)\right) \wedge \left(R_1(s) + (\tilde{\beta}_1 \otimes \beta_2)(t - s)\right)$$
$$\wedge \inf_{v \in [s,t]} [R(v) + \beta(t - v)]$$

Now $R_1(s) \geq R^*(s)$ thus

$$R^*(t) \geq$$
$$\left(R^*(s) + \tilde{\beta}_2(t-s) \right) \wedge \left(R^*(s) + (\tilde{\beta}_1 \otimes \beta_2)(t-s) \right)$$
$$\wedge \inf_{v \in [s,t]} [R(v) + \beta(t-v)]$$

□

Corollary 7.2.1. *If* $R_{i-1} \to (\tilde{\beta}_i, \beta_i) \to R_i$ *for* $i = 1$ *to* n *then* $R_0 \to (\tilde{\beta}, \beta) \to R_n$
with

$$\tilde{\beta} = \left(\tilde{\beta}_1 \otimes \beta_2 \otimes ... \otimes \beta_n \right) \wedge \left(\tilde{\beta}_2 \otimes \beta_3 \otimes ... \otimes \beta_n \right) \wedge ... \wedge \left(\tilde{\beta}_{n-1} \otimes \beta_n \right) \wedge \tilde{\beta}_n$$

and

$$\beta = \beta_1 \otimes ... \otimes \beta_n$$

Proof: Apply Theorem 7.2.2 iteratively and use Rule 6 in Theorem 3.1.5 on
Page 135.   □

Theorem 7.2.3 (Delay from Backlog). *If* $R \to (\tilde{\beta}, \beta) \to R^*$, *then the virtual delay
at time* t *is bounded by* $\tilde{\beta}^{-1}(Q(t))$, *where* $Q(t)$ *is the backlog at time* t, *and* $\tilde{\beta}^{-1}$ *is
the pseudo-inverse of* $\tilde{\beta}$ *(see Definition 3.1.7 on Page 129).*

Note that if the node is FIFO, then the virtual delay at time t is the real delay for
a bit arriving at time t.

Proof: If the virtual delay at time t is larger than $t + \tau$ for some $\tau \geq 0$, then we
must have
$$R^*(t + \tau) < R(t) \tag{7.5}$$

By hypothesis

$$R^*(t + \tau) \geq \left(R^*(t) + \tilde{\beta}(\tau) \right) \wedge \inf_{[u \in [t, t+\tau]]} [R(u) + \beta(t + \tau - u)] \tag{7.6}$$

now for $u \in [t, t + \tau]$

$$R(u) + \beta(t + \tau - u) \geq R(t) + \beta(0) \geq R^*(t + \tau)$$

thus Equation (7.6) implies that

$$R^*(t + \tau) \geq R^*(t) + \tilde{\beta}(\tau)$$

combining with Equation (7.5) gives

$$Q(t) = R(t) - R^*(t) \geq \tilde{\beta}(\tau)$$

thus the virtual delay is bounded by $\sup\{\tau : \tilde{\beta}(\tau) > Q(t)\}$ which is equal to $\tilde{\beta}^{-1}(Q(t))$. □

Consider a system (*bit-by-bit system*) with L-packetized input R and bit-by-bit output R^*, which is then L-packetized to produce a final packetized output R'. We call *combined system* the system that maps R into R'. Assume both systems are first-in-first-out and lossless. Remember from Theorem 1.7.1 that the per-packet delay for the combined system is equal the maximum virtual delay for the bit-by-bit system.

Theorem 7.2.4 (Packetizer and Adaptive Guarantee). *If the bit-by-bit system offers to the flow the adaptive guarantee $(\tilde{\beta}, \beta)$, then the combined system offers to the flow the adaptive guarantee $(\tilde{\beta}', \beta')$ with*

$$\tilde{\beta}'(t) = [\tilde{\beta}(t) - l_{\max}]^+$$

and

$$\beta'(t) = [\beta(t) - l_{\max}]^+$$

where $l_{\max}$ is the maximum packet size for the flow.

Proof: Let $s \leq t$. By hypothesis we have

$$R^*(t) \geq \left(R^*(s) + \tilde{\beta}(t - s)\right) \wedge \inf_{u \in [s,t]}[R(u) + \beta(t - u)]$$

We do the proof when the inf in the above formula is a minimum, and leave it to the alert reader to extend it to the general case. Thus assume that for some $u_0 \in [s, t]$:

$$\inf_{u \in [s,t]}[R(u) + \beta(t - u)] = R(u_0) + \beta(t - u_0)$$

it follows that either

$$R^*(t) - R^*(s) \geq \tilde{\beta}(t - s)$$

or

$$R^*(t) \geq R(u_0) + \beta(t - u_0)$$

Consider the former case. We have $R'(t) \geq R^*(t) - l_{\max}$ and $R'(s) \leq R^*(s)$ thus

$$R'(t) \geq R^*(t) - l_{\max} \geq R'(s) + \tilde{\beta}(t - s) - l_{\max}$$

Now also obviously $R'(t) \geq R'(s)$, thus finally

$$R'(t) \geq R'(s) + \max[0, \tilde{\beta}(t - s) - l_{\max}] = R'(s) + \tilde{\beta}'(t - s)$$

Consider now the latter case. A similar reasoning shows that

$$R'(t) \geq R(u_0) + \beta(t - u_0) - l_{\max}$$

but also

$$R^*(t) \geq R(u_0)$$

now the input is L-packetized. Thus

$$R'(t) = P^L(R^*(t)) \geq P^L(R(u_0)) = R(u_0)$$

from which we conclude that $R'(t) \geq R(u_0) + \beta'(t - u_0)$.

Combining the two cases provides the required adaptive guarantee.   □

7.3 Application to the Internet: Packet Scale Rate Guarantee

In this section we apply the concept of adaptive guarantee to practical schedulers used in the Internet.

7.3.1 Definition of Packet Scale Rate Guarantee

In Section 2.1.3 on Page 86 we have introduced the definition of guaranteed rate scheduler, which is the practical application of rate latency service curves. Consider a node where packets arrive at times $A_1 \geq 0, A_2, \ldots$ and leave at times $D_1, D_2, \ldots$. A guaranteed rate scheduler, with rate r and latency v requires that $D_i \leq T'_i + v$, where T'_i is defined iteratively by $T'_0 = 0$ and

$$T'_i = \max\{A_i, T'_{i-1}\} + \frac{l_i}{r}$$

where l_i is the length of the ith packet.

A *packet scale rate guarantee* is similar, but, much in the spirit of adaptive guarantees, avoids the limitations of the service curve concept discussed in Section 7.2.1. To that end, we would like that the deadline T'_i is reduced whenever a packet happens to be served early. This is done by replacing T'_{i-1} in the previous equation by $\min\{T'_i, D_i\}$. This gives the following definition.

Definition 7.3.1 (Packet Scale Rate Guarantee). *Consider a node that serves a flow of packets numbered $i = 1, 2, \ldots$. Call A_i, D_i, l_i the arrival time, departure time, and length in bits for the ith packet, in order of arrival. Assume $A_1 \geq 0$. We say that the node offers to the flow a packet scale rate guarantee with rate r and latency v if the departure times satisfy*

$$D_i \leq F_i + v$$

where F_i is defined by:

$$\begin{cases} F_0 = D_0 = 0 \\ F_i = \max\left\{A_i, \min\left(D_{i-1}, F_{i-1}\right)\right\} + \frac{l_i}{r} & \text{for all } i \geq 1 \end{cases} \qquad (7.7)$$

We now relate packet scale rate guarantee to an adaptive guarantee. We cannot expect an exact equivalence, since a packet scale rate guarantee does not specify what happens to bits at a time other than a packet departure or arrival. However, the concept of packetizer allows us to establish an equivalence.

Theorem 7.3.1 (Equivalence with adaptive guarantee). *Consider a node S with L-packetized input R and with output R^*.*

1. *If $R \to (\beta) \to R^*$, where $\beta = \beta_{r,v}$ is the rate-latency function with rate r and latency v, and if S is FIFO, then S offers to the flow the packet scale rate guarantee with rate r and latency v.*

2. *Conversely, if S offers to the flow the packet scale rate guarantee with rate r and latency v and if R^* is L-packetized, then S is the concatenation of a node S' offering the adaptive guarantee $\beta_{r,v}$ and the L-packetizer. If S is FIFO, then so is S'.*

The proof is long and is given in a separate section (Section 7.3.3). Note that the packet scale rate guarantee does not mandate that the node be FIFO; it is possible that $D_i < D_{i-1}$ in some cases. However, part 1 of the theorem requires the FIFO assumption in order for a condition on R, R^* to be translated into a condition on delays.

A special case of interest is when $v = 0$.

Corollary 7.3.1. *Consider a node with L-packetized input. Call A_i, D_i the arrival and departure times for packet i, with $i = 1, 2, ...$ and $A_1 \geq 0$. Let l_i be the size of packet i.*

1. *If the node guarantees a strict service curve λ_r and is FIFO then*

$$\begin{cases} D_0 = 0 \\ D_i \leq \max\{A_i, D_{i-1}\} + \frac{l_i}{r} \quad \text{for all } i \geq 1 \end{cases} \tag{7.8}$$

2. *Conversely if Equation (7.8) holds for all i, and if the output is L-packetized, then the node is the concatenation of a node guaranteeing a strict service curve λ_r and an L-packetizer.*

Proof: Apply Theorem 7.3.1 with $v = 0$ and note that $D_{i-1} \leq F_{i-1}$ in Equation (7.7). □

Definition 7.3.2. *We call* minimum rate server, *with rate r, a node for which Equation (7.8) holds for all i*

Thus, roughly speaking, a minimum rate server guarantees that during any busy period, the instantaneous output rate is at least r. A GPS node with total rate C and weight w_i for flow i is a minimum rate server for flow i, with rate $r_i = \frac{\phi_i C}{\sum_j \phi_j}$.

Since a packetizer does not add increase the per-packet delay, we can immediately derive the following property from Theorem 7.2.3 and Theorem 7.3.1:

Proposition 7.3.1 (Backlog from Delay). *For a FIFO node offering the packet scale rate guarantee with rate r and latency v, the delay for a packet present in the system at time t is bounded by $\frac{Q(t)}{r} + v$, where $Q(t)$ is the backlog at time t.*

Lastly, we have a concatenation result for FIFO systems:

Proposition 7.3.2. *Consider a concatenation of FIFO systems numbered 1 to n. The output of system $i - 1$ is the input of system i, for $i > 1$. Assume system i offers the packet scale rate guarantee with rate R_i and latency E_i. The global system offers the packet scale rate guarantee with rate $R = \min_{i=1,\dots,n} R_i$ and latency $E = \sum_{i=1,\dots,n} E_i + \sum_{i=1,\dots,n-1} \frac{L_{\max}}{R_i}$.*

Proof: By Theorem 7.3.1–(2), we can decompose system i into a concatenation $S_i, \mathcal{P}_i$, where S_i offers the adaptive guarantee β_{R_i, E_i} and $\mathcal{P}_i$ is a packetizer.

Call S the concatenation

$$S_1, \mathcal{P}_1, S_2, \mathcal{P}_2, \dots, S_{n-1}, \mathcal{P}_{n-1}, S_n$$

By Theorem 7.3.1–(2), S is FIFO. By Theorem 7.2.4, it provides the adaptive guarantee $\beta_{R,E}$. By Theorem 7.3.1–(1), it also provides the packet scale rate guarantee with rate R and latency E. Now $\mathcal{P}_n$ does not affect the finish time of the last bit of every packet.

□

7.3.2   Practical Realization of Packet Scale Rate Guarantee

We show in this section that a wide variety of schedulers provide the packet scale rate guarantee. More schedulers can be obtained by using the concatenation theorem in the previous section.

A simple but important realization is the priority scheduler.

Proposition 7.3.3. *Consider a non-preemptive priority scheduler in which all packets share a single FIFO queue with total output rate C. The high priority flow receives a packet scale rate guarantee with rate C and latency $v = \frac{l_{\max}}{C}$, where $l_{\max}$ is the maximum packet size of all low priority packets.*

Proof: By Proposition 1.3.7, the high priority traffic receives a strict service curve $\beta_{r,c}$.   □

We have already introduced in Section 2.1.3 a large number of schedulers that can be thought of as derived from GPS and we have modeled their behaviour with a rate-latency service curve. In order to give an adaptive guarantee for such schedulers, we need to define more.

Definition 7.3.3 (Accuracy of a scheduler with respect to rate r). *Consider a scheduler S and call D_i the time of the i-th departure. We say that the accuracy of S with respect to rate r is (v_1, v_2) if there is a minimum rate server with rate r and departure times G_i such that for all i*

$$G_i - v_1 \leq D_i \leq G_i + v_2 \tag{7.9}$$

We interpret this definition as a comparison to a hypothetical GPS reference scheduler that would serve the same flows. The term v_2 determines the maximum per-hop delay bound, whereas v_1 has an effect on the jitter at the output of the scheduler. For example, it is shown in [5] that $\mathrm{WF^2Q}$ satisfies $v_1(\mathrm{WF^2Q}) = l_{max}/r$, $v_2(\mathrm{WF^2Q}) = l_{max}/C$, where l_{max} is maximum packet size and C is the total output rate. In contrast, for PGPS [57] $v_2(\mathrm{PGPS}) = v_2(\mathrm{WF^2Q})$, while $v_1(\mathrm{PGPS})$ is linear in the number of queues in the scheduler. This illustrates that, while $\mathrm{WF^2Q}$ and PGPS have the same delay bounds, PGPS may result in substantially burstier departure patterns.

Theorem 7.3.2. *If a scheduler satisfies Equation (7.9), then it offers the packet scale rate guarantee with rate r and latency $v = v_1 + v_2$.*

Proof: We first prove that for all $i \geq 0$

$$F_i \geq G_i - v_1 \tag{7.10}$$

where F_i is defined by Equation (7.7). Indeed, if Equation (7.10) holds, then by Equation (7.9)):

$$D_i \leq G_i + v_2 \leq F_i + v_1 + v_2$$

which means that the scheduler offers the packet scale rate guarantee with rate r and latency $v = v_1 + v_2$.

Now we prove Equation (7.10) by induction. Equation (7.10) trivially holds for $i = 0$.

Suppose now that it holds for $i - 1$, namely,

$$F_{i-1} \geq G_{i-1} - v_1$$

By hypothesis, Equation (7.9) holds:

$$D_{i-1} \geq G_{i-1} - v_1$$

thus

$$\min[F_{i-1}, D_{i-1}] \geq G_{i-1} - v_1 \tag{7.11}$$

Combining this with Equation (7.7), we obtain

$$F_i \geq G_{i-1} - v_1 + \frac{L(i)}{R} \tag{7.12}$$

Again from Equation (7.7) we have

$$\begin{aligned} F_i &\geq A_i + \frac{l_i}{r} \\ &\geq A_i - v_1 + \frac{l_i}{r} \end{aligned} \tag{7.13}$$

Now by Equation (7.8)

$$G_i \leq \max[A_i, G_{i-1}] + \frac{l_i}{r} \tag{7.14}$$

Combining Equation (7.12)), Equation (7.13)) and (7.14) gives

$$F_i \geq G_i - v_1$$

$\square$

7.3.3   Proof of Theorem 7.3.1

The first part of Theorem 7.3.1 is based on a max-plus representation of the packet scale rate guarantee, which maps the (min-plus) definition of an adaptive guarantee. The second part relies on the reduction to the minimum rate server.

We use the same notation as in Definition 7.3.1. $L(i) = \sum_{j=1}^{i} l_j$ is the cumulative packet length.

Part 1:   Define the sequence of times F_k by Equation (7.7). Consider now some fixed but arbitrary packet index $i \geq 1$. By the FIFO assumption, it is sufficient to show that

$$R^*(t) \geq L(i) \tag{7.15}$$

with $t = F_i + v$. Define

$$j = \max \{ k \in \{1, ..., i\} : A_k \geq D_{k-1} \text{ or } A_k < D_{k-1} \leq F_{k-1} \}$$

Note that the set above is non-empty and $1 \leq j \leq i$. The definition of j implies

$$A_j \geq D_{j-1} \text{ or } A_j < D_{j-1} \leq F_{j-1} \tag{7.16}$$

and

$$A_k < D_{k-1} \text{ and } F_{k-1} < D_{k-1} \text{ for } j+1 \leq k \leq i \tag{7.17}$$

Note that the set of indices k to which the previous equation applies may be empty (in that case, $j = i$).

By Equation (7.16) and the definition of F_j, we have

$$F_j = s + \frac{l_j}{r} \tag{7.18}$$

with

$$s = A_j \vee D_{j-1}$$

Similarly, we derive from Equation (7.17) that for $j+1 \leq k \leq i$:

$$F_k = (A_k \vee F_{k-1}) + \frac{l_k}{r}$$

which can be re-written as

$$F_k = \left(A_k + \frac{l_k}{r} \right) \vee \left(F_{k-1} + \frac{l_k}{r} \right) \tag{7.19}$$

Now we obtain a max-plus expansion of F_i as follows. We substitute F_{i-1} from Equation (7.19) at $k = i - 1$ into Equation (7.19) at $k = i$ and obtain

$$F_i = \left(A_i + \frac{l_i}{r} \right) \vee \left(A_{i-1} + \frac{l_i + l_{i-1}}{r} \right) \vee \left(F_{i-2} + \frac{l_i + l_{i-1}}{r} \right)$$

We apply this iteratively until $k = j$ at which step we use Equation (7.18) instead of Equation (7.19). We obtain finally:

$$F_i = \left(s + \frac{L(i) - L(j-1)}{r} \right) \vee \max_{k=j+1}^{i} \left(A_k + \frac{L(i) - L(k-1)}{r} \right) \tag{7.20}$$

Let us apply the definition of an adaptive guarantee to the time interval $[s, t]$:

$$R^*(t) \geq A \wedge B$$

with

$$A := R^*(s) + r(t - s - v)^+ \text{ and } B := \inf_{u \in [s,t]} B(u)$$

where

$$B(u) := \left(R(u) + r(t - u - v)^+ \right)$$

Firstly, since $s \geq D_{j-1}$, we have $R^*(s) \geq L(j-1)$. By Equation (7.20), $F_i \geq s + \frac{L(i) - L(j-1)}{r}$ thus $t \geq s + \frac{L(i) - L(j-1)}{r} + v$. It follows that

$$t - s - v \geq \frac{L(i) - L(j-1)}{r}$$

and thus $A \geq L(i)$.

Secondly, we show that $B \geq L(i)$ as well. Consider some $u \in [s, t]$. If $u \geq A_i$ then $R(u) \geq L(i)$ thus $B(u) \geq L(i)$. Otherwise, $u < A_i$; since $s \geq A_j$, it follows that $A_{k-1} \leq u < A_k$ for some $k \in \{j+1, ..., i\}$ and $R(u) = L(k-1)$. By Equation (7.20),

$$F_i \geq A_k + \frac{L(i) - L(k-1)}{r}$$

thus

$$t - u - v \geq \frac{L(i) - L(k-1)}{r}$$

It follows that $B(u) \geq L(i)$ also in that case. Thus we have shown that $B \geq L(i)$. Combining the two shows that $R^*(t) \geq L(i)$ as required.

Part 2:   We use a reduction to a minimum rate server as follows. Let $D_i' :=$ $\min(D_i, F_i)$ for $i \geq 0$. By Equation (7.7) we have

$$A_i \leq D_i' \leq \max(A_i, D_{i-1}') + \frac{l_i}{r} \tag{7.21}$$

and

$$D_i' \leq D_i \leq D_i' + v \tag{7.22}$$

The idea of the proof is now to interpret D_i' as the output time for packet i out of a virtual minimum rate server. Of course, we cannot use Corollary 7.3.1.

Construct a virtual node $\mathcal{R}$ as follows. The input is the original input $R(t)$. The output is defined as follows. The number of bits of packet i that are output up to time t is $\psi_i(t)$, defined by

$$\begin{cases} \text{if } t > d'(i) \text{ then } \psi_i(t) = L(i) \\ \text{else if } a(i) < t \leq d'(i) \text{ then } \psi_i(t) = [L(i) - r(d'(i) - t)]^+ \\ \text{else } \psi_i(t) = 0 \end{cases}$$

so that the total output of $\mathcal{R}$ is $R_1(t) = \sum_{i \geq 1} \psi_i(t)$.

The start time for packet i is thus $\max[A_i, D_i' - \frac{l_i}{r}]$ and the finish time is D_i'. Thus $\mathcal{R}$ is causal (but not necessarily FIFO, even if the original system would be FIFO). We now show that during any busy period, $\mathcal{R}$ has an output rate at least equal to r.

Let t be during a busy period. Consider now some time t during a busy period. There must exist some i such that $A_i \leq t \leq D_i'$. Let i be the smallest index such that this is true. If $A_i \geq D_{i-1}'$ then by Equation (7.21) $D_i' - t \leq \frac{l_i}{r}$ and thus $\psi_r'(t) = r$ where ψ_r' is the derivative of ψ_i to the right. Thus the service rate at time t is at least r.

Otherwise, $A_i < D'i - 1$. Necessarily (because we number packets in order of increasing A_i's – this is not a FIFO assumption) $A_{i-1} \leq A_i$; since i is the smallest index such that $A_i \leq t < D_i'$, we must have $t \geq D_{i-1}'$. But then $D_i' - t \leq \frac{l_i}{r}$ and the service rate at time t is at least r. Thus, node $\mathcal{R}$ offers the strict service curve λ_r and

$$R \to (\lambda_r) \to R_1 \tag{7.23}$$

Now define node $\mathcal{D}$. Let $\delta(i) := D_i - D_i'$, so that $0 \leq \delta(i) \leq E$. The input of $\mathcal{D}$ is the output of $\mathcal{R}$. The output is as follows; let a bit of packet i arrive at time t; we have $t \leq D_i' \leq D_i$. The bit is output at time $t' = \max[\min[D_{i-1}, D_i], t + \delta_i]$. Thus all bits of packet i are delayed in $\mathcal{D}$ by at most $\delta(i)$, and if $D_{i-1} < D_i$ they depart after D_i. It follows that the last bit of packet i leaves $\mathcal{D}$ at time D_i. Also, since $t' \geq t$, $\mathcal{D}$ is causal. Lastly, if the original system is FIFO, then $D_{i-1} < D_i$, all bits of packet i depart after D_{i-1} and thus the concatenation of $\mathcal{R}$ and $\mathcal{D}$ is FIFO. Note that $\mathcal{R}$ is not necessarily FIFO, even if the original system would is FIFO.

The aggregate output of $\mathcal{D}$ is

$$R_2(t) \geq \sum_{i \geq 1} \psi_i(t - \delta(i)) \geq R_1(t - v)$$

thus the virtual delay for $\mathcal{D}$ is bounded by v and

$$R_1 \to (\delta_v) \to R_2 \qquad (7.24)$$

Now we plug the output of $\mathcal{D}$ into an L-packetizer. Since the last bit of packet i leaves $\mathcal{D}$ at time D_i, the final output is R^*. Now it follows from Equation (7.23), Equation (7.24) and Theorem 7.2.2 that

$$R \to (\lambda_r \otimes \delta_v) \to R_2$$

$\square$

7.4 Bibliographic Notes

The concept of adaptive service curve was introduced in Okino's dissertation in [55] and was published by Agrawal, Cruz, Okino and Rajan in [1], which contains most results in Section 7.2.3, as well as an application to a window flow control problem that extends Section 4.3.2 on Page 178. They call $\tilde{\beta}$ an "adaptive service curve" and β a "partial service curve".

The packet scale rate guarantee was first defined in a framework dependent of adaptive service guarantees in [4]. It serves as a basis for the definition of the Expedited Forwarding capability defined for the Internet.

7.5 Exercises

Exercise 7.1. *Assume that $R \to (\tilde{\beta}, \beta) \to R^*$.*

1. *Show that the node offers to the flow a strict service curve equal to $\tilde{\beta} \otimes \overline{\beta}$, where $\overline{\beta}$ is the sub-additive closure of β.*

2. *If $\tilde{\beta} = \beta$ is a rate-latency function, what is the value obtained for the strict service curve ?*

Exercise 7.2. *Consider a system with input R and output R^*. We call "input flow restarted at time t" the flow R_t defined for $u \geq 0$ by*

$$R_t(u) = R(t + u) - R^*(t) = R(t, u] + Q(t)$$

where $Q(t) := R(t) - R^*(t)$ is the backlog at time t. Similarly, let the "output flow restarted at time t" be the flow R_t^* defined for $u \geq 0$ by

$$R_t^*(u) = R^*(t + u) - R^*(t)$$

Assume that the node guarantees a service curve β to all couples of input, output flows (R_t, R_t^*). Show that $R \to (\beta) \to R^*$.

Chapter 8

Time Varying Shapers

8.1 Introduction

Throughout the book we usually assume that systems are idle at time 0. This is not a limitation for systems that have a renewal property, namely, which visit the idle state infinitely often – for such systems we choose the time origin as one such instant.

There are cases however where we are interested in the effect at time t of non zero initial conditions. This occurs for example for re-negotiable services, where the traffic contract is changed at periodic renegotiation moments. An example for this service is the Integrated Service of the IETF with the Resource reSerVation Protocol (RSVP), where the negotiated contract may be modified periodically [28]. A similar service is the ATM Available Bit Rate service (ABR). With a renegotiable service, the shaper employed by the source is time-varying. With ATM, this corresponds to the concept of Dynamic Generic Cell Rate Algorithm (DGCRA).. At renegotiation moments, the system cannot generally be assumed to be idle. This motivates the need for explicit formulae that describe the transient effect of non-zero initial condition.

In Section 8.2 we define time varying shapers. In general, there is not much we can say apart from a direct application of the fundamental min-plus theorems in Section 4.3. In contrast, for shapers made of a conjunction of leaky buckets, we can find some explicit formulas. In Section 8.3.1 we derive the equations describing a shaper with non-zero initial buffer. In Section 8.3.2 we add the constraint that the shaper has some history. Lastly, in Section 8.4, we apply this to analyze the case where the parameters of a shaper are periodically modified.

This chapter also provides an example of the use of time shifting.

8.2 Time Varying Shapers

We define a time varying shaper as follows.

Definition 8.2.1. *Consider a flow $R(t)$. Given a function of two time variables $H(t, s)$, a time varying shaper forces the output $R^*(t)$ to satisfy the condition*

$$R^*(t) \leq H(t, s) + R^*(s)$$

for all $s \leq t$, possibly at the expense of buffering some data. An optimal time varying shaper, or greedy time varying shaper, is one that maximizes its output among all possible shapers.

The existence of a greedy time varying shaper follows from the following proposition.

Proposition 8.2.1. *For an input flow $R(t)$ and a function of two time variables $H(t, s)$, among all flows $R^* \leq R$ satisfying*

$$R^*(t) \leq H(t, s) + R^*(s)$$

there is one flow that upper bounds all. It is given by

$$R^*(t) = \inf_{s \geq 0} \left[\overline{H}(t, s) + R(s) \right] \tag{8.1}$$

where $\overline{H}$ is the min-plus closure of H, defined in Equation (4.10) on Page 172.

Proof: The condition defining a shaper can be expressed as

$$\begin{cases} R^* \leq \mathcal{L}_H(R^*) \\ R^* \leq R \end{cases}$$

where $\mathcal{L}_H$ is the min-plus linear operator whose impulse response is H (Theorem 4.1.1). The existence of a maximum solution follows from Theorem 4.3.1 and from the fact that, being min-plus linear, $\mathcal{L}_H$ is upper-semi-continuous. The rest of the proposition follows from Theorem 4.2.1 and Theorem 4.3.1.   □

The output of the greedy shaper is given by Equation (8.1). A time invariant shaper is a special case; it corresponds to $H(s, t) = \sigma(t - s)$, where σ is the shaping curve. In that case we find the well-known result in Theorem 1.5.1.

In general, Proposition 8.2.1 does not help much. In the rest of this chapter, we specialize to the class of concave piecewise linear time varying shapers.

Proposition 8.2.2. *Consider a set of J leaky buckets with time varying rates $r_j(t)$ and bucket sizes $b_j(t)$. At time 0, all buckets are empty. A flow $R(t)$ satisfies the conjunction of the J leaky bucket constraints if and only if for all $0 \leq s \leq t$:*

$$R(t) \leq H(t, s) + R(s)$$

with

$$H(t, s) = \min_{1 \leq j \leq J} \{ b_j(t) + \int_s^t r_j(u) du \} \tag{8.2}$$

Proof: Consider the level of the jth bucket. It is the backlog of the variable capacity node (Section 1.3.2) with cumulative function

$$M_j(t) = \int_0^t r_j(u)du$$

We know from Chapter 4 that the output of the variable capacity node is given by

$$R'_j(t) = \inf_{0 \le s \le t} \{M_j(t) - M_j(s) + R(s)\}$$

The jth leaky bucket constraint is

$$R(t) - R'_j(t) \le b_j(t)$$

Combining the two expresses the jth constraint as

$$R(t) - R(s) \le M_j(t) - M_j(s) + b_j(t)$$

for all $0 \le s \le t$. The conjunction of all these constraints gives Equation (8.2).

In the rest of this chapter, we give a practical and explicit computation of $\overline{H}$ for H given in Equation (8.2), when the functions $r_j(t)$ and $b_j(t)$ are piecewise constant.

8.3 Time Invariant Shaper with Non-zero Initial Conditions

We consider in this section some time invariant shapers. We start with a general shaper with shaping curve σ, whose buffer is not assumed to be initially empty. Then we will apply this to analyze leaky bucket shapers with non-empty initial buckets.

8.3.1 Shaper with Non-empty Initial Buffer

Proposition 8.3.1 (Shaper with non-zero initial buffer). *Consider a shaper system with shaping curve σ. Assume that σ is a good function. Assume that the initial buffer content is w_0. Then the output R^* for a given input R is*

$$R^*(t) = \sigma(t) \wedge \inf_{0 \le s \le t} \{R(s) + w_0 + \sigma(t - s)\} \quad \text{for all } t \ge 0 \qquad (8.3)$$

Proof: First we derive the constraints on the output of the shaper. σ is the shaping function thus, for all $t \ge s \ge 0$

$$R^*(t) \le R^*(s) + \sigma(t - s)$$

and given that the bucket at time zero is not empty, for any $t \ge 0$, we have that

$$R^*(t) \le R(t) + w_0$$

At time $s = 0$, no data has left the system; this is expressed with

$$R^*(t) \leq \delta_0(t)$$

The output is thus constrained by

$$R^* \leq (\sigma \otimes R^*) \wedge (R + w_0) \wedge \delta_0$$

where $\otimes$ is the min-plus convolution operation, defined by $(f \otimes g)(t) = \inf_s f(s) + g(t - s)$. Since the shaper is an optimal shaper, the output is the maximum function satisfying this inequality. We know from Lemma 1.5.1 that

$$
\begin{aligned}
R^* &= \sigma \otimes [(R + w_0) \wedge \delta_0] \\
&= [\sigma \otimes (R + w_0)] \wedge [\sigma \otimes \delta_0] \\
&= [\sigma \otimes (R + w_0)] \wedge \sigma
\end{aligned}
$$

which after some expansion gives the formula in the proposition.   □.

Another way to look at the proposition consists in saying that the initial buffer content is represented by an instantaneous burst at time 0.

The following is an immediate consequence.

Corollary 8.3.1 (Backlog for a shaper with non-zero initial buffer). *The backlog of the shaper buffer with the initial buffer content w_0 is given by*

$$w(t) = (R(t) - \sigma(t) + w_0) \vee \sup_{0 < s \leq t} \{R(t) - R(s) - \sigma(t - s)\} \qquad (8.4)$$

8.3.2 Leaky Bucket Shapers with Non-zero Initial Bucket Level

Now we characterize a leaky-bucket shaper system with non-zero initial bucket levels.

Proposition 8.3.2 (Compliance with J leaky buckets with non-zero initial bucket levels). *A flow $S(t)$ is compliant with J leaky buckets with leaky bucket specifications (r_j, b_j), $j = 1, 2 \ldots J$ and initial bucket level q_j^0 if and only if*

$$
\begin{aligned}
S(t) - S(s) &\leq \min_{1 \leq j \leq J} [r_j \cdot (t - s) + b_j] &&\text{for all } 0 < s \leq t \\
S(t) &\leq \min_{1 \leq j \leq J} [r_j \cdot t + b_j - q_j^0] &&\text{for all } t \geq 0
\end{aligned}
$$

Proof: Apply Section 8.3.1 to each of the buckets.   □

Proposition 8.3.3 (Leaky-Bucket Shaper with non-zero initial bucket levels). *Consider a greedy shaper system defined by the conjunction of J leaky buckets (r_j, b_j), with $j = 1, 2 \ldots J$. Assume that the initial bucket level of the j-th bucket is q_j^0. The initial level of the shaping buffer is zero. The output R^* for a given input R is*

$$R^*(t) = \min[\sigma^0(t), (\sigma \otimes R)(t)] \qquad \text{for all } t \geq 0 \qquad (8.5)$$

where σ is the shaping function

$$\sigma(u) = \min_{1 \le j \le J}\{\sigma_j(u)\} = \min_{1 \le j \le J}\{r_j \cdot u + b_j\}$$

and σ^0 is defined as

$$\sigma^0(u) = \min_{1 \le j \le J}\{r_j \cdot u + b_j - q_j^0\}$$

Proof: By Corollary 8.3.2 applied to $S = R^*$, the condition that the output is compliant with the J leaky buckets is

$$R^*(t) - R^*(s) \le \sigma(t - s) \quad \text{for all } 0 < s \le t$$
$$R^*(t) \le \sigma^0(t) \quad\quad\quad\quad \text{for all } t \ge 0$$

Since $\sigma^0(u) \le \sigma(u)$ we can extend the validity of the first equation to $s = 0$. Thus we have the following constraint:

$$R^*(t) \le [(\sigma \otimes R^*) \wedge (R \wedge \sigma^0)](t)$$

Given that the system is a greedy shaper, $R^*(\cdot)$ is the maximal solution satisfying those constraints. Using the same min-plus result as in Proposition 8.3.1, we obtain:

$$R^* = \sigma \otimes (R \wedge \sigma^0) = (\sigma \otimes R) \wedge (\sigma \otimes \sigma^0)$$

As $\sigma^0 \le \sigma$, we obtain

$$R^* = (\sigma \otimes R) \wedge \sigma^0$$

□

We can now obtain the characterization of a leaky-bucket shaper with non-zero initial conditions.

Theorem 8.3.1 (Leaky-Bucket Shaper with non-zero initial conditions). *Consider a shaper defined by J leaky buckets (r_j, b_j), with $j = 1, 2 \ldots J$ (leaky-bucket shaper). Assume that the initial buffer level of is w_0 and the initial level of the jth bucket is q_j^0. The output R^* for a given input R is*

$$R^*(t) = \min\{\sigma^0(t), w_0 + \inf_{u > 0}\{R(u) + \sigma(t - u)\}\} \quad \text{for all } t \ge 0 \quad (8.6)$$

with

$$\sigma^0(u) = \min_{1 \le j \le J}(r_j \cdot u + b_j - q_j^0)$$

Proof: Apply Proposition 8.3.3 to the input $R' = (R + w_0) \wedge \delta_0$ and observe that $\sigma^0 \le \sigma$. □

An interpretation of Equation (8.6) is that the output of the shaper with non-zero initial conditions is either the output of the ordinary leaky-bucket shaper, taking into account the initial level of the buffer, or, if smaller, the output imposed by the initial conditions, independent of the input.

8.4   Time Varying Leaky-Bucket Shaper

We consider now time varying leaky-bucket shapers that are piecewise constant. The shaper is defined by a fixed number J of leaky buckets, whose parameters change at times t_i. For $t \in [t_i, t_{i+1}) := I_i$, we have thus

$$r_j(t) = r_j^i \text{ and } b_j(t) = b_j^i$$

At times t_i, where the leaky bucket parameters are changed, we keep the leaky bucket level $q_j(t_i)$ unchanged.

We say that $\sigma_i(u) := \min_{1 \leq j J}\{r_j^i u + b_j^i\}$ is the value of the time varying shaping curve during interval I_i. With the notation in Section 8.2, we have

$$H(t, t_i) = \sigma_i(t - t_i) \text{ if } t \in I_i$$

We can now use the results in the previous section.

Proposition 8.4.1 (Bucket Level). *Consider a piecewise constant time varying leaky-bucket shaper with output R^*. The bucket level $q_j(t)$ of the j-th bucket is, for $t \in I_i$:*

$$q_j(t) = \begin{aligned}[t] &[R^*(t) - R^*(t_i) - r_j^i \cdot (t - t_i) + q_j(t_i)] \vee \\ &\sup_{t_i < s \leq t}\{R^*(t) - R^*(s) - r_j^i \cdot (t - s)\} \end{aligned} \tag{8.7}$$

Proof: We use a time shift, defined as follows. Consider a fixed interval I_i and define

$$x^*(\tau) := R^*(t_i + \tau) - R^*(t_i)$$

Observe that $q_j(t_i + \tau)$ is the backlog at time τ (call it $w(\tau)$ at the shaper with shaping curve $\sigma(\tau) = r_j^i \cdot t$, fed with flow x^*, and with an initial buffer level $q_j(t_i)$. By Chapter 8.3.1 we have

$$w(\tau) = [x^*(\tau) - r_j^i \cdot \tau + q_j(t_i)] \vee \sup_{0 < s' \leq \tau} \{x^*(\tau) - x^*(s') - r_j^i \cdot (\tau - s')\}$$

which after re-introducing R^* gives Equation (8.7) $\square$

Theorem 8.4.1 (Time Varying Leaky-Bucket Shapers). *Consider a piecewise constant time varying leaky-bucket shaper with time varying shaping curve σ_i in the interval I_i. The output R^* for a given input R is*

$$R^*(t) = \min\left[\sigma_i^0(t - t_i) + R^*(t_i), \inf_{t_i < s \leq t}\{\sigma_i(t - s) + R(s)\}\right] \tag{8.8}$$

with σ_i^0 is defined by

$$\sigma_i^0(u) = \min_{1 \leq j \leq J}\left[r_j^i \cdot u + b_i^j - q_j(t_i)\right]$$

and $q_j(t_i)$ is defined recursively by Equation (8.7). The backlog at time t is defined recursively by

$$w(t) = \max \left[\begin{array}{c} \sup_{t_i < s \le t} \{R(t) - R(s) - \sigma_i(t-s)\}, \\ R(t) - R(t_i) - \sigma_i^0(t - t_i) + w(t_i) \end{array} \right] \quad t \in I_i \qquad (8.9)$$

Proof: Use the same notation as in the proof of Proposition 8.4.1 and define in addition

$$x(\tau) := R(t_i + \tau) - R(t_i)$$

We can now apply Theorem 8.3.1, with initial bucket levels equal to $q_j(t_i)$ as given in Equation (8.7) and with an initial buffer level equal to $w(t_i)$. The input-output characterization of this system is given by Equation (8.6), thus

$$x^*(\tau) = \sigma_i^0(\tau) \wedge [\sigma_i \otimes x'](\tau)$$

where

$$x'(\tau) = \left\{ \begin{array}{ll} x(\tau) + w(t_i) & \tau > 0 \\ x(\tau) & \tau \le 0 \end{array} \right.$$

Hence, re-introducing the original notation, we obtain

$$R^*(t) - R^*(t_i) = \left[\sigma_i^0(t - t_i) \wedge \inf_{t_i < s \le t} \{\sigma_i(t - s) + R(s) - R(t_i) + w(t_i)\} \right]$$

which gives Equation (8.8).

The backlog at time t follows immediately. $\qquad \square$

Note that Theorem 8.4.1 provides a representation of $\overline{\overline{H}}$. However, the representation is recursive: in order to compute $R^*(t)$, we need to compute $R^*(t_i)$ for all $t_i < t$.

8.5 Bibliographic Notes

[63] illustrates how the formulas in Section 8.4 form the basis for defining a renegotiable VBR service. It also illustrates that, if some inconsistency exists between network and user sides whether leaky buckets should be reset or not at every renegotiation step, then this may result in inacceptable losses (or service degradation) due to policing.

[11] analyzes the general concept of time varying shapers.

Chapter 9

Systems with Losses

All chapters have dealt up to now with lossless systems. This chapter shows that network calculus can also be applied to lossy systems, if we model them as a lossless system preceded by a 'clipper' [15, 16], which is a controller dropping some data when a buffer is full, or when a delay constraint would otherwise be violated. By applying once again Theorem 4.3.1, we obtain a representation formula for losses. We use this formula to compute various bounds. The first one is a bound on the loss rate in an element when both an arrival curve of the incoming traffic and a minimum service curve of the element are known. We use it next to bound losses in a complex with a complex service curve (e.g., VBR shapers) by means of losses with simpler service curves (e.g., CBR shapers). Finally, we extend the clipper, which models data drops due to buffer overflow, to a 'compensator', which models data accrual to prevent buffer underflow, and use it to compute explicit solutions to Skorokhod reflection mapping problem with two boundaries.

9.1 A Representation Formula for Losses

9.1.1 Losses in a Finite Storage Element

We consider a network element offering a service curve β, and having a finite storage capacity (buffer) X. We denote by a the incoming traffic.

We suppose that the buffer is not large enough to avoid losses for all possible input traffic patterns, and we would like to compute the amount of data lost at time t, with the convention that the system is empty at time $t = 0$. We model losses as shown in Figure 9.1, where $x(t)$ is the data that has actually entered the system in the time interval $[0, t]$. The amount of data lost during the same period is therefore $L(t) = a(t) - x(t)$.

The model of Figure 9.1 replaces the original lossy element, by an equivalent concatenation a controller or regulator that separates the incoming flow a in two separate flows, x and L, and that we call *clipper*, following the denomination introduced in [16], together with the original system, which is now lossless for flow x.

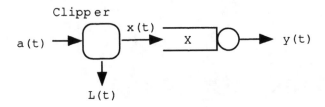

Figure 9.1: System with losses

The amount of data $(x(t) - x(s))$ that actually entered the system in any time interval $(s, t]$ is always bounded above by the total amount of data $(a(t) - a(s))$ that has arrived in the system during the same period. Therefore, for any $0 \le s \le t$, $x(t) \le x(s) + a(t) - a(s)$ or equivalently, using the linear idempotent operator introduced by Definition 4.1.5,

$$x(t) \le \inf_{0 \le s \le t} \{a(t) - a(s) + x(s)\} = h_a(x)(t). \tag{9.1}$$

On the other hand, x is the part of a that does actually enter the system. If y denotes its output, there is no loss for x if $x(t) - y(t) \le X$ for any t. We do not know the exact mapping $y = \Pi(x)$ realized by the system, but we assume that Π is isotone. So at any time t

$$x(t) \le y(t) + X = \Pi(x)(t) + X \tag{9.2}$$

The data x that actually enters the system is therefore the maximum solution to (9.1) and (9.2), which we can recast as

$$x \le a \wedge \{\Pi(x) + X\} \wedge h_a(x), \tag{9.3}$$

and which is precisely the same equation as (4.33) with $W = X$ and $M = a$. Its maximal solution is given by

$$x = \overline{(\{\Pi + X\} \wedge h_a)}(a),$$

or equivalently, after applying Corollary 4.2.1, by

$$x = \left(\overline{(h_a \circ (\Pi + X))} \circ h_a \right)(a) = \left(\overline{(h_a \circ (\Pi + X))} \right)(a) \tag{9.4}$$

where the last equality follows from $h_a(a) = a$.

We do not know the exact mapping Π, but we know that $\Pi \ge \mathcal{C}_\beta$. We have thus that

$$x \geq \overline{(h_a \circ C_{\beta+X})}(a). \tag{9.5}$$

The amount of lost data in the interval $[0, t]$ is therefore given by

$$L(t) = a(t) - x(t)$$

$$= a(t) - \overline{h_a \circ \{C_{\beta+X}\}}(a)(t) = a(t) - \inf_{n \in \mathbb{N}} \left\{ (h_a \circ C_{\beta+X})^{(n)} \right\}(a)(t)$$

$$= \sup_{n \in \mathbb{N}} \left\{ a(t) - (h_a \circ C_{\beta+X})^{(n)}(a)(t) \right\}$$

$$= \sup_{n \geq 0} \{ a(t) - \inf_{0 \leq s_{2n} \leq \ldots \leq s_2 \leq s_1 \leq t} \{ a(t) - a(s_1) + \beta(s_1 - s_2) + X$$

$$+ a(s_2) - \ldots + a(s_{2n}) \} \}$$

$$= \sup_{n \in \mathbb{N}} \{ \sup_{0 \leq s_{2n} \leq \ldots \leq s_2 \leq s_1 \leq t} \{ a(s_1) - \beta(s_1 - s_2) - a(s_2)$$

$$+ \ldots - a(s_{2n}) - nX \} \}.$$

Consequently, the loss process can be represented by the following formula:

$$L(t) \leq$$

$$\sup_{n \in \mathbb{N}} \left\{ \sup_{0 \leq s_{2n} \leq \ldots \leq s_2 \leq s_1 \leq t} \left\{ \sum_{i=1}^{n} [a(s_{2i-1}) - a(s_{2i}) - \beta(s_{2i-1} - s_{2i}) - X] \right\} \right\} \tag{9.6}$$

If the network element is a greedy shaper, with shaping curve β, then $\Pi(x) = C_\beta$, and the inequalities in (9.5) and (9.6) become equalities.

What the formula says is that losses up to time t are obtained by summing the losses over all intervals $[s_{2i-1}, s_{2i}]$, where s_{2i} marks the end of an overflow period, and where s_{2i-1} is the last time before s_{2i} when the buffer was empty. These intervals are therefore larger then the congestion intervals, and their number n is smaller or eqaul to the number of congestion intervals. Figure 9.2 shows an example where $n = 2$ and where there are three congestion periods.

We will see in the next sections how the losses representation formula (9.6), can help us to obtain deterministic bounds on the loss process in some systems.

9.1.2 Losses in a Bounded Delay Element

Before moving to these applications, we first derive a representation formula for a similar problem, where data are discarded not because of a finite buffer limit, but because of a delay constraint: any entering data must have exited the system after at most d unit of time, otherwise it is discarded. Such discarded data are called losses due to a delay constraint of d time units.

As above, let x be the part of a that does actually enter the system, and let y be its output. All the data $x(t)$ that has entered the system during $[0, t]$ must therefore have left at time $t + d$ at the latest, so that $x(t) - y(t + d) \leq 0$ for any t. Thus

$$x(t) \leq y(t + d) = \Pi(x)(t + d) = (S_{-d} \circ \Pi)(x)(t), \tag{9.7}$$

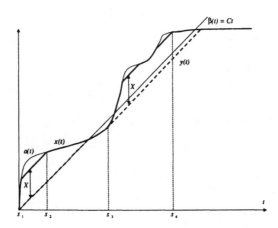

Figure 9.2: Losses in a constant rate shaper ($\beta = \lambda_C$). Fresh traffic a is represented with a thin, solid line; accepted traffic x is represented by a bold, solid line; the output process y is represented by a bold, dashed line.

where $\mathcal{S}_{-d}$ is the shift operator (with forward shift of d time units) given by Definition 4.1.7.

On the other hand, as in the previous example, the amount of data $(x(t) - x(s))$ that actually entered the system in any time interval $(s, t]$ is always bounded above by the total amount of data $(a(t) - a(s))$ that has arrived in the system during the same period. Therefore the data x that actually enters the system is therefore the maximum solution to

$$x \leq a \wedge (\mathcal{S}_{-d} \circ \Pi)(x) \wedge h_a(x), \tag{9.8}$$

which is

$$x = \overline{(\{\mathcal{S}_{-d} \circ \Pi\} \wedge h_a)}(a),$$

or equivalently, after applying Corollary 4.2.1, by

$$x = \left(\overline{h_a} \circ (\{\mathcal{S}_{-d} \circ \Pi\}) \circ h_a\right)(a) = \left(\overline{h_a} \circ \mathcal{S}_{-d} \circ \Pi\right)(a). \tag{9.9}$$

Since $\Pi \geq \mathcal{C}_\beta$, we also have,

$$x \geq \left(\overline{h_a} \circ \mathcal{S}_{-d} \circ \mathcal{C}_\beta\right)(a). \tag{9.10}$$

The amount of lost data in the interval $[0, t]$ is therefore given by

$$L(t) \leq \sup_{n \in \mathbb{N}} \left\{ a(t) - (h_a \circ \mathcal{S}_{-d} \circ \mathcal{C}_\beta)^{(n)}(a)(t) \right\}$$

which can be developed as

$$L(t) \leq$$

$$\sup_{n \in \mathbb{N}} \left\{ \sup_{0 \leq s_{2n} \leq \ldots \leq s_2 \leq s_1 \leq t} \left\{ \sum_{i=1}^{n} [a(s_{2i-1}) - a(s_{2i}) - \beta(s_{2i-1} + d - s_{2i})] \right\} \right\}$$

(9.11)

Once again, if $\Pi = \mathcal{C}_\beta$, then (9.11) becomes an equality.

We can also combine a delay constraint with a buffer constraint, and repeat the same reasoning, starting from

$$x \leq a \wedge \{\Pi(x) + X\} \wedge (\mathcal{S}_{-d} \circ \Pi)(x) \wedge h_a(x).$$

(9.12)

to obtain

$$L(t) \leq \sup_{n \in \mathbb{N}} \{ \sup_{0 \leq s_{2n} \leq \ldots \leq s_2 \leq s_1 \leq t} \{ \sum_{i=1}^{n} [a(s_{2i-1}) - a(s_{2i})$$
$$- (\beta(s_{2i-1} + d - s_{2i}) \wedge \{\beta(s_{2i-1} - s_{2i}) + X\})] \}\}.$$

(9.13)

This can be recast as a recursion on time if $t \in \mathbb{N}$, following the time method to solve (9.12) instead of the space method. This recurstion is established in [15].

9.2 Application 1: Bound on Loss Rate

Let us return to the case of losses due to buffer overflow, and suppose that in this section fresh traffic a is constrained by an arrival curve α.

The following theorem provide a bound on the loss rate $l(t) = L(t)/a(t)$, and is a direct consequence of the loss representation (9.6).

Theorem 9.2.1 (Bound on loss rate). *Consider a system with storage capacity X, offering a service curve β to a flow constrained by an arrival curve α. Then the loss rate $l(t) = L(t)/a(t)$ is bounded above by*

$$\hat{l}(t) = 1 - \inf_{0 < s \leq t} \frac{\beta(s) + X}{\alpha(s)}.$$

(9.14)

Proof: With $\hat{l}(t)$ defined by (9.14), we have that for any $0 \leq u < v \leq t$,

$$1 - \hat{l}(t) = \inf_{0 < s \leq t} \frac{\beta(s) + X}{\alpha(s)} \leq \frac{\beta(v - u) + X}{\alpha(v - u)} \leq \frac{\beta(v - u) + X}{a(v) - a(u)}$$

because $a(v) - a(u) \leq \alpha(v - u)$ by definition of an arrival curve. Therefore, for any $0 \leq u \leq v \leq t$,

$$a(v) - a(u) - \beta(v - u) - X \leq \hat{l}(t) \cdot [a(v) - a(u)].$$

For any $n \in \mathbb{N}_0 = \{1, 2, 3, ...\}$, and any sequence $\{s_k\}_{1 \le k \le 2n}$, with $0 \le s_{2n} \le \\ ... \le s_1 \le t$, setting $v = s_{2i-1}$ and $u = s_{2i}$ in the previous equation, and summing over i, we obtain

$$\sum_{i=1}^{n} [a(s_{2i-1}) - a(s_{2i}) - \beta(s_{2i-1} - s_{2i}) - X] \le \hat{l}(t) \cdot \sum_{i=1}^{n} [a(s_{2i-1}) - a(s_{2i})] .$$

Because the s_k are increasing with k, the right hand side of this inequality is always less than, or equal to, $\hat{l}(t) \cdot a(t)$. Therefore we have

$$
\begin{aligned}
L(t) & \le \sup_{n \in \mathbb{N}} \left\{ \sup_{0 \le s_{2n} \le ... \le s_1 \le t} \left\{ \sum_{i=1}^{n} [a(s_{2i-1}) - a(s_{2i}) - \beta(s_{2i-1} - s_{2i}) - X] \right\} \right\} \\
& \le \hat{l}(t) \cdot a(t),
\end{aligned}
$$

which shows that $\hat{l}(t) \ge l(t) = L(t)/a(t)$. $\square$

To have a bound independent of time t, we take the sup over all t of (9.14), to get

$$\hat{l} = \sup_{t \ge 0} \hat{l}(t) = 1 - \inf_{t > 0} \frac{\beta(t) + X}{\alpha(t)}, \tag{9.15}$$

and retrieve the result of Chuang and Chang [14].

A similar result for losses due to delay constraint d, instead of finite buffer X, can be easily obtained, too:

$$\hat{l}(t) = 1 - \inf_{0 < s \le t} \frac{\beta(s + d)}{\alpha(s)} \tag{9.16}$$

$$\hat{l} = 1 - \inf_{t > 0} \frac{\beta(t + d)}{\alpha(t)} . \tag{9.17}$$

9.3 Application 2: Bound on Losses in Complex Systems

As a particular application of the loss representation formula (9.6), we show how it is possible to bound the losses in a system offering a somewhat complex service curve β, by losses in simpler systems. The first application is the bound on the losses in a shaper by a system that segregates the resources (buffer, bandwidth) between a storage system and a policer. The second application deals with a VBR shaper, which is compared with two CBR shapers. For both applications, the losses in the original system are bounded along every sample path by the losses in the simpler systems. For congestion times however, the same conclusion does not always hold.

9.3.1 Bound on Losses by Segregation between Buffer and Policer

We will first compare the losses in two systems, having the same input flow $a(t)$.

The first system is the one of Figure 9.1 with service curve β and buffer X, whose losses $L(t)$ are therefore given by (9.6).

The second system is made of two parts, as shown in Figure 9.3(a). The first part is a system with storage capacity X, that realizes some mapping Π' of the input that is not explicitly given, but that is assumed to be isotone, and not smaller than Π ($\Pi' \geq \Pi$). We also know that a first clipper discards data as soon as the total backlogged data in this system exceeds X. This operation is called *buffer discard*. The amount of buffer discarded data in $[0, t]$ is denoted by $L_{\mathrm{Buf}}(t)$. The second part is a policer without buffer, whose output is the min-plus convolution of the accepted input traffic by the policer by β. A second clipper discards data as soon as the total output flow of the storage system exceeds the maximum input allowed by the policer. This operation is called *policing discard*. The amount of discarded data by policing in $[0, t]$ is denoted by $L_{\mathrm{Pol}}(t)$.

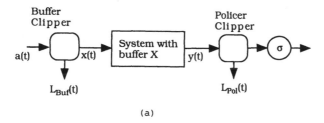

(a)

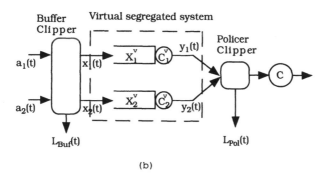

(b)

Figure 9.3: A storage/policer system with separation between losses due to buffer discard and to policing discard (a) A virtual segregated system for 2 classes of traffic, with buffer discard and policing discard, as used by Lo Presti et al [50] (b)

Theorem 9.3.1. *Let $L(t)$ be the amount of lost data in the original system, with service curve β and buffer X.*

Let $L_{\mathrm{Buf}}(t)$ (resp. $L_{\mathrm{Pol}}(t)$) be the amount of data lost in the time interval $[0,t]$ by buffer (resp. policing) discard, as defined above.

Then $L(t) \le L_{\mathrm{Buf}}(t) + L_{\mathrm{Pol}}(t)$.

Proof: Let x and y denote respectively the admitted and output flows of the buffered part of the second system. Then the policer implies that $y = \beta \otimes x$, and any time s we have

$$a(s) - L_{\mathrm{Buf}}(s) - X = x(s) - X \le y(s) \le x(s) = a(s) - L_{\mathrm{Buf}}(s).$$

which implies that for any $0 \le u \le v \le t$,

$$\begin{aligned}
y(v) &- y(u) - \beta(v - u) \\
&\ge (a(v) - L_{\mathrm{Buf}}(v) - X) - (a(u) - L_{\mathrm{Buf}}(u)) - \beta(v - u) \\
&= a(v) - a(u) - \beta(v - u) - X - (L_{\mathrm{Buf}}(v) - L_{\mathrm{Buf}}(u)).
\end{aligned}$$

We use the same reasoning as in the proof of Theorem 9.2.1: we pick any $n \in \mathbb{N}_0$ and any increasing sequence $\{s_k\}_{1 \le k \le 2n}$, with $0 \le s_{2n} \le \ldots \le s_1 \le t$. Then we set $v = s_{2i-1}$ and $u = s_{2i}$ in the previous inequality, and we sum over i, to obtain

$$\sum_{i=1}^{n} [y(s_{2i-1}) - y(s_{2i}) - \beta(s_{2i-1} - s_{2i})] \ge$$

$$\sum_{i=1}^{n} [a(s_{2i-1}) - a(s_{2i}) - \beta(s_{2i-1} - s_{2i}) - X]$$

$$- \sum_{i=1}^{n} [(L_{\mathrm{Buf}}(s_{2i-1}) - L_{\mathrm{Buf}}(s_{2i}))].$$

By taking the supremum over all n and all sequences $\{s_k\}_{1 \le k \le 2n}$, the left hand side is equal to $L_{\mathrm{Pol}}(t)$, because of (9.6) (we can replace the inequality in (9.6) by an equality, because the output of the policer is $y = \beta \otimes x$). Since $\{s_k\}$ is a wide-sense increasing sequence, and since L_{Buf} is a wide-sense increasing function, we obtain therefore

$$L_{\mathrm{Pol}}(t) \ge$$

$$\sup_{n \in \mathbb{N}} \left\{ \sup_{0 \le s_{2n} \le \ldots \le s_1 \le t} [a(s_{2i-1}) - a(s_{2i}) - \beta(s_{2i-1} - s_{2i}) - X] \right\} - L_{\mathrm{Buf}}(t)$$

$$= L(t) - L_{\mathrm{Buf}}(t),$$

which completes the proof.   □

Such a separation of resources between the "buffered system" and "policing system" is used in the estimation of loss probability for devising statistical CAC (Call Acceptance Control) algorithms as proposed by Elwalid et al [23], Lo Presti et al. [50]. The incoming traffic is separated in two classes. All variables relating to the first (resp. second) class are marked with an index 1 (resp. 2), so that $a(t) = a_1(t) + a_2(t)$. The original system is a CBR shaper ($\beta = \lambda_C$) and the storage system is a virtually segregated system as in Figure 9.3(b), made of 2 shapers with rates C_1^v and C_2^v and buffers X_1^v and X_2^v. The virtual shapers are large enough to ensure that no loss occurs for all possible arrival functions $a_1(t)$ and $a_2(t)$. The total buffer space (resp. bandwidth) is larger than the original buffer space (resp. bandwidth): $X_1^v + X_2^v \geq X$ ($C_1^v + C_2^v \geq C$). However, the buffer controller discards data as soon as the total backlogged data in the virtual system exceeds X and the policer controller discards data as soon as the total output rate of the virtual system exceeds C.

9.3.2 Bound on Losses in a VBR Shaper

In this second example, we consider of a "buffered leaky bucket" shaper [44] with buffer X, whose output must conform to a VBR shaping curve with peak rate P, sustainable rate M and burst tolerance B so that here the mapping of the element is $\Pi = \mathcal{C}_\beta$ with $\beta = \lambda_P \wedge \gamma_{M,B}$. We will consider two systems to bound these losses: first two CBR shapers in parallel (Figure 9.4(a)) and second two CBR shapers in tandem (Figure 9.4(b)). Similar results also holds for losses due to a delay constraint [47].

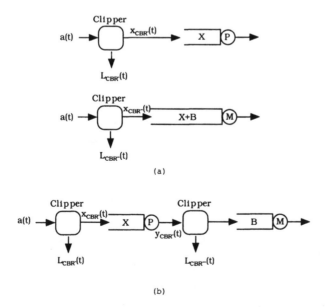

Figure 9.4: Two CBR shapers in parallel (a) and in tandem (b).

We will first show that the *amount of losses* during $[0, t]$ in this system is bounded by the sum of losses in two CBR shapers in parallel, as shown in Figure 9.4(a): the first one has buffer of size X and rate P, whereas the second one has buffer of size $X + B$ and rate M. Both receive the same arriving traffic a as the original VBR shaper.

Theorem 9.3.2. *Let $L_{VBR}(t)$ be the amount of lost data in the time interval $[0, t]$ in a VBR shaper with buffer X and shaping curve $\beta = \lambda_P \wedge \gamma_{M,B}$, when the data that has arrived in $[0, t]$ is $a(t)$.*

Let $L_{CBR'}(t)$ (resp. $L_{CBR''}(t)$) be the amount of lost data during $[0, t]$ in a CBR shaper with buffer X (resp. $(X + B)$) and shaping curve λ_P (resp. λ_M) with the same incoming traffic $a(t)$.

Then $L_{VBR}(t) \leq L_{CBR'}(t) + L_{CBR''}(t)$.

Proof: The proof is again a direct application of (9.6). Pick any $0 \leq u \leq v \leq t$. Since $\beta = \lambda_P \wedge \gamma_{M,B}$,

$$a(v) - a(u) - \beta(v - u) - X =$$
$$\{a(v) - a(u) - P(v - u) - X\} \vee \{a(v) - a(u) - M(v - u) - B - X\}$$

Pick any $n \in \mathbb{N}_0$ and any increasing sequence $\{s_k\}_{1 \leq k \leq 2n}$, with $0 \leq s_{2n} \leq \ldots \leq s_1 \leq t$. Set $v = s_{2i-1}$ and $u = s_{2i}$ in the previous equation, and sum over i, to obtain

$$\sum_{i=1}^{n} [a(s_{2i-1}) - a(s_{2i}) - \beta(s_{2i-1} - s_{2i}) - X]$$

$$= \sum_{i=1}^{n} [\{a(s_{2i-1}) - a(s_{2i}) - P(s_{2i-1} - s_{2i}) - X\}$$
$$\vee \{a(s_{2i-1}) - a(s_{2i}) - M(s_{2i-1} - s_{2i}) - B - X\}$$

$$\leq \sum_{i=1}^{n} [a(s_{2i-1}) - a(s_{2i}) - P(s_{2i-1} - s_{2i}) - X]$$

$$+ \sum_{i=1}^{n} [a(s_{2i-1}) - a(s_{2i}) - M(s_{2i-1} - s_{2i}) - B - X]$$

$$\leq L_{CBR'}(t) + L_{CBR''}(t),$$

because of (9.6). By taking the supremum over all n and all sequences $\{s_k\}_{1 \leq k \leq 2n}$ in the previous inequality, we get the desired result.   □

A similar exercise shows that the amount of losses during $[0, t]$ in the VBR system is also bounded above by the sum of losses in two CBR shapers in cascade as shown in Figure 9.4(b): the first one has buffer of size X and rate P, and receives the same arriving traffic a as the original VBR shaper, whereas its output is fed into the second one with buffer of size B and rate M.

Theorem 9.3.3. *Let $L_{VBR}(t)$ be the amount of lost data in the time interval $[0, t]$ in a VBR shaper with buffer X and shaping curve $\beta = \lambda_P \wedge \gamma_{M,B}$, when the data that has arrived in $[0, t]$ is $a(t)$.*

Let $L_{CBR'}(t)$ (resp. $L_{CBR''}(t)$) be the amount of lost data during $[0, t]$ in a CBR shaper with buffer X (resp. B) and shaping curve λ_P (resp. λ_M) with the same incoming traffic $a(t)$ (resp. the output traffic of the first CBR shaper).

Then $L_{VBR}(t) \leq L_{CBR'}(t) + L_{CBR''}(t)$.

The proof is left as an exercise.

Neither of the two systems in Figure 9.4 gives the better bound for any arbitrary traffic pattern. For example, suppose that the VBR system parameters are $P = 4$, $M = 1$, $B = 12$ and $X = 4$, and that the traffic is a single burst of data sent at rate R during four time units, so that

$$a(t) = \begin{cases} R \cdot t & \text{if} \quad 0 \leq t \leq 4 \\ 4R & \text{if} \quad t \geq 4 \end{cases}$$

If $R = 5$, both the VBR system and the parallel set of the two CBR' and CBR'' systems are lossless, whereas the amount of lost data after five units of time in the tandem of the two CBR' and CBR''' systems is equal to three.

On the other hand, if $R = 6$, the amount of lost data after five units of time in the VBR system, the parallel system (CBR' and CBR'') and the tandem system (CBR' and CBR''') are respectively equal to four, eight and seven.

Interestingly enough, whereas both systems of Figure 9.4 will bound the *amount of losses in the original system*, it is no longer so for the *congestion periods*, i.e. the time intervals during which losses occur. The tandem system does not offer a bound on the congestion periods, contrary to the parallel system [47].

9.4 Solution to Skohorkhod's Reflection Problem with Two Boundaries

To obtain the model of Figure 9.1, we have added a regulator – called *clipper* – before the system itself, whose input x is the maximal input ensuring a lossless service, given a finite storage capacity X. The clipper eliminates the fraction of fresh traffic a that exceeds x. We now generalize this model by adding a second regulator *after* the lossless system, whose output is denoted with y, as shown on Figure 9.5. This regulator complements y, so that the output of the full process is now a given function $b \in \mathcal{F}$. The resulting process $N = y - b$ is the amount of traffic that needs to be fed to prevent the storage system to enter in starvation. N compensates for possible buffer underflows, hence we name this second regulator *compensator*.

We can explicitly compute the loss process L and the "compensation" process N, from the arrival process a and the departure process b, using, once again, Theorem 4.3.1. We are looking for the maximal solution

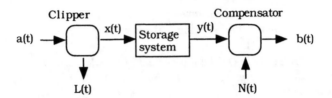

Figure 9.5: A storage system representing the variables used to solve Skorokhod's reflection problem with two boundaries

$$\vec{x}(t) = [x(t) \quad y(t)]^T,$$

where T denotes transposition, to the set of inequalities

$$x(t) \leq \inf_{0 \leq s \leq t}\{a(t) - a(s) + x(s)\} \tag{9.18}$$

$$x(t) \leq y(t) + X \tag{9.19}$$

$$y(t) \leq x(t) \tag{9.20}$$

$$y(t) \leq \inf_{0 \leq s \leq t}\{b(t) - b(s) + y(s)\}. \tag{9.21}$$

The two first inequalities are identical to (9.1) and to (9.2). The two last inequalities are the dual constraints on y. We can therefore recast this system as

$$x \leq a \wedge h_a(x) \wedge \{y + X\} \tag{9.22}$$

$$y \leq b \wedge x \wedge h_b(x). \tag{9.23}$$

This is a system of min-plus linear inequalities, whose solution is

$$\vec{x} = \overline{\mathcal{L}}_H(\vec{a}) = \mathcal{L}_{\overline{H}}(\vec{a}),$$

where H and $\vec{a}$ are defined as

$$\vec{a}(t) = [a(t) \quad b(t)]^T$$

$$H(t,s) = \begin{bmatrix} a(t) - a(s) & \delta_0(t-s) + X \\ \delta_0(t-s) & b(t) - b(s) \end{bmatrix}.$$

for all $0 \leq s \leq t$. Instead of computing $\overline{H}$, we go faster by first computing the maximal solution of (9.23). Using properties of the linear idempotent operator, we get

$$y = \overline{h}_b(x \wedge b) = h_b(x \wedge b) = h_b(x) \wedge h_b(b) = h_b(x).$$

Next we replace y by $h_b(x)$ in (9.22), and we compute its maximal solution, which is

$$x = \overline{h_a \wedge \{h_b + X\}}(a).$$

We work out the sub-additive closure using Corollary 4.2.1, and we obtain

$$x = \overline{(h_a \circ \{h_b + X\})}(a) \tag{9.24}$$

and thus

$$y = \left(h_b \circ \overline{h_a \circ \{h_b + X\}}\right)(a). \tag{9.25}$$

After some manipulations, we get

$$N(t) = b(t) - y(t) =$$

$$\sup_{n \in \mathbb{N}} \left\{ \sup_{0 \le s_{2n+1} \le \ldots \le s_2 \le s_1 \le t} \left\{ \sum_{i=1}^{2n+1} (-1)^i (a(s_i) - b(s_i)) \right\} - nX \right\} \tag{9.26}$$

$$L(t) = a(t) - x(t) =$$

$$\sup_{n \in \mathbb{N}} \left\{ \sup_{0 \le s_{2n} \le \ldots \le s_2 \le s_1 \le t} \left\{ \sum_{i=1}^{2n} (-1)^{i+1} (a(s_i) - b(s_i)) \right\} - nX \right\}. \tag{9.27}$$

Interestingly enough, these two functions are the solution of the so-called Skorokhod reflection problem with two fixed boundaries [66, 33].

Let us describe this reflection mapping problem following the exposition of [40]. We are given a lower boundary that will be taken here as the origin, an upper boundary $X > 0$, and a *free process* $z(t) \in \mathbb{R}$ such that $0 \le z(0-) \le X$. Skorokhod's reflection problem looks for functions $N(t)$ (*lower boundary process*) and $L(t)$ (*upper boundary process*) such that

1. The *reflected process*

$$W(t) = z(t) + N(t) - L(t) \tag{9.28}$$

is in $[0, X]$ for all $t \ge 0$.

2. Both $N(t)$ and $L(t)$ are non decreasing with $N(0-) = L(0-) = 0$, and $N(t)$ (resp. $L(t)$) increases only when $W(t) = 0$ (resp. $W(t) = X$), i.e., with 1_A denoting the indicator function of A

$$\int_0^\infty 1_{\{W(t)>0\}} dN(t) = 0 \tag{9.29}$$

$$\int_0^\infty 1_{\{W(t)<X\}} dL(t) = 0 \tag{9.30}$$

The solution to this problem exists and is unique [33]. When only one boundary is present, explicit formulas are available. For instance, if $X \to \infty$, then there is only one lower boundary, and the solution is easily found to be

$$N(t) = -\inf_{0 \le s \le t} \{z(s)\}$$

$$L(t) = 0.$$

If $X < \infty$, then the solution can be constructed by successive approximations but, to our knowledge, no solution has been explicitly obtained. The following theorem gives such explicit solutions for a continuous VF function $z(t)$. A VF function (VF standing for Variation Finie [33, 62]) $z(t)$ on $\mathbb{R}^+$ is a function such that for all $t > 0$

$$\sup_{n \in \mathbb{N}_0} \sup_{0=s_n < s_{n-1} < \ldots < s_1 < s_0 = t} \left\{ \sum_{i=0}^{n-1} |z(s_i) - z(s_{i+1})| \right\} < \infty.$$

VF functions have the following property [62]: $z(t)$ is a VF function on $\mathbb{R}^+$ if and only if it can be written as the difference of two wide-sense increasing functions on $\mathbb{R}^+$.

Theorem 9.4.1 (Skorokhod's reflection mapping). *Let the free process $z(t)$ be a continuous VF function on $\mathbb{R}^+$. Then the solution to Skorokhod's reflection problem on $[0, X]$ is*

$$N(t) = \sup_{n \in \mathbb{N}} \left\{ \sup_{0 \leq s_{2n+1} \leq \ldots \leq s_2 \leq s_1 \leq t} \left\{ \sum_{i=1}^{2n+1} (-1)^i z(s_i) \right\} - nX \right\} \quad (9.31)$$

$$L(t) = \sup_{n \in \mathbb{N}} \left\{ \sup_{0 \leq s_{2n} \leq \ldots \leq s_2 \leq s_1 \leq t} \left\{ \sum_{i=1}^{2n} (-1)^{i+1} z(s_i) \right\} - nX \right\}. \quad (9.32)$$

Proof: As $z(t)$ is a VF function on $[0, \infty)$, there exist two increasing functions $a(t)$ and $b(t)$ such that $z(t) = a(t) - b(t)$ for all $t \geq 0$. As $z(0) \geq 0$, we can take $b(0) = 0$ and $a(0) = z(0)$. Note that $a, b \in \mathcal{F}$.

We will show now that $L = a - x$ and $N = b - y$, where x and y are the maximal solutions of (9.22) and (9.23), are the solutions of Skorokhod's reflection problem.

First note that

$$W(t) = z(t) + N(t) - L(t) = (a(t) - b(t)) + (b(t) - y(t)) - (a(t) - x(t)) = x(t) - y(t)$$

is in $[0, X]$ for all $t \geq 0$ because of (9.19) and (9.20).

Second, because of (9.21), note that $N(0) = b(0) - y(0) = 0$ and that for any $t > 0$ and $0 \leq s < t$, $N(t) - N(s) = b(t) - b(s) + y(s) - y(t) \geq 0$, which shows that $N(t)$ is non decreasing. The same properties can be deduced for $L(t)$ from (9.18).

Finally, if $W(t) = x(t) - y(t) > 0$, there is some $s^\star \in [0, t]$ such that $y(t) = y(s^\star) + b(t) - b(s^\star)$ because y is the maximal solution satisfying (9.20) and (9.21). Therefore for all $s \in [s^\star, t]$,

$$0 \leq N(t) - N(s) \leq N(t) - N(s^\star) = b(t) - b(s^\star) + y(s^\star) - y(t) = 0$$

which shows that $N(t) - N(s) = 0$ and so that $N(t)$ is non increasing if $W(t) > 0$. A similar reasoning shows that $L(t)$ is non increasing if $W(t) < X$.

Consequently, $N(t)$ and $L(t)$ are the lower and upper reflected processes that we are looking for. We have already computed them: they are given by (9.26) and (9.27). Replacing $a(s_i) - b(s_i)$ in these two expressions by $z(s_i)$, we establish (9.31) and (9.32).   □

9.5 Bibliographic Notes

The clipper was introduced by Cruz and Tenaja, and was extended to get the loss representation formula presented in this chapter in [15, 47]. Explicit expressions when operator Π is a general, time-varying operator, can be found in [15]. We expect results of this chapter to form a starting point for obtaining bounds on probabilities of loss or congestion for lossy shapers with complex shaping functions; the method would consist in applying known bounds to virtual systems and take the minimum over a set of virtual systems.

Bibliography

[1] R. Agrawal, R. L. Cruz, C. Okino, and R. Rajan. A framework for adapative service guarantees. In *Proc. Allerton Conf on Comm, Control and Comp, Monticello, IL*, Sept 1998.

[2] R. Agrawal, R. L. Cruz, C. Okino, and R. Rajan. Performance bounds for flow control protocols. *IEEE/ACM Transactions on Networking (7) 3*, pages 310–323, June 1999.

[3] M. Andrews. Instability of fifo in session-oriented networks. In *Eleventh Annual ACM-SIAM Symposium on Discrete Algorithms (SODA 2000)*, January 2000.

[4] J. C. R. Bennett, Benson K., Charny A., Courtney W. F., and J.-Y. Le Boudec. Delay jitter bounds and packet scale rate guarantee for expedited forwarding. In *Proceedings of Infocom*, April 2001.

[5] J.C.R. Bennett and H. Zhang. Wf2q: Worst-case fair weighted fair queuing. In *Proceedings of Infocom*, Mar 1996.

[6] S. Blake, D. Black, M. Carlson, E. Davies, Z. Wang, and W. Weiss. An architecture for differentiated services, December 1998. RFC 2475, IETF.

[7] C. S. Chang. Stability, queue length and delay, part i: Deterministic queuing networks. Technical Report Technical Report RC 17708, IBM, 1992.

[8] C.-S. Chang, W.-J. Chen, and H.-Y. Hunag. On service guarantees for input buffered crossbar switches: A capacity decomposition approach by birkhoff and von neumann. In *Proc of IWQOS 99*, March 1999.

[9] C.S. Chang. On deterministic traffic regulation and service guarantee: A systematic approach by filtering. *IEEE Transactions on Information Theory*, 44:1096–1107, August 1998.

[10] C.S. Chang. *Performance Guarantees in Communication Networks*. Springer-Verlag, New York, 2000.

[11] C.S. Chang and R. L. Cruz. A time varying filtering theory for constrained traffic regulation and dynamic service guarantees. In *Preprint*, July 1998.

[12] A. Charny and J.-Y. Le Boudec. Delay bounds in a network with aggregate scheduling. In *First International Workshop on Quality of future Internet Services*, Berlin, Germany, September 2000.

[13] I. Chlamtac, A. Faragó, H. Zhang, and A. Fumagalli. A deterministic approach to the end-to-end analysis of packet flows in connection oriented networks. *IEEE/ACM transactions on networking*, (6)4:422–431, 08 1998.

[14] J.-F. Chuang, C.-M.and Chang. Deterministic loss ratio quality of service guarantees for high speed networks. *IEEE Communications Letters*, 4:236–238, July 2000.

[15] R. Cruz, C.-S. Chang, J.-Y. Le Boudec, and P. Thiran. A min-plus system theory for constrained traffic regulation and dynamic service guarantees. Technical Report SSC/1999/024, EPFL, July 1999.

[16] R. Cruz and M. Taneja. An analysis of traffic clipping. In *Proc 1998 Conf on Information Science & Systems, Princeton University*, 1998.

[17] R. L. Cruz. Sced+ : Efficient management of quality of service guarantees. In *IEEE Infocom'98, San Francisco*, March 1998.

[18] R.L. Cruz. A calculus for network delay, part i: Network elements in isolation. *IEEE Trans. Inform. Theory, vol 37-1*, pages 114–131, January 1991.

[19] R.L. Cruz. A calculus for network delay, part ii: Network analysis. *IEEE Trans. Inform. Theory, vol 37-1*, pages 132–141, January 1991.

[20] G. De Veciana, July 1996. Private Communication.

[21] A. Demers, S. Keshav, and S. Shenker. Analysis and simulation of a fair queuing algorithm. *Journal of Internetworking Research and Experience*, pages 3–26, Oct 1990.

[22] N. G. Duffield, K. K. Ramakrishan, and A. R. Reibman. Save: An algorithm for smoothed adaptative video over explicit rate networks. *IEEE/ACM Transactions on Networking*, 6:717–728, Dec 1998.

[23] A. Elwalid, Mitra D., and R. Wenworth. A new approach for allocating buffers and bandwidth to heterogeneous, regulated traffic in ATM node. *IEEE Journal of Selected Areas in Communications*, 13:1048–1056, August 1995.

[24] Baccelli F., Cohen G., Olsder G. J., , and Quadrat J.-P. *Synchronization and Linearity, An Algebra for Discrete Event Systems*. John Wiley and Sons, 1992.

[25] W.-C. Feng and J. Rexford. Performance evaluation of smoothing algorithms for transmitting variable-bit-rate video. *IEEE Transactions on Multimedia*, 1:302–312, Sept 1999.

[26] L. Georgiadis, R. Guérin, V. Peris, and R. Rajan. Efficient support of delay and rate guarantees in an internet. In *Proceedings of Sigcomm'96*, pages 106–116, August 1996.

[27] P. Goyal, S. S. Lam, and H. Vin. Determining end-to-end delay bounds in heterogeneous networks. In *5th Int Workshop on Network and Op. Sys support for Digital Audio and Video, Durham NH*, April 1995.

[28] R. Guérin and V. Peris. Quality-of-service in packet networks - basic mechanisms and directions. *Computer Networks and ISDN, Special issue on multimedia communications over packet-based networks*, 1998.

[29] R. Guérin and V. Pla. Aggregation and conformance in differentiated service networks – a case study. Technical Report Research Report, U Penn, http://www.seas.upenn.edu:8080/ guerin/publications/aggreg.pdf, August 2000.

[30] Jeremy Gunawardena. From max-plus algebra to nonexpansive mappings: a nonlinear theory for discrete event systems. *pre-print*, 1999.

[31] Sariowan H., Cruz R. L., and Polyzos G. C. Scheduling for quality of service guarantees via service curves. In *Proceedings ICCCN'95*, pages 512–520, Sept 1995.

[32] B. Hajek. Large bursts do not cause instability. *IEEE Trans on Aut Control*, 45:116–118, Jan 2000.

[33] J. M. Harrison. *Brownian Motion and Stochastic Flow Systems*. Wiley, New-York, 1985.

[34] J. Heinanen, F. Baker, W. Weiss, and J. Wroclawski. Assured forwarding phb group, June 1999. RFC 2597, IETF.

[35] Golestani S. J. A self clocked fair queuing scheme for high speed applications. In *Proceedings of Infocom '94*, 1994.

[36] F. Farkas J. Y. Le Boudec. A delay bound for a network with aggregate scheduling. In *Proceedings of the Sixteenth UK Teletraffic Symposium on Management of Quality of Service*, page 5, Harlow, UK, May 2000.

[37] V. Jacobson, K. Nichols, and K. Poduri. An expedited forwarding phb, June 1999. RFC 2598, IETF.

[38] C Kalmanek, H. Kanakia, and R. Restrick. Rate controlled servers for very high speed networks. In *IEEE Globecom'90, vol 1*, pages 12–20, 1990.

[39] Keshav. *Computer Networking: An Engineering Approach*. Prentice Hall, Englewood Cliffs, New Jersey 07632, 1996.

[40] T. Konstantopoulos and V. Anantharam. Optimal flow control schemes that regulate the burstiness of traffic. *IEEE/ACM Transactions on Networking*, 3:423–432, August 1995.

[41] Cruz R. L. and Okino C. M. Service guarantees for window flow control. In *34th Allerton Conf of Comm., Cont., and Comp. Monticello, IL*, Oct 1996.

[42] Gun L. and R. Guérin. Bandwidth management and congestion control framework of the broadband network architecture. *Bandwidth management and congestion control framework of the broadband network architecture, vol 26*, pages 61–78, 1993.

[43] Zhang L. A new traffic control algorithm for packet switching networks. In *Proceedings of ACM Sigcomm '90*, 1990.

[44] J.-Y. Le Boudec. Application of network calculus to guaranteed service networks. *IEEE Transactions on Information Theory*, 44:1087–1096, May 1998.

[45] J.-Y. Le Boudec. Some properties of variable length packet shapers. In *Proc ACM Sigmetrics / Performance '01*, 2001.

[46] J.-Y. Le Boudec and G. Hebuterne. Comment on a deterministic approach to the end-to-end analysis of packet flows in connection oriented network. *IEEE/ACM Transactions on Networking*, February 2000.

[47] J.-Y. Le Boudec and P. Thiran. Network calculus viewed as a min-plus system theory applied to communication networks. Technical Report SSC/1998/016, EPFL, April 1998.

[48] J.-Y. Le Boudec and O. Verscheure. Optimal smoothing for guaranteed service. Technical Report DSC2000/014, EPFL, March 2000.

[49] J. Liebeherr, D.E. Wrege, and Ferrari D. Exact admission control for networks with bounded delay services. *ACM/IEEE transactions on networking*, 4:885–901, 1996.

[50] F. Lo Presti, Z.-L. Zhang, D. Towsley, and J. Kurose. Source time scale and optimal buffer/bandwidth trade-off for regulated traffic in a traffic node. *IEEE/ACM Transactions on Networking*, 7:490–501, August 1999.

[51] S. H. Low and P. P. Varaiya. A simple theory of traffic and resource allocation in atm. In *Globecom'91*, pages 1633–1637, December 1991.

[52] J. M. McManus and K.W. Ross. Video-on-demand over ATM: Constant-rate transmission and transport. *IEEE Journal on Selected Areas in Communications*, 7:1087–1098, Aug 1996.

[53] J. Naudts. *A Scheme for Multiplexing ATM Sources*. Chapman Hill, 1996.

[54] J. Naudts. Towards real-time measurement of traffic control parameters. *Computer networks*, 34:157–167, 2000.

[55] Clayton M. Okino. A framework for performance guarantees in communication networks, 1998. Ph.D. Dissertation, UCSD.

[56] A. K. Parekh and R. G. Gallager. A generalized processor sharing approach to flow control in integrated services networks: The single node case. *IEEE/ACM Trans. Networking, vol 1-3*, pages 344–357, June 1993.

[57] A. K. Parekh and R. G. Gallager. A generalized processor sharing approach to flow control in integrated services networks: The multiple node case. *IEEE/ACM Trans. Networking, vol 2-2*, pages 137–150, April 1994.

[58] Vinod Peris. Architecture for guaranteed delay service in high speed networks, 1997. Ph.D. Dissertation, University of Maryland, http://www.isr.umd.edu.

[59] Fabrice P. Guillemin Pierre E. Boyer, Michel J. Servel. The spacer-controller: an efficient upc/npc for atm networks. In *ISS '92, Session A9.3, volume 2*, October 1992.

[60] Agrawal R. and Rajan R. Performance bounds for guaranteed and adaptive services, December 1996. IBM Technical Report RC 20649.

[61] J. Rexford and D. Towsley. Smoothing variable-bit-rate video in an internetwork. *IEEE/ACM Transactions on Networking*, 7:202–215, April 1999.

[62] H. L. Royden. *Real Analysis*. Mc-Millan, New-York, 2 edition, 1968.

[63] J. Y. Le Boudec S. Giordano. On a class of time varying shapers with application to the renegotiable variable bit rate service. *Journal on High Speed Networks*.

[64] J. D. Salehi, Z.-L. Zhang, J. F. Kurose, and D. Towsley. Supporting stored video: Reducing rate variability and end-to-end resource requirements through optimal smoothing. *IEEE/ACM Transactions on Networking*, 6:397–410, Dec 1998.

[65] H. Sariowan. A service curve approach to performance guarantees in integrated service networks, 1996. Ph.D. Dissertation, UCSD.

[66] A. Skorokhod. Stochastic equations for diffusion processes in a bounded region. *Theory of Probability and its Applications*, 6:264–274, 1961.

[67] D. Stiliadis and A. Varma. Rate latency servers: a general model for analysis of traffic scheduling algorithms. In *IEEE Infocom '96*, pages 647–654, 1991.

[68] Rockafellar R. T. *Convex Analysis*. Princeton University Press, Princeton, 1970.

[69] L. Tassiulas and L. Georgiadis. Any work conserving policy stabilizes the ring with spatial reuse. *IEEE/ACM Transactions on Networking*, pages 205–208, April 1996.

[70] Lothar Thiele, Samarjit Chakraborty, and Martin Naedele. Real-time calculus for scheduling hard real-time systems. In *ISCAS*, Geneva, May 2000.

[71] P. Thiran, J.-Y. Le Boudec, and F. Worm. Network calculus applied to optimal multimedia smoothing. In *Proc of Infocom 2001*, April 2001.

[72] D Verma, H. Zhang, and D. Ferrari. Guaranteeing delay jitter bounds in packet switching networks. In *Proceedings of Tricomm '91, Chapel Hill*, pages 35–46, April 1991.

[73] H. Zhang. Service disciplines for guaranteed performance service in packet switching networks. *Proceedings of the IEEE*, 1996.

[74] H. Zhang and D. Ferrari. Rate controlled service disciplines. *Journal of High Speed Networks*, 3 No 4:389–412, August 1994.

[75] Hongbiao Zhang. A note on deterministic end-to-end delay analysis in connection oriented networks. In *Proc of IEEE ICC'99, Vancouver, pp 1223–1227*, 1999.

Index

Lecture Notes in Computer Science

For information about Vols. 1–2025
please contact your bookseller or Springer-Verlag